Randi Baird

Tony Horwitz is the bestselling author of *A Voyage Long and Strange*, *Blue Latitudes*, *Confederates in the Attic*, and *Baghdad Without a Map*, and he is a Pulitzer Prize–winning journalist who has worked for *The Wall Street Journal* and *The New Yorker*. He has also been a fellow at the Radcliffe Institute for Advanced Study at Harvard University and a visiting scholar at the John Carter Brown Library at Brown University. He lives on Martha's Vineyard with his wife, Geraldine Brooks, and their two sons.

www.tonyhorwitz.com

Additional Praise for *Midnight Rising*

A *BOSTON GLOBE* BEST NONFICTION BOOK
A *CHRISTIAN SCIENCE MONITOR* BEST NONFICTION BOOK
A *NEW YORK TIMES* NOTABLE BOOK
A *LIBRARY JOURNAL* TOP TEN BOOK

"There's a brilliance to this book that put me in mind of Truman Capote's *In Cold Blood*, only Horwitz's *Midnight Rising* is set deeper in America's dark past. With stunning, vivid detail, he has captured the sheer drama and tragedy of John Brown and that bloody raid at Harpers Ferry that helped propel America toward civil war."

—Erik Larson, author of *The Devil in the White City*
and *In the Garden of Beasts*

"Horwitz, an exceptionally skilled and accomplished journalist, here turns his hand to pure history with admirable results. *Midnight Rising* is smoothly written, thoroughly researched, [and] places Brown within the context of his time and place."   —*The Washington Post*

"What do you call John Brown? Is he a terrorist (then, to many; now, to some) or a freedom fighter (then, to some; now, to many)? Was he fanatical or prescient, crazy or uncompromisingly principled? . . . A graceful narrative, ever engaging, with the reader allowed to connect Brown and his contemporaries to conflicts that continue to our day."

—*The Seattle Times*

"Tony Horwitz's gifts as a vivid narrator of dramatic events are on full display in this story of John Brown's wars in Kansas and his climactic Harpers Ferry raid in 1859. Brown's family and the men who joined him in these fights against slavery receive a more fully rounded treatment than in any other account. Of special note is the discussion of Brown's self-conscious emulation of Samson by pulling down the temple of bondage and dying a martyr in its ruins."

—James M. McPherson, author of *Battle Cry of Freedom*

"With his customary blend of rich archival research, on-location color, and lyrical prose, Tony Horwitz has delivered a John Brown book for our time. Part biography, part historical narrative, *Midnight Rising* is a riveting re-creation of the Harpers Ferry raid, told with an unblinking sense of Brown's tragic place in American history. Writing with enveloping detail and a storyteller's verve, Horwitz shows why Brown was—and still is—so troubling and important to our culture."
—David W. Blight, author of *American Oracle: The Civil War in the Civil Rights Era*

"A superb historical narrative . . . Horwitz has brought to life this delusional old man, with all his faults and foibles." —*Buffalo News*

"Horwitz's novelistic style and character development will appeal to a wide audience. Brown's raid was one of the critical factors leading an already-fractured nation to the brink of the Civil War, and *Midnight Rising* serves a noble purpose in reinterpreting this story for modern audiences." —*The Post and Courier* (Charleston)

"A probing look at the polarizing figure of preacher-terrorist John Brown . . . In captivating detail, Horwitz animates the wild-eyed, long-bearded crusader. . . . Whether Horwitz's book leaves you believing Brown was a terrorist or a hero (or both), he was ultimately prophetic." —*The Cleveland Plain Dealer*

"Tony Horwitz knows how to tell a story, and here his considerable gifts as a writer bring John Brown's raid on Harpers Ferry alive in a style that is just as electric as its subject." —Joseph J. Ellis, author of *Founding Brothers* and *First Family*

Midnight Rising

JOHN BROWN AND THE
RAID THAT SPARKED
THE CIVIL WAR

Tony Horwitz

PICADOR

HENRY HOLT AND COMPANY
NEW YORK

www.picadorusa.com
www.twitter.com/picadorusa • www.facebook.com/picadorusa

Picador® is a U.S. registered trademark and is used by Henry Holt and Company
under license from Pan Books Limited.

For book club information, please visit www.facebook.com/picadorbookclub
or e-mail marketing@picadorusa.com.

Maps by Gene Thorp/Cartographic Concepts, Inc.

Designed by Meryl Sussman Levavi

The Library of Congress has cataloged the Henry Holt edition as follows:

Horwitz, Tony, 1958–
    Midnight rising : John Brown and the raid that sparked the Civil War /
Tony Horwitz.—1st ed.
        p.   cm.
    Includes bibliographical references and index.
    ISBN 978-0-8050-9153-3
    1. Harpers Ferry (W. Va.)—History—John Brown's Raid, 1859.   2. Brown, John,
1800–1859.   3. Abolitionists—United States—Biography.   I. Title.
    E451.H77 2011
    973.7′116—dc22   2011015659

Picador ISBN 978-0-312-42926-3

First published in the United States by Henry Holt and Company

First Picador Edition: August 2012

20 19 18 17 16 15

To Nathaniel and Bizu,
my in-house insurrectionists

Sometimes there comes a crack in Time itself.
Sometimes the earth is torn by something blind.

STEPHEN VINCENT BENÉT,
"John Brown's Body"

Contents

PART THREE

THEY WILL BROWN US ALL

Midnight Rising

October 16, 1859

"**M**en, get on your arms," the Captain said. "We will proceed to the Ferry."

It was eight at night, an autumn Sunday, silent and dark in the Maryland hills. A horse-drawn wagon pulled up to the log house and the men loaded it with pikes, tools, torches, and gunpowder. The Captain put on the battered cap he'd worn in Bleeding Kansas. Then he climbed on the wagon and the men marched behind, down a dirt lane, past a snake-rail fence, onto the road to Harpers Ferry.

There were eighteen men, not counting the Captain. Almost all were in their twenties and had written farewell letters to family and lovers. Five of them were black, including a fugitive slave and a freedman whose wife and children were still in bondage. Two others were the Captain's sons. All had been formally inducted at the secluded log house as soldiers in the Provisional Army of the United States.

Their commander was fifty-nine, a sinewy man with gunmetal eyes and a white beard he'd grown to conceal his identity. He was wanted by state and federal authorities; President Buchanan had put a price on his head. While living underground, the Captain had drafted a constitution and a "Declaration of Liberty" for the revolutionary government that tonight's action would found.

"'When in the course of Human events, it becomes necessary' for an oppressed People to Rise, and assert their Natural Rights," the declaration began. If the opening sounded familiar, the close was not. "We will obtain these rights or die in the struggle," the document stated, before concluding: "Hung be the Heavens in Scarlet."

The road ran below a mountain ridge, through woods and rolling farmland. The mid-October night was cool and drizzly and dark, perfect weather for a surprise attack. There was no one else abroad and no sound, just the creak of the wagon's wooden wheels and the clop of hooves. Steam rose from the horse's flanks; behind the Captain's wagon the men marched in pairs, solemn and speechless, as if in a funeral cortège. Their orders were to make no noise and to conceal their rifles beneath gray shawls. Anyone they encountered was to be detained.

After three miles, the road descended steeply to the wide, swift Potomac River. On the far bank glowed the gas lamps of Harpers Ferry, Virginia, a factory town and the gateway to the largest slave state in the country. Two of the men crept ahead; soon they would cut the telegraph lines linking Harpers Ferry to the outside world. Two other men, hard veterans of Kansas, slipped onto the covered bridge over the Potomac and seized the night watchman who trolled back and forth with a lantern.

The Captain followed in his wagon, leading the others across the bridge. It was an hour before midnight when they emerged on the Virginia shore and entered the business district of Harpers Ferry. The wagon clattered across pavement, past a rail depot, a hotel, saloons, and shops, and up to the front gate of the U.S. armory. Behind its high wrought-iron fence stretched a massive industrial complex where the nation's newest weapons were manufactured.

"Open the gate!" one of the men shouted at a night guard within the armory fence. The watchman refused. Two of the men grabbed hold of him through the fence and pressed guns to his chest. Another man forced the gate's lock with a crowbar. Then the Captain rode into the armory yard and took the watchman prisoner.

"I came here from Kansas," he announced to his captive. "This is a slave state. I want to free all the Negroes in this state. I have possession now of the United States armory, and if the citizens interfere with me, I must only burn the town and have blood."

ON OCTOBER 16, 2009, I retraced the Captain's march with other pilgrims who had gathered for the hundred and fiftieth anniversary of John Brown's famous raid on Harpers Ferry. The night was appropriately cold and wet, and we followed a horse-drawn wagon through a landscape that has changed remarkably little since 1859. Brown's log hideout in Maryland still stands, as does the armory building in Harpers Ferry that became his headquarters and "fort." Though we didn't carry guns or wear nineteenth-century attire, I experienced a little of the time-travel high that Civil War reenactors call a "period rush."

But walking in the footsteps of history isn't the same as being there. I could tread where Brown's men did, glimpse some of what they saw, but the place I wanted to be was inside their heads. What led them to launch a brazen assault on their own government and countrymen? Why were millions of other Americans willing to kill and die in the civil war that followed? How did one event connect to the other?

My son's ninth-grade American history textbook offers little more insight than mine did in the 1970s. Harpers Ferry merits six paragraphs—a speed bump for students racing ahead to Fort Sumter and the Gettysburg Address. Recent history also provides a simplistic guide at best. Viewed through the lens of 9/11, Harpers Ferry seems an al-Qaeda prequel: a long-bearded fundamentalist, consumed by hatred of the U.S. government, launches nineteen men in a suicidal strike on a symbol of American power. A shocked nation plunges into war. We are still grappling with the consequences.

But John Brown wasn't a charismatic foreigner crusading from half a world away. He descended from Puritans and Revolutionary soldiers and believed he was fulfilling their struggle for freedom. Nor was he an alienated loner in the mold of recent homegrown terrorists such as Ted Kaczynski and Timothy McVeigh. Brown plotted while raising an enormous family; he also drew support from leading thinkers and activists of his day, including Frederick Douglass, Harriet Tubman, and Henry David

Thoreau. The covert group that funneled him money and guns, the so-called Secret Six, was composed of northern magnates and prominent Harvard men, two of them ministers.

Those who followed Brown into battle represented a cross section of mid-nineteenth-century America. In Kansas and, later, Virginia, he was joined by farm laborers, factory workers, tradesmen, teachers, an immigrant Jewish shopkeeper, a free black schooled at Oberlin, and two young women who acted as lookouts and camouflage at his hideout near Harpers Ferry. These foot soldiers often bristled at his leadership and rejected his orthodox Calvinism. Most who went with him to Harpers Ferry regarded themselves as nonbelieving "infidels."

Yet follow him they did, swearing allegiance to his revolutionary government and marching into Virginia to found a new order. Within two years, entire armies would cross the Potomac, and this obscured the magnitude of what happened in 1859. The street violence at Harpers Ferry came to seem almost quaint by comparison with the industrial-scale slaughter at Antietam and Gettysburg. In time, the uprising became known as John Brown's Raid, a minor-sounding affair, like one man's act of banditry.

But no one saw it that way at the time. A month after the attack, under the headline "HOW WOULD IT FIGURE IN HISTORY," a Baltimore newspaper listed the many labels given to the recent violence in Virginia. The most common were "Insurrection," "Rebellion," "Uprising," and "Invasion." Further down the list appeared "War," "Treason," and "Crusade." There were twenty-six terms in all. "Raid" was not among them.

THE UNITED STATES IN the late 1850s was a divided but peaceful country, with a standing army of only fifteen thousand men and a booming cotton trade that fed northern mills and accounted for three-quarters of the country's exports. Acts of political violence were rare. No president had yet been assassinated; the hundred thousand guns at Harpers Ferry were virtually unguarded. And the long-simmering conflict over slavery played out principally in Washington, where Southerners had held sway for most of the nation's history.

Though many Americans hated slavery, very few sought its abolition, or expected the institution to disappear anytime soon. "I do not suppose that in the most peaceful way ultimate extinction would occur in less than a hundred years at the least," Abraham Lincoln said in 1858. He advocated resettling free blacks in Africa and pledged to leave slavery alone in the states where it existed.

Harpers Ferry helped propel Lincoln into the White House, where he would ultimately fulfill Brown's mission. The midnight rising in Virginia also embroiled a host of future Confederates. Robert E. Lee and J.E.B. Stuart led troops against Brown; Thomas "Stonewall" Jackson guarded the abolitionist. So did John Wilkes Booth, who loathed Brown but took inspiration from his daring act of violence. Meanwhile, in Congress, Jefferson Davis cited the attack as grounds for Southerners to leave the Union, "even if it rushes us into a sea of blood." Harpers Ferry wasn't simply a prelude to secession and civil war. In many respects, it was a dress rehearsal.

This was true not only for participants but for the millions of Americans who followed the events from afar, through telegraphic dispatches that made Harpers Ferry one of the first breaking news stories in the nation. The debate and division stirred by the crisis unsettled decades of compromise and prevarication. On the subject of John Brown, there was no middle ground. North and South, citizens picked sides and braced for conflict that now seemed inevitable.

William Lloyd Garrison, America's leading abolitionist in the decades before the Civil War, had for thirty years waged an often lonely crusade to mobilize the moral force of the nation against slavery. As an ardent pacifist, he condemned Brown's violent act. But the passions and ruptures laid bare by Harpers Ferry compelled him to reconsider.

"In firing his gun, he has merely told us what time of day it is," Garrison said of Brown. "It is high noon, thank God!"

—◦◦◦—

PART ONE

The Road to Harpers Ferry

He was a stone,
A stone eroded to a cutting edge
By obstinacy, failure and cold prayers.

STEPHEN VINCENT BENÉT,
"John Brown's Body"

CHAPTER 1

~~~

School of Adversity

John Brown was born with the nineteenth century and didn't launch his attack on Virginia until he was nearly sixty. But almost from birth, he was marked in ways that would set him on the road to rebellion at Harpers Ferry.

Brown was named for his grandfather, a Connecticut farmer and Revolutionary War officer who marched off to fight the British in 1776. Captain John Brown died of dysentery a few weeks later, in a New York barn, leaving behind a pregnant widow and ten children. One of them was five-year-old Owen, who later wrote: "for want of help we lost our Crops and then our Cattle and so became poor."

Owen was forced "to live abroad" with neighbors and nearby relations, and went to work young, farming in summer and making shoes in winter. As a teenager he found religion and met a minister's daughter, Ruth Mills, pious and frugal like himself. Soon after their marriage, Ruth gave birth to "a very thrifty forward Child," a son who died before turning two. The Browns moved to a clapboard saltbox in the stony hills of Torrington, Connecticut, and had another son. "In 1800, May 9th John was born," Owen wrote, "nothing very uncommon."

A portrait of Owen Brown in later years depicts a thin-lipped, hawk-beaked man with penetrating eyes: an antique version of his famous son. Owen also bestowed on John his austere Calvinism, a faith ever vigilant against sin and undue attachment to the things of this world. In his late

John Brown's birthplace, in Torrington, Connecticut

seventies, after rising from childhood penury to become a prosperous landowner and respected civic leader known as Squire Brown, Owen wrote a brief autobiography for his family. It began: "my life has been of but little worth mostly fild up with vanity."

JOHN BROWN ALSO WROTE a short autobiography, in his case for a young admirer. Two years before the uprising at Harpers Ferry, while seeking money and guns for his campaign, he dined at the home of George Luther Stearns, a wealthy Massachusetts industrialist. Stearns's twelve-year-old son, Henry, was inspired by Brown's antislavery fervor and donated his pocket money (thirty cents) to the cause. In return— and after some prodding from Stearns senior—Brown wrote Henry a long letter describing his own youth in the early 1800s.

The letter was didactic in tone, doubtless intended to impress Henry's wealthy father as much as the boy himself. But it was nonetheless a telling account, delivered in the direct, emphatic, and grammatically irregular voice that distinguished so much of Brown's speech and writing.

"I cannot tell you of anything in the first Four years of John's life worth mentioning," Brown wrote, narrating his story in the third person, "save that at that <u>early age</u> he was tempted by Three large Brass Pins belonging to a girl who lived in the family & <u>stole them</u>. In this he was detected by his Mother; & after having a full day to think of the wrong; received from her a thorough whipping."

If Brown's earliest memory was of sin and chastisement, his next was of dislocation. When he was five, his family moved by oxcart to northeast Ohio. This territory, Connecticut's "Western Reserve," was pioneered by New Englanders seeking to extend their godly settlement. "I came with the determination," Brown's father wrote, "to build up and be a help in the seport of religion and civil order." He and his neighbors formed communities centered on Congregational churches and village greens, much like the world they left behind.

Young John's experience of Ohio was very different. When he was a boy, he wrote, the Western Reserve seemed a wondrously untamed place, "a wilderness filled with wild beasts, & Indians." He rambled in the woods, wore buckskins, learned to live rough (a skill that would serve him well in later years), and dressed the hides of deer, raccoons, and wolves. Those first few years in Ohio were the happiest and freest of his life.

"But about this period he was placed in the School of <u>adversity</u>," Brown wrote of himself, "the beginning of a severe but <u>much needed course</u> of dicipline." First, an Indian boy gave him a yellow marble, which he treasured but lost. Then he nursed and tamed a bobtail squirrel and grew to dote on his pet. "<u>This too he lost</u>," and "for a year or two John was <u>in mourning</u>." At the age of eight, he suffered a much greater trauma: the death of his mother in childbirth.

This loss "was complete & permanent," Brown wrote. Though his father quickly remarried "a very estimable woman," John "never <u>adopted her in feeling</u>; but continued to pine after his own Mother for years." The early loss of his mother made him shy and awkward around women. It also magnified the influence of his formidable father, who would marry a third time in his sixties and sire sixteen children.

From an early age, John hewed closely to his father's example of hard work and strict piety. He was prone to fibbing and "excessively fond of the hardest & roughest kind of plays," such as wrestling and snowball fights, but gave no sign of rebelliousness. A tall, strong boy, he was educated at a log school and went to work young, "ambitious to perform the full labour of a man." At twelve, he drove his father's cattle a hundred miles, on his own, and soon took up Owen's trade of leather tanning. He also became "a firm believer in the divine authenticity of the Bible," and briefly studied for the ministry. John "never attempted to dance," he wrote, never learned any card games, and "grew to a dislike of vain & frivolous conversation & persons."

John followed Owen in family matters, too. At twenty, "led by his own inclination & prompted also by his Father," Brown wrote, "he married a remarkably plain; but industrious & economical girl; of excellent character; earnest piety; & good practical common sense." Dianthe Lusk was nineteen, the daughter of Brown's housekeeper. A son was born a year after their marriage—the first of a brood that would grow, like Owen's, to almost biblical proportions.

Brown also raised animals, displaying a particular skill and tenderness with sheep. "As soon as circumstances would enable him he began to be a practical Shepherd," Brown wrote, "it being a calling for which in early life he had a kind of enthusiastic longing." But here, too, loss haunted him. One of the first creatures he tended, apart from his pet squirrel, was "a little Ewe Lamb which did finely till it was about Two Thirds grown; & then sickened and died. This brought another protracted mourning season."

Brown ended his brief autobiography with his entrance into manhood. At twenty-one, he was already a tannery owner, a family man, and, as some of his peers saw it, a bit of a prig. He quickly fell out with Dianthe's brother, who was only able to visit on Sundays. Brown disapproved of this. His church reserved the Sabbath for religious observance; even "worldly" conversation, visiting friends, and making cheese on Sunday were violations of Christian duty. (The church also excommunicated a deacon who "did open his house for the reception of a puppet show.") Brown required his tannery workers to attend church and a daily family worship. One apprentice later described his employer as sociable, so long as "the conversation did not turn on anything profane or vulgar." Scripture, the apprentice added, was "at his tongues end from one end to the other."

While demanding of others, Brown was hardest on himself. In his autobiographical letter, he wrote of young John's "haughty obstinate temper" and inability to endure reproach. He "habitually expected to <u>succeed</u> in his undertakings" and felt sure his plans were "right in themselves." This drive and confidence impressed elders he esteemed, which in turn fed his vanity. "He came forward to manhood quite full of self-conceit." Brown wrote that his younger brother often called him "a King against whom there is no rising up."

These traits—arrogance, self-certitude, a domineering manner—would bedevil Brown as he navigated the turbulent economy of the early nineteenth century. But they would also enable his late-life reincarnation as Captain John Brown, a revolutionary who took up arms in the cause of freedom, as his namesake had done two generations before him.

IN 1800, THE YEAR of Brown's birth in the thin-soiled hills of Connecticut, the United States was just entering its adolescence. The Constitution turned thirteen that year. For the first time, a president took up residence in the newly built White House, and Congress convened on Capitol Hill. The young nation barely extended beyond the Appalachians; its largest city, New York, had sixty thousand people, equal to present-day Bismarck, North Dakota.

In many respects, daily existence at the time of Brown's birth was closer to life in medieval Europe than modern-day America. Most people worked on farms and used wooden plows. Land travel moved at horse or foot speed on roads so awful that the carriage bringing First Lady Abigail Adams to Washington got lost in the woods near Baltimore. Crossing the ocean was a weeks-long ordeal. News wasn't new by the time it arrived.

In this preindustrial society of five million people, almost 900,000 were enslaved, and not only in the South. Though northern states had taken steps toward ending the institution, most of these measures provided for only gradual emancipation. Brown's home state had almost a thousand slaves at the time of his birth, and New York twenty times that number.

Slavery was also safeguarded by the Constitution, albeit in convoluted language. The Revolution had raised an awkward question: how to square human bondage with the self-evident truth that all men are created equal and endowed with certain inalienable rights? The Framers answered this, in part, by employing a semantic dodge. They produced a forty-four-hundred-word document that did not once use the term "slave" or "slavery," even though the subject arose right at the start.

Article I of the Constitution mandated that each state's delegation to the House of Representatives would be based on the number of free people added to "three fifths of all other Persons"—meaning slaves. In other words, every fifty slaves would be counted as thirty people, even though these "other Persons" couldn't vote and would magnify the representation of white men who owned them.

The Constitution also protected, for twenty years, the "importation of such Persons as any of the States now existing shall think proper." "Such Persons," of course, were African slaves. Furthermore, any "Person held to Service or Labour" who escaped to a free state—that is, any slave who ran away—had to be "delivered up" to his or her master.

These measures reflected the horse-trading needed to forge a nation from fractious states. Another deal, struck in 1790, led to the nation's capital being located on the Potomac River, between the slave states of Virginia and Maryland. In all, slaveholders had deftly entrenched their "species of property," as one South Carolina delegate euphemistically put it.

Even so, as the turn of the century approached, there were signs that slavery might wane. The exhaustion of the Chesapeake region's soil by tobacco weakened the economic basis for slavery in Maryland and Virginia, home to half of all southern slaves. A growing number of owners in these states were freeing their slaves, driven in part by evangelical fervor and the Revolution's emphasis on personal liberty. Other slave owners, such as Thomas Jefferson, acknowledged the "moral and political depravity" of the institution and expressed hope for its gradual end.

But all this would change markedly in the early decades of the nineteenth century, as John Brown came of age. The cotton gin, the steamboat, and the rapid growth of textile mills made it possible and hugely profitable to grow and ship millions of bales of what had previously been a minor crop. Andrew Jackson, himself a cotton planter, championed the policy of Indian "removal," dislodging southern tribes and opening vast tracts of new land for cultivation. This expansion, in turn, created a vibrant market for the Chesapeake's surplus slaves, who were sold by the thousands to gang-labor plantations in the Deep South.

Southerners also dominated government, largely because the three-fifths clause padded the representation of slave states in Congress and the electoral college, throughout the antebellum period. Southerners won thirteen of the first sixteen presidential contests, ruled the Supreme Court for all but eight years before the Civil War, and held similar sway over leadership posts in Congress.

But this clout—economic as well as political—depended on continual expansion. The South needed new lands to plant and new states to boost representation, to keep pace with the industrializing and more populous North. This inevitably sowed conflict as the nation spread west. With the settling of each new territory a contentious question arose: would it be slave or free?

The first serious strife flared in 1819, when Missouri sought statehood. Missouri had been settled mainly by Southerners; its admission to the Union would carry slavery well north and west of its existing boundaries and upset the numerical balance between slave and free states. After lengthy debate, Congress finessed the crisis by admitting Maine along with Missouri and by drawing a line across the continent, forbidding any further slavery north of the 36° 30' parallel. This deal—the Missouri Compromise of 1820—formed the basis for a three-decade détente over slavery's spread.

But Thomas Jefferson, then in his late seventies, immediately sensed the danger inherent in the agreement. In demarcating a border between slave and free, the compromise underscored the country's fault line and fixed the nation into two camps. "This momentous question, like a fire bell in the night, awakened and filled me with terror," Jefferson wrote of the debate over Missouri and slavery. "I considered it at once as the knell of the Union. It is hushed indeed for the moment, but this is a reprieve only, not a final sentence."

IN HIS AUTOBIOGRAPHICAL LETTER to young Henry Stearns, John Brown said he felt the first stirrings of his "Eternal war with Slavery" at age twelve, when he saw a slave boy beaten with iron shovels. "This brought John to reflect on the wretched, hopeless condition, of Fatherless & Motherless slave children," he wrote. Brown, who was also motherless and subject to childhood beatings, may have identified with the slave boy. But his burning hatred of racial oppression had another source. Like so much else in his life, it reflected the influence of his father.

In most respects, Owen Brown's religious faith harked back to his Puritan forebears, who believed they had a covenant with God to make America a moral beacon to the world. In the eighteenth century, Calvinist ministers began speaking of slavery as a threat to this special relationship— a breach of divine law that would bring down God's wrath upon the land. Owen was strongly affected by this preaching, and like many other New England emigrants, he carried his antislavery convictions to the Western Reserve.

He also displayed an unusual tolerance toward the native inhabitants of Ohio. "Some Persons seamed disposed to quarel with the Indians but I never was," he wrote. Nor did he proselytize, or damn natives as heathens, as Puritans of old would have done. Instead, he traded meal for fish and game; he also built a log shelter to protect local Indians from an enemy tribe. Young John "used to hang about" Indians as much as he could—the beginnings of a lifelong sympathy for natives that stood in stark contrast to the prevailing hostility of white Americans.

As Owen Brown established himself in Ohio, he and his neighbors helped fugitive slaves, making the town of Hudson a well-traveled stop on the Underground Railroad. John followed suit, aiding runaways who came to the log cabin he shared with a brother while he was still a bachelor. He continued to aid fugitive slaves after his marriage, but he had a great deal else to occupy him.

During the first four years of their union, Brown and his wife had three sons. Like his father before him, Brown pioneered new territory, taking his wife and toddlers to a sparsely settled section of northwestern Pennsylvania. He cleared land, built a tannery, raised stock, and, like Owen, became a civic leader, founding a school and church and serving as the area's first postmaster. "An inspired paternal ruler" was how one of his neighbors described him, "controlling and providing for the circle of which he was the head."

This circle quickly grew to include three more children. Brown, raised by disciplinarians, became one himself, hewing to the Calvinist belief in the depravity of human nature. His firstborn, John junior, was required to keep a ledger listing his sins and detailing the punishment due each: "unfaithfulness at work" earned three lashes; "disobeying mother" brought eight. The second born, Jason, had a vivid dream about petting a baby raccoon that was "as kind as a kitten," and described the encounter as if it had really happened. He was three or four at the time, and his father thrashed him for telling a "wicked lie." Five-year-old Ruth muddied her shoes while gathering pussy willows and then fibbed about how she'd gotten wet. Her father "switched me with the willow that had caused my sin," she recalled.

Corporal punishment was common at the time, but Brown dispensed the rod with especial vigor. He was determined to root out sin, not only in his offspring but also in himself and others. When he was a young man, this compulsion to punish wrongs was primarily manifest in small acts of moral policing. Brown apprehended two men he encountered on the road who were stealing apples, and smashed a neighbor's whiskey jug after taking a few sips and deciding the liquor had dangerous powers.

Despite his severity, Brown was beloved by his children, who also recalled his many acts of tenderness. He sang hymns to them at bedtime, recited maxims from Aesop and Benjamin Franklin ("Diligence is the mother of good luck"), cared for his "little folks" when they were ill, and was gentle with animals: he warmed frozen lambs in the family washtub.

Brown nursed his wife as well. Dianthe came from a family with a history of mental illness, and not long after her marriage she began to exhibit signs of what relatives called "strangeness." She also faltered physically, suffering from "a difficulty about her heart," Brown wrote.

Though the nature of her affliction isn't clear, it probably wasn't helped by bearing six children in nine years, one of whom, a son, died at the age of four. A year after his death, Dianthe went into labor a seventh time; the child, another boy, was stillborn and had to be extracted "with instruments," Brown wrote. After three days of "great bodily pain & distress," Dianthe also died, at the age of thirty-one. Brown buried her beside their unnamed son, beneath a tombstone bearing Dianthe's final words: "Farewell Earth."

THIS LOSS, WHICH ECHOED his mother's death in childbirth, appears to have sent Brown into shock. "I have been growing numb for a good while," he wrote a business partner. He also complained of vague physical symptoms. "Getting more & more unfit for any thing."

Brown and his five children—the youngest was not yet two—briefly moved in with another family. Upon returning to his own home, he hired a housekeeper, whose sixteen-year-old sister, Mary Day, often came along to help. Several months later, Brown proposed to Mary by letter. They married in July 1833, less than a year after Dianthe's death.

A tall, sturdy teenager of modest education, Mary was half her husband's age and only four years older than his eldest child. She would bear him thirteen more children and endure great economic hardship. Brown was a tireless worker and skilled at diverse trades: tanning, surveying, farming, cattle breeding, sheepherding. He won prizes for his fine wool, published articles about livestock ("Remedy for Bots or Grubs, in the heads of Sheep"), and filled a pocket diary with practical tips, such as rules for measuring hay in a barn and a farm lady's advice on making butter. ("In summer add plenty of cold water to the milk before churning. The slower the churning the better.")

But Brown's diligence and work ethic were repeatedly undone by his inability to manage money. This was a leitmotif of his earliest surviving letters, mostly to a partner in his tanning and cattle business. "I am running low for cash again," Brown wrote Seth Thompson in 1828. "I was unable to raise any cash towards the bank debt," he wrote in 1832. Then, later that year: "Unable to send you money as I intended." And in 1834, again: "I have been utterly unable to raise any money for you as yet." In these and many other letters, Brown expressed regret for his financial straits—and blamed them on forces beyond his control: the weather, ill health, the monetary policies of President Andrew Jackson.

Brown may also have been distracted by his budding concern for affairs other than business. It was in the early 1830s that he first wrote of his determination to help slaves. He also showed signs of a truculent and nonconformist spirit. Brown joined the Freemasons but quickly fell out with the secret society amid accusations that Masons had murdered one of their critics in New York. Far from being cowed by the controversy, Brown openly proclaimed his opposition to the group and circulated the published statement of a Mason who claimed that he'd been selected to cut the throat of a "brother" who revealed the order's secrets.

"I have aroused such a feeling towards me," Brown wrote his father in 1830, "as leads me for the present to avoid going about the streets at evening & alone." Brown knew his father would approve of his defiance, if not of the other measure he took. Owen was a committed pacifist; his son, a warrior at heart, acquired his first gun.

CHAPTER 2

—∕∕∕—

I Consecrate My Life

I n 1831, a decade after Missouri entered the Union, Jefferson's "fire bell in the night" rang again—this time in Southampton County, Virginia, close to where the first Africans had been sold to Jamestown colonists in 1619. Late one August night, a preacher named Nat Turner led a small band of fellow slaves from farm to farm, slaughtering whites. Other slaves joined in, and Turner's force killed about sixty people before militiamen quelled the uprising. Enraged whites then went on a rampage of their own, murdering hundreds of blacks and sticking their severed heads on roadside signposts as a warning.

Turner hid in the woods for two months before being captured. In prison, a lawyer recorded his chillingly eloquent confession. At an early age, Turner said, he "was ordained for some great purpose in the hands of the Almighty." Signs and visions gradually revealed what he considered his God-given mission: "I should arise and prepare myself, and slay my enemies with their own weapons."

Turner and his followers had done precisely that, using axes, fence rails, and captured arms to murder any whites they found, including women, schoolchildren, a baby sleeping in its cradle, and a man "who was to me a kind master," Turner said. He claimed to have had no design apart from killing. As his guiding "Spirit" had told him, "the time was fast approaching when the first should be last and the last should be first." At his trial, Turner pleaded not guilty, "saying to his counsel that

HORRID MASSACRE IN VIRGINIA·

Illustration in an 1831 pamphlet on the Nat Turner Rebellion

he did not feel so." Six days later, he was hanged and dismembered, his body parts distributed to family of the victims.

Though Turner failed to win any slaves their freedom, he stirred the deepest fear of southern whites: that blacks might at any moment rise up and slaughter them in their beds. This terror was particularly acute in plantation counties where slaves greatly outnumbered whites. That Turner was devout, and that his owners had treated him comparatively well, only made matters worse, for it upset the paternalistic fantasy that slaves were too docile and contented to revolt.

Turner's uprising also galvanized the newborn abolitionist movement, led by the fiery Boston editor William Lloyd Garrison. Previously, antislavery efforts in the United States had centered on the gradual emancipation of blacks and their "colonization" in Africa or the Caribbean. Jefferson and, later, Abraham Lincoln were among the adherents of this program, which was based on the belief that blacks could never live as equals to whites.

Garrison, by contrast, sought the immediate abolition of slavery and the extension of full rights to black Americans. He signaled his urgent, uncompromising stance in the inaugural issue of his abolitionist weekly, *The Liberator*, published just eight months before Turner's revolt. "Tell a man whose house is on fire to give a moderate alarm," he wrote. "I will not equivocate—I will not excuse—I will not retreat a single inch—AND I WILL BE HEARD."

There is no evidence that *The Liberator* reached or influenced Nat Turner. But in the wake of his uprising, white Southerners targeted the paper as part of a brutal crackdown on slaves and on anyone or anything that might feed their discontent. Southern states stepped up slave patrols and tightened slave codes; they barred blacks from learning to read or write, from preaching, from gathering in groups without white oversight. Southern officials also indicted Garrison, offering large rewards for his capture or, indeed, the apprehension of anyone distributing *The*

William Lloyd Garrison

Liberator, which Virginia's governor claimed was published "with the express intention of inciting the slaves."

This onslaught, in turn, fed Garrison fresh material for his crusade. In his view, the southern backlash gave evidence not only of slavery's cruelty but of the threat the institution posed to freedom of speech and the entire nation's liberty. Garrison sent salvo after salvo from *The Liberator,* each round prompting return fire from slavery's newly energized defenders, who began to espouse a brazenly unapologetic doctrine.

In earlier decades, Southerners had often spoken of slavery as a necessary evil, an uncomfortable inheritance from those who first brought Africans to the colonies. "I take higher ground," John Calhoun told Congress in 1837. "Instead of an evil," slavery was "a positive good." It was rooted in the Bible and racial difference, which made whites the natural and rightful masters of "savage" Africans. Slaves were secure and well cared for, unlike wage laborers in northern mills; white Southerners were freed from drudgery and class conflict.

George Fitzhugh, of Virginia, later took Calhoun's thesis to its logical extreme. In tracts such as *Cannibals All!,* he argued that if slavery was right, then the Founders themselves had been wrong. "All men are created equal" wasn't a manifest truth; it was a self-evident lie.

Ten days after Nat Turner's revolt, William Lloyd Garrison had written in *The Liberator*: "The first step of the earthquake, which is ultimately to shake down the fabric of oppression, leaving not one stone upon another, has been made." Garrison's words were to prove prophetic, though perhaps not in the way he imagined. In and of itself, Turner's revolt was a tremor. But it cracked open a rift between fundamentally opposed views of America's destiny. With each fresh denunciation and demonization, the chasm widened, until North and South came to regard each other not just as distinct regions but as separate peoples.

THE 1831 REVOLT AND its aftermath also stirred John Brown, who soon began plotting his own work against slavery. Bred of the same New England stock as William Lloyd Garrison and born the same year as Nat Turner, Brown shared essential traits with both the austere Yankee editor and the messianic slave preacher. In a sense, his antislavery career would trace an arc from one man to the other.

Brown's father was an early subscriber to *The Liberator* and shared it with his son, who often visited Owen in Ohio and would soon move his family back there. Owen also became an early supporter of organized abolitionism, which effectively emerged as a movement in the United States with the founding of the American Anti-Slavery Society in 1833, under Garrison's leadership.

The next year, Brown wrote his brother: "I have been trying to devise some means to do something in a practical way for my fellow-men who are in bondage." This is the earliest surviving mention of slavery in Brown's writing. He told his brother that he wanted to bring a black youth into his household, provide him an education, "and, above all, try to teach him the fear of God." He also hoped to start a school for blacks. Education, he wrote, would free blacks' minds and encourage Southerners to emancipate their slaves. "Perhaps we might, under God, in that way do more towards breaking their yoke effectually than in any other."

These words seem mild for a man who would later take up arms, but they meshed closely with the abolitionism espoused in *The Liberator*. Garrison believed education, moral suasion, and Christian uplift would convince Americans, North and South, that slavery was a sin and a stain on the nation that must be expunged. Though vehement in word, Garrison was nonviolent in deed, a passionate "non-resistant." He felt that violence, even in the cause of freedom, only recapitulated the sins of slave drivers. "I deny the right of any people to *fight* for liberty, and so far am a Quaker in principle."

Brown initially shared Garrison's pacifism. As a boy, he'd been so disgusted by what he saw of soldiers during the War of 1812 that he later refused to drill with local militias and paid fines to avoid military service. Throughout his life, he felt a strong affinity with Quakers, admiring their plainness, independent spirit, and long-standing opposition to slavery.

Brown and Garrison were also alike in their moral absolutism. Both hated compromise and felt "all on fire" to root out sin. Typical was their embrace of temperance, minus the moderation that word implies. Brown smashed jugs and barrels of whiskey; Garrison campaigned for abstinence that was "Total with a capital Tee"—the origin of the word "teetotaler."

But Brown's beliefs would part ways with Garrison's as conflict over slavery escalated from angry words and petitions to fists and clubs and guns. Garrison, heeding the New Testament admonition to "resist not evil," believed in turning the other cheek. Brown, more of an Old Testament Christian, sought divine retribution. He also displayed a visceral loathing of behavior he judged craven. Nothing galvanized him more than bullying that went unanswered.

The first sign of Brown's brewing militancy came in 1837, when a pro-slavery mob in Illinois killed an abolitionist editor, Elijah Lovejoy, and threw his printing press into the Mississippi. Garrison, who had narrowly escaped lynching two years before, disapproved of Lovejoy's arming himself in self-defense. Brown, at a church meeting called to protest Lovejoy's killing, lifted his right hand and declared: "Here before God, in the presence of these witnesses, from this time, I consecrate my life to the destruction of slavery."

Brown's father attended the same meeting and spoke in praise of Lovejoy. About this time, Owen also left his conservative church to join one affiliated with abolitionism. And he became an early trustee of Oberlin, a radical new college in Ohio that accepted blacks and women. One of Oberlin's first female graduates was Florella Brown, Owen's daughter by his second wife.

John Brown also broke with his church in the bold fashion that would become his hallmark. During a revival, he was angered to see the congregation's few black worshippers confined to the back of the church; he escorted them forward to his own family's pew and took their seats in back. Church deacons later reprimanded him.

Brown manifested his independence in another, more covert way. Abolitionists created scores of societies in the 1830s and 1840s, from national organizations to local knitting circles. Brown joined none of them. Instead, one night in the late 1830s, he gathered his wife and three teenaged sons by the fire and spoke of his determination to wage war on slavery. "He asked who of us were willing to make common cause with him in doing all in our power to 'break the jaws of the wicked and pluck the spoil out of his teeth,'" his eldest son wrote. "Are you, Mary, John, Jason and Owen?" As each family member assented, Brown knelt in prayer and administered an oath, pledging them to secrecy and devotion to slavery's defeat. He later brought his younger children into this secret army, including a daughter who would accompany him to Virginia.

But as imposing as Brown could be as a father, he wasn't a cult figure to his family. Nor did he command automatic obedience from his offspring. To the contrary, they often found amusement in his stern and ceaseless efforts to inculcate his beliefs. During the family's twice-daily prayers, his son Salmon recalled, Brown would become "dead to the world and to the pranks of his unregenerate boys, who slyly prodded each other with pins and trampled upon each other's toes to relieve the tension."

None of Brown's sons adopted their father's orthodox faith, and several openly challenged it—an apostasy that vexed him tremendously. But all seven of his "unregenerate boys" who survived childhood would take up arms against slavery. They "held firmly to the idea that father was right," Salmon recalled. "Where he had led we were glad to follow—and every one of us had the courage of his convictions." Brown's brothers, in-laws, and other kin would also lend support to his antislavery crusade. "There was a Brown family conspiracy," his eldest son said, "to break the power of slavery."

Over the course of this decades-long struggle, Brown drew inspiration from a number of Old Testament figures. But the one he returned to most often was Gideon. Called on by God to save Israel from the wicked Midianites, Gideon gathered a small force and crept up on his enemy's vast camp in the dark. Then he blew his trumpet and so did his men, raising their torches and crying, "The sword of the Lord, and of Gideon!" The Midianites "ran, and cried, and fled," until their leaders were hunted down and slain.

The story of Gideon embodied Brown's belief that a righteous band, boldly led, could bring divine wrath upon the wicked of the land. With God as his protector, he needed only a small tribe, beginning with the four family members he inducted by his hearth in the late 1830s.

BROWN'S INITIATION OF HIS wife and sons, however, coincided with a collapse in his worldly affairs. He'd moved back to Ohio in 1835, during a property boom in the Western Reserve that was fueled by easy credit and the many transportation projects under way in the rapidly expanding nation. Brown began speculating on land along a proposed canal route, borrowing money and subdividing lots and then borrowing again and buying more property.

This scheme collapsed when the canal company abruptly changed its plans. "I do think it is best to sell all out if we can at any thing like a fair rate," Brown wrote his long-suffering business partner, Seth Thompson, who wanted to cut their losses as prices spiraled down, "but I think the time unfavourable. If we have been crazy getting in, do try & let exercise a sound mind about the maner of getting out."

Brown's judgment proved disastrous: six months later, the economy crashed. During the "Panic of 1837," almost half the nation's banks closed, credit evaporated, and the United States entered its first economic depression. Brown, already in trouble, was now buried in debts and lawsuits.

"The prospect is rather dark," he finally conceded to Thompson in 1839, when he could no longer pay his taxes. "I feel rather more depressed than usual." Brown returned to tanning, cattle driving, and surveying—even breeding race horses to climb out of debt. But by 1840 he was "flat down" and unable to afford so much as postage.

Things got worse. Brown refused to vacate a piece of land to which he'd lost title. Instead, he armed his sons with muskets and holed up in a cabin on the property until he and two of his boys were arrested and briefly jailed. A year later, in 1842, an Ohio court declared Brown bankrupt and listed the household "necessaries" his family was allowed to keep for its survival. This meager inventory included "2 Earthen Crocks Broke," "3 Bags old," 20 pounds of lard, 11 Bibles, "8 Womens and childrens aprons," and a tin pail valued at 6 cents.

Brown's plight wasn't unusual: more than forty thousand Americans filed for bankruptcy under a new law enacted after the 1837 panic. But for a man who hated to "abandon anything he fixed his purpose upon," failure of this magnitude was especially galling. He'd fallen far short of his own exacting standards and had borrowed heavily from friends and family, including his beloved father, who lost his farm after underwriting one of John's loans. Brown also badly damaged his reputation by paying off land debts with money he'd been given to buy wool.

His letters from this period were self-lacerating. In one, he signed himself "Unworthily yours." In another, he asked his wife's forgiveness for his "many faults & foibles," and later addressed her as "the sharer of my poverty, trials, discredit, & sore afflictions."

A year after the bankruptcy, Brown's family was struck by an even greater catastrophe. Severe dysentery, possibly caused by cholera, swept the large household. Charles Brown, a "swift and strong" six-year-old, was the first to die. Soon after, on three consecutive days, three of his siblings perished. The oldest was nine-year-old Sarah.

"She seemed to have no idea of recovering from the first," Brown wrote, "nor did she ever express the least desire that she might." Ill himself, he buried Sarah and the others in a single grave. "They were all children towards whom perhaps we might have felt a little partial," he wrote his eldest son, John Brown, Jr., who was away at school, "but they all now lie in a little row together."

In the early 1800s, roughly a third of Americans died before reaching adulthood. Early death was so common that parents recycled their children's names; the Browns, having lost a Sarah, Frederick, and Ellen, named three newborns Sarah, Frederick, and Ellen. Of the twenty children Brown fathered, nine died before the age of ten, among them a baby girl accidentally scalded to death by an older sister.

Brown, though all too familiar with early death, had always taken losses exceptionally hard, beginning with his prolonged childhood mourning of pets and even of a marble. Burying four of his young flock in the fall of 1843 plunged him into a profound depression. It was "a calamity from which father never fully recovered," John junior wrote. The family's impoverishment, which had necessitated moving to a crowded and possibly unsanitary log house, may have deepened the wound. "I felt for a number of years," Brown later wrote in a letter to a young abolitionist, "a steady, strong desire: to die."

But in the same letter, he expressed his undying commitment to the destruction of slavery. "Certainly the cause is enough to live for," Brown wrote, and he was "now rather anxious to live for a few years more." He knew he would "endure hardness," as he had throughout his life. "But I expect to effect a mighty conquest, even though it be like the last victory of Samson."

A Warlike Spirit

In the 1840s, as Brown battled bankruptcy and depression, his eldest son became enamored of phrenology. This pseudoscience held that character could be read in the contours of the skull. John junior's father tended to be skeptical of the era's many heterodox notions, abolitionism excepted. But he consented to a "reading" by Orson Fowler, a well-known phrenologist.

Fowler may have been coached by John Brown, Jr., or he may have gleaned insight from the words and manner of his subject. In any event, his notes on Brown were for the most part astute. "You have a pretty good opinion of yourself—would rather lead than be led," Fowler wrote. "You like to have your own way, and to think and act for yourself . . . are positive in your likes and dislikes, 'go the whole figure or nothing' & want others to do the same." He added: "You like to do business on a large scale, and can make money better than save it."

Fowler wrote this in early 1847, as Brown embarked on a new and ambitious venture. A few years before, he had formed a partnership with a wealthy Akron man, to raise sheep and sell fine wool. Brown was a skilled shepherd and the partnership initially prospered. But as Fowler noted, Brown liked to think big and was very certain of his judgment. Others who knew him described this as "fixedness."

In this instance, Brown became fixed on the notion that textile

manufacturers were fleecing wool producers. He prevailed on his partner to establish a depot in Springfield, Massachusetts, where Brown
could buy and grade wool and sell it at a better price while collecting a
broker's commission.

He may have been right that producers were exploited. But fixedness
was a trait ill suited to the wildly fluctuating wool market of the late
1840s. When prices plunged, Brown refused to sell. Wool and unpaid
bills quickly piled up at the Springfield depot. Brown also gave signs of a
growing ambivalence about the enterprise in which he was engaged. This
was fed in part by his father's lifelong admonitions against vanity and
materialism.

"I sometimes have dreadful reflections about having fled to go down
to Tarshish," Brown wrote his father. Tarshish was the trade port that
Jonah set sail for in an attempt to escape God's will. En route he was
swallowed by a whale, then released to do the Lord's bidding as a preacher
to unbelievers.

But if Springfield tested (and found wanting) Brown's acumen and
dedication as a businessman, it proved an excellent place to pursue the
true mission he believed he had from God. The city had a large population of free blacks, many of them fugitives from slavery, and it was a
regular stop on the abolitionist circuit. Among those who visited Springfield was Frederick Douglass, the escaped slave, orator, and writer who
had become, alongside William Lloyd Garrison, the most prominent
abolitionist in the country.

Brown met Douglass in the winter of 1847–48 and invited him to his
home, which the visitor described as extremely humble, with furnishings
that "would have satisfied a Spartan." Douglass also gave a vivid description of Brown as he appeared in his late forties. Standing about five foot
ten, he was "lean, strong, and sinewy," and "straight and symmetrical as
a mountain pine." He had a prominent chin, coarse dark hair, and eyes
"full of light and fire." The earliest surviving portrait of Brown, a studio
daguerreotype, dates to the period of Douglass's visit. Brown's thin lips
are pressed firmly together, forming a slash across his angular face. His
deep-set eyes are piercing and hooded, his brow furrowed, his nose long
and sharp. Dark, bristly hair crowns his forehead.

Brown's pose is equally striking. His right hand is raised in oath, as if

John Brown ca. 1847, daguerreotype by Augustus Washington

pledging allegiance to a secret fraternity. His left hand clutches a banner that bore the letters "S.P.W." This stood for Subterranean Pass Way, shorthand for the radical scheme Brown had devised for slaves' liberation.

He shared this nascent plan with Frederick Douglass after their dinner in Springfield. Brown pointed to a map of the Allegheny Mountains, which run diagonally from Pennsylvania into Maryland and Virginia and deep into the South. Filled with natural forts and caves, these mountains, Brown said, had been placed by God "for the emancipation of the negro race." He planned to use the Alleghenies as a base for guerrillas, who would make lightning raids on the farm valleys below and "induce slaves to join them." As the insurgent army grew, it "would run off the slaves in large numbers," sending them north along the mountain chain to freedom.

Brown's main objective, he told Douglass, was to undermine slavery by "rendering such property insecure." He also believed his mission would focus national attention on slavery, as had happened after Nat Turner's revolt in 1831. The two men debated the scheme until three in the morning. Brown sought the black abolitionist's support; Douglass doubted the plan's feasibility. But he came away deeply impressed by the wool merchant's sincerity and commitment.

Douglass had begun his own abolitionist career as a protégé of Garrison's. But by the late 1840s, he'd come to question whether pacifism and moral suasion were sufficient tools for slaves' liberation. He also bristled at the prejudice and condescension displayed by many white abolitionists. Brown seemed remarkably free of this.

"Though a white gentleman," Douglass wrote in his abolitionist weekly, the *North Star*, soon after his Springfield visit, Brown "is in sympathy, a black man, and as deeply interested in our cause, as though his own soul had been pierced with the iron of slavery."

BROWN GAVE FURTHER EVIDENCE of this sympathy in 1848, when he sought the support of Gerrit Smith, one of the most exceptional, eccentric, and philanthropic men of his day. Born into the landed gentry of upstate New York, Smith profitably managed his family's estates while cycling through the many reform movements of the early 1800s, including temperance, women's rights, vegetarianism, and sexual "purity" (a creed advocated by Sylvester Graham, who claimed his coarse-grained crackers curbed lust and masturbation).

But Smith's abiding passion was abolitionism. He helped found the antislavery Liberty Party and ran as its presidential candidate in 1848 (receiving 0.1 percent of the vote). The small town his family founded in New York was so strongly abolitionist that a black visitor wrote Frederick Douglass, "There are yet two places where slaveholders cannot come, Heaven and Peterboro."

Smith also had a prior tie to Brown's family. Years before, the New Yorker had donated twenty thousand acres of his holdings in western Virginia to Oberlin, the radical new college in Ohio of which Owen Brown was a trustee. Owen arranged for his then destitute son to survey the land, and it was during this trip that Brown first visited the Allegheny Mountains.

Smith had since undertaken a utopian project: he granted free blacks thousands of acres in upstate New York, so they could farm and own

Gerrit Smith

enough property to qualify for the vote. But the land was poor and remote; the few blacks who settled in an Adirondacks colony called Timbucto struggled from the first.

Brown had a solution, which he proposed to Smith upon visiting the magnate's Peterboro mansion in 1848. He would move to upstate New York himself and help black pioneers survey, farm, and raise stock. "I can think of no place where I think I would sooner go," he wrote his father, "than to live with those poor despised Africans to try, & encourage them; & show them a little as far as I am capable."

Smith was impressed by the idealistic wool merchant and deeded him 244 acres at $1 an acre. In the spring of 1849, Brown settled near Lake Placid, in the village of North Elba. That June, Richard Henry Dana, the author of *Two Years Before the Mast*, was hiking in the Adirondacks when he stumbled on "a log-house and half-cleared farm"—the Browns' temporary home. Dana joined the family of nine for dinner. Two black neighbors were also at the table. Brown "called the negroes by their surnames, with the prefixes of Mr. and Mrs.," Dana observed. "It was plain they had not been so treated or spoken to often before."

The 1850 census listed a twenty-three-year-old black laborer from Florida, a fugitive slave, living with the Browns. Many black farm families dwelled close by. Brown's oldest daughter, Ruth—"a bonny, buxom young woman," Dana wrote, "with fair skin and red hair"—married a white neighbor, Henry Thompson, who would later join his father-in-law's abolitionist crusade, as would two of his brothers.

But Brown himself rarely stayed in North Elba for long. Soon after moving his family to upstate New York, he undertook a desperate scheme to wind up his wool business in Springfield. Rather than sell to domestic buyers at low prices, he shipped tons of his firm's finest wool to Great Britain, convinced he could break the American cartel.

Yet again, Brown's business instincts proved poor. British buyers scorned the American wool, forcing him to ship most of it back home, at great expense, for sale at ruinously low prices. His already troubled business collapsed, and Brown found himself mired in debt and lawsuits, just as he'd been a decade before. He would spend much of the next five years shuttling from court to court, contesting legal claims that "if lost will leave me nice and flat."

Meanwhile, Mary Brown had been left overseeing a cash-strapped household, in a land so harsh that snow still lay in the fields in late May. Since the loss of four children in 1843, Brown's wife had given birth to three more; two of them died as infants. Her frequently absent husband acknowledged the hardships she endured in an unusually tender letter in 1847, noting his "follies," "the verry considerable difference in our age," and the fact that "I sometimes chide you severely." The toll was evident to Richard Dana when he visited the Browns' Adirondack home; he described Mary, then just thirty-three, as "rather an invalid."

Later that summer, as Brown sailed for Britain, Mary decided "she must do something, at once, or she would not live but a little while," John junior wrote his father overseas. Leaving her stepdaughter Ruth in charge of her young children, Mary left North Elba for a "Water-Cure Infirmary" in Northampton, Massachusetts, where she was diagnosed as suffering from a nervous disorder and "a Scrofulous humour seated in her glands."

Mary Brown with daughters Annie and Sarah, ca. 1851

Mary wrote John junior complaining that his father "never believed there was any dissease about me," and had left her very little money. To extend her treatment ("plunge, douche, drenches, and spray baths") she pleaded with her stepson: "If you can send me twenty or twenty five dollars I should like it." Mary also mentioned a lecture by Lucy Stone, an abolitionist and suffragist. "I went to hear for the first time that I ever heard a Woman speak," she wrote, and she "liked her very well."

After her water cure, Mary recovered somewhat, bore another son, (who died aged three weeks), and gave birth a thirteenth and final time when she was thirty-eight. The one surviving photograph of her during her marriage shows a woman with strong cheekbones, severe hair, and downturned lips, seated between two bilious-looking girls.

AT MIDCENTURY, AS BROWN struggled to settle his family and finances, the fragile concord between free and slave states that had prevailed for three decades began to unravel. In the years since the Missouri Compromise, a new euphemism for slavery had emerged: "the peculiar institution."

In the early nineteenth century, this phrase connoted that slavery was "peculiar" or distinctive to the South. As long as it remained so, most Northerners chose to tolerate or ignore it. "It is an existing evil, for which we are not responsible," President Millard Fillmore said in 1850, expressing a common view. "We must endure it, and give it such protection as is guaranteed by the Constitution."

But Northerners recoiled whenever slavery threatened to bleed outside its existing boundaries. Their fear had much more to do with self-interest than with sympathy for blacks—indeed, the latter was so scarce that several northern states passed laws to exclude black immigrants altogether. At bottom, whites didn't want to compete with slave labor and see their own status and prospects diminished. *"The workingmen of the north, east, and west,"* Walt Whitman wrote in 1847, "shall *not* be sunk to the miserable level of what is little above brutishness—sunk to be like owned goods, and driven cattle!"

Whitman's outburst was prompted by national debate over the land grab under way during the Mexican War. Launched in 1846, under President James Polk—like Andrew Jackson, a slave-owning cotton planter—the war concluded in 1848 with the United States increasing its geographic size by a third at Mexico's expense. That same year, the gold rush to California began. This rapid expansion brought the slavery question to a fiercer boil than ever before. Could Southerners carry their "property" into the new territories, and would these territories become free states or slave?

After heated wrangling, Congress put off a reckoning by cutting a deal, just as it had done in 1820 over Missouri. The Compromise of 1850 carved the newly acquired land into three pieces: the free state of California and two territories, Utah and New Mexico, where the slavery question was left unresolved. In a major concession to Southerners, Congress also enacted a new and much tougher Fugitive Slave Act. Federal officials and ordinary citizens were now *required* to aid in the capture and return of runaways, even to the point of forming posses. In effect, every Northerner could be deputized as a slave catcher. Civil liberties were sharply curtailed, too, denying fugitive slaves the right to testify on their own behalf or to be tried before a jury.

This noxious statute instantly roused antislavery fury in the North. Boston mobs set upon slave hunters and freed captured fugitives. In

Pennsylvania, armed blacks, aided by local whites, fought off an attempt to recover four runaways and shot their owner dead. The Fugitive Slave Act also led Harriet Beecher Stowe to write *Uncle Tom's Cabin*, which sold three hundred thousand copies during its first year in print and brought the cruelties of slavery alive for a mainstream audience.

The furor reenergized John Brown as well. "It now seems that the Fugitive Slave Law was to be the means of making more Abolitionists than all the lectures we have had for years," he exulted in a letter to Mary in late 1850. Brown was back in Springfield at the time, trying to salvage what he could from his wool business. While there, he also devised a secret organization to fight slave catchers. He gave this self-defense group a telling name: the United States League of Gileadites. This referred to allies of Gideon, who guarded fords across the Jordan River and slew wicked Midianites fleeing across it.

Brown laid out his tactics in his "Words of Advice" to the Gileadites. He counseled them to act swiftly, secretly, and decisively, like Gideon. "Let the first blow be the signal for all to engage; and when engaged do not work by halves, but make clean work with your enemies." Brown also set out a stringent code of honor: never confess, never betray, never renounce the cause. "Stand by one another, and by your friends, while a drop of blood remains; and be hanged, if you must, but tell no tales out of school."

Forty-four people in Springfield, most if not all of them black, signed an agreement to form the first branch of the League of Gileadites. Little else is known of the group or of Brown's role beyond his "Words of Advice." But he had laid out a blueprint for future action, even to the point of anticipating his own dramatic end.

THE FUGITIVE SLAVE ACT of 1850 was just one of a series of provocations that propelled Brown toward violent action, and the nation toward disunion and conflict. Southern cotton production boomed in the 1840s and 1850s, supplying most of the world's demand and outstripping all other American exports combined. By the eve of the Civil War, the nation's twelve richest counties all lay in the South, a region that constituted, on its own, the fourth largest economy in the world.

The stereotypical "Old South" of columned mansions, hoop skirts, and endless rows of cotton was, in reality, new, and its bloom lasted for only the final decades of slavery's 246-year history in North America. But it gave little sign of withering in the years before the Civil War. To the contrary, slaveholders sought ceaselessly to expand their reach, proclaiming it the nation's manifest destiny to annex still more lands beyond those taken from Mexico and native tribes.

"Cuba must be ours," declared Mississippi senator Jefferson Davis. He also wanted the Yucatán peninsula, so that the Gulf of Mexico would become "a basin of water belonging to the United States." His fellow Mississippian, Senator Albert Brown, coveted Central America. "I want these countries for the spread of slavery," he said. "I would spread the blessings of slavery, like the religion of our Divine Master, to the uttermost ends of the earth."

In the 1850s, proslavery partisans known as "filibusters" invaded Cuba. They failed, but another filibuster, William Walker, briefly established the "Republic of Baja California" after seizing the peninsula from Mexico. Two years later, he led a private army into Nicaragua, installed himself as president, and reinstituted slavery (which had ended there in 1824).

Walker's dictatorship even won recognition from the White House, which was occupied in the 1850s by three of the weakest presidents in U.S. history. Millard Fillmore, Franklin Pierce, and James Buchanan were all Northerners who supported or appeased southern interests, a breed derisively known as "doughfaces"—half-baked and malleable in the hands of slave holders. This pliability was all the more exasperating to antislavery Northerners because of their region's dominance in other realms. By mid-century, the North was home to roughly 70 percent of the nation's free population and more than 80 percent of its industry.

This rapid expansion only heightened the South's insecurity—and the brashness of its leaders' demands for more slaveholding territory and even for the resumption of the transatlantic slave trade, outlawed by Constitutional decree since 1808. "Slavery," Horace Greeley wrote in the *New York Tribune*, "loves aggression, for when it ceases to be aggressive it stagnates and decays. It is the leper of modern civilization, but a leper whom no cry of 'unclean' will keep from intrusion into uninfected company."

GREELEY'S WORDS, in early 1854, were directed at a new and explosive threat to the nation's tenuous unity. Senator Stephen Douglas of Illinois (a powerful booster of the railroad, the Midwest, and himself) introduced a bill to open for settlement a vast stretch of prairie and plains comprising today's Kansas and Nebraska, as well as parts of six other western states. All of this territory lay north of the line demarcated in the Missouri Compromise, above which slavery was to be "forever prohibited." But to win southern votes in Congress, Douglas agreed to repeal the 1820 pact.

If the settlers of the new territories so chose, slavery might now extend across a swath of land reaching from Iowa and Minnesota to the Rockies. Signed into law by a compliant President Pierce in May 1854, the Kansas-Nebraska Act ignited a firestorm so intense that its author acknowledged, "I could travel from Boston to Chicago by the light of my own effigy."

President Pierce poured more oil on the flames that May by sending federal troops to enforce the Fugitive Slave Act against Anthony Burns, a runaway slave who had been captured and put under guard in a Boston courthouse. Abolitionists tried to free Burns by charging the courthouse

FORCING SLAVERY DOWN THE THROAT OF A FREESOILER

Political cartoon, showing Douglas and Pierce at left

with a battering ram. When this failed, he was taken under heavy guard to Boston Harbor, for shipment back to Virginia aboard a U.S. Navy vessel.

The bald spectacle of federal forces aiding in the return of a fugitive to bondage—and in Boston, the cradle of liberty, no less—pushed abolitionist fury to the bursting point. "My thoughts are murder to the state," Henry David Thoreau wrote in his journal, no longer able to reflect on nature during his long walks. A few weeks later, William Lloyd Garrison commemorated July 4 by publicly burning a copy of the U.S. Constitution, branding it "a covenant with death, and an agreement with hell." As the document went up in flames, he proclaimed, "So perish all compromises with tyranny!"

Abolitionists were still a small minority in the North, often mocked as cranks, scolds, and "ultras" or extremists, well outside the mainstream. But the Kansas-Nebraska Act, more than any previous event, gave substance to the specter of an insatiable "Slave Power," intent on devouring the liberties of all Americans. As a group of leading antislavery congressmen warned in a widely circulated appeal to the nation, the bill was "an atrocious plot," designed "to exclude from a vast unoccupied region, emigrants from the Old World and free laborers from our own States, and convert it into a dreary region of despotism, inhabited by masters and slaves."

In the wake of the Kansas-Nebraska debate, opponents of slavery's extension formed a new political coalition: the Republican Party. Societies also sprang up to recruit and assist emigrants to Kansas. Since the territory's status would be determined by popular vote, antislavery activists—and their proslavery counterparts—sought to fill Kansas with settlers sympathetic to their cause. In doing so, partisans on both sides resorted to scare tactics and crude stereotypes. Southerners conjured a tide of "grasping, skin-flint nigger stealing Yankees" washing over Kansas, while Northerners caricatured southern pioneers as "Pukes"—illiterate backwoodsmen with whiskey-red eyes, tobacco-stained teeth, and bowie knives.

IN THE SUMMER OF 1854, Kansas fever took hold in drought-stricken Ohio, where John Brown's grown sons owned farms and orchards. John junior told his father that he'd decided to sell out and move west. Brown approved, expressing praise of any family member "disposed to go to

Kansas or Nebraska, with a view to help defeat SATAN and his legions."
But he was unable to join in this laudable mission. "I feel committed to
operate in another part of the field," he wrote John junior on August 21.

At the time, Brown was living in Akron, where he'd moved his wife
and younger children in 1851 while contesting legal claims and wrapping
up his wool partnership. He now planned to return with his family to
North Elba, to resume work with black farmers in upstate New York, the
"part of the field" he referred to in his letter. Also, Mary Brown was eight
months pregnant and eager to settle after years of near nomadism. This
was no time for her fifty-four-year-old husband to set off on a western
adventure.

But the notion of going to Kansas clearly tempted Brown. "If I were
not so committed," he wrote John junior that August, "I would be on my
way this fall." In the autumn of 1854, his commitment wavered. By this
point, five of his sons had decided to head west, and they wanted their
father to join them. Brown acknowledged in a letter that going to Kansas
seemed "more likely to benefit the colored people on the whole." But he
still felt obliged to work with the black settlers in North Elba, having
"volunteered in their service."

That winter, his older sons trekked west with their families and livestock. In the spring of 1855, they staked claims near the Kansas hamlet of
Osawatomie, where Brown's half sister, Florella, had settled with her
missionary husband a few months before. The Brown sons plowed, planted,
and wrote long letters to their father about the dire political situation in
the territory.

"Every Slaveholding State," John junior wrote in May, "is furnishing
men and money to fasten Slavery upon this glorious land, by means no
matter how foul." The worst threat came from "Border Ruffians" based in
neighboring Missouri who moved in and out of Kansas, harassing anyone who showed free-soil leanings. The Border Ruffians were particularly adept at voter fraud and intimidation. A territorial census in early
1855 found 2,905 eligible voters in Kansas. Yet proslavery forces "won" an
early election that March with 5,427 votes.

By late spring, a proslavery army was rumored to be massing in Missouri for a full-scale invasion. Yet free-state settlers in Kansas "exhibit the
most abject and cowardly spirit, whenever their dearest rights are invaded

and trampled down," John junior wrote. He and his brothers were prepared to take the lead in forming free-state militias to fight back, if only
they had arms. "We need them more than we do bread." In another letter
that May, John junior echoed his father's biblical language. "Every day
strengthens my belief that the sword, that final arbiter of all the great questions that have stirred mankind, will soon be called on to give its verdict."

If Brown needed any final prompt to head for Kansas, this was it. His
family was in peril and so was the cause of freedom. Yet no one was
standing up to the Slave Power's bullying. In June 1855, after finally settling Mary and four children in an unfinished farmhouse in North Elba,
he carried John junior's letter to a convention of radical abolitionists in
Syracuse. Brown spoke of the crisis in Kansas and raised money to buy
guns. In August, he left New York State for Kansas; on the way, he stopped
in Ohio, where he collected more money and weapons.

He also went to see his father, who was eighty-four years old and in fail-
ing health. Owen Brown's mind, however, remained sharp. In a letter to his
daughter in Osawatomie, Owen expressed parental concern about John's
state of mind on the eve of his departure for Kansas. "He has something of
a warlike spiret," Owen wrote. "I think as much as necessary for defence
I will hope nothing more."

A few days later, Owen gave John $40 and said goodbye to his eldest
son. He would never see him again.

CHAPTER 4

—∽—

First Blood

Brown's family members in Kansas had written home not only about politics, but also of the land and its promise. Like emigrants everywhere, eager to lure friends and family to join them, they painted their new surrounds as a pioneer paradise.

"I *certainly* never saw any region to compare in beauty and in richness of soil," wrote Wealthy Brown, John junior's wife. Timber and water abounded, and there was "any quantity of nice prairie where there is not a stone or a stump to prevent ploughing." Grapes grew wild and large; steady breezes cooled the June air.

"The prairies are covered with grass which begins to wave in the wind most beautifully," John junior added. A town site had been laid out, on a gentle slope with open country all around. "The view from this ground is beautiful beyond measure."

All this may have been true in the early summer of 1855. But in October, when John Brown arrived, eastern Kansas appeared far less pleasant. He found his sons and their families still living in tents and wagons, "shivering over their little fires all exposed to the dreadfuly cutting Winds Morning and Evening, & stormy days," he wrote. Almost everyone was sick, too feverish and feeble to bring in crops. Nor were cold and wind the only blight. "We were all out a good part of the night last," John reported to Mary soon after his arrival, "helping to keep the Prairie fires from destroying every thing."

Brown had reached Kansas in poor shape himself. He'd traveled with his teenaged son Oliver, his son-in-law, Henry Thompson, and a horse and wagon purchased in Chicago. The men walked much of the way because the horse was sick and the wagon's load heavy. Its contents included the weapons Brown had collected in New York and Ohio, and the corpse of his four-year-old grandson, who had died en route to Kansas with his family the previous spring and been hastily buried. Brown stopped to disinter the child and bring his remains to Kansas, "thinking it would afford some relief to the broken hearted Father & Mother," he wrote.

By the time Brown reached Kansas, he and his companions were down to sixty cents. Brown, who had turned fifty-five in May, was so exhausted that he camped for the night just a mile or two short of his family's settlement, letting Oliver and Henry go ahead without him.

In the course of this difficult journey, Brown had reflected on his pilgrimage in a letter to Mary, writing from a tent near the Mississippi as he cooked prairie chickens over a fire: "I think, could I hope in any other way to answer the end of my being; I would be quite content to be at North Elba."

Answering "the end of my being" was critical to Calvinists like Brown, who believed in predestination. What path had God charted for me, and was I among his Elect? Though Brown had qualms about leaving his wife and young children in a harsh land with little money, he'd come to believe that battling slavery in Kansas was his God-given destiny. And he was impatient to meet it by the time he reached the territory.

"You are all very dear to me & I humbly trust we may be kept & spared; to meet again on Earth," he wrote Mary and their children in his first letter home after arriving at the Browns' settlement, "but if not let us all endeavor earnestly to secure admission to that Eternal Home where will be no more bitter seperations, 'where the wicked shall cease from troubling; & the weary be at rest.'"

BROWN DIDN'T WAIT LONG to take up arms in the battle he'd come to join. A few weeks before his arrival, the territory's proslavery legislature—"elected" amid rampant fraud—put into force some of the most extreme laws in antebellum America. Anyone who expressed antislavery views was guilty of a felony, punishable by two years' hard labor. Aiding a fugitive slave brought ten years' imprisonment; inciting blacks to rebel brought death. As if this weren't draconian enough, a proslavery editor warned: "We will continue to tar and feather, drown, lynch and hang every white-livered abolitionist who dares to pollute our soil."

Free-state settlers refused to recognize the territory's legislature and scheduled an election of their own for October 9, 1855, just two days after Brown's arrival. Border Ruffians from Missouri had disrupted previous votes with fists and bowie knives; it was feared they would do so again. This gave Brown an opportunity to unpack the special freight—"Guns, Revolvers, Swords, Powder, Caps"—he'd brought west.

"Hearing that trouble was expected we turned out powerfully armed," he wrote his father, a few days after the vote. All the Brown men took part in this show of force, except one who was too sick to carry a gun. "No enemy appeared," Brown added, with evident regret.

Two months later, after helping his sons bring in crops and build log "shanties," Brown leaped at another chance to confront the enemy. Proslavery Missourians had laid siege to the free-state stronghold of Lawrence, Kansas, and the Browns hurried forty miles to join the town's defense. Brown's zeal earned him a commission as captain of the Liberty Guards, a company of twenty men, four of them his sons.

The unit, however, never fired a shot. Following a last-minute treaty, the Missourians pulled back. The newly anointed Captain Brown nonetheless returned home exultant. Free-staters, he believed, had finally faced down their thuggish foes, and his own family had shown its mettle. He also made sure that the world learned of the Liberty Guards, writing at length about the short campaign not only to his family but in a letter to an Ohio newspaper. He took particular pride in telling how he and his men, pistols stuck conspicuously in their belts, had marched onto a bridge guarded by Missourians, who "silently suffered us to pass." Free-state men, he concluded, had acted with coolness and determination, "sustaining the high character of the Revolutionary Fathers."

These and other actions quickly earned the Browns and their Kansas settlement, Brown's Station, a reputation for militancy. Most free-state settlers were antislavery but also antiblack; they wanted Kansas to be a free state for whites only. Also, most free-state leaders discouraged armed resistance, believing that nonviolence would elevate their cause in the eyes of the nation.

The Browns believed in full equality for blacks and were determined to fight for it. John junior became active in free-state politics, while his father maintained a consistently bellicose presence. "Our men have so much <u>war</u> and <u>elections</u> to attend to," wrote Wealthy Brown in January 1856, "that it seems as though we were a great while getting into a house."

In fact, Wealthy, her husband, and their young son were still sleeping in a tent and three-sided shed with a fire at the open end—hardly shelter enough against the heavy snows, severe winds, and thirty-below temperatures during the exceptionally harsh winter of 1855–56. Several of the Browns were laid up with frostbitten feet and the family was forced "to live rather slim," wrote sixteen-year-old Oliver, "having nothing but beans + Johny cake + Johny cake + beans with a very little milk."

Brown had to ask his father in Ohio for more money, as did his destitute wife, who wrote her husband that "we got on our last loaf & I did not know what to do." Brown also trekked back and forth to Missouri through heavy snow to get provisions for his Kansas clan. "Father seems to be as rugged as I ever saw him," Wealthy wrote of Brown. "I guess 'roughing it' agrees with him."

All the while, Brown remained alert for rumblings of war. Hearing a rumor of another planned attack on Lawrence, he wrote Mary: "<u>Should</u> that take place we may soon again be called uppon to 'buckle on our armor,' which by the help of God we will do."

While the weather muffled major conflict, the winter was marked by sporadic violence and constant sniping between Kansas's proslavery and free-state legislatures, which sought statehood for the territory on opposed platforms. The antislavery camp appeared to be gaining ground, since most of the settlers pouring into Kansas were Northerners. But their foes found a powerful ally in President Franklin Pierce, whose half-southern cabinet was dominated by a Mississippian: Jefferson Davis, secretary of war and future head of the Confederacy.

Early in 1856, news reached Kansas that Pierce had endorsed the territory's proslavery legislature as "legitimate," declared resistance to it "treasonable," and threatened to use federal troops against free-state agi-

tators. Pierce also blamed the nation's deepening divide on "wild and chimerical schemes of social change" and "a fanatical devotion to the supposed interests of the relatively few Africans in the United States." Rarely had the U.S. government's acquiescence to the Slave Power been so plainly expressed—and done so by a dough-faced Yankee from New Hampshire.

Brown was incensed. In a letter to an abolitionist congressman in Ohio, he decried the notion that federal troops might enforce the "Hellish enactments" of Kansas's proslavery legislature, and demanded to know "Will anything be done?" Privately, however, he welcomed the outrages committed by Pierce and his southern allies.

"I have no desire," he wrote Mary, "to have the Slave power cease from its acts of aggression. 'Their foot shall slide in due time.'" Brown was quoting a passage from Deuteronomy about the Lord's punishment of the wicked and unsuspecting: "To me belongeth vengeance and recompense; their foot shall slide in due time; for the day of their calamity is at hand."

APRIL 1856 BROUGHT SHOOTS of grass and fresh portents of conflict. A territorial judge arrived to hold court at Dutch Henry's Crossing, a proslavery outpost on Pottawatomie Creek, near Brown's Station. Rumors flew that arrest warrants would be issued for the Browns, who had flagrantly defied proslavery statutes. But the family wasn't about to cower before "bogus" Kansas law. Instead, several of the Brown men sat in on the court session and then stepped outside, loudly calling together a newly formed local militia, the Pottawatomie Rifles. They pledged to resist by force any attempt to enforce proslavery laws and presented this determination in writing to the judge. He adjourned the court the next day without arresting any of them.

Whether or not the judge had been intimidated by the Browns' display, it greatly enhanced their notoriety and deepened the enmity of their proslavery neighbors, a number of whom served as court officers or jurors. The day after the court standoff, Brown wrote a relative: "Matters are a fair way of comeing to a head."

They would do so in May, a month that opened with a menacing arrival. Four hundred Southerners rode into eastern Kansas, led by an

Alabama major, Jefferson Buford, who had recruited "men capable of bearing arms" to colonize the territory and defend it from "the free-soil hordes." The legion's banner proclaimed "The Supremacy of the White Race." On entering Kansas, Buford's men camped near Dutch Henry's Crossing, within easy striking distance of the Browns and other free-state settlers who lived in scattered cabins and hamlets between the Osage River and Pottawatomie Creek.

"We are constantly exposed and have almost no protection," Florella Adair wrote on May 16. The vulnerable free-state enclave, she added, "is known and called an 'abolitionist nest.'"

In the event, the proslavery forces struck first at a much bigger nest: the abolitionist bastion of Lawrence. When free-state leaders in the town resisted arrest on charges of treason, a U.S. marshal called on "law-abiding citizens" in Kansas to form a posse "for the proper execution of the law." His call was promptly answered—by Border Ruffians from Missouri, Buford's band of Alabamans, and others who relished a chance to invade the free-state Gomorrah at Lawrence.

"Draw your revolvers & bowie knives, & cool them in the heart's blood of all those damned dogs, that dare defend that damned breathing hole of hell," David Atchison, a former U.S. senator from Missouri, told cheering Southerners encamped outside Lawrence on May 21, "never to slacken or stop until every spark of free-state, free-speech, free-niggers, or free in any shape is quenched out of Kansas!"

When news of the threat to Lawrence reached Brown's Station the next day, John junior, who was head of the Pottawatomie Rifles, quickly mobilized his thirty-four men and set off for the besieged town. His father and four of his brothers formed a separate squad; two other militias joined en route. The free-state men marched through the night and part of the next day before learning they were too late. A rider from Lawrence reported that Border Ruffians had taken the town without resistance and were proceeding to loot and burn it. The free-state men marched on, until they heard from a second rider that federal troops had taken control of the ruined town from its southern pillagers.

Brown was enraged. *Had no one put up a fight?* As the free-state men made camp and deliberated over what to do, Jason Brown overheard his father talking to two men about their proslavery neighbors back at Dutch Henry's Crossing, on Pottawatomie Creek. "Now something *must* be done," Brown said. "Something *is going to be done now.*"

He spoke to others in camp, seeking men for a secret mission under his command. John junior argued against dividing the free-state force and cautioned his father to "commit no rash act." But four other sons—Owen, Frederick, Salmon, and Oliver—joined their father, as did their brother-in law, Henry Thompson. Brown also recruited the two men he'd spoken to over breakfast. Theodore Weiner, a Polish Jew, ran a store near Dutch Henry's and had been harassed by its inhabitants. James Townsley, a painter, knew the proslavery settlement well and offered to carry Brown's band to the Pottawatomie in his two-horse wagon.

The eight men were well armed with rifles and revolvers. But before heading off to the enemy encampment, they used a grindstone to sharpen the short, heavy broadswords that Brown had acquired in Ohio. "There was a signal understood," his son Owen later said. "When my father was to raise a sword—then we were to begin."

THOUGH BROWN NEEDED NO further spur to carry out his Gideon-like mission, the pillaging of Lawrence coincided with another shocking assault by the proslavery camp. Earlier that week, on the floor of the U.S. Senate, Charles Sumner of Massachusetts had delivered a five-hour diatribe about Kansas, accusing the "Slave Power" of perpetrating "the rape of a Virgin Territory" by "hirelings picked from the drunken spew and vomit of an uneasy civilization." Sumner also heaped invective on Senator Andrew Butler of South Carolina, whom he mocked for making great claims to chivalry while taking as his mistress "the harlot, Slavery."

Butler was ill and absent from the chamber. But a kinsman from South Carolina, Congressman Preston Brooks, accosted Sumner on the floor of the Senate on May 22, as Lawrence smoldered. Brooks told Sumner his speech was "a libel on South Carolina and against my relative Senator Butler." Then he beat the Massachusetts senator hard enough to splinter the gold-headed cane he used to do it. Sumner fell to the floor, bloodied and unconscious, so badly hurt that he did not return to the Senate for three years. Brooks, meanwhile, became an instant southern celebrity, hailed for having "lashed into submission" the Senate's most vocal abolitionist.

Salmon Brown, one of the sons who joined his father's secret mission to the Pottawatomie, later stated that news of Sumner's brutal beating reached the war party as it was en route to its destination. "The men went crazy—crazy," he recalled. "It seemed to be the finishing, decisive touch."

Salmon's memory may have been clouded. Brooks's attack occurred just a day before Brown set off for the Pottawatomie. It's doubtful that news from the nation's capital could have reached frontier Kansas that quickly. But the two events, the "sack of Lawrence" and the beating of Sumner, were strikingly parallel in their symbolism. Southerners, in both Kansas and the Capitol Building, could bully and beat with impunity, like plantation slave drivers.

Something *must* be done. And it must be done *now*.

AT ABOUT ELEVEN P.M. on the brightly moonlit night of May 24, 1856, James Doyle, his wife, Mahala, and their five children were in bed when they heard a noise in the yard. Then came a rap at the door of their cabin on Mosquito Creek, a tributary of the Pottawatomie. A voice outside asked the way to a neighbor's home. When Doyle opened the door, several men burst in, armed with pistols and large knives. They said they were from the "Northern army" and had come to take Doyle and three of his sons prisoner.

The Doyles, a poor family from Tennessee, owned no slaves. But since moving to Kansas the preceding autumn, James and his two oldest sons had joined a proslavery party and strongly supported the southern cause. Two of the Doyles had served on the court convened the month before at Dutch Henry's Crossing, a mile along the creek.

Mahala Doyle pleaded tearfully with the intruders to release their youngest captive, her sixteen-year-old son, John. They let him go and then led the others out of the cabin and into the night. "My husband and two boys, my sons, did not come back," Mahala later testified.

She and her son John didn't know the identity of the men who came to their door, but they'd glimpsed their faces in the candlelight. "An old man commanded the party," John Doyle testified; "his face was slim." He added: "These men talked exactly like eastern men and northern men talk."

Before leaving, the strangers asked the Doyles about a neighbor, Allen Wilkinson, who lived about half a mile away with his wife, Louisa Jane, and two children. Like the Doyles, they had come from Tennessee and owned no slaves. Unlike them, Wilkinson could read and write. He was a member of Kansas's proslavery legislature, and his cabin served as the local post office.

After midnight, Louisa Jane, who was sick with measles, heard a barking dog and woke her husband. He said it was nothing and went back to sleep. Then the dog began barking furiously and Louisa Jane heard footsteps and a knock. She woke her husband again; he called out, asking who was there.

"I want you to tell me the way to Dutch Henry's," a voice replied.

When Wilkinson began to give directions, the man said, "Come out and show us." His wife wouldn't let him. The stranger then asked if Wilkinson was an opponent of the free-state cause. "I am," he said.

"You are our prisoner," came the reply. Four armed men poured into the cabin, took Wilkinson's gun, and told him to get dressed. Louisa Jane begged the men to let her husband stay: she was sick and helpless, with two small children.

"You have neighbors?" asked an older man who appeared to be in command. He wore soiled clothes and a straw hat pulled down over his narrow face. Louisa Jane told him she had neighbors, but couldn't go for them. "It matters not," he said. Unshod, her husband was led outside. Louisa Jane thought she heard her husband's voice a moment later "in complaint," but then all was still.

DUTCH HENRY'S CROSSING WAS named for Henry Sherman, a German immigrant who had settled the ford on the Pottawatomie. He traded cattle to westward pioneers and ran a tavern and store that served as a gathering place for proslavery men. He and his brother, William, were feared by free-state families for their drunken and threatening behavior.

On the night of the Northern army's visit to the Pottawatomie, Dutch

Henry was out on the prairie looking for stray cattle. But one of his employees who lived at the crossing, James Harris, was asleep with his wife and child when men burst in carrying swords and revolvers. They demanded the surrender of Harris and three other men who were spending the night in his one-room cabin. Two were travelers who had come to buy a cow; the third was Dutch Henry's brother, William.

Harris and the two travelers were questioned individually outside the cabin, and then returned inside, having been found innocent of aiding the proslavery cause. Then William Sherman was escorted from the cabin. About fifteen minutes later, Harris heard a pistol shot; the men who had been guarding the cabin left, having taken a horse, a saddle, and weapons.

It was now Sunday morning, about two or three A.M. The terrified settlers along the Pottawatomie waited until dawn to venture outside. At the Doyles', the first house visited in the night, sixteen-year-old John found his father, James, and his oldest brother, twenty-two-year-old William, lying dead in the road about two hundred yards from their cabin. Both men had multiple wounds; William's head was cut open and his jaw and side slashed. John found his other brother, twenty-year-old Drury, lying dead nearby.

"His fingers were cut off; and his arms were cut off," John said in an affidavit. "His head was cut open; there was a hole in his breast." Mahala Doyle, having glanced at the bodies of her husband and older son, could not look at Drury. "I was so much overcome that I went to the house," she said.

Down the creek, locals who went to the Wilkinsons' cabin to collect their mail found Louisa Jane Wilkinson in tears. She had heard about the Doyles and could not bring herself to go outside, for fear of what she might find. Neighbors discovered Allen Wilkinson lying dead in brush about a hundred and fifty yards from the cabin, his head and side gashed, his throat cut.

At Dutch Henry's Crossing, James Harris had also gone looking for his overnight guest, William Sherman. He found him lying in the creek. "Sherman's skull was split open in two places and some of his brains was washed out by the water," Harris testified. "A large hole was cut in his breast, and his left hand was cut off except a little piece of skin on one side."

NEWS OF THE MURDERS along the Pottawatomie spread quickly through the district. A day after the killings, when John Brown and his party rejoined the free-state force they'd left three days before, he was immediately confronted by his son Jason. A gentle man known as the "tenderfoot" of the Brown clan, Jason had stayed behind with his brother John junior while the others headed to Dutch Henry's.

"Did you have anything to do with the killing of those men on the Pottawatomie?" Jason demanded of his father.

"I did not do it, but I approved of it," Brown answered.

"I think it was an uncalled for, wicked act," Jason said.

"God is my judge," his father replied. "We were justified under the circumstances."

This was about as clear a statement as Brown would ever make about what became known as the Pottawatomie Massacre. He spoke of it rarely, and then only in vague terms that suggested he was culpable without having personally shed any blood. His family hewed to this line. "Father never had any thing to do with the killing but he run the whole business," said Salmon, the most talkative of the four sons present. "The work was so hot, & so absorbing, that I did not at the time know where each actor was, exactly, or exactly what each man was doing."

The Browns and their allies cast the killings as an act of self-defense: a preemptive strike against proslavery zealots who had threatened their free-state neighbors and intended to harm them. The Browns' defenders also denied any intent on their part to mutilate the Kansans. Broadswords had been used to avoid making noise and raising an alarm; the gruesome wounds resulted from the victims' attempts to ward off sword blows.

But this version of events didn't accord with evidence gathered after the killings. Mahala Doyle and James Harris both testified that they heard shots in the night. And "old man Doyle" was found with a bullet hole in his forehead, to go with a stab wound to his chest.

Years later, the wagon driver in Brown's party, James Townsley, issued a confession in which he said John Brown had shot old man Doyle as the settler's sons were being killed with swords. Salmon Brown, late in his life, admitted to a researcher that he'd lied in claiming that his father took no active part in the bloodshed. But he insisted that Brown shot Doyle late in the night, when the settler was already stone dead. "For what purpose I never knew," Salmon said, "but I always thought it was for a signal for all the crowd to get together and go to our camp."

This absolved his father of actual killing, and among Brown's defenders it became the accepted explanation of Doyle's bullet wound. But it made little sense. If a signal shot was all Brown intended, he could have fired in the air, instead of shooting a dead man in the face. Other statements in Brown's defense were likewise dubious. Broadswords, it was claimed, had been used for the sake of quiet, not with intent to mutilate. But if Brown wanted to avoid raising an alarm, why did witnesses report hearing gunshots, including the one that left a bullet in Doyle's forehead?

The most plausible account of Brown's actions that night came from a family member who wasn't there: John junior. Though initially opposed to his father's mission, he later wrote a lengthy defense of it. Until late May 1856, proslavery forces in Kansas had committed almost all the violence, killing six free-state men without reprisal. Lawrence's sacking was the last straw. As the Browns and their free-state allies stewed in camp, John junior said, they realized the enemy needed shock treatment— "death for death."

But the Pottawatomie attack wasn't simply a matter of evening the score in Kansas. Those sentenced to die must be slain "in such manner as should be likely to cause a restraining fear," John junior wrote. In other words, the killing should so terrorize the proslavery camp as to deter future violence.

In this light, the massacre made grisly sense. Like Nat Turner, the most haunting figure in the southern imagination, Brown's "Northern army" came in the night and dragged whites from their beds, hacking open heads and lopping off limbs. The killers wore no masks, plainly stated their allegiance, and left maimed victims lying in the road or creek. Pottawatomie was, in essence, a public execution and the message it sent was chilling.

"I left for fear of my life," Louisa Jane Wilkinson testified in Missouri, where she took refuge after her husband's killing. The Doyles also fled a day after the slaughter. So did many of their neighbors. And news that five proslavery men had been "taken from their beds and almost litterly heived to peices with broad swords" spread like prairie fire across Kansas.

"I never lie down without taking the precaution to fasten my door," a settler from South Carolina wrote his sister soon after the killings. "I have my rifle, revolver, and old home-stocked pistol where I can lay my hand on them in an instant, besides a hatchet & axe. I take this precaution to guard against the midnight attacks of the Abolitionists, who never make an attack in open daylight."

Pottawatomie had clearly succeeded in sowing terror. But it failed to produce the "restraining fear" that John junior believed to be its intent. Instead of deterring violence, the massacre incited it.

"LET SLIP THE DOGS OF WAR!" read the headline in a Missouri border paper, reporting on the deaths. Up to that point, the Kansas conflict had generated a great deal of heat but relatively little bloodshed. Now, in a single strike, Brown had almost doubled the body count and inflamed his already rabid foes, who needed little spur to violence.

Not for the last time, Brown acted as an accelerant, igniting a much broader and bloodier conflict than had flared before. "He wanted to *hurry up the fight*, always," Salmon Brown observed of his father. "*We struck merely to begin the fight* that we saw was being forced upon us."

IF IT WAS BROWN'S intent to bring on a full-fledged conflict, he got his wish. The number of killings escalated dramatically in the months that followed, earning the territory the nickname "Bleeding Kansas." But this widespread violence came at considerable cost to Brown's family, beginning with the murders that May night along the Pottawatomie. The intimate butchering of five grown men, as if they were so much livestock, was traumatic for his sons. Owen Brown, the oldest son present, was initially opposed to taking part, but later said he was swayed by his father, who "thought it a matter of duty that there should be a little bloodletting." After the massacre, Owen "felt terribly conscience stricken because he had killed one of the Doyles," Salmon said. "He cried and took on at an agonizing rate."

The next oldest sibling at the scene, Frederick Brown, also wept, telling another brother: "When I came to see what manner of work it was, I *could not* do it." Frederick, one of four sons from Brown's first marriage, showed signs of having inherited his mother's mental illness. He was so prone to severe headaches and "spells" of wildness that his father had taken him to an alienist. The treatment didn't work; a year before going to Kansas, Frederick "subjected himself to a most dreadful Surgical operation (his taking away of the greater part of the ———)," Brown wrote: the reference is apparently to self-castration.

Frederick's older brothers, John junior and Jason, weren't quite so conspicuously unstable, but both had brittle psyches that began to crack in the wake of Pottawatomie. Though Jason hadn't been present at the massacre, hearing that his beloved father and brothers were implicated in the brutal killings was "the most terrible shock" of his life, he said, and "nearly deprived me of my reason." John junior broke down completely in the days after the massacre. Anxious, exhausted, and unable to sleep, "he became quite insane," his father wrote.

John junior's condition made him easy prey for a proslavery posse that went in search of the Browns. He was quickly captured (as was Jason), and then beaten, chained, and held for three months on treason and other charges. A proslavery militia also burned the Browns' dwellings and drove off their livestock, reducing a year of labor and most of the family's possessions to weeds and ashes.

The clan's women and children were forced to take refuge in the one-room cabin of Brown's half sister, Florella, and her husband, Samuel Adair, who disapproved of the killings and felt badly exposed by his family's ties to Pottawatomie. "You cannot easily imagine our situation when it is known all abroad that our relatives have a hand in this affair," he wrote.

Brown, meanwhile, took to the woods and ravines of eastern Kansas with his remaining sons and other allies to plot his next move. He also launched a publicity campaign, in concert with a young Scottish-born correspondent, James Redpath. The line between journalist and partisan in Kansas was extremely thin, and Redpath, who wrote for antislavery papers in the East, made little secret of his ardent abolitionism. A week after Pottawatomie, he managed to find his way to Brown's creekside bivouac.

"Never before had I met such a band of men," Redpath wrote, describing a rustic encampment of "fine-looking" youths in coarse blue shirts, with pistols and bowie knives stuck in their belts, their horses saddled and ready. "Old Brown," sleeves rolled up and toes protruding from his boots, was cooking a pig.

"Give me men of good principles," Redpath quoted Brown as saying, a dozen "God-fearing men," and he would fight a hundred southern "ruffians." As for the "Pottawatomie affair," Brown declined to comment and Redpath obligingly drew a veil over the massacre, except to later write that the abolitionist had no hand in it. Many other northern correspondents followed his lead, leaving their readers in the dark about what had happened.

Instead, Redpath drew Brown as a selfless freedom fighter, "acting in obedience to the will of the Lord" in combating the Slave Power. "I left this sacred spot with a far higher respect for the Great Struggle than ever I had felt before," Redpath later wrote of his hour-long stay in Brown's camp. "I had seen the predestined leader of the second and holier American Revolution."

IN EARLY JUNE 1856, ten days after Pottawatomie, Brown struck again, joining his band with other free-state fighters in a bold dawn attack on a much larger force of proslavery men. This marked the first open-field combat in Kansas, and the first instance of organized units of white men fighting over slavery, five years before the Civil War. The Battle of Black Jack, as it became known, was a confused half-day clash involving about a hundred combatants. It ended with the surrender of the proslavery men, who were fooled into believing they were outnumbered. "I went to take Old Brown, and Old Brown took me," the proslavery commander later conceded. He surrendered not only his men but also a valuable store of guns, horses, and provisions.

Black Jack also brought greater attention to Brown, who kept the northern press abreast of his campaign, sometimes taking antislavery journalists with him in the field. One of these was William Phillips, a *New York Tribune* correspondent who rode with Brown after the battle. "He is not a man to be trifled with," Phillips wrote, "and there is no one for whom the border ruffians entertain a more wholesome dread than Captain Brown."

Phillips, however, was less adulatory than Redpath in his depiction of Brown's character. "He is a strange, resolute, repulsive, iron-willed inexorable old man," possessing "a fiery nature and a cold temper, and a cool head, —a volcano beneath a covering of snow."

Brown's growing renown came, once again, at great cost to his family. His son-in-law, Henry Thompson, was shot in the side at Black Jack, and nineteen-year-old Salmon Brown sustained a gunshot to the shoulder soon after the battle. Life on the run, subsisting on gooseberries, bran flour, and creek water flavored with a little molasses and ginger, also wore down the outlaw band. "We have, like David of old, had our dwelling with the serpents of the rocks and wild beasts of the wilderness," Brown wrote his wife in June. Three of his sons became so debilitated by illness that in August he escorted them to Nebraska to recover in safety.

By then, conflict raged across eastern Kansas. Partisans on both sides spent the summer raiding, robbing, burning, and murdering, while federal troops struggled to contain the anarchy. The violence climaxed in late August, when several hundred proslavery fighters, armed with cannon, descended on the free-state settlement at Osawatomie, where Brown's sister and other family members lived. With just forty men, Brown led a spirited defense of Osawatomie, inflicting a number of casualties on the proslavery force. Though he was ultimately forced to retreat, Brown scored another propaganda victory by fearlessly battling a much larger and better-armed foe.

"This has proven most unmistakably that 'Yankees' *will* fight," John junior wrote of the reaction to Osawatomie. His father, slightly wounded in the combat, was initially reported dead, a mistake that only enhanced his aura. The battle also gave the Captain a new title. As a noted guerrilla and wanted man, he would adopt a number of aliases over the next three years. But the nom de guerre that stuck in public imagination was "Osawatomie Brown," a tribute to his Kansas stand.

The name also evoked his family's continued sacrifice in the cause of freedom. Early in the morning before the battle at Osawatomie, proslavery scouts riding into the free-state settlement encountered Frederick Brown on his way to feed horses. Believing himself on friendly ground, Frederick evidently identified himself to the riders. One of them was a proslavery preacher who blamed the Browns for attacks on his property, and he replied by shooting Frederick in the chest. The twenty-five-year-old died in the road.

His father learned of the slaying while rallying his small force to repel Osawatomie's invaders. Frederick's older brother Jason took part in the battle, and at its end, he stood with his father on the bank of the Osage River, watching smoke and flames rise in the distance as their foes torched the free-state settlement they'd fought so hard to defend.

"God sees it," Brown told Jason. "I will die fighting for this cause." He had made similar pledges before. But this time Brown was in tears, and he mentioned a new field of battle to his son. "I will carry the war into Africa," he said. This cryptic phrase spoke clearly to Jason, who knew "Africa" was his father's code for the slaveholding South.

———

CHAPTER 5

Secret Service

I n early October 1856, five weeks after the battle at Osawatomie, Brown left Kansas in the back of a wagon, desperately ill with dysentery and fever. Winter approached, he had nowhere to live, and most of his family had already retreated east, exhausted by the fighting.

Brown had entered Kansas exactly a year before, a weary pioneer with a broken-down horse and sixty cents in his pocket. His health, financial and physical, wasn't any better upon his departure from the territory. But the failed businessman and virtual unknown who had arrived in Kansas the previous year was leaving it as "Captain Brown of Osawatomie," a hero to abolitionists and slavery's great scourge. Brown's name now carried weight and he intended to make the most of it.

"You need not be anxious about me if I am some time on the road," Brown wrote his wife upon reaching Iowa, "as I have to stop at several places; & go some out of my way; having left partly on business expecting to return if the troubles continue in Kansas."

By "business," Brown no longer meant wool selling or any of the other trades he'd pursued. His new vocation was guerrilla warfare, and to wage it he needed men, money, and weapons. This mission would keep him in constant motion for the next three years, as he shuttled from Kansas to New England to Canada and points between, preparing his crusade "into Africa."

Brown made one of his first stops in northern Ohio, where his father,

Owen, had died that May, a few weeks before his family's bloody rampage on the Pottawatomie. Though Brown hadn't learned of his father's death until after the massacre, Owen had written in late March that he felt "death was at the dore" and asked his family to pray for his salvation, signing his last letter, "Your unfaithful Parent." In one of his final letters to his father, Brown expressed the hope that Owen would live "to witness the triumph of that cause you have laboured to promote." Owen's impending death may have hardened Brown's resolve to strike a blow against slavery, and at the same time freed him to take up arms—a measure his father disapproved of, except in defense.

From Ohio, Brown continued east, in full freedom-fighter persona. He carried props from his frontier combat, including a bowie knife taken from the proslavery leader he'd defeated at Black Jack and a chain his foes had used to shackle his eldest son. He'd embarked on an "errand from the territory," Brown wrote in his speaking notes, "to enable me to continue my efforts in the cause of Freedom."

He also carried a letter of introduction to a young man who would prove critical to his mission. At twenty-five, Franklin Sanborn was already one of the best-connected abolitionists in New England, a recent Harvard graduate who was as smooth as Brown was rough. Darkly handsome, fluent in Greek and Latin, Sanborn had married his sickly teenaged love on her deathbed. This Byronic mien both masked and served his keen ambition. Sanborn made an art of attaching himself to famous men; Ralph Waldo Emerson invited him to run a school in Concord, the citadel of Transcendentalism. Sanborn's pupils included Emerson's children, a son of Nathaniel Hawthorne's, and the brothers of Henry James.

In addition, Sanborn served as secretary of the Massachusetts State Kansas Committee, among the most prominent groups that had sprung up to aid the free-state cause. It was in this capacity that he met Brown in early 1857. Sanborn immediately grasped the rough-hewn warrior's potential—an insight he would brag of for the rest of his long life. "There is a divining quality in youth and in genius which lets them behold in simple men more than the callous veteran may discern," Sanborn wrote of his first interview with Brown. "He had a purpose, knew what it was, and meant to achieve it."

So did Sanborn. The idealistic young striver became Brown's speaking

Franklin Sanborn in the 1850s

agent and social liaison, providing entrée to the upper reaches of New England society. Over time, he would also become one of Brown's closest confidants and co-conspirators—and, later, his devoted hagiographer.

Brown had been living rough for eighteen months; now, under Sanborn's management, he spent the first half of 1857 touring the lecture halls and salons of the antislavery establishment. He spoke to the National Kansas Committee at the Astor House in New York; to Massachusetts legislators at the State House in Boston (where Sanborn introduced him as the Miles Standish of Kansas); and to Transcendentalists at the town hall in Concord, where he dined at the homes of Emerson and Henry David Thoreau.

"He did not overstate anything, but spoke within bounds," Thoreau wrote of Brown, "paring away his speech, like an experienced soldier, keeping a reserve of force and meaning." Brown's "pent-up fire" also struck Thoreau's neighbor, the writer and philosopher Bronson Alcott. He noted Brown's set lips, "suppressed yet metallic" voice, and strong watchful air, "the countenance and frame charged with power throughout." If Brown appeared potent yet contained, Alcott was not: "I think him about the manliest man I have ever seen."

Brown in late 1856, shortly before his eastern tour

Brown's austerity of speech and manner and his unbending faith in himself and his mission evoked frequent comparisons to the Puritan warrior Oliver Cromwell. Brown's rigidly erect bearing and weather-beaten face added to the impression, as did his deacon-fighter attire: high-collared white shirt, brown broadcloth suit, gray military-style cape.

Brandishing the captured bowie knife strapped just above his boot, or loading a revolver as he warned of federal marshals on his trail, Brown also introduced a frisson to the genteel parlors of New England. "I should hate to spoil these carpets," he told one Boston hostess, "but you know I cannot be taken alive."

Another hostess was struck by his "moral magnetism" and ability to stir the conscience of wealthy abolitionists. Upon hearing of his sacrifices and devotion to the cause, Mary Stearns wrote, "it suddenly seemed mean and unworthy—not to say wicked—to be living in luxury while such a man was struggling for a few thousands to carry out his cherished plan."

BUT LARGER AUDIENCES WEREN'T always so impressed. Brown's public speaking voice tended to be flat and nasal. And the notes he carried on his 1857 lecture tour amounted to a rambling, self-pitying recitation of his deeds and losses in Kansas. "John Brown, a flame of fire in action, was dull in speech," wrote a minister who heard him in Worcester.

Brown was also vague about his intentions. He said he wanted to equip and train a hundred "Minute Men" to repel Border Ruffians and defend free-state Kansas. But beyond that he revealed little. "I do not expose my plans," he said, when asked whether the weapons he solicited might be used beyond Kansas's borders. "I will not be interrogated; if you wish to give me anything I want you to give it freely. I have no other purpose but to serve the cause of liberty."

Brown's pitch, delivered dozens of times in 1857, brought modest returns, mostly small contributions or pledges of cash, clothing, and other supplies. But the Massachusetts Kansas Committee, of which Sanborn was secretary, gave Brown custody of the two hundred Sharps rifles and ammunition it had stored in Iowa. And the committee chairman, George Luther Stearns—husband of the admiring Mary—paid from his own pocket for two hundred revolvers, additionally pledging thousands of dollars to the Kansas fight.

Brown also tapped his wealthy backers for aid to his beleaguered family. "I have no other income for their support," he wrote one donor, assuring him that the money would be carefully spent, "my Wife being a good economist, & a real old fashioned business woman. She has gone through the Two past winters in our open cold house: unfinished outside; & not plastered."

This was true, and Mary wasn't at all pleased about it. Though rarely expressed, her discontent was evident in the apologetic tone of Brown's letters to her from the time he'd first set off for Kansas: "I fully sympathize with you in all the hardships. . . . You may be assured you are not alone in having trials to meet . . . those here are not altogether in Paradise; while you have to stay in that miserable Frosty region. . . . I think much too of your kind of Widowed state." Upon returning east, Brown had spent only a few days in North Elba before establishing a home away from home at the Massasoit Hotel in Springfield, owned by abolitionist admirers. While there, in March 1857, he received a bracing letter from Mary: their sons, she informed him, had resolved "to learn, & practice war no more."

Brown's reply was defensive. Of "the boys" and war, he wrote, "it was not at my solicitation that they engaged in it at the first." But he admitted having "wholly forgotten" how much he'd borrowed from one of his sons, and sent him a bank draft for thirty dollars, all he could spare. A few days later, he also made a gesture of atonement toward his youngest child, two-year-old Ellen, giving her a Bible inscribed "in remembrance of her father (of whose care and attentions she was deprived in her infancy), he being absent in the territory of Kansas."

Before returning to the field, he attended to another family matter. On a speaking trip to his native Connecticut, he found the grave of his Revolutionary namesake, Captain John Brown, and arranged to have the headstone shipped to North Elba. "I prize it very highly," he wrote Mary, asking that the granite be "inscribed in memory of our poor Fredk, who sleeps in Kansas."

The gravestone was still on his mind weeks later, as he headed west to resume his war on slavery. "If I should never return," he wrote Mary, "it is my particular request that no other monument be used to keep me in remembrance than the same plain old one that records the death of my Grandfather & Son & that a short story like those already on it be told of John Brown." He wanted this inscription so his descendants "should not only remember their parentage, but also the cause they labored in."

AS IT HAPPENED, NOT all Brown's sons had resolved to "practice war no more." Six of them had fought in Kansas, along with a son-in-law. Of these, one was dead, two wounded, and two badly shaken by the experience. But one of Brown's sons, thirty-two-year-old Owen, chose to return west with his father in the summer of 1857. A quirky bachelor who signed his rare letters "OX"—which a friend joked was short for "Oxentricity"—he was partly crippled in his right arm and hand from a boyhood accident. Though he often bickered with his domineering father, Owen was nonetheless a reliable aide-de-camp. Above all, he was extremely loyal and discreet, traits that Brown particularly prized.

In late June 1857, the two men left Ohio in a mule-drawn wagon and headed for the Iowa town of Tabor, close to the Kansas line. This was to be Brown's base, where he would collect his weapons and train volunteers. But his plans went awry almost from the start. By the time he and Owen arrived, in early August, having eaten little but soda crackers and herring for weeks, they were down to just $25. Despite months of fundraising, Brown was returning to the field little better off than he'd been upon leaving it a year before.

In part, this penury was beyond his control. He'd concluded his eastern tour just as the worst financial panic in twenty years hit the nation, and much of the money pledged to him was never paid. But Brown's chronic inability to manage funds also dogged him. Upon raising several thousand dollars, he'd immediately succumbed to the grandiosity and poor judgment that doomed his earlier career as a land developer and wool trader.

Among the Connecticut admirers to whom Brown had showed off his fearsome bowie knife in March 1857 was a skilled forge master, Charles Blair. Brown wondered whether the long two-edged blade could be affixed to a six-foot shaft. This Cromwellian pike, he announced, would be the perfect defensive weapon "for the settlers of Kansas to keep in their log cabins."

Never one for half measures, Brown promptly contracted with Blair to make a thousand of the spears. He also arranged for his teenaged son Oliver to work in Blair's shop. But after paying an initial $550 and receiving samples, Brown failed to come up with the balance due. Blair kept the money he'd been paid and stopped work on the "Kansas butter knifes," as Oliver coyly called them. Brown, who rarely gave up on his own ideas, was to revive the pike project at a later date, for use in a different theater.

He undertook a much costlier folly soon after his Connecticut visit. In New York City, he met Hugh Forbes, a British fencing teacher and soldier of fortune who had served with the Italian revolutionary Giuseppe Garibaldi. The flamboyant "colonel," as Forbes styled himself, struck Brown as the perfect drillmaster for the volunteer force he planned to train. He hired Forbes and advanced him six months' pay, part of it as compensation for a manual on guerrilla tactics the colonel promised to deliver.

Months later, Brown was still waiting for the manual, and for Forbes to come train his Minute Men. "I furnished that money in the full expectation of having your <u>personal assistance</u> this present time," Brown wrote, in a vain effort to recover his payment. Very belatedly, Forbes finished the manual and made an appearance in Iowa—but by then, Brown was too broke to pay him any more. The disgruntled and erratic mercenary would soon decamp, taking with him a great deal of damaging information about Brown's secret plans.

In any event, there was no one for Forbes to train, apart from Brown and Owen; other volunteers had yet to materialize. This was, in large part, because Kansas had changed during the year Brown was away. A new territorial governor had succeeded in calming the violence, and the continuing influx of northern settlers was shifting the balance of power toward the free-state camp. As a result, there was no longer a clear need for the defense force Brown had proposed. This, in turn, eroded his persistent efforts to drum up financial support back East. "It is not easy to raise money for your operations," Franklin Sanborn wrote, "so long as there is peace."

By the late summer of 1857, Brown could no longer afford his board in Iowa. He had ample guns, but still lacked knapsacks, saddlebags, and other equipment needed to outfit his phantom army. The inaction and delay had also sapped Brown's customary drive and sense of direction. "<u>How to act now</u>," he wrote his brother-in-law in Kansas. "I do not know."

This paralysis didn't last long. Throughout his life, Brown searched for clues to his destiny, the path he must follow "to answer the end of my being." Everything had meaning, a hidden divine purpose—even his Iowa funk in the summer of 1857. He had believed that his God-given mission led back to Kansas. But if that was not so, then it must be time to put in motion his much more ambitious plan.

"In <u>immediate</u> want of from Five Hundred to One Thousand Dollars for <u>secret service & no questions asked</u>," he wrote one of his eastern patrons late that summer. Brown had always been inclined to the clandestine, but secrecy now became his watchword. He had recently adopted the first of several aliases, "Nelson Hawkins," the name of a family friend in Ohio. Writing to Sanborn, Brown reported that Hugh Forbes had arrived and opened a "small school." Baffled, Sanborn replied: "Do you mean a children's school, or a school for drilling?"

Brown also became ever more evasive about his movements and

intentions. In November 1857, he finally returned to Kansas, but only briefly and mysteriously. He quietly convened a small group of veteran fighters around a campfire on the prairie, seeking to enlist them for a strike against slavery. "If you want hard fighting you'll get plenty of it," he said, offering few other details.

Nine men agreed to follow him back to his training base in Iowa. Only then did he reveal the mission that would cost most of them their lives. As one of the recruits later stated in a jailhouse confession, *"Here we found that Capt. Brown's ultimate destination was the State of Virginia."*

BROWN HAD LONG PLANNED to carry his crusade against slavery into "Africa," and his efforts to raise a Kansas defense force were one means to that end—a way to acquire arms, train a crack unit, and make trial incursions into neighboring Missouri. But in the summer of 1857, marooned without money or men, he had refined his scheme and resolved to accelerate its execution.

Brown also homed in on a specific target. Over the years, he canvassed a number of possible sites for a first strike, considering locales as distant as New Orleans. But with characteristic "fixedness," he kept returning to a terrain that had long enchanted him: the rugged mountain corridor linking Pennsylvania to the South.

Brown's preoccupation with the Alleghenies may have dated to 1840, when he surveyed Oberlin's landholdings in western Virginia and briefly considered settling there. He returned to the region as a wool merchant, and he had mentioned the Alleghenies to Frederick Douglass in the winter of 1847–48, when he disclosed his nascent plan for launching raids to free slaves and funnel them north along the mountains.

Brown's thinking had since grown far bolder. A student of military history and slave revolts, he took time during his wool-selling trip to Europe to tour battlefields and fortifications on the Continent. By the summer of 1857, he was poring over maps of the South, listing strategic locations and making notes on historical examples of small, mountain-based units successfully battling conventional armies. "Guerrilla warfare See Life of Lord Wellington Page 71 to Page 75," he wrote in his pocket diary, referring to a passage about Spanish partisans in the Napoleonic Wars.

Brown's years in Springfield also exposed him to an industry for which that city was renowned: gun manufacturing. Most of the weapons were produced for the government at a massive federal factory in the city. There was only one other such facility in the nation, to which Springfield had close ties: the U.S. Armory at Harpers Ferry, Virginia.

In the 1790s, as the United States sought to free itself from dependence on foreign and privately made arms, President George Washington had determined that his young country needed to establish at least two armories. Springfield, an early milling center with a preexisting arsenal, seemed an obvious choice. But Harpers Ferry was quite the opposite, a frontier hamlet in the Blue Ridge Mountains, located at the confluence of the Shenandoah and Potomac Rivers. This water gap, known to early pioneers as the Hole, was so dramatic and untamed that Thomas Jefferson judged it "one of the most stupendous scenes in nature," a vista "worth a voyage across the Atlantic."

Washington took a more utilitarian view. A man of many parts, he was among other things a land speculator and transportation booster with grand visions for the river that ran past his plantation at Mount Vernon. He had long dreamed of making the Potomac a busy corridor between the Atlantic Seaboard and the Ohio Valley; upon becoming president, he touted Harpers Ferry as an ideal site for a national armory.

"This spot affords every advantage that could be wished for," Washington wrote his secretary of war in 1795. The Shenandoah and Potomac provided endless water power; the surrounding hills abounded with timber and iron ore for gunstocks and barrels. And Harpers Ferry was just sixty miles from the new nation's capital, roughly in the middle of the country as it then existed.

As a military strategist, Washington was also mindful of defense. Harpers Ferry—well inland, walled by mountains, and moated by rivers— was the most secure place imaginable to manufacture and store the nation's guns.

"There is not a spot in the United States, which combines more or greater requisites," Washington wrote, "considered either as a place of immense strength," or as "inaccessible by an enemy."

U.S. armory at Harpers Ferry, 1803

The nation's first president had in mind a European threat: soldiers arriving by sea, as they'd done in the Revolutionary War and would do again during the War of 1812. In Washington's day, it was impossible to imagine that the attack on the armory, when it came, would be launched by an enemy within.

WHEN, PRECISELY, BROWN FIXED on Harpers Ferry as a target isn't clear, but he first mentioned it in 1857, during his sojourn in Tabor, Iowa. Though he had no one for Hugh Forbes to drill, Brown used the former Garibaldi partisan as a sounding board for his military plotting when Forbes arrived in Iowa. The plan of attack he disclosed was similar in its opening to his original scheme: a party of twenty-five to fifty guerrillas would strike a slave district in Virginia, inducing hundreds of slaves to join his mountain band. But what Brown expected would come after this was novel.

Brown planned to give mounts to eighty or a hundred of the freed slaves and "make a dash" at the Harpers Ferry armory, destroying whatever guns he couldn't carry off. Other parties would conduct additional raids on slave districts, which in turn would swell the guerrillas' ranks. Brown thought he "could easily maintain himself in the Alleghanies" against the U.S. troops that would likely arrive within a few days. Finally, and most grandiosely, Brown believed his New England allies *would in the meantime call a Northern Convention to restore tranquility and overthrow the pro-Slavery Administration."*

This was a very different scheme from the Subterranean Pass Way to freedom Brown had described to Frederick Douglass a decade earlier. In some respects, his new strategy resembled that of the proslavery "filibusters" who invaded Latin America in the 1850s. Like them, he envisioned leading a small private army with the ultimate goal of toppling the government. The obvious difference was that he sought to destroy slavery in his own country, while filibusters aimed to expand it beyond the nation's borders.

Hugh Forbes—whose letters are the only documentation of the Tabor strategy session—raised a number of objections to Brown's plan. Unless slaves were forewarned of the plot, he told Brown, the "invitation to rise" would "meet with no response or a feeble one." If an uprising did occur, it would be "either a flash in the pan, or would leap beyond his control or any control." Forbes had even less faith in a Northern Convention. "Brown's New-England friends would not have the courage to show themselves, so long as the issue was doubtful," he wrote.

Forbes also proposed an alternative plan, close to Brown's earlier scheme: hit-and-run raids along slavery's frontier, to "stampede" slaves to Canada and make the institution untenable in border regions. This battle line could then be pushed slowly southward, further destabilizing the peculiar institution.

After days of debate, the two men forged a "mixed plan" and agreed that its execution would be overseen by a "Committee of Management." Or so Forbes claimed to believe. He was first and foremost an opportunist, intent on using the intelligence he gathered at Tabor to enrich himself. And he was shrewd enough to know that compromise and shared leadership were anathema to Brown, a man whose plans were never "mixed" or managed by committee.

Forbes also grasped that Brown's zeal was impervious to military doubts. "He was very pious, and had been deeply impressed for years with the Bible story of Gideon," Forbes wrote, "believing that he with a handful of men could strike down slavery."

THE NINE RECRUITS WHO followed Brown back to Tabor in the autumn of 1857, just after Forbes's departure, were cut from very different cloth than their leader. One was an English poet, who styled himself a "protégé" of Lord Byron's widow. Another was an Army bugler who had been sentenced to death for "drunken riot and mutiny." Several were Spiritualists who rejected traditional Christianity. None was married, and most had migrated west seeking work or adventure before getting caught up in the Kansas struggle.

This experience had imbued them with a militant commitment to fighting slavery—the quality Brown most sought. "The persons I have with me are mostly well tried men," he wrote Mary, "& all of them are pledged to stand by the work."

But they weren't in thrall to Brown or to his strategy. In fact, several of the men voiced strong objections upon learning that Brown's mysterious strike against slavery was aimed at Virginia. "Some warm words passed between him and myself in regard to the plan, which I had supposed was to be confined entirely to Kansas and Missouri," one of the men later wrote. At this point, there was no mention of Harpers Ferry; Brown said only that the men would go east to prepare for their mission. Only "after a good deal of wrangling," one of the dissidents wrote, did the nine men agree to go ahead.

In early December 1857, Brown, his son Owen, and the new volunteers loaded covered wagons with the weapons stored in a Tabor barn and began a slow trek east across Iowa. The "11 desperadoes," as Owen referred to the band in his diary, walked beside the wagons, through heavy snow, and spent nights around a log fire, singing and picking at lice. They also held "Lyceums or discussions of some question," one of the men wrote, usually a topic proposed by Brown and "he always presiding."

Owen made notes on these extraordinary sessions in his journal. "Cold, wet and snowy; hot discussion upon the Bible and war," he wrote.

"Warm argument upon the effects of the abolition of Slavery upon the Southern States, Northern States, commerce and manufactures, also upon the British provinces and the civilized world; whence came our civilization and origin? talk about prejudices against color; question proposed for debate—greatest general, Washington or Napoleon. Very cold night; prairie wolves howl nobly."

In late December, the band reached a railhead in eastern Iowa and shipped their arms to Ohio, where Brown planned to train his men before embarking for Virginia in the spring. But, unable to sell his horse and wagons to raise money for the onward journey, he swapped them for winter board at a farm near Springdale, a mostly Quaker community that was a well-traveled stop on the Underground Railroad.

Quartered in the farmhouse attic, the men commenced training at what Owen wryly called their "War College." Since Hugh Forbes was no longer available, the job of drillmaster fell to the Army deserter in Brown's ranks, who went by the alias Colonel Whipple. He oversaw maneuvers in a field behind the farmhouse, including drills with wooden swords, and calisthenics to harden the men for mountain operations. They also studied Forbes's manual on guerrilla tactics.

Neighboring Iowans weren't sure what to make of these paramilitary exercises. As Quakers, they disapproved of violence, but they also hated slavery. Most locals believed the men were preparing to return to Kansas; others, curiously, thought the strangers were a band of Mormon spies.

Over time, however, relations became closer. On snowbound days and long winter nights, the men grew restless. Some played chess, checkers, and cards; others were skilled debaters and began holding mock legislative sessions in a local schoolhouse. Following parliamentary rules of order, the men introduced and voted on bills related to slavery, women's rights, temperance, and other questions. These "legislatures" became popular entertainment for neighboring Iowans.

The men, all bachelors, also started courting local women. This led to the mock "censure" of one of Brown's men, "for hugging girls in Springdale Legislature." Another man evidently took far greater liberties. Months later, a Quaker couple wrote to demand details of his relationship with their daughter and ask whether she was "the worse for their intimacy."

BROWN STERNLY DISAPPROVED OF such licentious behavior, but he wasn't present to monitor it. Within a few weeks of the band's arrival in Springdale, he went east to raise money. This time, he went about his fund-raising very differently. Rather than speak in public venues, seeking aid from all quarters, he cloaked his movements and sought discreet support from the few men he believed willing to back his "secret service."

One of his first stops, in late January 1858, was at the Rochester, New York, home of Frederick Douglass. He stayed three weeks and seemed possessed by his mission, drawing up plans and drafting a "constitution" for the revolutionary state he intended to found in the mountains of Virginia. "His whole time and thought were given to this subject," Douglass wrote. "It was the first thing in the morning, and the last thing at night; till, I confess, it began to be something of a bore to me."

Brown's feverish planning included sketches of mountain redoubts. "These forts were to be so arranged as to connect one with the other by secret passages, so that if one was carried another could be easily fallen back upon," Douglass said. "I was less interested in these drawings than my children were."

Brown was on fire in his correspondence as well. "Courage, courage, courage!" he wrote his wife and children in North Elba, in a letter filled with exclamation points, urging them to be stalwart as he undertook "the great work of my life." He also remobilized John junior, who, in an effort to calm his shattered nerves, had turned to a quiet life of farming in Ohio. "Kansas is daugerotyped upon my heart," John junior wrote that February, "a stormy yet glorious picture."

Though no longer fit for armed service, the son answered his father's call to help with logistics. Brown gave him instructions about the weapons he'd shipped from Iowa, which were initially hidden beneath coffins in a furniture warehouse near John junior's house. Brown also urged him to travel to Gettysburg, Chambersburg, and other towns in southern Pennsylvania to quietly seek out allies. "When you look at the location of those places you will readily perceive the advantage of getting up some acquaintances in those parts."

Brown then spilled out another page of orders, asking John junior to visit Washington as well. "I want to get good maps, & State statistics of

Thomas Wentworth Higginson

Theodore Parker

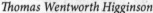

the different Southern States," he wrote. Brown was sometimes scolding of John junior, but he closed this letter with encouraging words for his fragile son: "I have no doubt you would by <u>diligence & patient persever-ence</u> fully succeed in raising the wind."

Brown deployed a similar mix of flattery and exhortation in his letters seeking financial support. To Thomas Wentworth Higginson—a militant minister who believed in breaking apart the Union to destroy slavery—Brown wrote: "I now want to get for the perfecting of <u>by far</u> the most <u>important</u> undertaking of my whole life from $500 to $800 within the next sixty days. Hope this is my last effort in the begging line."

The fiery Higginson replied: "I am always ready to invest money in treason, but at present have none to invest." He also pointed out that he was already attempting to raise money for the Underground Railroad.

"Rail Road business on a <u>somewhat extended scale</u> is the <u>identical</u> object for which I am trying to get means," Brown shot back. He appealed to the minister's considerable vanity as well. "I have been told you are both a true <u>man</u> & a true <u>abolitionist,</u>" he wrote, at the same time questioning whether this was so of others in their circle.

The same day, Brown sent a separate letter to Theodore Parker—one of the men named in his note to Higginson—and played the identical game. "I have written to some of our mutual friends," Brown told Parker, "but none of them understand my views so well as you do." Brown added that he wasn't certain these other friends were "deeply-dyed Abolitionists," as Parker most assuredly was.

THESE SLY, STROKING APPEALS had their intended effect. In early 1858, Higginson, Parker, and four other men agreed to form a cadre to support Brown's mission. Though the group would later become known as the Secret Six, it was composed of very public and prominent figures. Four were Harvard graduates, the most distinguished of them Parker, a leading Transcendentalist and radical Boston minister. Among other bold acts, he had harbored and then married a fugitive slave couple, handing the groom a sword to guard against slave catchers. Parker was also an eloquent orator—his was the famous declaration that the arc of the moral universe "bends towards justice."

Higginson, a protégé of Parker's, was another Harvard Divinity School graduate and clergyman, as well as a writer (he later became the mentor of Emily Dickinson). But his literary and spiritual pursuits were coupled with a temperament that resembled Brown's. Higginson was one of the abolitionists who had battered down the door of a Boston courthouse in 1854 to free the fugitive slave Anthony Burns. He was also a boxing and bodybuilding enthusiast, intolerant of weakness and impatient for muscular action. In one letter to Brown, he wrote: "I long to see you with adequate funds in your hands, set free from timid advisers, & able to act in your own way."

Samuel Gridley Howe was another well-bred man of action. The grandson of a participant in the Boston Tea Party, he graduated from Harvard Medical School and was inspired by Lord Byron to join Greece's revolution against Turkey as a soldier-surgeon. He later aided Polish insurgents fighting Russia. Returning to Boston, Howe became a pioneer in the care of the

Samuel Gridley Howe *George Luther Stearns*

blind, deaf, and mentally disabled. He also married the poet Julia Ward Howe, who would immortalize Brown's spirit in the "Battle Hymn of the Republic"—and who was so dispirited by her dashing, unfaithful husband that she wrote, "Hope died as I was led, / Unto my marriage bed."

While Parker, Higginson, and Howe brought ideological fire to Brown's cause, George Luther Stearns provided money and guns. A self-made magnate, enriched by the manufacture of linseed oil and lead pipe, he was the Kansas Committee chair who had paid on his own to send Brown two hundred revolvers, while also pledging thousands of dollars. On his doctor's advice, Stearns wore an extravagant beard to warm his chest and throat and protect them from bronchial problems. In other respects, he was the most conventional and businesslike of the Secret Six—in the words of Ralph Waldo Emerson, "no boaster or pretender, but a man for up-hill work."

The last two members of the Secret Six were already close associates of Brown: his upstate New York patron, Gerrit Smith, and the Concord teacher Franklin Sanborn. It was to them, at Smith's estate in late February,

that Brown first unveiled the nature of his "secret service." Sanborn immediately scribbled a note to Higginson, filled with the aliases and coded language that Brown so often employed.

"Our friend Hawkins," he wrote, is "entering largely into the wool
business, in which he has been more or less engaged all his life. He now
has a plan—the result of many years' study." On the back of the letter
were Brown's penciled sketches of his mountain forts, labeled "Woollen
machinery."

A month later, in March 1858, the "secret committee" of six was established, its mission to raise money and other aid for Brown and his men.
But the alliance was delicate from the start. The Secret Six shared Brown's
seething hatred of slavery and his scorn for pacifist remedies. In most
other respects, they were poles apart. Brown was a religious conservative,
whose faith differed greatly from the unorthodox theology that Parker and
Higginson espoused. A man of very modest means, he resented begging in
Brahmin parlors, amid what he called the "wealth, luxury, and extrava-
gance of this 'Heaven exalted' people." And he resisted his backers' strategic advice, instead relying on his own judgment and the "unseen Hand" of
Providence.

This obstinacy became evident when Brown first shared his "wool
business" plans at Gerrit Smith's home in Peterboro. Sanborn and Smith
immediately raised concerns about the "manifest hopelessness" of defeat-
ing slavery with a small band. To which Brown confidently replied: "If
God be for us, who can be against us?"

Sanborn and Smith mulled the matter during a walk through the snowy
fields of the Peterboro estate. They regarded Brown's mission as "dangerous, and even desperate," Sanborn wrote. Most of the other members of the
Secret Six also harbored doubts about Brown's chances of success. But it was
obvious that nothing would deter him from going ahead. "We cannot give
him up to die alone; we must support him," Smith declared.

This humane sentiment wasn't the only motive for backing Brown.
The danger and desperation of his plan appealed to the Secret Six, as did
his faith that he was God's instrument. Brown was no "milk-and-water"
abolitionist, believing in talk and moral suasion. He was a blunt and righteous weapon, like Higginson's battering ram. Even if he failed, Brown's

assault on the Slave Power might bring on the great conflict necessary to vanquish it.

"He is of the stuff of which martyrs are made," Samuel Gridley Howe wrote a wealthy associate he hoped would give money to Brown. "Under his natural and unaffected simplicity and modesty there is an irresistible propensity to war upon injustice and wrong."

Gerrit Smith, least secret of the Six, was more explicit. In March, as the conspirators formed their committee, he wrote an abolitionist congressman: "The slave will be delivered by the shedding of blood, and the signs are multiplying that his deliverance is at hand."

CHAPTER 6

—ᴍᴍ—

This Spark of Fire

In April 1858, Brown returned to Iowa to collect the volunteers he'd recruited for his "wool business," as Sanborn continued to call it. The "flock of sheep" in Springdale had grown by two during Brown's absence, but was still too small to put the "mill" into operation. Brown hoped to find more men, and another asset he deemed essential, by taking a detour north—to Canada.

Before traveling back to Iowa, he'd scouted across the border and chosen the town of Chatham, for "a very quiet convention." Fifty miles east of Detroit, Chatham was a terminus of the Underground Railroad and home to more than a thousand blacks, many of them former slaves. Brown distributed a circular seeking "true friends of freedom." In early May, he returned to Canada, this time with his "flock"; about thirty-five men joined them at a Baptist church for a gathering disguised as a meeting to establish a black Masonic lodge.

In reality, Brown had convened a latter-day Constitutional Convention: the secret creation of a new American government. The delegates—all black, apart from Brown and eleven of his Iowa cohort—included a printer, a gunsmith, a schoolmaster, a minister, a poet, and the pioneering black nationalist Martin Delany, a physician and editor who was soon to lead the "Niger Valley Exploring Party" to found a colony of American blacks in Africa.

A secretary took notes as Dr. Delany made a motion for Brown "to state the object of the convention," which he did "at length." For many years, Brown said, the idea of freeing the slaves "had possessed him like a passion," and he'd "read all the books upon insurrectionary warfare which he could lay his hands upon." The mountain-based guerrilla action he now planned, and which he outlined, would cause slaves to "immediately rise all over the Southern States." As they did so, a new social order would emerge, with its own schools, churches, and government.

Brown then presented "a plan for organization" for this new society, entitled "Provisional Constitution and Ordinances for the People of the United States." In many respects, it mimicked the existing U.S. Constitution, including a preamble and articles ordered by Roman numerals. But the language was more John Brown than James Madison.

"Whereas, Slavery, throughout its entire existence in the United States, is none other than a most barbarous, unprovoked, and unjustifiable War of one portion of its citizens upon another portion," the preamble began, "WE, CITIZENS OF THE UNITED STATES, AND THE OPPRESSED PEOPLE . . . ORDAIN AND ESTABLISH FOR OURSELVES, THE FOLLOWING PROVISIONAL CONSTITUTION."

Brown's redrafting of one of the nation's founding documents wasn't in itself bizarre. Antebellum reformers and Utopians did so routinely; a statement of women's rights, for instance, was modeled on the Declaration of Independence. Abolitionists were especially prone to challenging the sanctity of the Constitution, and never more so than in the late 1850s, following the Supreme Court's notorious ruling in the *Dred Scott* case, a year before the Chatham Convention.

Dred Scott, a Missouri slave, sued for his freedom on the basis of living for many years in free territory, where he had been taken by an owner who was posted in the North as a military officer. Not only did the Court rule against Scott, it also declared that the Founders had never intended for blacks—free or slave—to have *any* of the privileges of U.S. citizens. As the staunchly proslavery chief justice, Roger Taney, wrote in his opinion, blacks had "no rights that white men were bound to respect."

John Brown cited this infamous ruling in his constitution's preamble, which explained why a new government was needed "to protect our persons, property, lives, and liberties." But the forty-eight articles that followed were less concerned with rights than with the command structure of Brown's highly militarized state. The role of its weak president and Congress was mainly to advise a powerful commander-in-chief, who could tap the treasury as needed for money and valuables "captured by honorable warfare." Article XL was directed toward another preoccupation of Brown's. It forbade "filthy conversation," "indecent behavior," "intoxication," and "unlawful intercourse."

The constitution was read aloud at Chatham, debated, and signed the same day. "Every man was anxious to have his name at the head," wrote one of Brown's Iowa party. But the delegates showed distinctly less enthusiasm two days later, when they reconvened to elect officials. The black men nominated for the presidency declined to stand; the post was left vacant, along with many others. Only two congressmen were appointed, and the cabinet was filled by Iowa recruits. Brown, unsurprisingly, was "elected by acclamation" as commander-in-chief.

"Had a good Abolition convention here," he wrote his wife two days later. "Great unanimity prevailed." In a narrow sense, this was true. He'd sought black approval for his war on slavery and received it, with the delegates enthusiastically signing his constitution. But he'd hoped for much fuller participation in his campaign, writing upon his arrival in Canada: "There is the most abundant material; & of the right quality: in this quarter."

Brown was also keen to enlist one woman: Harriet Tubman, who had escaped slavery in Maryland and courageously slipped back into the South many times to guide other fugitives to freedom. She lived in Canada part of the year and seemed to Brown an ideal partner, able to recruit foot soldiers and advise him on infiltrating the northern borderlands of slavery. After meeting with her on his reconnaissance trip to Canada, Brown felt certain of her support.

"Hariet Tubman hooked on his whole team at once," he exulted in a letter to John junior, referring to Tubman in masculine terms as a mark of his respect. "He Hariet is the most of a man naturally; that I ever met with."

But to Brown's dismay, Tubman didn't appear at the Chatham meeting. Nor did several other black leaders he'd invited. In the end, his Canadian sojourn yielded only one fully committed recruit: Osborne

Anderson, a Pennsylvania-born printer who was named to Brown's provisional congress and later joined him in the field.

Many blacks in Chatham and the nearby towns would volunteer to fight in the Civil War. But they were painfully familiar with slavery, from their own experience or that of people close to them. Brown's vision and ardor inspired more admiration for him than confidence in his chances of success—or in the chances of anyone who went with him.

BROWN ENCOUNTERED SIMILAR RESISTANCE from his own family. Some were no longer fit for active duty, others reluctant. Jason, like his older brother, John, "had the blues very bad" after Kansas and needed to settle down or risk what he called "a crazy spell." Salmon had healed from the gunshot wound he sustained in Kansas but felt he must "quit running around" and had married a North Elba woman. Brown hoped to enlist her brothers, but they also declined.

"I should be most glad to have <u>Three</u> come on from North Elba <u>at least</u>," he wrote, as the pool of possible recruits dwindled. Saying no to the "old man" wasn't easy. Though his son-in-law, Henry Thompson, had three young children and a bullet still lodged in his back from the Battle of Black Jack, Brown pleaded with his wife. "O my daughter Ruth! Could any plan be devised whereby you could let Henry go 'to school,'" he wrote, in his customary code. "I would rather now have him 'for another term' than to have a hundred average scholars."

"Dear father, you have asked me rather a hard question," Ruth wrote back. "I cannot bear the thought of Henry leaving me again, yet I feel selfish. When I think of my poor, despised sisters, that are deprived of both husband and children, I feel deeply for them."

Brown kept pressing, until Henry replied himself. "My whole heart is in the work," he wrote in late April, but he feared that if he joined Brown and failed to return, his family would be left destitute. "<u>Nothing</u> but three little helpless children keeps me at home."

Ruth appended an apologetic note of her own. "I hope you will not blame me," she wrote. "I should like to have him go with you if I could feel that he would live to come back." Lest her father think she lacked faith,

Ruth added: "I do feel that God has been with you thus far, and will still be with you in *your great and benevolent work.*"

But she undercut this vote of confidence in the letter's last line: quoting her son, Ruth wrote, "Johnny says 'tell Grandfather that I hope he will live to come back here again.'"

A FEW WEEKS LATER, the issue became moot, at least for the time being. Brown had originally intended to launch his attack right after the Chatham Convention, which ended on May 10. But this plan was never realistic and it began to unravel even before he left Canada. The root cause, characteristically, was Brown's money management, compounded by his poor judgment of personnel.

Brown's disgruntled drillmaster, Hugh Forbes, had turned to blackmail. After leaving Iowa, Forbes wrote to members of the Secret Six, demanding money, which he said Brown had promised was forthcoming from "New England humanitarians." When these importunings failed, Forbes spread his net wider, even accosting an abolitionist congressman on the floor of the U.S. Senate. He disclosed elements of Brown's plans and named several of the men who had provided him money and arms.

This threw the Secret Six into a panic. They feared Forbes would go fully public, exposing Brown's plans and their own complicity. Gerrit Smith, the most skittish of the Six, argued that they should abandon the plot altogether. Others suggested a delay. Thomas Wentworth Higginson wanted to plunge ahead regardless, as did Brown, who complained to the pugnacious minister that the others had lost their nerve because "they were not men of action."

But the majority won out. In mid-May, over Higginson's objections, the Secret Six suspended funding of Brown's mission until the following winter or spring. In the interim, Brown should return to Kansas, to "blind" Forbes and discredit any claims he might make about a southern attack. The Six also sought distance from the conspiracy itself. "I do not wish to know Captain Brown's plans," Smith wrote Sanborn. "I hope he will keep them to himself."

THIS POSTPONEMENT WAS A blow not only to Brown but to the dozen soldiers he'd thus far recruited. Following the Chatham Convention, most of them had holed up in a Cleveland boardinghouse, restlessly awaiting orders. In early June 1858, Brown informed them that Forbes's betrayal had choked off funding. He had no choice but to disband the party and let the men find work where they could until he called them into service again.

Some of the volunteers chose to follow Brown back to Kansas. Others became disillusioned and drifted off, never to rejoin the unit. But one man headed in a different direction. John Cook, born to a well-to-do family in Connecticut, was a reckless and romantic figure even by the standards of Brown's extraordinary band. Earlier in life, Cook had trained for the law, but at twenty-five he fled his staid eastern roots for Kansas, where he gained renown as a crack shot and daring free-state fighter. When Brown went to Kansas in late 1857 to recruit soldiers for his secret mission, the Connecticut Yankee was the first man he sought.

Cook was also a blond, blue-eyed charmer who sent his female admirers letters filled with flower petals and florid verse. "He would have a girl in a corner telling them stories or repeating poetry to them in such a high faluting manner that they would laugh to kill themselves," Salmon Brown recalled. Another Kansas fighter described Cook as "suavity itself."

But his "rage for talking" became a source of unease for Brown's clandestine band. As they hid out in Cleveland after the Chatham Convention, Cook behaved "in a manner well calculated to arouse suspicion," one recruit warned Brown. He brandished his guns, boasted of being on a "secret expedition," and "talked a great deal too much" to a "lady friend."

Cook was so impatient and gung-ho that he proposed to three of his companions that they head south on their own. This didn't happen. But when Brown came to Cleveland in June and announced an indefinite postponement, he consented to a solo mission. Cook would go ahead alone to Harpers Ferry, "to see how things were there, and to gain information."

Brown had qualms about this plan, and cautioned his cocky and garrulous scout to say nothing of their ultimate objective. But Cook proved to be a talented spy. His large personality played better in Virginia than it did in the close confines of Brown's secret army—in part because of the unusual territory he went to reconnoiter.

CONTRARY TO STEREOTYPE, THE antebellum South wasn't a uniformly agrarian and insular society. Its cities and industry, though smaller than the North's, were growing rapidly, and the region's economy was well integrated with national and global markets. Even so, Harpers Ferry stood out. It was a bustling crossroads of industry and innovation, and its history was emblematic of the nation's development.

In 1803, just a few years after George Washington established a federal armory in the Virginia village, President Jefferson concluded the Louisiana Purchase, more than doubling the geographic size of the United States. The man he dispatched to explore this vast territory, Meriwether Lewis, went first to Harpers Ferry to buy "Rifles, Tomahawks & knives" for his expedition, as well as a collapsible iron boat frame that could be covered in hides—a vessel he called "the Experiment."

In 1819, an inventor named John Hall came to town and undertook a pioneering advance in America's industrial revolution. Previously, muskets had been produced by highly skilled gunsmiths who made and assembled each part and weapon themselves—"lock, stock, and barrel." Hall began manufacturing guns from interchangeable parts, employing "common hands," even children, to run machines at his pilot factory.

Harpers Ferry also became a hub of the transport revolution. In the 1820s, stagecoaches arrived, traveling on turnpikes that had been newly macadamized, or paved with small broken stones. The Chesapeake & Ohio Canal reached town in 1833; the Baltimore & Ohio Railroad came the next year. New industries arose along the water and rail lines, as did hotels, shops, and restaurants. George Washington's dream of the Potomac becoming a corridor of commerce seemed close to fulfillment.

But Harpers Ferry also offered a preview of the ills that afflicted the nation as it rapidly expanded and industrialized. In 1836, a visitor complained of the "coal smoke and clanking of hammers" that filled the "most abominable" town. Harpers Ferry officials urged citizens to clear piles of "offensive matter" from the streets, and struggled to rein in prostitution, cockfighting, brawling, "hallooing or rioting," and "throwing stones."

Panorama of Harpers Ferry from the Maryland shore

Some of those rowdy workmen were not happy. Many were skilled craftsmen who had once controlled the pace of their work; now they toiled through ten-hour shifts beneath factory clocks. In the 1840s, they went on strike and sent a delegation to the White House, complaining of being turned into "mere machines of labor."

One disgruntled workman shot an armory superintendent who tried to curtail drinking and gambling on the job. The victim was found in his office "with a ghastly wound in the stomach, through which protruded portions of the dinner he had eaten a few minutes before." Though the murderer was hanged, he lived on in local memory, a symbol of resistance to anyone who challenged the proud and fiercely independent workmen of Harpers Ferry.

The town's rough-and-tumble atmosphere had calmed somewhat by the summer of 1858, when Cook arrived. But Harpers Ferry remained a fluid and heterogeneous place, accustomed to strangers from the North and abroad. Cook, a versatile and well-schooled young man, soon found employment at a variety of jobs, joined a debating society, and acquainted himself with a wide range of locals, from Irish canal workers to patrician slave owners. He also worked his considerable charms on women, including the wives of leading armory employees, none of whom suspected an underground abolitionist cell was taking root in their midst.

"I was really pleased with him, he spoke so fluently and intelligently and had all the nice little graces of a gentleman," one woman wrote her daughter, whose beauty Cook had complimented. "He seems to have made a favorable impression upon every one."

As cook embarked on his covert operation that summer, Brown's western mission was going less well. He returned to Kansas with a fresh alias—Shubel Morgan, the first name meaning "captive of God"—and a flowing white beard, which a journalist called "his patriarchal disguise." The beard made Brown look older than his fifty-eight years, as did his deepening stoop. Decades of hardship had taken a toll on him.

A few years earlier, planning the house he wanted built in North Elba, Brown had written that he meant to place it very close to a stream to avoid lugging water uphill: "I have done a great deal of that." Since then, he'd lived rough for long stretches and suffered frequent bouts of "ague," a recurrent fever that was probably malarial. On returning west in the summer of 1858, he was incapacitated for weeks by severe shakes and other symptoms; he wrote to John junior that he "was never more sick" in his life.

As he recovered, though, Brown became impatient to resume his Virginia work. In August, Kansas voters had overwhelmingly rejected a proslavery constitution and thus guaranteed the territory's eventual entry into the Union as a free state. Though violence continued near the border with Missouri, Brown once again lacked a clear purpose other than to dispel any rumors that Hugh Forbes might spread regarding his secret plans.

Then, in December, a new mission suddenly presented itself. A Missouri slave named Jim Daniels crossed into Kansas, on the pretext of selling brooms. Meeting one of Brown's men on patrol near the border, Daniels said that he and other slaves were about to be sold and desperately needed help.

Brown answered this appeal by leading eighteen guerrillas into Missouri the next night. One party under his command raided the farmhouse of Daniels's master, liberating five slaves at gunpoint. They then freed five more slaves at a neighboring property. A separate party burst into another home and freed a slave, but in so doing shot her owner dead. The two groups of raiders also carried off oxen, horses, food, clothes, and other material, as well as two white hostages, before crossing back into Kansas.

This daring midnight strike caused an immediate sensation, much like the one following Brown's Pottawatomie attack two years earlier. Proslavery posses quickly formed and as the identity of the raid's instigator became known, both the governor of Missouri and President Buchanan offered rewards for Brown's capture. The cross-border rescue also met with opprobrium from many in the antislavery camp. Defending free-state Kansans was one thing; it was quite another to invade a southern state, steal property, and kill a civilian.

Brown, ever the propagandist, mocked his critics in a letter to the *New York Tribune*. The previous May, he observed, a proslavery band had massacred five free-state settlers in Kansas, and authorities had done nothing. Yet when "eleven persons are forcibly restored to their 'natural and inalienable rights,'" the government and much of the public "are filled with holy horror."

Brown also kept himself in the news by embarking on a dramatic midwinter trek. He escorted the liberated slaves north, with posses and federal marshals in hot pursuit. Near Lawrence, Kansas, he eluded capture by switching getaway wagons, from an oxcart he'd taken in Missouri to a wagon drawn by horses. A few days later, an eighty-man posse intercepted his convoy at a ford. With just twenty-two men of his own, Brown marched straight at his foes, causing them to fall back in panic. "The closer we got to the ford the farther they got from it," one of his men wrote. Brown's band gave chase, capturing horses and taking several prisoners.

In February 1859, Brown left Kansas territory, leading his caravan across Iowa. At the eastern end of the state, the liberated slaves were secreted onto a boxcar bound for Chicago, then taken from there to Detroit, where they boarded a ferry. BROWN'S RESCUED NEGROES LANDED IN CANADA, read the March 18 headline in the *New York Tribune*. The long journey from bondage to freedom had taken eighty-two days and covered eleven hundred miles, mostly by wagon. One of the formerly enslaved women, the *Tribune* reported, had been owned by six different masters. Another had given birth since being freed in Missouri. "The child has been christened John Brown," the newspaper said.

The infant's white namesake could hardly have composed a more laudatory narrative. "Osawatomie Brown" had hugely enlarged his celebrity as a bold and seemingly invincible warrior who took the fight to his enemies. Best of all, he had turned the hated Fugitive Slave Act on its head. Instead of slave catchers trespassing on free territory, Northerners had invaded a slave state to liberate bondspeople. Brown had acted, he wrote a newspaper editor that March, because the "most ready and effectual way" to fight for freedom was "to meddle directly with the peculiar institution."

THE MISSOURI RESCUE ALSO reinvigorated the Secret Six, whose faith had flagged due to delays in Brown's mission and his ceaseless demands for money. "He has begun the work in earnest," Sanborn wrote Higginson. "I think we may look for great results from this spark of fire." Gerrit Smith, who had completely lost his nerve the year before, was now exultant, seeing the Missouri raid as a rehearsal for the plan Brown intended "to pursue *elsewhere*."

Brown's thoughts ran along a parallel track. He resumed his preparations even before completing the trek from Kansas. On reaching Iowa, he wrote the Secret Six that he was now ready with new men to "set his mill in operation," and wanted the cash promised him the year before. "The entire success of our experiment ought (I think) to convince every capitalist."

In mid-March, immediately after putting the fugitives on a ferry to Canada, Brown rushed to Cleveland. There he delivered a fund-raising lecture and theatrically auctioned off horses he'd "liberated" from Missouri. He also scoffed at posters in Cleveland advertising the president's reward for his arrest, saying he "would give two dollars and fifty cents for the safe delivery of the body of James Buchanan in any jail of the Free States."

Continuing east, Brown collected fresh funds from Gerrit Smith and stayed with Franklin Sanborn in Concord, where he spoke at the town hall before Emerson, Thoreau, and other luminaries. "The Captain leaves us much in the dark concerning his destination and designs for the coming months," Bronson Alcott wrote in his diary. "Yet he does not conceal

John Brown in Boston, May 1859

his hatred of slavery, nor his readiness to strike a blow for freedom. . . . I think him equal to anything he dares, —the man to do the deed, if it must be done."

Alcott also noted Brown's changed appearance, writing that his long white beard gave him a "soldierly air, and the port of an apostle." Others who saw him that spring were struck not only by his facial hair but by his fevered manner. John Forbes, a Boston businessman at whose home Brown stayed, thought his guest's "glittering gray-blue eyes" had "a little touch of insanity." Amos Lawrence, another businessman, wrote in his diary that Brown exhibited a "monomania" about "stealing negroes."

These impressions may have been influenced by Lawrence's disapproval of the Missouri raid, and by Brown's ague, which continued to trouble him. But one of the men closest to Brown during the 1859 slave rescue also questioned the abolitionist's state of mind. George Gill was a young adventurer and former whaler who had joined Brown's band in Iowa and become secretary of the treasury in his provisional government. At the Chatham Convention, Gill wrote, a preacher kept exclaiming of Brown, "This is the Moses, whom God has sent to conduct the children of Israel through the Red Sea." Other blacks often hailed Brown in similar terms; "it would elate him through and through."

The Missouri rescue completed Brown's identification with Moses: the long-bearded prophet leading slaves to freedom as Pharaoh's legions gave chase. Gill was intimately involved in this latter-day Exodus. He was the man on patrol who first encountered Jim Daniels, bringing the desperate slave to Brown's attention; he also took part in the Missouri raid and traveled by his commander's side during much of the long journey north.

"He seemed strangely attached to me," Gill wrote. "I was a verdant innocent-looking fellow with but little to say to him." But this quiet young follower came to wonder whether success had gone to his leader's already swollen head. "In time he believed that he was Gods chosen instrument— and the *only one*," Gill later wrote. "Whatever methods he used, God would be his guard and shield, rendering the most illogical movements into a grand success."

By the time the convoy reached eastern Iowa, Gill had fallen sick and was unable to continue. A few months later, the call came for him to mobilize for the long-delayed Virginia mission. To Brown's great surprise and disappointment, his once-loyal lieutenant and treasury secretary never appeared.

IN EARLY JUNE, AFTER raising money in New York and New England, Brown turned up at the door of the Connecticut forge master he'd long ago hired to manufacture a thousand pikes. "I have been unable, sir, to fulfill my contract with you up to this time," Brown told Charles Blair, "now I am able to do so."

Blair was reluctant: his workmen were fully employed and he'd been disappointed by Brown two years earlier. He also couldn't understand why the abolitionist wanted him to finish work on the pikes, which had been intended for free-state families. "Kansas matters are all settled," he told Brown, "what earthly use can they be to you now?"

Brown replied that the pikes were worth nothing unfinished, but that he "could dispose of them in some way" once they were fully assembled. And so, a week later, upon receipt of the $450 still outstanding, Blair wrote Brown that he would finish the job. "Wishing you peace and prosperity," he said in closing.

Brown by then was in North Elba, visiting his family; a daughter-in-law trimmed his extravagant beard. He stayed only a week before heading to Ohio, where most of his soldiers and guns were quartered. Then, accompanied by two sons and another man, he traveled to southern Pennsylvania. A fourth accomplice—John Kagi, a veteran of the partisan battles in Kansas—was to rendezvous with the advance party at its final destination.

"We leave here to day for Harpers Ferry," Brown wrote Kagi on June 30, 1859, from a town just north of the Mason-Dixon Line. "We shall be looking for cheap lands near the Rail Road in all probability."

He signed himself with a new alias: "Yours in truth I. Smith."

—~~~—

PART TWO

Into Africa

He was a stone, this man who lies so still,
A stone flung from a sling against a wall,
A sacrificial instrument of kill.

STEPHEN VINCENT BENÉT,
"John Brown's Body"

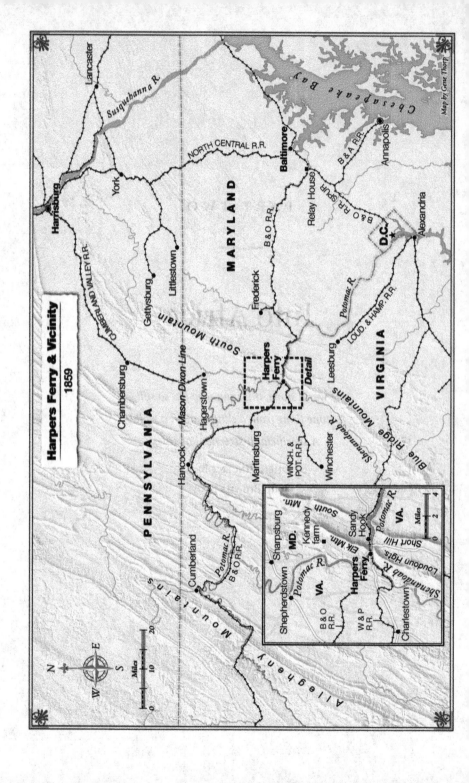

CHAPTER 7

───── ∞ ─────

My Invisibles

On July 4, 1859, John Unseld was riding to Harpers Ferry from his farm in Maryland when he encountered four strangers on the road. "Good morning, gentlemen," Unseld called out, "how do you do?"

The eldest of the party introduced himself as Smith, without giving his first name. He said two of the young men with him were his sons, the other a Mr. Anderson. They'd arrived by rail in Harpers Ferry the evening before, inquired about cheap lodging, and been directed to the village of Sandy Hook, just across the Potomac River in Maryland.

"I suppose you are out hunting mineral, gold, and silver?" Unseld asked.

"No, we are not," Smith replied, "we are out looking for land." He said the weather in northern New York had recently been so severe that they'd decided to sell their farmland and try their luck farther south.

Unseld rode on to Harpers Ferry and met the men again on his return trip. Smith told him he was impressed by the countryside he'd seen so far and asked about property for sale or rent. Unseld knew of a vacant farmhouse and guided Smith as far as his own home, where he invited the newcomer in for dinner. Smith declined, not even taking a drink.

"If you follow up this road along the foot of the mountain," Unseld told him, "it is shady and pleasant and you will come out at a church up here about three miles, and then you can see the house."

Smith saw the place and liked it, whereupon Unseld directed him to its owner, a widow named Kennedy who lived in Sharpsburg, Maryland, a short way north along Antietam Creek. When Unseld next saw Smith, the New Yorker said he'd rented the Kennedy farm until the following March and showed him the receipt. Unseld thought it odd that the man wanted him to see the piece of paper. "It is nothing to me," he said.

Over the next few months, the genial Marylander often stopped by the Kennedy farm, an isolated place with a log house set well back from the road and a separate cabin hidden by summer growth. Unseld never saw the interior. Since Smith always declined Unseld's invitations to enter his own home, the Marylander did likewise. In any event, Smith told him they had no chairs to sit on, only boxes.

So during his visits, Unseld remained on his horse in the yard, chatting with Smith or with two young women of the family who appeared that July. The newcomers cut some hay and acquired a few farm animals. Unseld also learned that Smith planned to buy fat cattle and drive them north to New York for sale.

"There was nothing which induced me to suppose that his purpose was anything different from what he stated," Unseld said, months later, in sworn testimony before the U.S. Senate. Nor did the slave-owning Marylander suspect that "Smith" was an assumed name, and that the reticent New York farmer he'd helped to find lodging on Independence Day was America's most notorious abolitionist—"Old Ossawattomie Brown, from Kansas," as Unseld called him.

MR. ANDERSON, THE NONFAMILY member of the "Smith" party, was a midwestern farmer, first name Jeremiah, and he recorded his impression of Independence Day in the South in a letter he wrote on July 5 to his brother in Iowa.

"Nothing going on here except drinking and dancing, and fighting," he wrote. However, he praised the mountain scenery and the wild berries he'd collected by the road. "I am going to be on a farm about 5 miles from the Ferry up the Potomac engaged in agricultural pursuits," he told his brother. "I am going to work on the farm for Mr. *Smith* who expects to rent until he finds land to buy."

His employer's words were likewise anodyne. In a letter to "John Henrie Esquire," an associate in Smith & Sons, a diversified firm that required workmen and the shipment of heavy boxes, Brown wrote: "Dear Sir, Please forward enclosed at once + write us on first arrival of freight or of hands to work on the job." When the freight arrived, his associate formally replied: "I await your directions in the matter. Respectfully, John Henrie."

By the summer of 1859, "Mr. Smith" and "Mr. Henrie"—real name, John Henry Kagi—were old hands at this sort of subterfuge. Since Brown's recruitment of Kagi two years before, the two had worked closely together on covert missions and cycled through a number of aliases. Brown didn't always choose his aides wisely—Hugh Forbes being a glaring example— but in John Kagi, his secretary of war, he'd found a loyal and versatile lieutenant.

Born in Ohio to a blacksmith from Virginia, Kagi was a precocious youth who began teaching school at seventeen in the Shenandoah Valley, sixty miles from Harpers Ferry. A freethinker, vegetarian, and abolitionist, he was forced to leave his job because of his antislavery views. Kagi headed west, earning a law degree and becoming a newspaper correspondent and free-state partisan in Kansas. Before joining Brown's band in Tabor, Iowa, he was twice imprisoned, and was badly wounded in a shootout with a proslavery judge.

As Brown's second-in-command, Kagi possessed attributes his leader did not. He was young, like most of the recruits, extremely personable, and deft at logistics and communication, traits that suited him well for the delicate task he undertook in the summer of 1859.

Having chosen as a forward post the isolated Kennedy farm, five miles from Harpers Ferry, Brown needed a staging area where he could safely receive men and weapons from the North. He found it in Chambersburg, Pennsylvania, a railroad hub just north of the Mason-Dixon Line. The town had a large population of free blacks who were active in the Underground Railroad, and it lay forty miles by country road from Brown's Maryland hideout, allowing for the discreet forwarding of supplies and personnel.

"John Henrie" found lodging by the railroad tracks in Chambersburg at the boardinghouse of an abolitionist sympathizer, Mary Ritner. He enlisted the help of local blacks "to receive company," and coordinated

John Henry Kagi

the shipment of "freight" from agents in other states. Anyone who opened this correspondence would find opaque discussions of "prospecting," "mining tools," and "hands." Kagi's clerklike demeanor also gave nothing away. One man who shared his small Chambersburg boardinghouse that summer later remarked that the agreeable young fellow, who spent most of his time in his room writing, "had far more of the appearance of a Divinity student than of a Warrior."

WHILE KAGI QUIETLY SETTLED in southern Pennsylvania, and Brown planted himself at the Kennedy farm in Maryland, another agent operated inside Virginia—albeit in very different style. Since going ahead to Harpers Ferry the year before, John Cook had kept his own name and utilized rather than cloaked his expansive personality. He worked as a teacher, as a book peddler, and as a canal lock keeper; he published poetry in a local paper; and he gained entrée to homes, workplaces, and outlying plantations.

He also charmed his landlady's eighteen-year-old daughter, Virginia, whom he married on April 18, 1859, atop Jefferson's Rock, a scenic perch overlooking Harpers Ferry. There is no evidence that Cook wed Virginia to deepen his local cover; the bride was five months pregnant. But he did use the occasion to gather intelligence, asking the clerk who issued their marriage license how many slaves lived in the county. Cook said he had a bet with a friend about the total and the clerk gave him the official figure.

By the time Brown arrived in Harpers Ferry on July 3, his high-spirited spy was bursting to make use of the information he'd collected over the past twelve months. "Tomorrow is the Fourth! The glorious day which gave *our* Freedom birth—but left sad hearts beneath the Slave Lash," Cook wrote an Iowa family he'd befriended the year before. "Oh! How I wish I could be with you once again. But that's a joy I may never know, till I have filled the humble post allotted to me, in the great mission now before us."

Cook wasn't alone in believing action to be imminent. Brown had intimated to the Secret Six that he might open his "wool business" on July 4, a date Harriet Tubman had suggested "as a good time to 'raise the mill.'" In the event, he reached Harpers Ferry too late to make this happen. Even so, he hoped to launch his campaign quickly and wanted to "have the freight sent" as soon as possible.

There was, however, a hitch in the supply chain—"John Smith," head of Smith & Sons' Ohio branch and the eldest son of its founder, "Isaac." At thirty-eight, John Brown, Jr., was an erudite and erratic man who had abandoned careers as a teacher and lecturer. He had never fully recovered from his breakdown in Kansas; in 1858, he described himself as so melancholic that he was "almost disqualified for anything which is engrossing in its nature."

But he remained dedicated to his father's cause and eager for his approval. "Please say to Mr. S_____ I am still ready to serve," he wrote Kagi in the early summer of 1859. Brown didn't call on his fragile son to come south, but he did entrust him with a critical behind-the-lines role. Brown's rifles, pistols, and other supplies were now stored in a hay barn near John junior's home in a rural district east of Cleveland. This staunchly abolitionist area also served as a hideout and muster station for many of Brown's scattered men. On July 5, the day after finding quarters at the Kennedy farm, Brown sent word for all "hands" and "<u>freight</u>" to be collected and forwarded south, "as near <u>together</u> as possible," so he wouldn't have to conceal them for long.

Instead, Brown's men and arms dribbled in piecemeal over the course of months rather than weeks. John junior took his time shipping heavy boxes labeled "Hardware + Castings," which traveled a circuitous route via wagon, canal, and rail to Kagi in Chambersburg. He also fumbled the forwarding of men, having somehow misunderstood his father's "mining" schedule. "I had supposed you would not think it best to commence opening the coal banks before spring," John junior wrote Kagi in late summer, in response to yet another urgent call for manpower. "Shall strain every nerve to accomplish this."

Brown's supply problems weren't entirely his son's fault. He could be too cryptic in his communiqués, and the many false starts in his mission had made some recruits lose heart—and money. "I expected to have joined in the dance long before this," Luke Parsons wrote Kagi upon receiving the call to come south. "Were I to see Uncle John now & he to ask me to go, I should tell him that I owed $230, & must pay that first." Parsons, who had joined Brown in Iowa and gone with him to Canada, was on his way to dig gold at Pike's Peak. Though he considered rejoining the band, his mother helped dissuade him. "Don't you do it," she wrote her son. "They are bad men; you have got away from them keep away from them."

BROWN, WHILE TRYING TO mobilize his troops, also realized that he needed recruits of another sort at the Kennedy farm—not guerrilla fighters, but innocent-seeming civilians. Otherwise, his Maryland neighbors might grow suspicious of the young men and wagon loads of freight arriving at the all-male compound. "I find it will be indispensable to have some women of our own family with us," Brown wrote his wife, urging her to come for a "short visit" with their teenaged daughter, Annie. "It will be <u>likely to prove</u> the most valuable service you can ever render in the world."

At the time, Mary Brown still had four children living at home, the youngest of whom was four. Two of her three sons, Oliver and Watson, and a stepson, Owen, were already pledged to her husband's dangerous cause. She was evidently unhappy at his request for still more family sacrifice. "Mother *would not go*," Annie later wrote. But she herself was eager to do so, and her sister-in-law, Martha Brown, was willing to join her in Mary's stead.

In mid-July, Oliver Brown—Martha's husband and Annie's older brother—escorted the young women by boat down the Hudson River to New York and then by rail to Harpers Ferry. Annie was just fifteen, Martha only a year older. A dignified teenager with pale brown hair and blue-gray eyes, Martha had married Oliver despite her family's strong dislike of abolitionists. Her twenty-year-old husband was a sensitive, bookish man who had hoped to study natural philosophy in New York City. But he felt obligated to help provide for the North Elba clan—and, now, to serve beside his father as he'd done in Kansas.

Oliver doted on his young bride; he carried a lock of her hair and a piece

Oliver and Martha Brown

of her wedding dress, and he sent her soulful letters when he was away. The couple was so enraptured "in the enjoyment of each other," Annie Brown wrote, "that they did not feel the need of much of this world's goods."

They would have very few such goods during their time together at the Kennedy farm. To furnish the tiny room the couple shared with Annie, the women made bed ticks from coarse cotton filled with straw and laid them on the floor, without pillows. "Sometimes in the night I could hear Oliver and Martha up stirring and beating their bed," Annie wrote, "and would ask them what they were doing. Martha would say, 'We are just trying to stir a little soft into our bed.'" She would give birth to a daughter early the next year.

By day at the Kennedy farm, Annie and Martha kept house, though theirs was no ordinary domestic duty. While cooking and cleaning, they watched constantly for neighbors or passersby who might cast a curious eye on the "Smith" household and its comings and goings that summer. If anyone stopped in, the women were instructed to be sociable and act like ordinary farm folk.

Martha, as the elder of the pair, anointed herself mistress of the household, except when it came to company. "I always blush and act like I was guilty of something," she told Annie, "while you can chatter and talk nonsense so that no one would ever suspect that you know anything."

Annie mildly resented Martha's pulling rank on the basis of a mere year in age. But she took to her role as lookout and decoy, and came to think of herself as "the outlaw girl." She washed dishes by the window or by the open door of the kitchen so she could keep watch; she sat sewing on the farmhouse's high front porch, which overlooked the yard, garden, and road. She occupied this post in the evening, too, enjoying the southern fireflies. And when the landlady's son stopped by and asked about Mr. Smith's absent wife, Annie blithely lied that her mother had stayed behind in New York to sell their property.

The Smiths' closest neighbors, a poor family named Huffmaster, presented more of a problem. They had rented a garden just behind the Kennedy farmhouse. As a result, Annie wrote, Mrs. Huffmaster and her four young children, the whole family barefoot, "had a good excuse for coming at all times to look at the garden—and at us." As the summer wore on

The Kennedy farmhouse, 1859

and the Kennedy farm filled with "freight" and "hands," Mrs. Huffmaster and her frequent visits became the "plague and torment" of Annie's existence.

A FEW WEEKS AFTER Annie and Martha arrived in Maryland, they were joined by another contingent from North Elba. Watson Brown was the only male member of the family who hadn't fought along with his father in Kansas, having stayed behind to manage the farm. He'd also married into the neighboring Thompson clan, like his older sister Ruth, whose husband, Henry, had fought with Brown on the frontier. Henry still resisted his father-in-law's pleas to rejoin him, but two of his brothers, William and Dauphin, had been inspired by Brown to take up the cause and they traveled south with Watson.

None of the three young men fit the mold of tough guerrilla fighter. Twenty-three-year-old Watson was tall and slender, with "earnest, kind-looking blue eyes," Annie wrote, and "as good and mild as he looked."

Watson Brown   *William Thompson*   *Dauphin Thompson*

He'd once tried to set off for California, only to be sold a bogus ticket in New York City, losing all his money. Watson had delayed traveling south to Harpers Ferry until his wife, Isabella, gave birth to their first child. "After bidding us good bye," Ruth Brown wrote of her brother's departure, "he rushed out of the house crying as though his heart would break."

William Thompson, who also left behind a young wife, was a gentle jokester, "a sort of merry Andrew," Annie Brown wrote. She described William's younger brother, Dauphin, just twenty, as "much more like a girl than a warrior, with his light yellow, curly hair and innocent blue eyes and face as smooth as a baby's." Dauphin found himself at the Kennedy farm among much harder men, some of whom considered the baby-faced farm boy "too womanish and tenderhearted to go on such an expedition."

One of these doubters was Albert Hazlett, a hardscrabble Kansas veteran who had eagerly answered the call back to service. "i Received your letter a few minuets ago," he wrote Kagi on July 14 from a farm in Pennsylvania. "i Will Bee Ready When you Want mee." The day after he arrived, Annie Brown found pools of tobacco spit under the table where the men played cards. When she complained, Hazlett confessed that the spit was his and told her "that he had nearly always lived in camp or amongst rough men."

Another arrival that summer was Aaron Stevens, the most fearsome and physically striking of Brown's fighters. A "chronic roamer" from

Connecticut, he'd volunteered at sixteen to serve in the Mexican War and later returned west, writing his sister that New England was "no place for a young man," despite the allure of his mother's baked beans and hot apple pie. He became a bugler and Indian-fighting dragoon, until his hot temper derailed his military career. In Taos, in the New Mexico Territory, he drew a gun on a major; court-martialed for "drunken riot" and mutiny, he was sentenced to die before a firing squad.

The penalty was commuted to three years' hard labor with ball and chain at Fort Leavenworth, in Kansas. Stevens served less than six months before escaping and becoming a free-state guerrilla under the alias Colonel Whipple. "The grate battle is begun," he wrote his brother shortly before joining Brown, "you will alwase find me on the side of human freedom." It was Stevens who had served as drillmaster at Brown's "military college" in Iowa, and he who had shot a slave owner dead during the raid to free slaves in Missouri.

Tall, dark, extremely muscular and broad-shouldered—"the finest specimen of physical manhood I have ever seen in my life," a reporter later called him—Stevens was Brown's third-in-command, a brawny warrior to Kagi's brainy strategist. He also had a beautiful singing voice and wrote passionate letters to Jennie Dunbar, a music teacher he'd fallen for in Ohio while awaiting the call to Virginia.

"Jenny if I thought you loved me as I do you, it would be the happyes moment in my life," Stevens wrote soon after reaching Maryland. "I mean what I say, no *soft sope* about me."

THE MAIN HOUSE AT the Kennedy farm had just four small rooms: a kitchen, a room for eating and sitting, the bedroom used by Martha, Oliver, and Annie, and a low, slope-ceilinged attic where the men slept side by side on the floor. By late August, about fifteen men had gathered. "We are rather thick here," Stevens told Jennie Dunbar, blaming his poor writing on there being "so much noys."

The men also had to make room for large crates of "freight," which finally began reaching Chambersburg from Ohio on August 11 and were moved by covered wagon to Maryland. Boxes of rifles, marked "furniture," served as benches in the eating area. A box of pistols became Martha

Brown's dressing table. If visitors asked about the unopened crates, Annie told them her mother was "very particular" and had asked "us to not unpack her furniture until she arrived."

The presence of so many strange men was harder to explain. As much as possible, Annie and Martha tried to keep the recruits out of sight. If all seemed safe, the men would help with the wash or "skulk into the kitchen and stay and visit Martha awhile to relieve the monotony," Annie wrote. Mostly, though, they stayed cloistered in the small eating/sitting room, or in the loft above, playing checkers and cards, or reading from a small library that included Thomas Paine's *Age of Reason* and the manual on guerrilla warfare that Hugh Forbes had prepared for Brown. Annie came to think of the attic tenants as her personal secret and responsibility—"my invisibles," she called them.

However invisible they might be, the men weren't very good at keeping quiet, as revealed by the dozens of letters they sent and received via Kagi in Chambersburg. "Press nobly on," a female admirer urged a recruit named Charles Tidd, who corresponded with women in several states, so "millions may have the pleasure of singing the song of liberty." Another member of Brown's small army, Edwin Coppoc, heard from a friend in Iowa: "all no where you was a going som of them glory in your spunk an others think you ar a gone boy." The friend urged Coppoc to dodge bullets "like the d———l and show them you can come [home] without a hole in your hide."

William Leeman, a third recruit, was only slightly more discreet in letters to his impoverished family. A shoe factory worker from Maine, he had joined Brown's band in Kansas at the age of seventeen and often promised his family he would return home, where one sister worked in a cotton mill while the other looked after their frail parents. "I suppose you all think I am unworthy the Name of a son or Brother to stay away from you so long and not to render you some assistance," he wrote that August, "but have Patience a little longer and you shall know all and then you will not Blame me for I am Engaged in a Cause that will make us above want if I succeed & I know we shall." In a later letter, he confided that he belonged to "a Secret Asosiation" whose members were "privately gathered in a Slave State."

When Brown caught wind of his men's indiscretions, he was furious.

"I do hope all corresponding except on business of the Co: will be droped for the present," he wrote in a mid-August memorandum to Kagi, who acted as postmaster. "If every one must write some girl; or some other extra friend telling, or showing our location; & telling (as some have done) all about our matters; we might as well get the whole published at once, in the New York Herald. Any person is a stupid fool who expects his friends to keep for him; that which he cannot keep himself. All our friends have each got their special friends; and they again have theirs; and it would not be right to lay the burden of keeping a secret on any one; at the end of a long string."

Brown had reason to be fearful. There was indeed a lengthening string of people aware of his plans, at least in general terms, and several were about to reveal what they knew. But the "fool" who had set this disclosure in motion was Brown himself.

In Springdale, Iowa, he'd confided in several Quakers who aided his band in the winter of 1857–58 and again the next year when Brown passed through with the slaves he'd freed from Missouri. These Quaker confidants, in turn, talked to other Friends. Though fiercely opposed to slavery, they feared Brown's mission would end in disaster and the death of him and his men. To forestall this tragedy, a few of them decided to compose an anonymous letter to the U.S. secretary of war, John Floyd.

"I have discovered the existence of a secret association, having for its object the liberation of the slaves at the South by a general insurrection. The leader of the movement is 'old John Brown,' late of Kansas." The letter stated that small companies of men would "pass down through Pennsylvania and Maryland, and enter Virginia at Harper's Ferry." It also warned of a mountain rendezvous in Virginia and a spy placed at an armory in Maryland.

The letter reached the secretary of war in late August 1859, when Floyd had fled the Washington summer for Red Sweet Springs, a mountain spa in Virginia. He knew there was no armory in Maryland, and this small mistake in the letter led him to regard it as a hoax. "Besides, I was satisfied in my own mind that a scheme of such wickedness and outrage could not be entertained by any citizens of the United States," Floyd later stated, in testimony before a Senate committee. "I put the letter away, and thought no more of it."

THOUGH BROWN HAD NARROWLY avoided exposure thanks to an error of geography and the inattention of a vacationing official, he faced a number of other threats to his mission that August. The thousand pikes he'd ordered from Connecticut had yet to be shipped because of a problem finding parts. His other "freight" had begun arriving from Ohio, but the shipping bills were much higher than anticipated. This, and the cost of sustaining his men during the delay, had almost exhausted the money he'd raised that spring in expectation of quickly launching his campaign.

"I begin to be apprehensive of getting into a tight spot for want of a little more funds," he wrote John junior, sounding very much like the cash-strapped businessman of old. He told his son that he had only $180 still on hand, and wondered "how I can keep my little wheels in motion for a few days more." Though Brown found it "terribly humiliating" to seek funds yet again, he asked John junior to "solicit for me a little more assistance while attending to your other business."

This "other business" referred to Brown's continuing effort to make up his shortfall of men. And so, having at last shipped the stored weapons, the hapless John junior embarked on a final recruitment and fundraising drive that was notable mainly for its self-congratulation. In Boston he called on members of the Secret Six and crowed in a letter to Kagi: "They were all in short, *very much* gratified, and have had their Faith & Hopes much strengthened." His solicitations, however, yielded only $50 from Brown's increasingly anxious backers.

John junior went on to Canada, where he attempted to mobilize troops with the assistance of a black recruiter, who, he wrote, was "too fat" to be of much use. He nonetheless boasted of forming "associations" in several Canadian towns, to "*hunt up good workmen.*" At Chatham, site of Brown's constitutional convention, "I met with a hearty response," John junior said. But only one workman proved willing to set off for Chambersburg—Osborne Anderson, whom Brown had recruited the year before.

John junior forged on to Detroit, where he met with even less success and shed his fat companion, regretting that "I spent so much money in transporting so much *inert* adipose matter." Turning toward his home in

Ohio, he wrote Kagi that he was still eager "to devote my whole time if I can to the work," adding, however: "If friend 'Isaac' wishes me to go any where else, I shall need more means, as I have only enough to get back with."

WHILE JOHN JUNIOR CONDUCTED his futile and expensive "Northern tour," Brown confronted a near mutiny at his Maryland hideout. The crisis, this time, wasn't precipitated by money or delays or the danger of exposure; it was ignited by the nature of the mission itself.

Most of the men gathered at the Kennedy farm were well acquainted with Brown; five were his sons or neighbors, and the others had joined him in Kansas or Iowa. They were accustomed to his secretive ways and had come south with dedication and few questions asked. "It is my chief desire to add fuel to the fire," a recruit named Steward Taylor wrote, upon receiving the summons in early July at the wheat farm where he worked in Illinois. "My ardent passion for the gold field is my thoughts by day and my dreams by night."

Apart from Kagi, none of the members of Brown's band knew exactly what he planned, and the clues the men had received were mixed. In the summer of 1858, Kagi had told one Kansas fighter that the Virginia mission would start small and "seem a slave stampede, or local outbreak at most," with the guerrillas pulling back to the mountains, accompanied by freed slaves. "Harper's Ferry was mentioned as a point to be seized— but not held." A few months after this parley, Brown launched his Missouri raid. "It seemed to be the impression of most of the men," Annie Brown wrote of the Kennedy farm tenants, "that they had come there to make another such a raid, only on a larger scale."

Instead, in late summer, Brown revealed that Harpers Ferry itself would be the first and primary target. Only after seizing the town and its sprawling weapons works would the raiders begin freeing slaves and moving through the mountains.

This news did not go over well. Almost "all of our men," Owen Brown said of those present, "were opposed to striking the first blow" at Harpers Ferry. Brown's sons were among the loudest critics. Owen, Oliver, and Watson were known locally as the offspring of "Mr. Smith," and they were freer than the others to move about and see the challenges Harpers Ferry presented as a target. Owen at one point likened his father's plan to Napoleon's disastrous march on Moscow.

Charles Tidd was another determined foe. A hotheaded Kansas veteran, he'd once smashed the tobacco pipes of his fellow recruits while he was trying to quit smoking in the cramped quarters the band shared in Iowa. Now, he expressed his ire by storming out of the farmhouse and going to stay with John Cook, who lived with his wife in Harpers Ferry. "It nearly broke up the camp," Tidd later said of the dissent over Brown's plan.

In the third week of August, Brown convened an emergency meeting at the Kennedy farm, with Kagi coming down from Chambersburg and Cook from Harpers Ferry. Kagi stood by his commander's plan, as did Cook (who further bolstered Brown's confidence with optimistic reports on his contacts with locals). Brown also turned the debate into a test of loyalty: since so many opposed him, he insisted on resigning as commander so the men could choose another.

Within five minutes, he was reinstated as leader. Shortly thereafter, the dissidents reluctantly consented to his plan—on condition, Tidd later said, that railroad bridges near the town would be burned, making it much more difficult for anyone to come to its defense. On August 18, Owen, who often acted as intermediary between his father and the other men, drafted a formal if rather strained endorsement of Brown's continued leadership.

Dear Sir,

We have all agreed to sustain your decisions, untill you have *proved incompetent*, & many of us will adhere to your decisions as long as you will.

Your Friend,
OWEN SMITH.

BY THE NEXT DAY, Brown was in Chambersburg, wooing another reluctant ally. Ever since conceiving his war on slavery, Brown had courted black support, believing it both critical to his success and morally imperative. Though the sin of slavery weighed heavily on white Americans, it could be expunged only if blacks took part in their own liberation. "Give a slave a pike and you make him a man," he said. "Deprive him of the means of resistance, and you keep him down."

This belief had always set Brown apart from the mainstream of white abolitionists, many of whom regarded blacks as too pitiable and submissive to fight. He was also exceptional in practicing what he preached. Brown took blacks into his home and stayed at theirs; sought blacks' financial and logistical support; recruited them into his army; and communicated his egalitarian and tough-minded ethos to all those under his command.

"There was no milk and water sentimentality—no offensive contempt for the negro, while working in his cause," wrote Osborne Anderson, the black printer who attended the Chatham Convention and made his way to the Kennedy farm in the fall of 1859. "In John Brown's house, and in John Brown's presence, men from widely different parts of the continent met and united in one company, wherein no hateful prejudice dared intrude its ugly self—no ghost of a distinction found space to enter."

Brown's ardor in the cause of racial justice was a powerful source of his ability to inspire others. But it may have clouded his strategic judgment. As a fiery crusader, he naturally appealed to black militants such as Charles Langston, an Oberlin-educated abolitionist who forcibly freed a fugitive slave from a federal marshal and hailed Brown for trying to "put to death" those "who steal men and sell them." He also drew support from a shadowy self-defense group in Detroit called African Mysteries and an allied organization in Ohio whose leader showed one of Brown's men an impressive arsenal and claimed, "they were only waiting for Brown or someone else to make a successful initiative move when their forces would be put in motion."

This was the message Brown most wanted to hear: blacks were not only desperate for freedom but ready and able to fight. All they needed was a spark. But the militants who urged him on weren't much more representative of blacks than Brown was of whites. Brown's limited experience of the slaveholding South wasn't a reliable guide, either. He'd visited only the region's borderlands while working as a surveyor and wool merchant in far western Virginia—where many whites had little stake in the institution— and along the raw frontier of Missouri and Kansas. The whites he'd battled there were minimally trained and loosely organized.

Brown, in short, was ill equipped to gauge how either blacks or whites might react to a full-scale assault on a system of property and social control that had been entrenched and brutally enforced for generations. "He thought the slaves would flock to him," Annie Brown wrote, "and that the masters would be so paralyzed with fear that they would make no resistance."

Her father had also convinced himself that black leaders would join him in Virginia and be there to guide the liberated slaves. Throughout the summer of 1859, he and his backers tried to contact Harriet Tubman and bring her south. When she was finally located, in New Bedford, Massachusetts, she was evidently too ill to travel.

Frederick Douglass, however, responded to an August summons from Brown and traveled to southern Pennsylvania, accompanied by Shields Green, a fugitive slave he'd taken into his home and introduced to the white abolitionist. Reaching Chambersburg on August 19, Douglass contacted one of John Kagi's local "friends," a black barber who directed him to a secret meeting place: an abandoned stone quarry at the edge of town. Approaching the quarry, Douglass spotted Brown in an old hat, carrying a

Frederick Douglass

fishing rod as camouflage. "His face wore an anxious expression, and he was much worn by thought and exposure," Douglass later wrote. The two men "sat down among the rocks" and resumed the debate they'd inaugurated a dozen years before, at their first meeting in Springfield.

Douglass knew Brown's plans had evolved, but up to this point, he had believed they were still aimed at siphoning off slaves in a gradual way that would alarm owners and undermine the institution. Now, during their conversation at the quarry, Brown instead unveiled his bold plan for seizing Harpers Ferry. Brown said this dramatic strike would "instantly rouse the country," Douglass later wrote, serving as a "notice to the slaves that their friends had come, and a trumpet to rally them to his standard."

Douglass, like the men at the Kennedy farm, "at once opposed the measure." He argued that opening the campaign with an attack on a federal armory "would array the whole country against us," rather than rallying Americans to the antislavery cause. Brown shrugged this off. "It seemed to him that something startling was just what the nation needed."

Douglass raised military objections, too, arguing that Brown and his men would be easily surrounded in Harpers Ferry. Again, Brown seemed unperturbed. He said he could "find means for cutting his way out," but wouldn't need to, because he planned to take prominent citizens hostage. That way, if worse came to worst, he could "dictate terms" to his foes. This confidence astonished Douglass, who believed Virginians would blow Brown and his hostages "sky-high" rather than let abolitionists hold Harpers Ferry.

There in the old quarry, the two men debated through that day and part of the next, with Douglass, a formidable orator, mustering "all the arguments at my command." None of them moved Brown. He was utterly fixed in his course. "Come with me, Douglass," he finally said, wrapping his arms tightly around his friend. "I want you for a special purpose. When I strike the bees will begin to swarm, and I shall want you to help hive them."

But Douglass could see nothing but menace in Harpers Ferry. "All his arguments, and all his descriptions of the place, convinced me that he was going into a perfect steel trap," Douglass wrote, "and that once in he would never get out alive." Having escaped slavery as a young man, Douglass also had no illusions about his own prospects if he went along. "My discretion or my cowardice," he admitted, "determined my course." He would not go with Brown.

As he got up to leave the quarry, Douglass turned to his companion, Shields Green, who, along with Kagi, had sat in on the conference. In Rochester, the fugitive slave from South Carolina had been moved by Brown's antislavery fervor and said he intended to join him. Now, Douglass told Green: "Shields, you have heard our discussion. If in view of it, you do not wish to stay, you have but to say so, and you can go back with me."

To Douglass's surprise, Green coolly replied, in his Lowcountry patois, "I b'leve I'll go wid de ole man."

THOUGH DISAPPOINTED IN DOUGLASS's decision, Brown at last had his first black recruit at the Kennedy farm. Shields Green's addition to the ranks, however, greatly increased the risk of exposure. The narrow, hilly borderland between Pennsylvania and the Potomac River made a natural highway for fugitives, and it was closely watched by southern patrols and slave catchers who collected bounties for apprehending runaways. Soon after the meeting in the quarry, as Owen Brown was escorting Green from Chambersburg to the farmhouse in Maryland, they encountered several men who became suspicious and gave chase with dogs. Owen and Green— who, reversing the usual pattern, was trying to slip back into the South— had to bushwhack through the woods and hills to elude their pursuers.

Green also became a conspicuous presence at the Kennedy farm, where Annie Brown was already struggling to keep her "invisibles" out of sight. Only her father, her brothers, and Jeremiah Anderson ventured out freely, traveling in the wagon to Chambersburg for "freight" or to Harpers Ferry to pick up provisions. They otherwise mixed little with locals, though Brown attended the nearby church of a small German sect and at one point performed minor surgery on a neighbor, lancing a "wen" on her neck. In gratitude, the family gave Brown a mongrel pup named Cuffee. The dog, along with a cow and horse and a few pigs, gave the Kennedy farm an air of rural normality.

But maintaining this façade required constant vigilance. One day, while Annie and her father went to church, those left keeping watch weren't careful enough. Green, a garrulous man who in Rochester had cleaned clothes for a living, came down from the loft to help Martha with the ironing. No one noticed the approach of their nosy neighbor, Mrs. Huffmaster. Coming to the door, she saw Green, as well as two unfamiliar white men, before Martha managed to hustle her out onto the porch.

When Brown returned from church, he immediately sent Annie to find out what their neighbor knew, and to "buy her off" with some milk. Mrs. Huffmaster told Annie she thought the black man was a fugitive, escaping with the aid of the white strangers she'd seen. Annie tried to convince her "they were some friends of ours, but that they had gone where she would not see them and asked her to not say anything." The woman promised to do so, but "used her power over me every time she thought of anything she wanted, that we had," Annie wrote. "We lived in constant fear and dread after that."

The men also lived in even greater confinement to avoid another sighting. Most mornings, they gathered downstairs as Brown read from the Bible and led them in prayer. Then they would retreat to the loft and stay cooped up all day, coming down only for meals. If Mrs. Huffmaster approached the farmhouse as they were eating, Annie or Martha would intercept her on the porch while the men hurried upstairs, "taking the dishes, victuals, tablecloth and all with them."

Only at night were the men free to roam outside. And only in certain weather did they feel safe enough to break the quiet. "When there was a thunderstorm they would jump about and play, making all kinds of noise," Annie wrote, "as they thought no one could hear them."

A WEEK OR TWO after the arrival of Shields Green, a second black volunteer came to the farm: Dangerfield Newby, who differed in several key respects from the other men. He was about forty, much older than his fellow recruits, and he hadn't been with Brown in Kansas or Iowa or Canada. For Newby, the mission ahead was also unusually personal. Virginia-born, he'd been freed in 1858 after his owner moved to Ohio. But Newby's wife and children remained enslaved in Virginia, some fifty miles from Harpers Ferry. "He was impatient to have operations commenced," Annie wrote, "for he was anxious to get them."

Newby had already gone to great lengths to try and free his family. A

Dangerfield Newby, ca. 1858

blacksmith and canal worker, he'd saved money and asked others for contributions so he could buy his wife and children from their owner. By the summer of 1859, he had certificates of deposit in an Ohio bank worth more than $700—a considerable sum for a former slave, equal to about $17,000 today. But Harriett Newby's owner, who had earlier agreed to a price, raised it or decided not to sell. Harriett responded with a series of wrenching letters to her husband.

"Oh, Dear Dangerfield *com* this fall with out fail *monny* or no *monney*," she wrote in April 1859. "I want to see you so much. That is the one bright hope I have before me." A house slave, she had to care night and day for her mistress, who had just given birth. "Nothing more at present but remain Your affectionate wife, Harriett Newby."

A few weeks later, she wrote again, this time to report that her own baby "commenced to *Crall* to-day; it is very delicate." The infant, a girl, was their sixth child. "Dear Dangerfield, you cannot *amagine* how much I want to see you. It is the grates Comfort I have is thinking of the *promist* time when you will be here oh that bless hour when I shall see you once more."

By summer, Harriett was desperate. "I want you to buy me as soon as possible, for if you do not get me some body else will," she wrote. "It is said Master is in want of money. If so, I know not what time he may sell me *an* then all my bright *hops* of the *futer* are blasted, for *their* has ben one bright hope to cheer me in all my troubles, that is to be with you." Their little girl, she added, wasn't walking yet but could "step around" by holding on to things. Harriett closed: "you mus write soon and say when you think you can Come."

This letter was dated August 16, 1859. By the time it reached northern Ohio, where Dangerfield Newby had met some of John Brown's men and decided to join their cause, he had already set off, leaving his bank deposits behind. Money or no money, he was coming to Virginia that fall.

SEPTEMBER AT THE KENNEDY farm brought cooler weather, the arrival of the pikes from Connecticut, and a sobering atmosphere as the mission drew near. On the first of the month, in a letter from a place he identified only as "Post of Duty," Aaron Stevens declared his love for the Ohio music teacher, Jennie Dunbar: "if I live to get through *with this* and you live I hope I shall have the pleasure of hearing *you play and sing again* if nothing more." In a postscript, he added: "you may not get a letter from me for some time . . . hoping to meet you again in this world."

A few days later, Dauphin Thompson wrote his brother and sister from "Parts unknown." He described sitting in the door of a small cabin on the Kennedy farm, where four of the men took up residence once the pikes had arrived and been stored in the outbuilding's loft. "Probably you will hear from us about the first of october if not before," he wrote, referring to the "operations" that would soon commence. "I suppose the folk think we are a set of fools but they will find out we know what we are about."

Watson Brown wrote to his wife, Belle, who was back in North Elba with Frederick, a newborn named for the uncle killed in Kansas. "I think of you all day, and dream of you at night," Watson wrote. "I would gladly come home and stay with you always but for the cause which brought me here, —a desire to do something for others, and not live wholly for my own happiness."

Other men confided their growing apprehension to the two young women at the farm. "They nearly all seemed to be impressed with the idea that they were going to their death," Annie wrote. One man, Steward Taylor, described his own end for her, having seen it in a vision or dream. "He knew he would be shot at the taking of Harper's Ferry, and be one of the first ones too."

With the arrival of Osborne Anderson from Canada in September, Brown had seventeen soldiers on hand, still fewer than the twenty-five or so he believed was the minimum needed. Desperately short of funds, he had to borrow $40 from one of his men. Even so, as the end of the month approached, Brown took a step that signaled the attack was imminent. He sent Martha and Annie home to North Elba.

For the women as well as the men, it was a difficult parting. Martha, now several months pregnant, would be separated from her husband. Annie, though homesick, had become "very intimate" with her invisibles, she later wrote. She shared with the men not only the extremely close quarters, but also faith in their cause and the secret of their mission. This was a heady and romantic experience for a teenaged farm girl. So was the attention of so many young men, most of whom were striking in appearance, at least to judge by their photographs and Annie's descriptions of them as "tall," "fine-looking," "gentlemanly," "very attractive," or "really handsome."

Her sister Ruth later said that Annie's "first lover" was one of the men at the Kennedy farm, though she didn't say which. If Ruth was correct, then the likeliest candidates were Annie's young neighbor from North Elba, Dauphin Thompson ("a perfect blond," she called him, "good size, well-proportioned—a handsome young man"); the darkly attractive Jeremiah Anderson (to whom, Annie's family later hinted, she "took a fancy"); and the passionate Kansas fighter Charles Tidd, of whom Annie later wrote to Franklin Sanborn, "I know your sister thought we were 'lovers.'" Annie denied this. "A soldier could understand the tie that bound us without explanation."

Whether these ties were soldierly, sisterly, or otherwise, the women's presence at the Kennedy farm had been a great solace to the men. They enjoyed teasing Martha and Oliver as "Mother and Father," played pranks on Annie, and confided in her about "mothers, sisters, friends, and

Charles Tidd   *Jeremiah Anderson*

homes." The women also brightened the men's confinement by gathering flowers, wild fruit, and nuts. "We were, while the ladies remained, often relieved of much of the dullness," Osborne Anderson wrote.

On the afternoon before their departure, Annie gave Mrs. Huffmaster a crock of bacon grease to cook with, saying she and Martha were going to see relatives in Pennsylvania and would be away several weeks. "Of course you will not want to come here while we are gone," Annie told her, "as the men are going to 'keep bachelors hall.'"

That night, the men sang "Home Again" to Martha and Annie, and in the morning the young women rode off in Brown's wagon to a train depot in Pennsylvania. Annie said goodbye to her father on a railway platform. The next day, he wrote a letter to his family with particular words for his daughter: "I want you, first of all, to become a sincere, humble, earnest, and consistent Christian; and then acquire good and efficient business habits. Save this letter to remember your father by, Anne."

He also addressed practical matters, saying he hoped to send the family $50, adding, "Perhaps you can keep your animals in good condition through the winter on potatoes mostly, much cheaper than any other feed." In closing, he told them to read the newspaper carefully and to send any future correspondence to John junior in Ohio. "God Almighty bless and save you all!"

IN EARLY OCTOBER, THE men began preparing for their mission in earnest. They browned the barrels of their rifles, readied belts and holsters, and assembled the pikes from Connecticut—these had arrived with the shafts separate from the heads, so as to pass off the shafts as hayfork handles. The men also studied Hugh Forbes's manual—"Sharp's rifle loads from the breech by drawing back a lever, which causes the bottom of the breech to slide down so that the cartridge can be put in"—and went through quiet drills under the instruction of Aaron Stevens.

Brown, meanwhile, went over his plans with Kagi at the Ritner boardinghouse in Chambersburg, as he'd done throughout the summer. Their conferences led one of the Ritner girls and a playmate to suspect the men were counterfeiters. One day, the girls peeked through the keyhole of an upstairs bedroom where the men were quietly conversing; to the girls' disappointment, the two were only studying a map.

As the date neared for the assault, Kagi drafted a document headed "General Orders," which laid out the organization of the "Provisional Army" that Brown envisioned would arise once his operation was under way. Each company was to consist of fifty-six privates, fifteen officers, and a surgeon. Four such companies would constitute a battalion, and so on, to the regiment and brigade level, with the largest units entitled to a commissary and musician. These orders were dated October 10, when Brown could not yet muster three "bands" of eight men each.

Equally ambitious was Brown's political manifesto, a fiery companion piece to his constitution entitled "A Declaration of Liberty By the Representatives of the Slave Population of the United States of America." Loosely modeled on "that Sacred Instrument" signed in 1776, the declaration proclaimed a new revolution, to "secure equal rights, privileges, & Justice to all," black and white, slave and free, "Irrespective of Sex." It also called for punishing those guilty of "oppressing their fellow Men," condemned "Our President and other Leeches," and repudiated allegiance to a government that had betrayed the original Declaration of Independence by protecting slave owners and traffickers.

The declaration was written in large letters on sheets of foolscap, with each page pasted onto white cloth. The fabric was then rolled around a stick and tied with a string, like a Torah scroll. This was Brown's Sacred

Instrument, which he would bring down from the mountains to fulfill God's will and the destiny of his chosen nation.

The commencement of this second American Revolution, originally planned for the Fourth of July, was finally set for the third week of October. In a letter to John junior, Kagi explained why this was "just the right time" to attack. Crops had been harvested and stored, meaning food would be available to a roving army. Slaves, having worked hardest in late summer and early fall, "are discontented at this season more than at any other." And an autumn church revival was in progress, which Kagi believed made whites more open to questioning the morality of slavery.

A more urgent impetus to action was financial. "We have not $5 left, and the men must be given work or they will find it themselves," Kagi wrote. Brown's penniless and restive recruits were also at growing risk of exposure. Kagi informed John junior on October 10 that he was leaving Chambersburg "for good" and closed his letter: "This must be our last for a time."

As it happened, last-minute aid arrived that same day, in the unlikely figure of a sickly, one-eyed Bostonian. Francis Jackson Meriam came from a prominent abolitionist family and had gone the previous year to Haiti, to investigate the condition of its formerly enslaved population. Upon hearing of Brown's mission, he rushed to join the band—and also to report back to Brown's worried backers. "He goes to look into matters a little for the stockholders," Sanborn wrote Thomas Wentworth Higginson on October 6.

Apart from his loathing of slavery, nothing recommended Meriam for service in the field. He was physically frail and had no experience as a fighter. Higginson thought him "half-crazy," and Meriam looked it, with one glass eye and a face blotched by syphilis. But Meriam brought with him an asset that none of Brown's other volunteers could supply. He carried $600 in gold coins, money he'd inherited and was eager to give to the cause. He spent about half of this fund buying percussion caps and other supplies for the men. The rest gave Brown a badly needed reservoir to draw on during the long campaign he anticipated.

Suddenly flush, the band was also bolstered by the arrival of two final

Lewis Leary   *John Copeland*

volunteers, both of them free blacks born in North Carolina who had moved to the abolitionist hotbed of Oberlin, Ohio. Lewis Leary was a harness maker with a wife and baby daughter; he had left them without giving any hint of his mission. His nephew, John Copeland, had studied at Oberlin College and been indicted for helping rescue a captured fugitive. Like Brown, he took inspiration from the American Revolution. It wasn't "white men alone who fought for the freedom of this country," Copeland wrote his brother, "the very first blood that was spilt was that of a negro"—a reference to Crispus Attucks, killed by the British in the Boston Massacre.

Leary and Copeland had been delayed in departing Ohio by lack of money. Traveling in the dark from Chambersburg to avoid detection, they arrived at the Kennedy farm at daybreak on Saturday, October 15. This gave Brown twenty-one men; it was still fewer than he'd anticipated, but the risk of waiting any longer was too great. Brown may also have learned from Meriam of the impatience and anxiety of the Secret Six.

On October 13, Sanborn giddily reported to Higginson that he'd heard from Meriam that the "business operation" would commence within three days. "Though the mills of *John* grind slowly, yet they grind exceedingly small," Sanborn wrote.

AS THE LAST PIECES of the operation fell into place that October, Brown's men attended to final business of their own. Charles Tidd wrote his parents telling them where to find his possessions, since "this is perhaps the last letter you will ever receive from your son. The next time you hear from me, will probably be through the public prints. If we succeed the world will call us heroes; if we fail, we shall hang between the Heavens and earth."

William Leeman used his last letter to unburden himself of the secret he'd kept from his poor family in Maine. "I am now in a Southern Slave State and before I leave it will be a free State Mother," he wrote, revealing that for three years he'd belonged to a secret group dedicated to "the Extermination of Slavery." This was why "I have staid away from you so long why I have never helped you when I knew you was in want and why I have not Explained to you before. I dared not divulge it before for fear of my Life now we are about to commence it does not make any diference."

Last, like every son writing his mother, he urged her not "to worrie yourself." Danger was "Natural to me," he wrote, and should he die, it would be "in a good Cause" of which he knew she approved. "Beside Mother it will bring me a Name & Fortune. If we succeed we will not want anymore."

Oliver Brown, in a letter datelined "Home," fretted about Martha's "peculiar condition" and urged his pregnant wife to get plenty of sleep and exercise. "Finally, Martha, do try to enjoy yourself; make the most of everything." His brother Watson wasn't quite so cheerful. He'd left North Elba in tears that summer, just after his son's birth, and confided in a last letter to his wife, Belle, "I sometimes think perhaps we shall not meet again. If we should not, you have an object to live for, —to be a mother to our little Fred. He is not quite a reality to me yet." He expected to leave the Kennedy farm for the last time that afternoon or the following day. "I can but commend you to yourself and your friends if I should never see you again. Believe me yours wholly and forever in love. Your husband, Watson Brown."

Aaron Stevens also wrote "a few more lines" to his beloved, knowing that "it may be the last time." Jennie Dunbar had yet to answer his sudden declaration of love from afar, and he regretted "that I did not get better acquainted with you" before leaving Ohio. "Jenny I doo long to see you so that I am allmost dead."

Whatever happened now, Stevens believed, "we have not lived for naught," since "insted of keeping our fellow beings back, we have healped them forward." He also expressed hope that "I shall live to see thy lovly face wonce more." But a hard fight lay ahead and he signed the letter using his old battle alias.

With meny good wishes I *remain for ever your love.*

C. Whipple

Good By

CHAPTER 8

Into the Breach

O n October 15, the Kennedy farm, which had served Brown's men as a barracks, arsenal, summer camp, and safe house, acquired a new status: "HEAD-QUARTERS WAR-DEPARTMENT, Near Harpers Ferry."

These words were emblazoned on military papers issued the men before battle. "In pursuance of the authority vested in US," one of the documents stated, "We do hereby Appoint and Commission the said Watson Brown a Captain." The commission was signed by "Secretary of War" John Kagi and "Commander in Chief" John Brown.

On Sunday morning, October 16, another formal induction took place at the "War Department" headquarters. Some of the men were newcomers to Brown's band and unfamiliar with the constitution adopted at Chatham. So Aaron Stevens read the document aloud, with Brown administering an oath of loyalty. Brown also read a Bible chapter "applicable to the condition of the slaves," and "offered up a fervent prayer to God to assist in the liberation of the bondmen."

In the afternoon, Brown gave final orders for the mission ahead. The three men least fit for hard fighting would stay at the farm to guard weapons and bring them forward at the appropriate time: Owen Brown, crippled in one arm; Francis Meriam, the sickly Bostonian; and Barclay Coppoc, an Iowa Quaker with bad lungs who was judged less energetic and determined than his brother Edwin.

The others would march to Harpers Ferry, with Charles Tidd and John Cook slipping ahead to cut down telegraph lines. Kagi and Stevens would seize the night watchman on the railroad bridge over the Potomac River, and the rest would follow, along the wagon road that ran beside the tracks and over the Potomac. Once in Harpers Ferry, the invaders would fan out, securing another bridge, the U.S. armory and arsenal, and several plantations outside town.

Having received their orders, the men had only to wait for dark. "Throughout the entire day," Osborne Anderson wrote, "a deep solemnity pervaded the place." Of Brown's twenty-one followers, all but two were in their twenties and only a third of them had seen real fighting in Kansas. None had participated in an operation as complex and ambitious as the one they were about to undertake.

On Sunday evening, Brown offered a few last words to his men. "You all know how dear life is to you, and how dear your life is to your friends,"

Harpers Ferry in 1859, from a hill behind town, Potomac bridge at center

he said. "Do not, therefore, take the life of any one if you can possibly avoid it; but if it is necessary to take life in order to save your own, then make sure work of it."

Finally, at eight o'clock, he gave the command: "Men, get on your arms; we will proceed to the Ferry." As Brown climbed onto the horse-drawn wagon, Barclay Coppoc kissed and embraced his brother Edwin.

"Come, boys!" John Brown called out, leading the wagon away from the log house and onto the road to Harpers Ferry. The men walked in pairs, widely separated, keeping as quiet as possible. One of the men later told Annie Brown what this solemn procession had been like. "They all felt," he said, "like they were marching to their own funeral."

ON THE NIGHT OF October 16, Patrick Higgins was running late. A watchman on the B & O Railroad bridge across the Potomac, the Irishman was paid a dollar a day for twelve hours of guard duty. His shift was due to begin at midnight, at which time he would relieve a fellow guard, Bill Williams. But it was ten minutes after midnight when Higgins reached the Maryland end of the bridge; as he did, he noticed that the lamps hanging at the entrance had been extinguished. And there was no sign of Williams, who was supposed to stick a peg in a time clock every thirty minutes as he patrolled the bridge. Higgins saw that the last peg had been placed at ten thirty P.M., more than ninety minutes earlier.

Higgins waited twenty minutes before starting across the bridge to look for Williams. Designed by Benjamin Latrobe, the architect of the U.S. Capitol, the bridge was enclosed with weatherboard siding and a tin roof. It ran for over a thousand feet, so that crossing the covered span felt like passing through a long dark tunnel. While walking along the bridge, Higgins carried a lantern but no weapon, since his primary job was to watch for fire sparked by locomotives and to make sure track switches were correctly set.

As Higgins neared the Virginia end of the bridge, two men loomed in the dark, holding what looked like to him like spears and carrying short rifles beneath their long gray shawls.

"Which way?" one of the men asked him.

Unbeknownst to Higgins, this was a demand for a password. Higgins answered it literally: "Not far; I am at my station."

In reply the stranger announced that Higgins was his prisoner and grasped the watchman's lantern. The Irishman swung his free hand at his captor's face, causing the stranger to stumble and let go of him. Higgins then ran to the end of the bridge and hurled himself through the window of a hotel by the railroad tracks, as two shots rang out behind him. "Lock your doors," he told the hotel clerk, "there are robbers on the bridge."

HIGGINS'S PARTNER, BILL WILLIAMS, had been similarly surprised and confused two hours earlier. First, a pair of armed strangers accosted him on the bridge, and then seventeen more men appeared, two of whom he recognized: the affable John Cook, who worked at a canal lock close to the bridge, and Isaac Smith, the bearded New York farmer who had crossed the Potomac from time to time since July. When Smith and his men told Williams that he was now their prisoner, he at first thought they were joking.

The men escorted Williams from the covered bridge and straight into Harpers Ferry, moving past the railroad depot and up to the granite and iron gate of the nearby armory. Its night watchman, Daniel Whelan, heard a wagon approaching and stepped out of his guardhouse just inside the armory gate. Whelan saw someone trying to open the padlocked entrance and thought this must be the head watchman. As he moved forward to help, a stranger called on him to open the gate; when he refused, armed men threatened him and used a crowbar to break in.

"I was nearly scared to death with so many guns about me," Whelan later testified. Though he guarded a gun factory, Whelan carried only a sword. Like the bridge guards, he was mainly charged with watching for fire, in his case by making sure the armory's many forges had been safely extinguished at the end of the workday. In fact, the entire government works at Harpers Ferry—a massive complex that included the main armory, a second rifle factory, and the arsenal where finished weapons were stored—was protected only by walls, fences, and a few elderly or unskilled men, such as Whelan.

Brown was well aware of this, because John Cook had scouted the armory and talked to its employees. "I knew Cook well," Whelan testified, and it was Cook who took the watchman's sword as other men swarmed into the armory yard on the night of October 16.

But Whelan quickly saw that Cook was not in charge. "The head man of them," an older bearded figure Whelan didn't know, posted guards by the gate and dispatched his other men out of the yard to secure the arsenal across the street, as well as Hall's Rifle Works, half a mile away, and the bridge across the Shenandoah River. All this was swiftly accomplished, without firing a shot or raising an alarm.

By midnight, Brown and his band of eighteen men had control of Harpers Ferry's guns (about a hundred thousand in all), rail lines, and river bridges, and they had cut telegraphic contact with the outside world. For the moment, Brown had reason to feel buoyant about the bold scheme he'd plotted in secret for so many years. And for the first time he shared it publicly, albeit before an audience of only two: the captured watchmen, Bill Williams and Daniel Whelan, alone with him in the armory yard.

"I want to free all the Negroes in this state," he told his prisoners, further warning them, "if the citizens interfere with me, I must only burn the town and have blood."

BROWN HAD WORRIED ALL summer that his plan would be exposed—by prying neighbors, by his men's indiscretions, or as a result of some other slip. But on the night of October 16, 1859, he caught Harpers Ferry entirely unawares. One reason was the sheer audacity and outlandishness of his attack. Southerners might dread a repetition of Nat Turner's uprising in 1831, but they had no reason to suspect that a war of liberation would be launched by a white man leading a small interracial band, striking an industrial mountain town where slaves were scarce.

A significant portion of Harpers Ferry wasn't even Virginia soil—much of the town belonged to the U.S. government, which owned not only the sprawling gun works but the town hall, dozens of houses and commercial buildings, and the grounds of schools, churches, public squares, and graveyards. Blacks, barred from skilled factory jobs, made up less than 10 percent of the population, and a third of them were free—unusual ratios for a southern town. Also atypical was the large sprinkling of immigrants and northern-born workmen. All told, in a community of almost three thousand, only about fifty male slaves were available for Brown to free and arm.

But Harpers Ferry was peculiar in another respect: it lay close to a

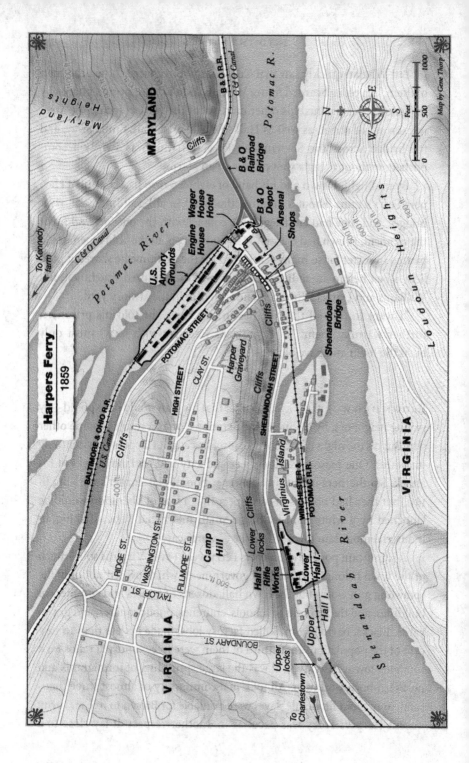

Harpers Ferry
1859

Map by Gene Thorp

MARYLAND

Maryland Heights

Potomac River

C & O Canal

B & O R.R.

Cliffs

To Kennedy farm

C & O Canal

Potomac River

B & O Railroad Bridge

Potomac R.

Wager House Hotel

Engine House

U.S. Armory Grounds

B & O Depot

Arsenal

Shops

Shenandoah Bridge

POTOMAC STREET

Loudoun Heights

HIGH STREET

CLAY ST.

Harper Graveyard

Cliffs

SHENANDOAH STREET

BALTIMORE & OHIO R.R.

U.S. Canal

Cliffs

400 ft.

Camp Hill

Virginius Island

WINCHESTER & POTOMAC R.R.

RIDGE ST.

WASHINGTON ST.

TAYLOR ST.

FILLMORE ST.

500 ft.

Lower Cliffs

Lower locks

Hall's Rifle Works

Lower Hall I.

VIRGINIA

Shenandoah River

BOUNDARY ST.

Upper Hall I.

Upper locks

To Charlestown

VIRGINIA

N E W S

Feet

0   500   1000

very different landscape. Just west of town, the area's steep shale cliffs and river gorges gave way to the gently rolling farmland of the Shenandoah Valley. This part of Jefferson County, Virginia, was fairly typical of the upcountry South, a mostly rural society with a few wealthy landowners, a large class of yeoman farmers, and 40 percent of its population enslaved. It was into this territory that Brown, after securing the gun works and bridges in Harpers Ferry, dispatched a wagonload of men to begin the real work of liberation.

AT ABOUT ONE THIRTY on the morning of October 17, Lewis Washington awoke to a low voice calling his name from the hallway outside his bedroom. A forty-six-year-old widower with grown children, Washington lived at Beallair, his 670-acre estate five miles west of Harpers Ferry. He described himself as a farmer, but this was misleading. The great-grandnephew of George Washington, he was also a close associate of Virginia's governor, an honorary colonel, and one of the wealthiest and most prominent citizens of Jefferson County.

When Washington heard someone summoning him in the night, he thought a traveling friend had arrived late and been let in a back door "by the servants." These "servants" were, of course, his slaves, who were a commodity

Lewis Washington and his home, Beallair

as well as a workforce in antebellum Virginia. In just the past year, Washington had sold nine slaves for $7,300 and "hired" two servants, meaning he paid another slave owner for the year's use of their labor. Washington recorded these transactions in his diary, alongside his notations about the purchase and sale of bacon, potatoes, and cord wood. In July 1859, he noted in the same diary that he was decamping for a mountain spa until September, leaving his overseer and slaves to toil in the summer heat.

Early that fall, soon after his return to Jefferson County, Washington visited Harpers Ferry and was approached in the street by a young stranger. "I believe you have a great many interesting relics at your house," the man said, and asked if he could come out to Beallair and see them.

Washington, who was fond of displaying his possessions and assumed the man was a gunsmith at the armory with an interest in firearms, invited him to visit. When the man appeared at Beallair, Washington showed him several heirlooms, including a pistol that the Marquis de Lafayette had presented to George Washington. His visitor, in turn, showed Washington two heavy Colt revolvers, which he said he'd carried as a buffalo hunter in Kansas. One of them was etched with the name John Cook, which Washington later learned was that of his guest.

The visitor then suggested a shooting contest with the Colts. Washington agreed, and they went outside and fired two dozen rounds at a target. Washington hadn't handled the revolver before and his shooting skills were rusty. Cook, though he chose not to show it that day, was a crack marksman. The colonel managed to win the contest. "He told me I was the best shot he had ever met," Washington said.

Pleased with this flattering young gun enthusiast, the colonel sought him out that October on a return trip to Harpers Ferry. Told that Cook had left town, Washington assumed that he had departed for Kansas, as he had mentioned his intention to return to the territory soon.

The colonel was therefore greatly surprised to meet Cook again, this time at one thirty in the morning of October 17, when Washington went to his bedroom door at Beallair in nightshirt and slippers. He was greeted by Cook and several other men carrying guns. One held a pine torch that lit the hallway; he brandished a large revolver and informed Washington, "You are our prisoner." This was Aaron Stevens, the toughest and most experienced of Brown's soldiers.

Stevens ordered Washington to get dressed. The Virginia gentleman took his time, pausing to express concern about bits of fire falling from the intruders' torch. "I asked them to come in my room and light my candles, so as to prevent my house from being burnt," he later stated.

Washington also coolly inquired about their purpose. "You are a very bold looking set of fellows," he said, noting that each man carried a rifle and two pistols stuck in his belt. "Possibly you will have the courtesy to tell me what this means."

"We have come here for the purpose of liberating all the slaves of the South," Stevens replied. Washington didn't believe him. When he and his uninvited guests repaired to the dining room, Cook directed Stevens to a gun closet he'd seen on his previous visit. The intruders took several of the weapons inside, including a fowling piece, the pistol given George Washington by Lafayette, and a dress sword that had allegedly been presented to the first president by Prussia's Frederick the Great.

Stevens also asked for Colonel Washington's watch, which he refused to surrender. "You told me your purpose was philanthropic," he said to Stevens, "but you did not mention at the same time that it was robbery and rascality."

Stepping outside, Washington found that still more of his property was in the hands of the intruders. The colonel's carriage came up to the door with an unfamiliar black man in the driver's seat. This was Shields Green, the fugitive slave in Brown's band. Hitched behind the carriage were four horses and Washington's farm wagon, with several of his male slaves inside. The colonel climbed aboard his carriage and took a seat beside Cook, at which point the caravan of raiders, freed slaves, and their newly unfree master trotted off toward Harpers Ferry.

En route, the ever affable Cook asked Washington if he had done any shooting since their contest earlier that fall. He also apologized for taking his host prisoner after being so hospitably treated on his previous visit to Beallair.

This cordial exchange was interrupted when the caravan halted beside the home of John Allstadt, another prominent landowner and slaveholder. In the dark, Washington listened as his captors took a heavy log from a rail fence by the turnpike and used it to batter open the door of Allstadt's home. "In a few moments there was a shout of murder and general commotion in the house," Washington later said.

Unlike the colonel, Allstadt had family living with him, and it was his daughter and a female cousin whom Washington heard shouting "Murder!" from a second-floor window. Downstairs, three armed men had burst in and ordered Allstadt to get dressed and come with them. They also seized his eighteen-year-old son.

Stepping onto the porch, Allstadt found a number of his slaves already gathered. At Washington's estate, most of the slaves had been away visiting family, as was generally permitted on Sunday nights. But all seven of Allstadt's male slaves were present. They, along with Allstadt and his son, were loaded into the farm wagon, which resumed its journey to Harpers Ferry.

Even then, Colonel Washington wasn't convinced that his captors had come to free slaves. He still thought that they were "merely a robbing party" and at this point they were probably returning to their lodging at Harpers Ferry. "I did not take the thing as very serious at all until we drove to the armory gate."

There, one of the armed men on the front seat of the carriage said, "All's well." A sentinel gave the countersign and opened the gate. The carriage then drove into the armory yard and up to the small brick guardhouse. As Washington disembarked, he was greeted by a man he would learn was John Brown. "You will find a fire in here, sir," he said to the colonel, "it is rather cool this morning."

It was also still dark, hours before dawn. At first light, Brown said, he would ask Washington to "write to some of your friends to send a stout, able-bodied Negro" as ransom. Brown also told Washington why he'd been the first slave owner taken. "I wanted you particularly for the moral effect it would give our cause, having one of your name as a prisoner."

Three months later, the members of a Senate committee would question Washington closely about this conversation.

Question. Did he tell you what his purpose was; what "cause" he was in?
Answer. He spoke generally of it. He said, perhaps, "this thing must be put a stop to," or something of that sort. He used general terms.
Question. "This thing," alluding to what?
Answer. Alluding to slavery.

The colonel soon realized that Brown was in deadly earnest. Upon arriving at the armory, Washington and Allstadt had been separated from their slaves and put by the stove in the guardroom. When the black men reappeared, the relationship between master and servant had changed. "They came in repeatedly to warm themselves," Washington testified, "each Negro having a pike in his hand."

THOUGH BROWN WAS FINALLY realizing his dream of freeing and arming slaves, not all had gone as planned while his raiding party traveled into the countryside of Jefferson County. The first hitch came just after midnight, when Patrick Higgins went to start his guard shift on the Potomac bridge and then fled the armed men who accosted and fired at him.

The Wager House Hotel, where Higgins had taken refuge, anchored the busiest wedge of transport and commerce in Harpers Ferry, a cramped

Train coming off the Potomac bridge and passing the Wager House, at rear

district known as the Point, where the rivers and railroad lines converged. Three and a half stories tall, the massive hotel had two parlors, a restaurant capable of seating hundreds, and a checkered reputation, having gone to seed in recent years and become popular mainly for its bar. But a new proprietor had just taken over and begun trying to upgrade the image of his establishment. Three days before Brown's attack, a newspaper advertisement touted the "newly fitted up" Wager House, "in the romantic Village of Harper's Ferry," where patrons could "rest assured no effort will be spared to render satisfaction and promote their comfort."

Gunfire after midnight probably wasn't what the proprietor had in mind. Then again, Harpers Ferry was a boisterous town, and the night clerk at the hotel, William Throckmorton, wasn't unduly alarmed. An hour or so earlier, he'd noticed a covered wagon roll past the hotel toward the armory, followed by four or five men; he'd concluded it was a "gypsy wagon." Now, when Patrick Higgins burst in and warned him of robbers on the bridge, he decided the excitable watchman had been alarmed by "some rowdies from the canal locks," just over the river in Maryland.

Still, Throckmorton thought it prudent to visit the nearby railroad office, where the night porter kept a pistol. He didn't find the porter, but on his way back to the hotel, Throckmorton saw two men on the bridge carrying guns. Whatever was going on, it looked more serious than canal rowdies or passing Gypsies.

At 1:25 A.M., when the express train from Wheeling to Baltimore pulled up at the platform by the Wager House, Throckmorton and Higgins warned the crew that armed strangers were on the bridge. The train's conductor, Andrew Phelps, went to investigate with four other men, one of whom carried a lantern. As they entered the covered bridge, the train followed slowly behind.

About fifty yards inside the bridge, a voice called out: "Stand and deliver!" Phelps could make out rifle muzzles in the dark and saw that they were pointed at his party. Then someone snatched the lantern away from one of his companions and extinguished it.

Phelps immediately turned and retreated, ordering the engineer to back the train off the bridge. As he reached the end of the span, he heard gunfire behind him. Moments later, a tall black man staggered out from the covered bridge, crying, "I am shot."

Heyward Shepherd was a free black baggage master at the Harpers Ferry depot. He had charge not only of the B & O depot at night, but also of the pistol Throckmorton had gone looking for earlier. Apparently, he wasn't carrying it when he ventured onto the bridge at about the same time as Phelps, in an effort to see what was going on.

Like the others, Shepherd reported that he had been ordered to halt. When he turned and fled instead, one of the sentinels on the bridge fired. The bullet tore through Shepherd's back and came out his chest, just below his left nipple. He was carried to the nearby railroad office and laid on a plank between two chairs, where a doctor examined him and judged the wound fatal. John Brown's campaign to liberate slaves had claimed as its first casualty a free black man, shot down while defying the orders of armed whites.

Who fired the shot, and why, wasn't clear. Patrick Higgins, the bridge watchman, later identified the armed pair he'd encountered earlier on the bridge as Oliver Brown and William Thompson. But during the night, others joined them, including Steward Taylor, who had told Annie Brown about envisioning his own death at Harpers Ferry. Hours after Shepherd's shooting, one of Brown's men found Taylor by the bridge, pale and trembling. Taylor said he had shot a man and believed he had killed him.

Whether it was Taylor or someone else who shot Shepherd, the reason was almost certainly skittishness. As a number of men approached their post on the dark bridge with a train chugging slowly behind, Brown's sentries couldn't easily see who the men were or whether they were armed. It's also unlikely that they could tell whether the men were black or white. Shepherd was described as being very large; when he turned and ran, he presented a ready target to a nervous young man with a cocked gun in his hand and orders to hold the bridge at all costs.

The shooter couldn't anticipate the havoc his single bullet would unleash, either. At first, the response was shock, as Shepherd lay slowly dying in the railroad office and the train crew and passengers struggled to make sense of the attack. Then, a few minutes after the shooting, one of Brown's sentries came off the bridge and headed toward the armory. "There he goes now!" someone shouted. The hotel clerk, Throckmorton, who had succeeded in borrowing a pistol, fired several shots. The sentry fired back, as did two men by the armory gate. No one was hit in the exchange.

But the gunfire turned what was already a tense and confused situation into wholesale panic. "Passengers were at this time running around in excitement and women and children screaming in the cars," Throckmorton said. Many of them crowded into the Wager House, where the doors were barricaded and the lights put out. From the upper windows of the tall hotel, observers could easily see armed men stationed in the lamplit yard of the armory, just across the road.

"It was filled with Men that had helped themselves to arms," S. F. Seely, an Ohio storekeeper on the train, wrote his wife later that day. Those around Seely offered "a thousand conjectures who they were or what they wanted."

One rumor suggested that the men were disgruntled armory workers launching a strike. Others believed they were angry laborers who'd been working on a government dam, a troubled project whose contractor had recently absconded with money due his employees. Or they were robbers who had come after $15,000 believed to be in the armory paymaster's safe. No one yet guessed that the midnight raiders were abolitionists.

The gunfire in the night also awoke a young and intrepid doctor, John Starry, who lived at the Point. After examining Heyward Shepherd's wound, Starry took it upon himself to learn all he could about the armed strangers. He spent the rest of the night in close surveillance, creeping as near the insurgents as he could, even questioning Brown's sentinels on the bridge and at the armory gate, asking what they were doing. "Never mind, you will find out in a day or two," one told him.

Starry also observed the traffic in and out of the armory. Shortly before dawn, he saw a heavy wagon roll out of the gate and head across the Potomac bridge toward Maryland. Several men stood in the bed of the wagon holding spears, while others walked beside, carrying rifles. Starry decided to get on his horse and raise the alarm, which hadn't yet spread beyond the Wager House and train platform, some distance from where most of the townspeople lived.

ON A NORMAL MONDAY morning in Harpers Ferry, the armory bell rang at six thirty to mark the beginning of the work week. But on October 17, 1859, the armory bell didn't sound. The man whose job it was to ring the bell had been taken prisoner, along with a number of other employees who showed up early for work only to be seized by armed strangers at the gate. In the night, Brown's sentinels had also detained several passersby, including two men returning late from a church meeting and another man coming home after putting a lady friend on the canal boat to Washington. By dawn, about forty men were being held under guard in the armory.

Brown made it clear to his hostages that he meant them no harm. His object, he assured Armistead Ball, the armory's master machinist, "was to free the slaves—not to make war on the people." He even let Ball, escorted by two guards, to go home to tell his family he was safe, and to eat breakfast. Breakfast wasn't yet ready, so Ball was permitted to return home again later. The wives and daughters of other hostages were allowed to bring them food at the armory.

Brown also provided victuals for the rest of his prisoners, sending an early-morning note to the Wager House: "You will furnish forty-five men with a good breakfast." This request astonished the hotel clerk, William Throckmorton, who had exchanged gunfire with the insurgents just a few hours before. He told Brown that breakfast would "have to be rather rough, as we had not expected anything like this, and were not prepared." After delivering pots of coffee and baskets of rolls and butter, Throckmorton asked about pay. Brown told him he would want another meal that afternoon, "for perhaps 200 men, and he would pay for the whole then."

Early that morning, Brown also met with Andrew Phelps, the conductor of the B & O train, and assured him it was safe to cross the Potomac. Phelps wasn't convinced. To guarantee safe passage, he asked Brown—whom townspeople at this point knew only as "Smith" or "the Captain"—to walk with him ahead of the train as it went over the bridge. Brown complied, and as the two men reached the Maryland shore, he said something that stuck with Phelps.

"You no doubt wonder that a man of my age should be here with a band of armed men," he told the conductor, "but if you knew my past history you would not wonder at it so much."

Brown also disclosed his purpose in coming to Harpers Ferry, which Phelps conveyed to his superiors as soon as his train reached a station with telegraph lines intact. At 7:05 A.M., from Monocacy, Maryland, Phelps wired a message that began: "Express train bound east, under my charge, was stopped this morning at Harper's Ferry by armed abolitionists. They say they have come to free the slaves and intend to do it at all hazards."

Phelps reported the insurgents' possession of the bridge and armory, the shooting of Shepherd, and the size of the occupying force, which he estimated at 150. "The leader of those men requested me to say to you that this is the last train that shall pass the bridge either East or West," Phelps reported. "It has been suggested you had better notify the Secretary of War at once."

Who "suggested" this to Phelps wasn't made clear. It might have been a crewman or passenger. But Brown knew his words would be widely disseminated, and he had tailored them for maximum effect. In a second telegram, Phelps reported that "the Captain" had said "he expected a reinforcement of 1500 men."

Brown made the same claim to his armory prisoners, and told one hostage that he had a picket line eighteen miles wide, extending all the way to the Mississippi. By keeping his eighteen men in constant motion, he also masked the size of the force he'd brought to Harpers Ferry. In the dark, as shawl-clad gunmen patrolled the streets, bridges, and government works, and as wagons rumbled in and out of the armory yard, estimates of the raiding party's numbers grew, until rumors spread that Brown's men were no fewer than 750.

The presence of armed blacks added to the confusion and panic. Some witnesses claimed they had seen hundreds of blacks in the night, including "strapping negroes who occasionally shouted out that they longed for liberty, as they had been in bondage long enough." Others believed the blacks were actually white robbers in disguise, feigning a slave uprising so they could more easily "escape with their booty."

The terrified train passengers carried these wild rumors east on Monday morning, flinging notes out the train windows to alert residents of the Maryland countryside. By the time they reached Baltimore, a little after noon, a throng had gathered at the station, including journalists who quickly telegraphed the news to papers in New York and other cities. The headlines given these first dispatches reflected the sensation Brown had caused in just twelve hours, and with only eighteen men.

FEARFUL AND EXCITING INTELLIGENCE . . .

INSURRECTION AT HARPER'S FERRY . . .

EXTENSIVE NEGRO CONSPIRACY IN VIRGINIA AND
    MARYLAND . . .

GENERAL STAMPEDE OF SLAVES . . .

As Brown had told Frederick Douglass at the Chambersburg quarry two months before, he thought "something startling" was just what the nation needed. By releasing the B & O train early on the morning of October 17, he delivered this shock treatment with extraordinary speed and impact. Brown had also spoken to Douglass and others of the military counterattack he anticipated. This, too, was certain to be hastened by his decision to use Phelps and his passengers as messenger pigeons.

But Brown had done enough research to know that the peacetime military of 1859 was far from a swift or well-oiled machine. The nation's standing army had fewer than twenty thousand men—three-quarters of them posted west of the Mississippi, the others scattered across forts, barracks, and other installations. It would almost certainly take the better part of a day, if not longer, for federal troops to mobilize and make their way to Harpers Ferry.

In the meantime, Brown had little to fear, or so it appeared at daybreak on Monday morning when he let the train continue its trip east. No local opposition had surfaced, apart from the potshots fired by the Wager House clerk hours earlier. The situation was now calm and Brown and his men were in control, with most townspeople still unaware of the trouble down by the armory and railroad bridge. Even some of those who had been awakened by gunfire thought little of it and went back to sleep. This was, after all, a community accustomed to factory hammers, locomotive whistles, "canal rowdies," and other disturbances. A few bangs in the night weren't necessarily cause for alarm.

Among the town's unsuspecting residents was Thomas Boerly, an Irish tavern keeper and grocer who went to open his shop as usual at about seven o'clock that Monday morning. As he did so, a neighbor ran up and told Boerly he had just escaped several armed men who tried to seize him down by the armory. The two townsmen grabbed shotguns and went to confront them.

Boerly was a large and combative man. On reaching Shenandoah Street, the main thoroughfare by the river, he blasted buckshot at sentinels posted by the arsenal gate. One of Brown's men returned fire with his much more accurate rifle, hitting the two-hundred-pound Boerly in the groin. Mortally wounded, the grocer staggered into a jewelry shop and lay bleeding on the floor, living long enough to receive last rites from a local priest. Boerly was forty-five. He left a wife, three children, and an orphaned niece he'd adopted.

News of the shooting circulated just as townspeople awoke to the trouble in Harpers Ferry. The alert was thanks largely to John Starry, the young doctor who had jumped on his horse to sound the alarm. He had roused armory officials and workmen and asked one of them to ring the bells at the Lutheran church, "to get the citizens together to see what sort of arms they had and to see what we could do to get rid of these fellows." By seven A.M., a number of people had gathered on Camp Hill, a steep rise overlooking the industrial and commercial areas by the rivers.

What Starry learned was disheartening. Per capita, Harpers Ferry housed more weapons than just about anyplace in America—roughly a hundred guns for every adult white male. But almost all these arms were housed in the arsenal and the gun factories, which were now in the hands of mysterious attackers. All the citizenry could muster was a handful of squirrel rifles and shotguns like the one Boerly had died firing.

After the conference on Camp Hill, Starry concluded that he had better get on his horse again, and he rode off to seek reinforcements in the county seat of Charlestown, eight miles away.

EARLY THAT SAME MORNING, another rider headed toward Harpers Ferry, unaware of the turmoil in town. Terence Byrne lived in Maryland, not far from the Kennedy farm, and he'd ridden about a mile from his home when he encountered a heavy farm wagon coming the other way. As the Marylander passed it, a voice called out, "Mr. Byrne, stop."

Reining in his horse, Byrne turned and saw John Cook, a familiar figure in the neighborhood. "I am very sorry to inform you that you are my prisoner," Cook told him.

"You are certainly joking," Byrne replied.

"I am not."

Byrne glimpsed a rifle poking from beneath Cook's coat. Another man came up and also pointed his gun at Byrne. "You must go with us to your place," he said. "We want your Negroes."

This was Charles Tidd, whom Brown had sent across the Potomac with Cook, William Leeman, and about five of the slaves liberated from the plantations in Virginia. Brown's men and the newly freed slaves rode in Lewis Washington's wagon; one of the slaves carried the colonel's fowling piece, while the others carried pikes. This was the well-armed party that John Starry had seen leave the armory at about five A.M. before he rode off to rouse other townspeople.

The men had been sent to Maryland on a dual mission: to start bringing forward weapons from the Kennedy farm and to collect more slaves and take their masters hostage. Byrne, who with his brother owned a farm and a number of slaves, had ridden right into their hands.

Unlike Lewis Washington, Byrne took the men at their word when they said they'd come to free slaves. He also worried about what this might portend. As he returned home in his captors' custody, Byrne saw his brother standing on the porch and tried to warn him. "I whispered to him, 'civil war,'" Byrne later testified. "Perhaps I said 'servile war.'"

Brown's men entered the house and seated themselves, uninvited, while Byrne nervously paced. "Cook commenced making a kind of speech," Byrne later testified. "He said that all men were created equal" and went on at some length. Byrne was too rattled to take much of it in. He also summoned a visiting cousin, "as she was a lady of considerable nerve." Indeed, upon coming downstairs, she told Byrne he should "cowhide those scoundrels out of the house."

Byrne didn't take this advice: the men carried rifles and revolvers. But they were thwarted in their primary mission, since Byrne's male slaves had gone off on Saturday night and not yet returned. Cook and the others nonetheless held to their orders to take Byrne hostage, loading him into the wagon beside a number of heavy boxes retrieved from the nearby Kennedy farm. The four-horse wagon then set off toward Harpers Ferry, pulling heavily in the damp morning air.

After traveling a mile or two, the wagon stopped beside a log schoolhouse, which Brown had chosen as a forward depot for his weapons.

The Maryland schoolhouse and arsenal

Perched near the head of a ravine running down to the Potomac, the secluded school was accessible to Harpers Ferry and also defensible, a potential redoubt for Brown's men if they chose to pull back into the Maryland hills.

But there was one complication: by the time the first wagonload of weapons arrived, about ten o'clock on Monday morning, school was already in session. There were some twenty-five pupils inside the one-room building, along with a young schoolteacher named Lind Currie.

Cook, nonchalant as always, walked in and informed the teacher that he needed part of the schoolroom to store boxes of weapons. Equally startling was Cook's request that Currie continue with his lessons; the teacher, Cook said, "should not be interrupted."

Cook carried a rifle and had a bowie knife and two revolvers stuck in his belt. Tidd and Leeman were similarly armed, while the black men carried pikes. When this party appeared, Currie's students grew wide-eyed and "very much alarmed," the teacher later testified. As he drily informed Cook, his pupils "were not in a condition to engage in their usual duties."

After trying to calm the students himself, Cook agreed to let them go and allowed Currie to escort home a frightened little boy. When the teacher returned, the wagon had been unloaded and was on its way back to the Kennedy farm for more weapons, leaving Cook and one of Lewis Washington's former slaves to guard the school. Currie found Cook "rather cooler" than before, and guessed this was because the insurgent had learned that the teacher, who lived just a mile from Colonel Washington, was a slaveholding farmer as well.

Currie also realized he was now "detained" and had no choice other than to stay. But Cook was incapable of sustaining a chill. "He became rather more communicative, and spoke of a great many things," Currie testified. Over the hours that followed, the two young men from Connecticut and Virginia engaged in "long and varied" conversation, on topics such as "the feeling entertained towards the south by the north generally."

A CURIOUS INTIMACY ALSO developed between Terence Byrne and twenty-year-old William Leeman, the man assigned to escort the Maryland slave owner the rest of the way to Harpers Ferry. The two men hadn't walked far from the school when rain began to pour down. "I had an umbrella," Byrne later testified, "and proposed to him to sit up close to me, and my umbrella would be some protection to him." As the hostage and his armed guard huddled together by the road, Leeman disclosed that his commander, "Captain Smith," was actually the notorious John Brown of Kansas.

Byrne, already extremely anxious, now grew even more so. "I was fearful of a bloody civil war," he said. "I was under the impression that, unless they were in great numbers, they would not be foolish enough to make an attack on the borders of two slaveholding States."

But he also sensed that his young bodyguard had doubts about the mission. At Byrne's house earlier that morning, while Cook speechified about the coming triumph of freedom, Byrne noticed that Leeman had hunched quietly by the fire, his head resting against the mantel and his cap drawn down. Now, as Leeman waited out the rain shower with his hostage, "he appeared to be very serious," Byrne said. "I am inclined to think he was meditating his escape."

The Marylander sensed no such anxiety in another member of Brown's band he met that morning. When William Thompson, one of the Potomac bridge guards, passed Leeman and his captive on the road, he "came up smiling," extended his hand, and said, "How are you, Byrne?" To which the Marylander replied with feigned heartiness: "Good morning, Mr. Thompson; I am well; how are you?"

The cheerful young man told Byrne about the situation in town, where a lull had prevailed since the early-morning gunfire. He had just given a similar message to the guards at the schoolhouse. "Thompson came up from the Ferry and reported that everything was all right," Cook later stated. The courier then hurried back down to his post on the bridge.

This dispatch was delivered at about eleven o'clock on Monday morning. A short time later, Cook received a fresh report from the Ferry, though this one was not delivered in person. "I heard a good deal of firing," Cook said, "and became anxious to know the cause."

FROM THE MOMENT HE arrived in Harpers Ferry, Brown had sought to assure the townspeople that he did not regard them as his enemy. He had come to free slaves and intended to hurt no one, unless he met with resistance. Following the gunfire that broke out in the night, Brown repeatedly sent peace emissaries to frightened train passengers and citizens at the Wager House. He expressed regret for the shooting of the railroad porter, Heyward Shepherd, blaming it on "bad management" by his sentinels on the bridge and telling Conductor Phelps, "It was not his intention that any blood be spilled."

He'd also indicated to his band that he anticipated some support from white townspeople. "From Brown," one of them later stated, "I understood that there were laboring men at Harper's Ferry who wished to get rid of slaves and would aid in running them off." At the least, Brown appears to have believed that most whites would stay out of the fray rather than take up arms in defense of the slaveholding gentry.

This belief was bolstered by the intelligence he had received from Cook, who found the community welcoming, even to a Northerner who sometimes told his acquaintances of his sympathy for the free-state cause in Kansas. Relatively few townspeople owned slaves, and they seemed to live and work peaceably alongside free blacks. Thomas Boerly, for instance, rented part of his property to a black family. The black baggage master, Heyward Shepherd, was employed at the B & O depot by the town's mayor, who had also helped another free man buy his wife and children out of slavery.

But this interracial cooperation didn't translate into sympathy for Brown's cause. Nor were many people in Harpers Ferry aware of his intentions, at least initially. The shooting of a free black man confused matters, as did the mixed signals Brown seemed to convey. He said he meant no harm to citizens—yet seized their town at night, took hostages, claimed command of a vast army, and brought with him barrels of gunpowder and torches that one hostage described as "sticks wrapped with cotton waste and dipped in burning fluid." His men also carried Sharps rifles, a new kind of carbine named for a gunsmith who had once worked at Harpers Ferry. Compact, quick-loading, and renowned for its range and accuracy, the Sharps was the deadliest firearm of its day, and the origin of the word "sharpshooter."

Unsurprisingly, townspeople doubted Brown's peaceful overtures—particularly after the shooting of Shepherd and then Boerly, news of which quickly reached the locals who had convened that morning on Camp Hill. As John Starry rode off to seek aid in the county seat, townsmen set about arming themselves.

First, someone realized that not all the government weapons were under the watch of the invaders. A few weeks earlier, when flooding threatened the low ground by the Shenandoah, scores of rifles had been moved from the arsenal to a storeroom on the armory grounds, which stretched for half a mile beyond Brown's headquarters by the gate. Two townsmen succeeded in reaching the storeroom and they returned with rifles, percussion caps, and a few bullet molds.

Meanwhile, women and children helped gather all the lead they could find, including pewter plates and spoons, to melt on stoves and form into ammunition. "Father and the others were putting bullets into their pockets, hot from the moulds," recalled Jennie Chambers, a fifteen-year-old armorer's daughter and schoolgirl in Harpers Ferry.

Another relative of Jennie's, George Chambers, was the proprietor of the Gault House, a wooden saloon near the Wager House that overlooked both the arsenal and the armory grounds. Chambers posted himself in an upper story of the ramshackle building and began delivering sporadic harassing fire. A few others followed suit.

Though no one was hit, this sniping forced Brown's men to take cover and dodge between their separate posts at the bridges, armory, arsenal, and the more distant Hall's Rifle Works, where John Kagi was posted. As local opposition emerged, Brown's second-in-command sent a messenger to the armory, urging that Brown and his force withdraw from Harpers Ferry before it was too late. Kagi received no answer.

TEN MILES WEST OF Harpers Ferry, James Hooff was working in a field that morning, supervising slaves as they seeded and harrowed, when John Starry "rode out in haste." The doctor told him "whites and Negroes had possession of the Ferry & were killing the citizens," Hooff wrote in his diary. The farmer immediately mounted his horse, gathered "all the arms I could get," and rode off to nearby Charlestown, the seat of Jefferson County.

Others did the same, alerted by Starry, by an overseer at Lewis Washington's plantation, and by tolling bells in Charlestown, a sound that on non-church days normally signified an emergency such as a fire. The town was also the base for a modestly equipped and trained militia. One of its principal roles was to act as a slave patrol and guard against revolt—a source of keen anxiety following Nat Turner's insurrection, when many such civilian units were organized and the Virginia Military Institute established.

While Brown anticipated sympathy from some factory workers in Harpers Ferry, he could expect none from the farming heartland of Jefferson County, centered on Charlestown. Just three months before Brown's attack, the town had enacted a new ordinance forbidding "any negro" to be on the street after nine P.M. In addition: "Not more than five negroes shall at any one time stand together on a sidewalk, or at or near the corner of a street, and negroes shall never stand on a sidewalk, to the inconvenience of white persons having to pass by, and any negro who shall violate this order will be punished by stripes not exceeding fifteen." Slaves were regularly auctioned at the door of the county courthouse in Charlestown. So were free blacks, sold into slavery "for remaining in the Commonwealth contrary to law." (Freed blacks were required to leave Virginia within a year, unless granted a special permit.)

By ten A.M. on the morning of October 17, about a hundred volunteers had gathered in Charlestown, some of them militiamen, many not. All were ready to oppose the shadowy interracial mob that had kidnapped their neighbor Lewis Washington and taken hold of Harpers Ferry. Boarding a train, they disembarked at a rail spur halfway to their destination, so the cars could be sent to bring additional militia from Winchester, a short distance west. Couriers were also dispatched to other Virginia towns.

When the Charlestown contingent marched into Harpers Ferry, at about eleven thirty A.M., they joined a group of local men on Camp Hill who had found enough guns and bullets to fight. Officers in the Charlestown militia took charge of this combined force, now numbering about 150, and divided it into five units. One squad was sent on a flanking maneuver and ordered to cross the Potomac a mile above the Ferry so it could attack the B & O bridge from the Maryland side. Another snaked down through town to slip into the Gault House and reinforce its saloonkeeper turned sniper, George Chambers. A third party occupied other tall buildings near the government works. The remainder went to secure the Shenandoah bridge and the road leading to Hall's Rifle Works, half a mile from Brown's headquarters at the armory.

These maneuvers were executed in heavy mist and rain by men who— except for a handful of Mexican War veterans—had never seen combat. They were haphazardly armed and knew nothing of their foes, apart from wild rumors that suggested the insurgents numbered in the hundreds, including "armed bands of maddened blacks."

The twenty men sent to flank Brown's force had to work their way north of town and pole across the shallow Potomac in flatboats. Reaching the Maryland bank, they then crept along a towpath toward the railroad bridge, unable to see the Virginia shore because of the mist. To their left loomed a cloud-shrouded cliff; they feared that insurgents stood atop it, waiting to shower down boulders or bullets.

"Every man," one of the Charlestown volunteers later wrote, "felt when he reached the Maryland end of the Potomac Bridge that he had literally 'run the gauntlet,' and we were all glad to be alive."

The Virginians then poured onto the bridge, firing wildly. Brown's

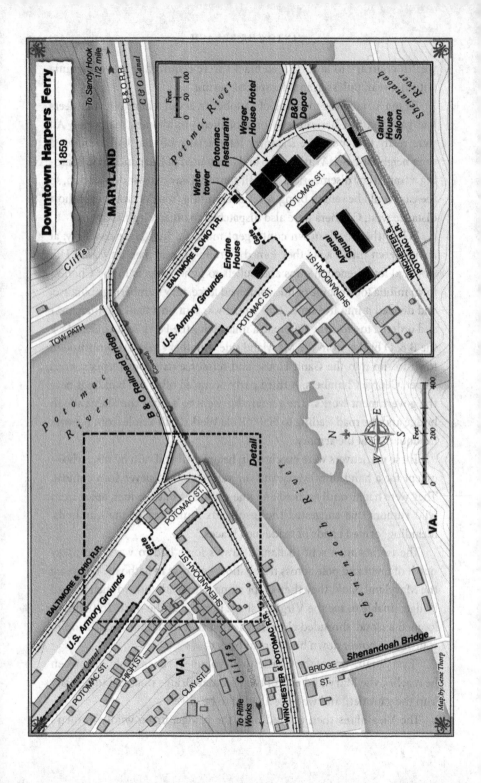

Downtown Harpers Ferry
1859

Map by Gene Thorp

sentinels, badly outnumbered and caught by surprise, quickly fell back across the Potomac toward Harpers Ferry. Spilling out of the covered bridge on the Virginia side, they ran for the armory, only sixty yards away. The last stretch was open pavement, exposed to the fire of gunmen who had occupied the upper stories of buildings overlooking the street.

Some of Brown's men at the armory and arsenal rushed from their sheltered posts to defend their retreating comrades. In the confused moments that followed, one of the insurgents raced down Shenandoah Street, between the arsenal and armory. From a window high above, a gunman fired down at him, apparently having loaded his rifle with a crude slug or spike instead of a bullet. The steeply angled shot tore through the running man's neck and throat, dropping him dead on the pavement.

Brown's other men dodged to safety but were unable to retrieve their fallen compatriot, who was left exposed on the street for townspeople to gawk at. Locals didn't know his name, but recognized him as a tall mulatto who had been seen earlier at the arsenal gate, firing his Sharps rifle. No one dared to collect his body, which lay in a gutter near the center of the fighting that now raged around the armory.

Later that day, hogs came to root in the slain man's gaping neck wound. Angry and inebriated townspeople poked sticks in the wound and used pocket knives to cut off pieces of the dead man's ears as gruesome souvenirs. By the time the mutilated body was finally taken away and dumped in an unmarked pit, little remained to identify the deceased as Dangerfield Newby, the former slave who had hoped to free his family still in bondage in Virginia.

Remarkably, the desperate letters Newby had received from his wife survived, having been taken from his pockets or from among his possessions found later. "if I thought I shoul never see you this earth would have no charms for me," Harriett had written Dangerfield in her last message, begging him to rescue her before she was sold south. "Do all you Can for me, witch I have no doubt you will."

Her determined husband fell just inside Virginia, fifty miles from Harriett, and his death extinguished her dream of freedom. A few months later, she was sold to a new master, in Louisiana. Her husband's estate—including the $741 he'd saved to free her—was distributed among his relatives in Ohio.

NEWBY'S DEATH ALSO MARKED a turn in the broader campaign of liberation he'd joined. He was shot just as Brown's men lost control of the Potomac bridge, a setback that isolated the small invasion force and exposed the deep flaws in its commander's plan.

Among Brown's idiosyncrasies as a military thinker were some curious notions regarding topography. On a carriage ride with Franklin Sanborn in 1857, he surveyed the New England landscape and told the Concord teacher that the strongest positions weren't hilltops, as usually supposed. Rather, a ravine "well guarded on the flanks, was often a better military post," he said.

This "strange doctrine," as Sanborn called it, also turned up in the notes Brown took on his military reading. "Some valuable hints," he wrote in his diary, listing book passages on guerrilla warfare, including one that mentioned "deep and narrow defiles where 300 men would suffise to check an army."

Harpers Ferry fit Brown's belief that ravines could serve as ideal redoubts. Occupying a point of land at the bottom of a gorge, the town was enclosed by rivers and steep mountains. Brown believed he could choke off the few approach points and defend what he considered an impregnable fortress against a much larger force. But if this doubtful strategy had any merit, it vanished the moment Virginians flanked Brown at midday on October 17.

The loss of the Potomac bridge cut Brown off from his men and material in Maryland. Having retreated from the Shenandoah bridge at about the same time, the band in Harpers Ferry now had no clear avenue of escape. Brown and his men also became vulnerable to attack from above. Since buildable land was scarce in the hilly, flood-prone town, most of the structures stood close together and were generally tall, three stories or more. Those on the steep hill behind the armory and arsenal loomed much higher. Once gunmen occupied buildings overlooking the "Lower Town," as the riverside area was known, Harpers Ferry became a virtual shooting gallery.

Badly exposed, Brown's men in the town were also isolated from one another. Instead of one mobile unit, they now constituted three separated squads: at the armory, arsenal, and rifle works. Anyone who tried to move between these outposts risked the fate that had befallen Danger-field Newby.

Late the previous night, Brown had sent a party under John Kagi to secure and hold Hall's Rifle Works, half a mile from the armory. Kagi and his men stayed there through the night and morning, patrolling the factory grounds and awaiting further orders. None came, nor did Brown respond to Kagi's message urging a withdrawal. Kagi and his men were left stranded and in the dark as gunmen mobilized on the ridge over-looking their position.

Also waiting anxiously for Brown's orders was Charles Tidd, who had spent most of the day in Maryland, transporting weapons from the Kennedy farm to the log schoolhouse. That summer, when Tidd had angrily left the farm upon learning of his commander's plan to seize Harpers Ferry, he had been mollified by Brown's agreement to send men "in each direction to burn RR bridges & return with slaves," as Tidd later described

Front gate of the U.S. armory; the engine house is the first building on the left

the revised plan. These measures would presumably give the band much-needed reinforcement and make it harder for counterattacking troops to reach the scene. But if Brown did in fact make such a promise to Tidd, he didn't follow through on it. Instead, he stayed put in Harpers Ferry all morning, until the "steel trap" Frederick Douglass had warned of began to close, leaving his men to wonder: What was the old man up to?

To THOSE AT HIS side early that afternoon, Brown betrayed no sign of panic or indecision over his deteriorating military position. In Kansas, he'd earned a reputation for coolness under fire; here too he seemed in control, even as militiamen and armed citizens seized the bridge, killed one of his men, and began directing steady fire at his small force holed up in the armory.

As the shooting commenced, Brown put his hand on Terence Byrne, one of the forty or so prisoners held in the armory guard room. "I want you, sir," he said, also selecting nine other men, including prominent armory officials and Byrne's fellow farmers and slaveholders, Lewis Washington and John Allstadt. The ten prisoners were taken to a larger space adjoining the guardroom. This stablelike chamber had thick brick walls, heavy wooden doors, and very high windows. Designed to house the armory's two fire engines, it would now become Brown's command post and the holding cell for his most valuable hostages.

The prisoners were positioned at the rear of the engine house, behind the fire carts. Their captors manned the doors, which opened inward and could be pulled back a few inches to peer or shoot out of. Brown also put one of Allstadt's freed slaves, Phil Luckum, to work drilling at the building's brick walls to create openings for rifles. "You are a pretty stout looking fellow," he said to Luckum, "can't you knock a hole through there for me?" Using mason's tools, Luckum worked until a bullet sent brick and mortar flying back in his face. "It's getting too hot," he declared, leaving Brown to finish the job.

With bullets thudding against the engine house and crashing through the high windows, Brown's hostages agreed to help broker a cease-fire. A leading citizen was sent out with a flag of truce, escorted by William

Thompson, who had buoyantly told John Cook a short while ago that "everything was all right" at the Ferry.

Earlier in the day, Brown had sent out emissaries without incident. But the gunmen now surrounding the armory were in no mood to negotiate. They promptly seized Thompson and dragged him into the Wager House, tying his hands and feet to an armchair in the parlor. As the first of Brown's men to be captured, Thompson was set upon by interrogators who asked about his motivation and the meaning of the attack.

"His answers were invariably the same," said Christine Fouke, the sister of the hotel's proprietor. Thompson told his captors he had been "taught to believe the Negroes were cruelly treated and would gladly avail themselves of the first opportunity to obtain their freedom." He'd also been led to believe that once Brown and his men took possession of the armory, "the colored people would come in a mass, backed by the non-slaveholders of the Valley of Virginia."

THOMPSON'S SEIZURE, UNDER A flag of truce, angered Brown and enraged his second-in-command at the armory, Aaron Stevens. Tender in his lovelorn letters to the Ohio music teacher Jennie Dunbar, Stevens was a ferocious fighter and dangerously hotheaded when crossed. His court-martial, five years before, was due to Stevens having felt insulted by a superior officer, which prompted him to draw his gun, declare "I am as good a man as you," and threaten to blow out the officer's "damned brains." Since arriving in Harpers Ferry, he'd spoken sharply to Lewis Washington, the patrician plantation master, and told another hostage who expressed support of slavery, "You would be the first fellow I would hang." Now, he wanted violent retribution against Thompson's captors.

Stevens was dissuaded from this course of action by the most prominent of the local hostages, Archibald Kitzmiller, the acting superintendent of the armory. (His superior was away on business.) Kitzmiller had been the first man awakened by John Starry, who had alerted him that the armory "was in possession of an armed band." Going to investigate, Kitzmiller had been seized and held ever since.

As Brown and Stevens mulled how to respond to Thompson's capture,

Kitzmiller said, "I can possibly accommodate matters." He then offered to go out as a peace broker himself, with Stevens as escort. Despite what had happened to Thompson, Brown agreed, sending not only Stevens but also his son Watson as a second bodyguard.

Stevens and Watson walked out of the gate behind Kitzmiller, who waved his handkerchief at armory workers he saw posted by the Potomac bridge. The three men then proceeded down a narrow street that formed a sort of canyon between tall commercial buildings on either side. This lane dead-ended at a raised railroad trestle, above which loomed the Gault House saloon. As Kitzmiller and his two escorts neared it, the saloon-keeper, George Chambers, smashed an upper-story window so he could shoot unobstructed. Then he and a fellow gunman opened fire.

Their first volley hit Watson Brown. A moment later, Stevens was also struck. He swore and fired back; hit again and again, he finally collapsed. Lying bloodied on the pavement, Stevens called out to Kitzmiller, who had urged him to attempt a peaceful negotiation. "I have been cruelly deceived," Stevens said.

Kitzmiller, who had been dragged from his bed before dawn and then taken hostage, replied: "I wish I had remained at home."

Watson Brown, meanwhile, had staggered back to the armory, vomiting blood from a stomach wound. He hoisted his rifle and for a time resumed his post at the engine house, until he became too weak and lay down on the floor. His father could do little except give him water and fume over the barbarity of his assailants. He began to "show temper," one of the hostages later testified, and "said he had it in his power to destroy that place in half an hour."

Brown regarded himself as a soldier, subject to traditional rules of battlefield conduct. His hostages, for the most part, abided by this canon, and not only because they were terrified. A number of them later testified to Brown's sincere and respectful treatment of them. Virginians prided themselves on their code of honor, and Brown seemed a man whose word was his bond. Hostages who left the armory as emissaries pledged to return—and did so. Archibald Kitzmiller was a rare exception. Caught in the firefight that felled Aaron Stevens, he "did not consider" his pledge to return "binding under the circumstances," as he later put it. Instead, he took cover in the Wager House.

The bullet-riddled Stevens was left crumpled on the pavement out-side, exposed to a hard rain and the horrified gaze of onlookers. "I seen big beefs killed and they did not lose more blood," Patrick Higgins, the bridge watchman, later stated.

But the strapping warrior wasn't yet dead. After lying still for a few min-utes, Stevens began to move and groan. Brown, having now lost three men under flags of truce, couldn't risk sending out another to assist his wounded lieutenant. But a hostage volunteered to go to Stevens's aid. Joseph Brua had served earlier as a peace envoy. Now he went into the bullet-raked street, helped Stevens into the Wager House, and returned once again to captivity. In an extraordinary day that mixed cruelty and kindness, dishonor and courage, Brua's act was among the most remarkable.

Also astonishing was the fortitude of the man Brua rescued. Stevens had already commanded notice from townspeople for his fearsome and unflinching defense of an exposed position at the armory gate. Now, lying half naked on a bed in the Wager House, where a doctor dressed the wounds to his face, chest, and limbs, Stevens became a figure of awe for his majestic physique. "A large, exceedingly athletic man, a perfect Samson in appearance," one person wrote. Another described his "brawny shoulders and large sinewy limbs, all the muscles finely developed and hard."

His manner was just as imposing. Though shot six times and sur-rounded by armed interrogators, he remained composed and defiant. Ste-vens told his captors, as Thompson had, that Brown believed "the Negroes would flock to them by the thousands, and they would soon have force enough for their purposes." Stevens now realized that Brown "had been greatly deceived," but he expressed no regret and was fully prepared to die for the cause of freedom. "One life for many," he said. Believing himself close to death, Stevens gazed at a picture he wore around his neck, an image of his beloved Jennie Dunbar posing with a little girl in Ohio they both adored.

NOT ALL OF BROWN's men behaved quite so staunchly on the after-noon of October 17, as their position grew ever more perilous. Earlier in the day, the Maryland farmer Terence Byrne had sensed doubt and appre-hension in his guard, William Leeman, the youngest of Brown's men. Just twenty, the former shoe factory worker was tall and lean, regarded by his peers as a "Devil may care kind of fellow," hard to control but a tough fighter. He was one of the Kansas veterans who'd teased Dauphin Thompson at the Kennedy farm, questioning whether the baby-faced novice was suited for combat.

But in the midst of battle, it was Leeman who faltered. From his many letters, it appeared that he'd joined Brown out of a youthful mix of idealism, ambition, and adventure-seeking. As he'd written his impoverished mother just before the attack, he expected the Harpers Ferry mission to bring such fame and fortune that "we will not want anymore."

The prospects for this success were fading fast on the afternoon of October 17. At about one o'clock, while the combatants' attention was focused on the engine house and the street outside the armory gate, Leeman slipped away, dodging between buildings in the vast armory yard that stretched behind the engine house and ran parallel to the Potomac. Crossing the railroad tracks, he ducked through a culvert and into the river, wading about sixty yards before being spotted. Gunmen on the bridge and

William Leeman

on shore opened fire, while two others scrambled down to the riverbank and splashed in after Leeman.

As usual in autumn, the Potomac was low, its bed filled with rocks. Midway across, Leeman slipped and fell, losing his rifle in the water. He plunged on until he reached a large rock, where he drew a bowie knife and cut the straps holding his cartridge box and pistols, probably so he could swim more easily. But his two pursuers were closing fast.

"Don't shoot!" he cried, throwing up his hands. One of the men approached the rock, raised his gun, and shot Leeman in the face.

Before returning to shore, the gunman went through Leeman's pockets, finding his two-day-old commission as a captain in Brown's army and a letter from his teenaged sister, Lizzie. She told of the family's poverty and pleaded with him to come home to Maine. "Oh my dear brother," she wrote, "I hope you are as good as you were when you went from your home, and I know you are, for you would not do anything wrong."

Leeman, like Dangerfield Newby, was left where he fell. Sprawled on a large rock in the middle of the Potomac, his body lay in plain sight of gunmen on the bridge and in buildings overlooking the river. They pumped dozens of bullets into the corpse until finally, an observer wrote, the body slipped from the rock and drifted in the shallow river, Leeman's black hair "floating upon the surface and waving with every ripple."

FROM THE TIME BROWN'S men first crossed the Potomac late on Sunday night, the fighting at Harpers Ferry had been confined to a tiny geographic area near the armory and arsenal. Townspeople were aware that insurgents also held Hall's Rifle Works. But it was hard for them to judge how many men were holed up in the factory, and where inside the walled nine-building complex they were headquartered. Not until two thirty in the afternoon on Monday did a local man succeed in sneaking up and spotting their hideout in one of the workshops. He and others immediately volunteered to form a party to flush the insurgents out.

The attack plan called for gunmen to occupy a bluff opposite, from which they would commence the assault with a barrage through the windows of the workshop. But as soon as they took up position, five men raced out of the targeted building. John Kagi had seen the attackers mobilizing and given the order to evacuate. As the men on the bluff opened fire, Kagi led a retreat out the back of the rifle works and toward the nearby Shenandoah.

In 1859, this stretch of the riverfront was crowded with mills, railroad tracks, and industrial waterways used to power factory turbines. Kagi may have hoped to follow the Potomac's bank toward town and rejoin whatever he could find of Brown's party. But the way was blocked by gunmen posted in buildings beside the rifle works. The only path open was straight ahead, into the Shenandoah.

Kagi waded into the river, followed by two of his men. But gunmen quickly appeared on the far shore, while others ran down to the bank the insurgents had just fled. Some of them pursued Kagi and his men into the river. The rest unleashed a watery cross fire.

A local woman witnessed the scene from her house overlooking the Shenandoah and described it moments later in a letter to her daughter. "Our men chased them in the river just below here and I saw them shot down like dogs," Mary Mauzy wrote of the "ruffians" who had fled the rifle works. "I saw one poor wrech rise above the water and some one strike him with a club he sank again and in a moment they dragged him out a Corpse."

This was Kagi, who had struggled two-thirds of the way across the Shenandoah before he was shot and fell under the water. A diary found in his pocket told of final preparations the week before in Chambersburg, where he'd written a last letter to his family: "Be cheerful my dear father and sisters—dont *imagine* dangers, all will be well."

Close behind Kagi in the river was Lewis Leary, the free black harness maker from Oberlin, who had arrived at the Kennedy farm only two days before. He climbed atop a rock in the Shenandoah and was shot in the back. Dragged ashore, Leary begged for warmth and was laid beside a stove in a workshop by the river, where he lingered in great pain for twelve hours.

Leary asked his captors to send word of his death to his young wife, Mary, back in Ohio with their baby daughter. Leary hadn't told her of his plans; she thought he was going to see family in Pennsylvania. But Mary had wondered why he was so emotional on departing, having taken their baby in his arms and "wept like a child," she later said.

Leary's kinsman from Oberlin, John Copeland, was behind Leary and Kagi as they tried to cross the Shenandoah. After seeing his two comrades shot, Copeland floated down behind some rocks, hoping to hide there until the gunmen "thought that we were all killed," he later wrote. Copeland was quickly discovered and hauled ashore, where men stood knotting handkerchiefs together and shouting for the young black man to be lynched. But John Starry, the ubiquitous doctor, happened to be on the scene and shielded Copeland with his horse until an officer arrived and took the captured insurgent to jail in Charlestown.

Also taken prisoner was a slave from John Allstadt's estate named Ben, who had been sent to guard the rifle works with Kagi and the others. Rather than run into the river, he'd thrown down his pike and surrendered— only to be threatened, like Copeland, with summary execution. In Ben's case, it was a local minister who intervened. "So enraged were the multitude," the churchman wrote, "that it was with difficulty they were restrained from hanging & shooting several on the spot."

One other slave had been posted at the rifle works: Jim, a young coachman hired by Lewis Washington from an owner in Winchester. Unlike Ben, Jim ran for the river, but he didn't make it. He was found floating in a millrace; unable to swim, or weighed down by his gear, he'd drowned in the stone-lined channel. Jim was thus the fourth black man, and the first slave, to die in Brown's war of liberation.

THAT AFTERNOON, THE ATMOSPHERE around Brown's position in the armory also grew ugly and anarchic. During the course of the day, armed men had continued flowing into Harpers Ferry, most of them aligned with no organized unit but "fighting on my own hook," as one man put it. Many fortified themselves at the Gault House and other bars in and around the Point. Emboldened by drink, they were further incited that afternoon by the deaths of three well-known individuals.

The first was George Turner, a West Point graduate, Seminole War veteran, prominent slave owner, and intimate of Lewis Washington's. Upon riding into town, Turner had taken up a position on High Street, the main road climbing the hill above the armory and arsenal. He was taking aim when, before a number of onlookers, a shot to the neck struck him dead. Soon after, frenzied locals started seizing anyone who seemed the least bit suspicious, including a railroad director from Pennsylvania who had disembarked from his stalled train to see what was happening in Harpers Ferry. Though he carried only a train ticket, a diary, and a French novel, the Northerner was hauled off by drunken guards to the county jail.

Turner's death, early in the afternoon, was followed by that of Heyward Shepherd, the black baggage master who had been shot in the back on the Potomac bridge the night before. He had lingered for more than twelve hours in the railroad office, begging for water and groaning in pain until his death at about three o'clock. This had a profound effect on his employer and patron, Fontaine Beckham, the B & O agent for Harpers Ferry who also served as mayor. Though free, Shepherd had needed white sponsorship to work and stay in the town, since his legal residence lay in another county. Beckham, a sixty-year-old slave owner, provided this legal guardianship.

"The old man had had him ten or twelve years, and liked him very much," said William Throckmorton, the Wager House clerk, in a statement that spoke to the murky and insecure status of "free" blacks in Virginia. When Shepherd died, Throckmorton added, Beckham became "greatly excited" and went out on the railroad platform with a pistol in his pocket. Others pulled him back. But Beckham went out again, this time reaching a water pumping station directly across from the armory engine house. Brown's men had taken fire from the direction of the pumping station and could now see a figure peering around it, about thirty yards off.

"If he keeps on peeking I'm going to shoot," said Edwin Coppoc, crouched behind the engine house's folding doors, which had been pulled open a crack so Brown's men could see out. When the figure behind the pumping station reappeared, Coppoc fired. After he fired a second shot, Brown declared, "That man is down."

Brown and Coppoc had no way of knowing "that man" was the town's mayor and one of Jefferson County's most respected and well-connected citizens. Shot in the chest, Beckham fell dead on the railroad trestle, a site so exposed that no one was able to recover his body.

"When Beckham was shot our men became almost frantic," Throckmorton said. Some of them rushed into the Wager House, where William Thompson was still tied to a chair. "Shoot him!" "Kill him!" they cried. The two men at the head of this mob were George Chambers, the saloonkeeper-sniper at the Gault House, and Henry Hunter, a nephew of Fontaine Beckham's. They leveled cocked guns at Thompson's head and were about to shoot when a woman intervened. According to Hunter's court testimony, she sat in Thompson's lap, "covered his face with her arms and shielded him," crying out, "For God's sake wait and let the law take its course."

The woman who intervened was Christine Fouke, the sister of the Wager House's proprietor, and she gave a slightly different version of events. At the time, she said, her sister-in-law was lying in the next room, afflicted by a "nervous chill, from sheer fright." Fouke feared the shooting of Thompson so close by would prove "fatal to her." Also, "I considered it a great outrage to kill the man in the house, however much he deserved to die." But she denied having intervened in the intimate fashion Hunter described. Fouke shielded Thompson, *without touching him,*" she said, until an officer came up and assured her the prisoner would "not be shot in the house. This was all I desired."

Thompson's assailants complied. Instead of shooting him in the parlor, they dragged him outside to the railroad bridge and began searching for a rope suitable for lynching. At first, Thompson begged for his life. Then he became defiant, telling Hunter: "You may kill me, but it will be revenged; there are eighty thousand persons sworn to carry this work."

These were Thompson's final words. Unable to find a rope, Hunter and Chambers raised their guns and fired. "Before he fell, a dozen or more balls were buried in him," Hunter said. The gunmen then threw Thompson into the river, where he somehow managed to flail forward a few feet before another fusillade stilled him. Hunter expressed no regret for the killing, stating in court that he was "fired and excited by the cowardly, savage manner in which Mr. Beckham's life had been taken."

Nor were the vigilantes satisfied: they marched back into the Wager House to take revenge on Aaron Stevens as well. Lying badly wounded in bed, Stevens folded his arms across his chest and stared in silent contempt at the men threatening to kill him. Since he was "probably dying,"

Hunter testified, "we concluded to spare him, and start after others, and shoot all we could find."

THE MAJORITY OF BROWN'S remaining men were sixty yards away, in and around the squat brick engine house, just behind the armory gate. From there, the armory complex stretched more than five hundred yards north, between raised railroad tracks and the Potomac on one side and a high wall on the other. If well-patrolled, the facility was hard to breach. But the armory's northern end now lay far beyond Brown's sight or reach, and late that afternoon, it was occupied by newly arrived volunteers from Martinsburg, a Virginia town twenty miles from Harpers Ferry. Most of the reinforcements were railroad men who worked on heavy-tonnage trains, and they were led by a Mexican War veteran, Captain Ephraim Alburtis.

At about four o'clock, Alburtis marched his force south through the armory yard until they came under fire from Brown's men, a few of whom had taken up sheltered positions outside the engine house. The Martinsburg men returned fire and pressed forward, driving the defenders back inside their fortress.

At midday, Brown had moved his ten most prominent hostages into the engine house, leaving the other thirty or so prisoners in the adjoining guardroom. With the help of Alburtis's men, these prisoners smashed a window and escaped around the side of the building as shooting continued at the front.

At this point, Alburtis later stated, he felt "we could have ended the business" with a coordinated assault by his men and those positioned outside the armory gate. But their efforts were piecemeal, and a brief charge at the gate in support of the Martinsburg men was repulsed.

The ill-organized gunmen besieging the armory also came under fire from an unexpected direction. All that afternoon, John Cook had listened to the gunshots in Harpers Ferry from his post at the Maryland schoolhouse, a mile or so away. He had strict orders to remain there, guarding the arms with one of Lewis Washington's freed slaves. He also kept watch on the schoolteacher, Lind Currie, who later said that Cook initially showed no anxiety about the sound of battle from across the river. Whenever gunfire erupted, Currie testified, Cook would turn to his fellow guard and say, "There, that's another one of your oppressors gone."

But as the day went on and the firing became "very rapid and continuous," Cook couldn't sit still any longer. On the promise that the teacher would say nothing of what he'd seen, Cook released Currie and then headed down to the Potomac. From two women he spoke to at a canal lock, Cook learned that "our men were hemmed in, and that several of them had been shot." Determined to do what he could to help them, Cook scrambled up the precipitous ridge rising behind the Potomac's Maryland bank.

From there, he could see that Brown's force was encircled and that gunmen on the high ground in Harpers Ferry, directly opposite him, were firing down at his comrades in the armory. Raising his rifle, he took aim across the river. "I thought I would draw their fire on myself," he later explained.

The men he targeted were about half a mile distant. They quickly returned fire. Several rounds were exchanged across the river until smoke from Cook's gun helped his foes locate him. A bullet cut the tree limb Cook was clutching for balance, pitching him down the steep ridge, "by which I was severely bruised and my flesh somewhat lacerated."

But his ploy had worked. Cook not only drew fire away from the armory, he spooked the Virginians, who knew little about Brown's overall force and feared he might yet command a large body of men in Maryland. In the drizzly late-day gloom, townspeople also worried that continued assaults on the engine house would endanger the hostages inside. The Martinsburg men and the other attackers drew back. Eight of them had been wounded in the fray, including two shot in the face and two others permanently disabled.

Brown's much smaller force had also sustained casualties. His men fired most of their shots while kneeling and aiming through a crack in the engine-house doors. This presented a narrow but predictable target to gunmen outside. During the battle that afternoon, one hostage reported, a man crouching at the door was shot in the chest and tumbled back, exclaiming "It's all up with me." Another man was also hit while shooting from the same position.

"We could not administer to their needs," wrote one of their comrades, Edwin Coppoc, "for we were surrounded by the troops who were firing volley after volley, so that we had to keep up a brisk fire in return to keep them from charging upon us."

One of the men shot by the door was twenty-three-year-old Steward Taylor, who had told Annie Brown about visions of his death at Harpers Ferry. Before meeting it, Coppoc wrote, "he suffered very much and begged us to kill him." Coppoc also described the second casualty: Brown's youngest son, Oliver, who, in the minutes after being shot, "spoke no word, but yielded calmly to his fate."

Oliver was just twenty, and in early October he had escorted his pregnant wife, Martha, part of the way home from the Kennedy farm. "You can hardly think how I want to see you, or how lonesome I was the day I left you," he wrote her upon his return to the Maryland hideout. But he took solace in her picture. "I have made a morocco case for it and carry it close to my body." He would doubtless have been carrying Martha's picture a week later, as he lay dying on the floor of the engine house.

Their child, born early the following year, was named Olive in memory of her father. But the baby lived only two days, and Martha soon fell ill with childbed fever. "She had been a wife, a mother, and a childless widow at seventeen," Annie Brown wrote. Martha now declared she had nothing more to live for; she gave away her few possessions, and died a month after giving birth. "She was willing to go," Mary Brown wrote, "said she wanted to go where Oliver & her baby was."

BY FOUR THIRTY OR five o'clock on that Monday afternoon, the firing at Harpers Ferry had petered out. As it did so, the antagonists cautiously opened negotiations. Despite the day's vicious fighting, the two sides now parleyed in a decorous and formal manner. One emissary approached the engine house carrying an old umbrella with a white handkerchief tied to the ferrule. "Who commands this fortification?" he demanded. Another appeal, this one written, came from Colonel Robert Baylor, a Virginia officer who had taken overall command of the troops that had converged on the town. Addressing Brown as "Captain," the note discussed "terms of capitulation" and the release of prisoners. "Sir," Colonel Baylor wrote, "I say to you, if you will set at liberty our citizens, we will leave the government to deal with you concerning their property, as it may think most advisable."

In reply, Baylor received an astonishing proposal, one that Brown had twice tried to deliver under flag of truce earlier that day. "In consideration of all my men, whether living or dead, or wounded, being soon safely in and delivered up to me at this point, with all their arms and ammunition, we will then take our prisoners and cross the Potomac bridge, a little beyond which we will set them at liberty." This wasn't all: "We require the delivery of our horse and harness at the hotel."

Brown elaborated on this proposal in a separate parley with two officers from a Maryland unit that had just reached town and been posted at the armory. He told them that once he reached the far side of the river and released the prisoners, the troops opposing him would be free to "take him if we could." Brown also said, "He had fought Uncle Sam before, and was willing to do it again." But he then added one final condition: "that he & his men should not be shot down instantly by a body of men posted for the purpose, but on being allowed a brief period for preparing for fight, he was willing to take his chances for death or escape."

Brown, in short, demanded that he be given a fighting chance—a duel, almost, on the opposite bank of the Potomac. He may have hoped to make a fighting retreat along the ravine leading up to the log schoolhouse, where he could expect to collect more arms and be reinforced by his men in Maryland. Brown believed he merited this chance not only because he held hostages, but also because he had fought honorably rather than massacring civilians or burning the town. As one of the Maryland officers reported: "He thought he was entitled to some terms."

In the view of Brown's foes, this was preposterous: he deserved no concessions and was in no position to demand them. The armory was surrounded and reinforcements were en route. "The terms you propose I cannot accept," Colonel Baylor wrote in a curt reply. But he decided to postpone any further action until morning, rather than risk an attack in the dark. In his official report, Baylor gave an additional reason for suspending operations: "Our troops by this time required some refreshment, having been on active duty, and exposed to a heavy fall of rain all day."

Baylor, however, had only loose command of the hundreds of armed men in Harpers Ferry, many of whom had long since sought refreshment on their own. By the time Captain John Sinn of the Frederick, Maryland, militia arrived on Monday evening, he found the town in a state of drunken mayhem. "Every man had a gun, and four-fifths of them were under no command," he reported. "The military had ceased firing, but men who were intoxicated were firing their guns in the air, and others at the engine-house."

Still others were stumbling from the saloons to desecrate the corpse of Dangerfield Newby, or to taunt the wounded Aaron Stevens in his bed at the Wager House. Captain Sinn found young men threatening to shoot Stevens and shamed them by saying, "If the man could stand on his feet with a pistol in his hand they would all jump out of the window."

Sinn also arranged for a surgeon in his unit to go to the engine house and tend to Brown's wounded son Watson. By the time the surgeon arrived, late Monday night, the scene inside the engine house was ghastly. On one side of the cramped interior—a room just twenty foot square—stretched the bloodied corpses of Steward Taylor and Oliver Brown. Near them lay Watson, in such agony that he begged his comrades to shoot him. The surgeon could do little for his stomach wound, but promised to return in the morning.

BROWN'S UNINJURED MEN, COOPED up in the engine house with the dead and wounded, were in poor shape as well. They had marched and fought with little or no food or sleep since leaving the Kennedy farm more than twenty-four hours before. With a drunken mob howling and firing potshots outside the armory's gate, there wasn't much prospect of rest during the long night ahead.

The same was true for Brown's hostages, some of whom had refused breakfast—the only meal that day—fearing it might be drugged. The engine house was cold and dark and the only place to lie down was the brick floor. Though the hostages occupied the safest part of the building, behind the fire engines, there was still the danger of bullets ricocheting through the doors or windows. Armistead Ball, the hostage who was a master machinist at the armory, sought shelter by wedging himself in a corner of the brick structure, but found he was too large. "For the first time in my life," he later said, "I wished I was a thin man."

Even more uncomfortable was the situation of the black Virginians in the engine house. Though ostensibly liberated, they now had, in effect, three sets of masters. First, Brown and his men, who had thrust pikes into their hands and put them at great peril inside the engine house. Second, the white hostages sequestered with them, including their owners, who were alert to any sign of cooperation or complicity with the insurgents. And third, the mob outside, which was unlikely to show mercy toward armed slaves caught in the presence of abolitionists. To Armistead Ball, the black men in the engine house seemed, like himself, "badly scared."

Brown, on the other hand, appeared as cool and composed as he had been throughout the battle. At day's end, when the firing subsided, he had straightened the limbs of his dead son Oliver and removed his gear. Then, through the night, he tried to comfort Watson, who kept crying out in pain and begging to be put out of his misery. "No, my son, have patience: I think you will get well," one hostage heard Brown say. "If you die, you die in a glorious cause." Another hostage heard Brown tell Watson "to endure a little longer and he might die as befitted a man."

Brown also tried to hold together what remained of his shattered army. Of the eighteen men who had crossed the Potomac with him Sunday night, half were dead, dying, or captured, including his lead lieutenants, Kagi and Stevens. Two other tested fighters, Tidd and Cook, were in Maryland, while two men posted to the arsenal were unaccounted for. That left Brown in direct command of only one Kansas veteran, Jeremiah Anderson, and three novices, all in their early twenties: the fugitive slave Shields Green, the Iowa Quaker Edwin Coppoc, and the smooth-cheeked Dauphin Thompson, whose older brother, William, had been brutally slain within sight of the engine house that afternoon.

Some of them lost heart in the course of the night. When the Maryland officer, Captain Sinn, brought a surgeon to the engine house, he also delivered the news that U.S. troops had arrived and occupied the armory yard. This prompted one of Brown's men to ask if he would be committing "treason against his country in resisting" federal soldiers. Upon being told that this would be so, "the man then said, 'I'll fight no longer,'" one of the hostages testified. "He thought he was merely fighting to liberate slaves." At least one of the other men also wanted to give up.

But Brown refused to surrender. At one point late that night, Captain Sinn promised to provide the insurgents safe conduct to jail if they laid down their arms. Brown scorned the offer, the officer reported, "saying he knew his fate, and he preferred meeting it with his rifle in his hands to dying for the amusement of a crowd." The machinist Armistead Ball also appealed to Brown, on grounds of humanity, to surrender rather than risk more bloodshed. Brown replied that he had already been "proclaimed an outlaw," had a reward on his head, and knew the consequences of his actions.

As he awaited daylight, Brown paced the brick floor carrying George Washington's sword, which his men had taken from the president's great-grandnephew. The sword's owner, still hostage in the engine house, hated everything Brown stood for. But even Lewis Washington admired the abolitionist's "extraordinary nerve," he later acknowledged. Brown never quailed, Washington said, "though he admitted during the night that escape was impossible and he would have to die."

CHAPTER 9

~~~

I Am Nearly Disposed of Now

W hen word of trouble in Harpers Ferry first spread on the morning of October 17, the response of white Virginians nearby was swift and instinctive. Their neighbors were under attack, blacks were rumored to be rising up, and that was all any able-bodied man needed to know before grabbing a gun and rushing to the scene.

But this wasn't true of parties more distant from the fight. When Andrew Phelps telegraphed the B & O office in Baltimore at 7:05 and reported that "armed abolitionists" had seized the armory and the Potomac bridge, stopped his train, shot a railroad porter, and pledged to free the slaves "at all hazards," the response was skeptical.

"Your dispatch is evidently exaggerated and written under excitement," the B & O master of transportation, W. P. Smith, wired Phelps two hours later. "Why should our trains be stopped by Abolitionists, and how do you know they are such and that they number one hundred or more? What is their object? Let me know at once before we proceed to extremities."

Phelps shot back: "My dispatch was not exaggerated, neither was it written under excitement as you suppose. I have not made it half as bad as it is."

Smith, whose sole concern was keeping trains running, remained unconvinced. He wired a railroad official in Wheeling, where Phelps had started his trip, to keep sending trains east. "Matter is probably much exaggerated and we fear it may injure us if prematurely published."

But Smith did inform his own superior of Phelps's warning, and the B & O president began to notify state and federal authorities. He telegraphed a Maryland commander, the governor of Virginia, the U.S. secretary of war, and, finally, "*His Excellency, James Buchanan, Pres't U.S.*," informing him that the armory was "in the possession of rioters" and troops were needed "for the safety of Government property, and of the mails."

This message was sent at ten thirty A.M., more than three hours after the conductor's first alert. The secretary of war responded by calling out three companies of federal artillery. These units, however, were posted at a coastal fort in the southeast corner of Virginia, hundreds of miles from Harpers Ferry. The only U.S. troops readily available were ninety marines barracked at the Navy Yard in Washington—a small, inexperienced force that hardly seemed adequate to quell an uprising by insurgents now rumored to number more than seven hundred.

But the War Department was lucky: it so happened that two extraordinary soldiers were close at hand. One of them was a lieutenant from Virginia named James Ewell Brown Stuart, better known as Jeb, a fast-rising young cavalryman on leave from service in Kansas. On October 17, he was visiting the War Department, trying to sell it on a scabbard strap he'd designed. Overhearing talk of trouble at Harpers Ferry, he volunteered his services and was promptly sent with a summons for one of the Army's best officers, Colonel Robert E. Lee, whose son was a close friend of Stuart's.

Lee, an acclaimed military engineer and Mexican War veteran, was living at his family's mansion in Arlington, Virginia, directly across the Potomac from Washington. Stuart quickly located the colonel at an Alexandria apothecary shop and hurried him back to the capital.

Then fifty-two, Lee was in the midst of an unwelcome hiatus in his military career, having returned from the field upon the death of his father-in-law, George Washington Custis. The grandson of Martha Washington by her first marriage, Custis had been raised at Mount Vernon and inherited tremendous wealth, but he wasn't an attentive manager. As his father-in-law's executor, Lee found himself mired in the tedious business of untangling a vast and ill-run estate that included three plantations and two hundred slaves.

"He has left me an unpleasant legacy," Lee wrote his son in the summer of 1859, reporting on the capture of two escaped slaves from one of the Custis properties. This incident brought the colonel unwanted attention when northern newspapers claimed he had whipped the runaways.

Lee regarded slavery with distaste, but he staunchly defended Southerners' right to maintain their peculiar institution. He abhorred abolitionists and believed emancipation should be left to "a wise Merciful Providence." He also didn't hasten to carry out the instruction in his father-in-law's will to free the Custis slaves, a number of whom expressed their displeasure by running away or otherwise rebelling. Lee finally freed his father-in-law's slaves in 1862, by which time he was commanding a Confederate army, with Jeb Stuart at his side.

In 1859, however, the two future secessionists were loyal U.S. soldiers, and now they were charged with putting down rebels who had seized a federal armory. Lee was put in command of the ninety marines from the Navy Yard, with Stuart accompanying him as an aide. On Monday afternoon, the two men boarded a special locomotive to catch up with the marines, who were already en route to "the scene of difficulty," as Stuart

J.E.B. Stuart   *Robert E. Lee*

called it. "I had barely time to borrow a un.'.f. coat and a saber." Lee wore only his civilian clothes.

At about eleven P.M., they reached the depot at Sandy Hook, Maryland, just across the Potomac from Harpers Ferry. This station was now a crowded staging area for soldiers and others who had converged on the scene, including the aggrieved B & O official W. P. Smith. "Have given telegraph up to reporters, who are in force strong as military," he wired his superiors on Monday night.

Taking command of the ninety marines, Lee marched them into Harpers Ferry in a light rain, reaching the town about midnight. He coolly assessed the situation and immediately grasped that rumors of a mass uprising were wildly overblown. There was only "a party of Banditti" holed up in the armory, he wrote. After sending word that no further troops were needed, he posted the marines around the engine house, choosing not to endanger the hostages with a nighttime attack.

Lee also drafted a formal message to "the persons" inside the engine house, to be delivered at daybreak. "If they will peaceably surrender themselves and restore the pillaged property, they shall be kept in safety to await the orders of the President," the document read. "Colonel Lee represents to them, in all frankness, that it is impossible for them to escape; that the armory is surrounded on all sides by troops; and that if he is compelled to take them by force he cannot answer for their safety."

Lee expected that his demand for surrender would be refused. In that event, he planned to launch an immediate attack so the gunmen in the engine house wouldn't have additional time to prepare, or to harm the hostages. To further guard the captives' safety, Lee ordered his men to attack with bayonets and "cautioned the stormers particularly to discriminate between the insurgents & their prisoners."

This may have sounded straightforward in theory, but it presented considerable challenges in practice. Few of the marines had seen combat. The engine house was small and crowded. And its defenders had already shown themselves resolute fighters, prepared to die if necessary.

The mob surrounding the armory yard also posed a problem. "The people are terribly excited and threats are made of killing all in the morning," a railroad official telegraphed late that night. By daybreak, a throng of about two thousand people had crowded every window, doorway, and other vantage point within sight of the engine house. "All eyes were directed to one spot," wrote Edward White, a young teacher in Harpers Ferry. "All were awaiting the final act of the drama."

SOON AFTER SUNRISE ON Tuesday, October 18, Jeb Stuart approached the engine house under a flag of truce and announced that he had a message from Colonel Lee. A gunman "opened the door about four inches," Stuart wrote, "and placed his body against the crack with a cocked carbine in his hand." Stuart recognized the man, having encountered him while serving in the U.S. cavalry out west.

"You are Osawatomie Brown, of Kansas?" Stuart asked.

"Well, they do call me that sometimes, Lieutenant."

Brown's presence in Harpers Ferry had been widely rumored for the past twenty-four hours, but Stuart was the first Virginian able to positively identify him.

"This is a bad business you are engaged in, Captain," Stuart said. "The United States troops have arrived, and I am sent to demand your surrender."

"Upon what terms?" Brown asked.

Stuart then delivered Lee's message, promising protection to Brown and his men until the president determined their fate. Brown countered with his own now-familiar proposition—that he and his men be granted a chance to escape across the river.

"I have no authority to agree to such an arrangement," Stuart said, "my orders being to demand your surrender on the terms I have stated."

This Brown refused to do. Knowing "he could expect no leniency," Brown told Stuart, he preferred to die fighting and "would sell his life as dearly as possible."

The exchange at the door greatly alarmed the hostages. Some of them begged Stuart to bring Colonel Lee into the parley. But Stuart's orders were to avoid negotiations, and to signal any refusal to surrender as quickly as possible.

"Is that your final answer, Captain?" Stuart asked Brown.

"Yes."

Stepping away from the door, Stuart waved his cap—the sign agreed upon for the marines to attack. A storming party of twelve men stood ready against the side wall of the engine house. Three of them now sprang to the front of the building and battered the heavy wooden doors with sledgehammers.

As Lee had hoped, the swiftness of the assault caught Brown by surprise. "It was evident he did not expect an attack so soon," Lewis Washington said. But the previous day's siege had given the engine-house defenders ample time to fortify their position. They'd placed the two fire carts against the entrance as a brace, and fastened the double doors with ropes. This gave the doors spring, so that each blow of the sledgehammers pushed the heavy wood in without shattering it.

The marines' pounding "reechoed from the rocky sides of the lofty mountains," one spectator said. Finally, after several minutes, the marines stopped their futile hammering and withdrew; there followed "a brief pause of oppressive silence" for those crowded around the armory.

Though the initial assault had failed, the thunderous banging terrified the men inside the engine house, who couldn't see out and had no clear idea what was happening. "There was a cessation for a moment or two," Terence Byrne later testified, "and during this time one of Brown's men turned round to him and said, 'Captain, I believe I will surrender.'"

"Sir, you can do as you please," Brown replied.

A few of the hostages began shouting, "One man surrenders!" But they couldn't be heard in the confusion, and, moments later, there was another awful thud at the door.

The marines had tossed aside their sledgehammers and taken hold of a heavy ladder in the armory yard, deploying it as a battering ram. A dozen soldiers clutched the ladder and rushed at the engine house. Their first charge did not so much as dent the doors. With Brown's men now firing from inside, the marines stepped back, hoisted the ladder, and rushed forward a second time. Again, nothing happened. Then, on their third charge, the attackers stove in one of the doors, splintering open a breach just large enough to charge through, one man at a time.

The leader of the storming party, Lieutenant Israel Green, leaped on the inward-leaning door and darted inside. He was followed by a marine paymaster who wielded only a rattan switch. The firing was now heavy on both sides, despite Lee's order that the men use only bayonets. The

Newspaper illustration of marines storming engine-house

third marine rushing into the engine house fell back with a gunshot to his stomach. The next took a bullet in the face.

The huge crowd around the armory could see little except marines in powder-blue uniforms vanishing into the smoke and noise. The frightened hostages in the engine house also looked on in confusion, their view partly obscured by the fire carts and gun smoke. "When I heard the door breaking in," said Armistead Ball, the portly machinist, "I thought I was a goner." Lewis Washington urged his fellow prisoners to throw up their hands, so the storming party could more easily distinguish them.

Two of Brown's men also "cried for quarter and laid down their arms," a hostage testified. But as marines poured in, "they picked them up again and resumed the fight." These two unnamed men were almost certainly Dauphin Thompson and Jeremiah Anderson. A third, Edwin Coppoc, later stated that he, too, had wanted to surrender but fought on in the heat of the moment, with a gun that misfired. Shields Green, according to Coppoc and the testimony of a hostage, put down his rifle and cartridge box and joined the six slaves in the engine house, hoping to be mistaken for one of them.

Only Brown appeared committed to fighting to the end. Israel Green, the marine lieutenant who was the first man to burst into the engine house, ran to one side of a fire cart positioned just behind the shattered door. As he came around the rear of it, Lewis Washington pointed at a crouched figure near the front of the building, between the two fire engines. "There's Brown!" Washington cried. Perched on one knee, pants tucked into his boots, Brown was pulling a lever to reload his carbine.

"Quicker than thought," Lieutenant Green said, "I brought my saber down with all my strength upon his head." Brown was moving as Green struck. The sword blow gashed his neck. He fell to the floor and rolled onto his back. "Instinctively as Brown fell I gave him a saber thrust in the left breast," Green said.

This blow could easily have pierced Brown's heart or lung. But Green, in nervous haste that day, had armed himself with a light dress sword rather than a combat saber. He also seems to have struck a strap or buckle that deflected the thrust. Instead of penetrating, the light sword blade bent double. Green kept flailing at Brown, stabbing at him and beating his head with the sword's hilt until he lay motionless on the floor.

The other marines pouring into the engine house had gone after Brown's men. One of the attackers bayoneted Dauphin Thompson, who had taken cover under a fire engine. Another thrust his bayonet so fiercely into Jeremiah Anderson that the insurgent was pinned to the rear wall of the engine house and twisted almost upside down in his agony.

Other marines quickly seized Edwin Coppoc and Shields Green without injury. The hostages in the engine house, and the black men briefly liberated from slavery, also escaped harm. Robert E. Lee, who had engineered the storming and observed it from behind a pillar near the armory gate, dispassionately summarized the attack for his superiors. "The whole was over in a few minutes," he wrote in his official report.

MUCH MORE EMOTIONAL WAS the response of the many spectators who had watched the marines rush in and anxiously awaited the outcome. When the hostages emerged unhurt, "the breathless silence outside was broken, and from thousands of throats rose a shout," one witness recalled. Even W. P. Smith, the laconic B & O official, was momentarily overcome. "I never saw so thrilling a scene," he telegraphed the railroad president immediately after the fray ended.

The most visibly ecstatic man was Armistead Ball, who had believed himself "a goner" just moments before. "I embraced my friends eagerly and in fact, everybody," he said. "I never was so happy in my life." Lewis Washington, on the other hand, maintained an air of unruffled dignity. Before leaving the engine house, he collected the sword belonging to his great-granduncle, which Brown had laid on one of the fire engines. Then he "stepped daintily out, carefully drawing on a pair of kid gloves," wrote Edward White, the local teacher. According to another witness, "Colonel Washington emerged from his prison-house looking as well dressed as usual, and seemed as cool as if nothing had happened. He said he would like some breakfast."

The cheers and hugs that welcomed the freed hostages were in sharp contrast to the reception given the captured insurgents as they were brought out of the engine house. "The crowd, nearly every man of which carried a gun, swayed with tumultuous excitement, and cries of 'Shoot them!' 'Shoot them!' rang from every side," a newspaper correspondent wrote.

Marines also carried out the dead and wounded and laid them in front of the engine house. Dauphin Thompson died almost instantly from his bayonet wound. Jeremiah Anderson, having been unpinned from the wall, was still alive, although "vomiting gore." As the crowd pressed forward to stare, a spectator with a woman on each arm asked, "Gentlemen, can't you stand back and let the ladies see the corpses?"

Others weren't so genteel. One spat tobacco juice into Anderson's face. Another stared at the dying man in disgust, walked away, and then returned, telling him: "Well it takes you a hell of a long time to die." In Anderson's pockets were found his commission as captain and a letter from his brother in Iowa, urging him to move there and study law. From the pockets of other insurgents, scavengers took an empty wallet, a lock of a woman's hair, a copy of Brown's Provisional Constitution, and a love letter from a lady in Illinois.

Watson Brown, still alive after a night of anguish in the engine house, received somewhat gentler treatment. Taken to the guardroom adjoining the engine house, he was laid on a bench with two pairs of overalls placed under his head. C. W. Tayleure, a militiaman and correspondent for a Baltimore newspaper, gave him a cup of water and asked what had brought him to Harpers Ferry.

"Duty, sir," he replied. "I did my duty as I saw it."

Watson "feelingly enquired whether his father was alive," Tayleure wrote, and "affirmed his conviction of the justness of the cause in which he had been so disastrously engaged." Watson lingered through that Tuesday and died early the next morning, leaving his widow, Belle, with their two-month-old baby. "Keep up good courage," he'd written her two days before the attack, "there is a better day a-coming."

Watson's father had been carried to the nearby paymaster's office and laid on the floor beside his badly wounded lieutenant, Aaron Stevens, moved there from the Wager House. In the same building, on the other side of a low partition, lay a dying marine, Luke Quinn, whom Brown or one of his men had shot in the stomach as the twenty-four-year-old stormed the engine house. A priest administered last rites to the Irish-born Quinn, "a mere boy," one reporter wrote, whose "cries and screams made one's flesh creep."

Also curdling were the cries from outside, where a crowd bayed for the lynching of the surviving insurgents. To those inside the paymaster's office, it seemed unlikely that Stevens and Brown would live long enough to be hanged, legally or otherwise. Stevens lay "with his hands folded helplessly across his breast and giving no sign of life except his slow labored breathing and occasional quivering of the eyelids," wrote David Strother, a reporter and artist who sketched the scene. Brown, "gaunt, grim & grizzled," writhed atop a wretched shakedown. He was covered by a dirty quilt, his head resting on a carpetbag.

"The old man's strongly marked face, iron grey hair and white beard were grimed and matted with blood," Strother wrote, "and fresh puddles oozing from wounds in his head collected on the floor and traveling bag." Jeb Stuart, who seemed to harbor an especial loathing for the abolitionist, assisted Strother in his work, "giving Brown a round cursing & roughly ordered him to pull down his blanket that we might have a better view of his face."

Though Brown was initially judged unlikely to survive, Robert E. Lee informed the secretary of war in a follow-up telegram that "upon a more

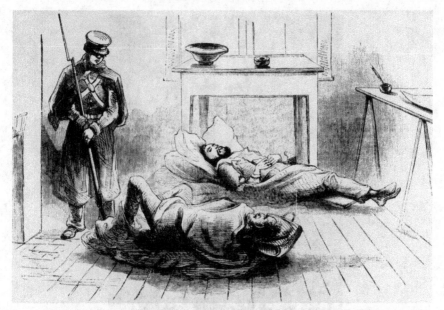

David Strother sketch of Brown and Stevens in paymaster's office

deliberate examination," his injuries "are believed not to be mortal. He has three wounds, but they are not considered by the surgeon as bad as first reported."

Lee treated the wounded prisoners with solicitude. When people crowded into the paymaster's office to question the leader of the insurrection, Lee said he would clear the room "if the wounded men were annoyed or pained by them," a reporter wrote. "Brown said he was by no means annoyed; on the contrary he was glad to be able to make himself and his motives clearly understood."

HE WOULD SOON DO SO, in a remarkable performance that marked yet another twist in his volatile career. By all appearances, the mission he called "the great work of my life" had just ended in abject failure. Instead of a months-long campaign reaching across the South, his attack had withered in thirty-two hours, a stone's throw inside Virginia. The climactic battle lasted five minutes, with the insurrectionists' brick citadel easily breached and its commander beaten to the floor with a parade-ground

Henry Wise

sword. The few slaves Brown had briefly liberated were now returning to bondage. And two more of his sons had been sacrificed, along with their in-laws, the Thompsons, and a number of other young men Brown had led.

As he lay bleeding on the floor, Brown also faced the prospect of his own imminent and ignoble death. Even if he survived his wounds and the lynch mob outside, he could anticipate summary execution under martial law, or a show trial and hasty transit to the gallows like that given Nat Turner in 1831. Either way, the audience gathering in the paymaster's office might be his last.

This audience also included a new and formidable adversary in the figure of Henry Wise, the governor of Virginia and a man as driven as the bloodied abolitionist to make the most of the opportunity at hand. Tall, sallow, and gaunt, with deep-set gray eyes, the cadaverous governor was an electric orator who spoke like "a corpse galvanized," one contemporary said. Wise had shot his first political opponent in a duel, and he had since maneuvered his way into consideration for the presidency. Though his political positions were renowned for their shiftiness, Wise could always be counted on to seize center stage, which he had done the moment he heard of the trouble in Harpers Ferry. After ordering out the state's militia, Wise boarded a troop train in Richmond, hoping to lead Virginians in a valiant recapture of the town.

But his train was delayed; after sixteen frustrating hours, Wise arrived to find the fight had just ended. "The Governor," a Virginia reporter wrote, "looked like a man who in a violent passion has kicked at a door & found it open."

Wise was nonetheless determined to take command of the battle's aftermath. Following a briefing by Colonel Lee, he hurried with his entourage to the paymaster's office, eager to interrogate the author of this great crime against his state.

"Old Brown received him with the utmost composure, though evidently suffering much from his wounds," wrote a reporter for the *Richmond Enquirer*, a paper edited by Wise's son. "He said, 'Well, Governor, I suppose you think me a depraved criminal. Well sir, we have our opinions of each other.' The remark was made with no disrespect whatsoever."

Wise officiously replied, "You are in the hands of the State, and I have questions to ask, which you can answer or not." Brown said he had nothing to conceal, though he refused to speak about any of his men still at large. "He was singularly free and communicative," wrote a lawyer who accompanied Wise. "He told us of the plan of government he was going to set up here, and also where his carpetbag was that had in it all the documents, i.e., the form of government, with lists of the officers, etc." When a copy of the Provisional Constitution was retrieved and read aloud, Brown proudly acknowledged authorship.

Few other details of this interview survive. But Brown's bold and unapologetic words made a strong impression on Wise. "He is the gamest man I ever saw," the governor told a reporter. A few days later, in his first public speech about the attack on Harpers Ferry, Wise spoke even more fulsomely. "He is a bundle of the best nerves I ever saw cut and thrust and bleeding and in bonds," Wise declared. "He is a fanatic, vain and garrulous, but firm, and truthful, and intelligent."

Brown had a similar effect on a second, larger set of interrogators at the paymaster's office. This time, the audience included Robert E. Lee, Jeb Stuart, Lewis Washington, and three proslavery congressmen. Among the latter was Senator James Mason of Virginia, who had drafted the Fugitive Slave Act. Also present were several journalists for pro-southern papers who took note of Brown's extraordinary manner.

"No sign of weakness was exhibited," reported the *Baltimore American*, even though he lay smeared with blood, "in the midst of enemies, whose homes he had invaded; wounded, and a prisoner; surrounded by a small army of officials, and a more desperate army of angry men; with the gallows staring him full in the face."

The reporters gave a verbatim transcript of the questioning, which was initially led by Senator Mason and, despite Brown's weakened condition, lasted three hours. Typical was the following exchange:

SEN. MASON—How do you justify your acts?

BROWN—I think, my friend, you are guilty of a great wrong against God and humanity. I say that without wishing to be offensive. It would be perfectly right for any one to interfere with you, so far as to free those you willfully and wickedly hold in bondage. I do not say this insultingly.

MR. MASON—I understand that.

BROWN—I think I did right, and that others will do right who interfere with you at any time, and all times. I hold that the golden rule, do unto others as you would that others should do unto you, applies to all who would help others to gain their liberty.

Brown maintained this mix of courtesy and defiance throughout the extraordinary session, parrying every thrust, including several by angry bystanders. When one cried out, "I think you are fanatical," Brown retorted: "And I think you are fanatical. 'Whom the Gods would destroy they first make mad.'"

Brown also succeeded in steering the interrogation away from specific queries about his funding and supporters, returning instead to his central argument. "I want you to understand, gentlemen," he said, "that I respect the rights of the poorest and weakest of colored people, oppressed by the slave system, just as much as I do those of the most wealthy and powerful. That is the idea that has moved me, and that alone."

Near the end of the long interview, Brown turned to the reporters in the room and made what amounted to a closing statement. "You had better—all you people at the South—prepare yourselves for a settlement of that question that must come up," he said. "You may dispose of me very easily; I am nearly disposed of now; but this question is still to be settled—this Negro question I mean—the end of that is not yet."

PART THREE

They Will Brown Us All

He could not have been tried by a jury of his peers, because his peers did not exist.

—HENRY DAVID THOREAU
"A Plea for Captain John Brown"

His Despised Poor

Journalists arriving in Harpers Ferry on Tuesday, October 18, found gruesome proof of the violence that had just ended. David Strother, who wrote and sketched for *Harper's Weekly*, visited the railroad trestle where the town's mayor, Fontaine Beckham, had lain for hours after being shot. "The boards were stained with dark blood marks and tufts of white hair were visible sticking to them," he wrote. Beckham's exposed body had finally been carted away in a wheelbarrow by Christine Fouke, the same woman who kept gunmen from shooting one of Brown's men held prisoner in the Wager House.

No one had yet bothered to collect the slain insurgents, most conspicuously Dangerfield Newby, whose maimed corpse still lay on the pavement, twenty-four hours after he became the first of Brown's men to die. "A dog was smelling the mass of coagulated blood which surrounded his head and a couple of pigs were rooting at the body," Strother wrote. The bullet-riddled bodies of John Kagi, William Leeman, and William Thompson floated in the Potomac and Shenandoah.

Six other insurgents lay dead or dying near the rifle works and engine house. When the bayoneted Jeremiah Anderson finally expired in the armory yard, his body was crammed into a barrel and taken away for dissection at a medical school in nearby Winchester. The same fate befell Watson Brown. The other eight dead, most of them still wrapped in the shawls they'd worn into battle, were piled into a pair of pine storage boxes. A local man, paid $5 to bury them in an out-of-the-way location, carted the boxes half a mile up the Shenandoah, and dumped them in shallow unmarked pits.

With the fighting over, the dead disposed of, and the surviving insurgents under heavy guard, the disturbance at Harpers Ferry appeared at be at an end. "The work is done," W. P. Smith telegraphed the B & O president, soon after Brown's capture. "No difficulties have attended our trains except their slight irregularity by the interruption."

Even before the marines stormed the engine house, Robert E. Lee had turned back additional federal troops headed to Harpers Ferry, judging reinforcements unnecessary. Now that the fight was over, he expected to return to Washington with the marines and prepared a report that minimized the significance of Brown's actions. "The result proves that the plan was the attempt of a fanatic or madman, which could only end in failure," Lee wrote, "and its temporary success was owing to the panic and confusion he succeeded in creating by magnifying his numbers."

Lee's tactical analysis was acute. But the panic and confusion he mentioned went deeper than he realized. Locals' anxiety resurfaced immediately after Brown's capture, when Sharps rifles were found in the cellar of a house by the Shenandoah. They'd been left there by two insurgents, Albert Hazlett and Osborne Anderson, who had managed to slip away from their posts at the arsenal and escape in a stolen boat. From Maryland, reports also filtered in that John Cook and an unknown number of insurgents were still at large in the hills near Harpers Ferry. Townspeople were so jittery that even the "shaking of a tree on the mountain opposite" sparked a rumor that guerrillas were "throwing up entrenchments," the *New York Herald* reported.

The panic crested on the night of October 19, thirty-six hours after Brown's capture, when a man rode into Harpers Ferry crying, "To arms! To arms! They are murdering the women and children!" The herald told of hearing gunfire and screams from a neighbor's farmhouse in Pleasant Valley, Maryland, five miles east of Harpers Ferry, and he claimed to have seen slaves running off to the mountains. On the way to the Ferry, he'd sounded the alarm in Sandy Hook, the Maryland community just across the Potomac, causing families to stream across the river in search of refuge.

Colonel Lee, characteristically, responded with calm dispatch. Though he doubted the report, he set off with Jeb Stuart and twenty-five marines "for the scene of the alleged outrage." Upon reaching Pleasant Valley, he found its residents "safe and asleep."

Lee also sent troops to the Maryland school and the Kennedy farm, where locals believed Brown's men might still be holed up. These rumors proved unfounded: both buildings were vacant, except for the dog that had been given to the Browns, which someone had left tied to the porch rail of the Kennedy farmhouse. The soldiers nonetheless made a series of astonishing discoveries. Butting in the door of the log schoolhouse, they found sixteen heavy boxes of rifles, revolvers, bayonets, swords, and ammunition. At the Kennedy farm, they found tents, blankets, axes, knives, boxes of clothing, and almost a thousand pikes, which Brown had planned to put in the hands of freed slaves.

Carried in wagons back to Harpers Ferry, the combined haul from the school and farm constituted a formidable arsenal. In addition to hundreds of carbines and revolvers, the hoard included 23,000 percussion rifle caps, a heavy swivel gun, fourteen pounds of lead shot, and enough clothing, tools, and other supplies to outfit a large mountain army—"all the necessaries for a campaign," Lee wrote. In light of these finds, Brown's claim that he had expected a long operation and thousands of reinforcements seemed more than an idle boast.

The Kennedy farm yielded an additional cache: trunks and carpetbags stuffed with letters and other documents that revealed the breadth of Brown's ambitions. Among the papers were thousands of copies of his Provisional Constitution ("done up in small bundles, apparently for convenient distribution," a reporter wrote); hundreds of copies of Hugh Forbes's manual on guerrilla tactics; and, most ominously, large maps of southern states, with cross marks and census figures denoting counties where blacks greatly outnumbered whites. These maps, carefully mounted on thick cambric cloth, appeared to offer a blueprint for a far-reaching invasion of the slaveholding South.

The soldiers who ransacked the Kennedy farm also uncovered troubling correspondence, including a letter from the U.S. Ordnance Department in Washington, "answering inquiries as to the disposition of the United States troops." Other letters pointed to a network of prominent northern supporters, such as Gerrit Smith and Frederick Douglass. Some letters were entirely in code. All told, the papers suggested "the existence of an extensive and thoroughly organized conspiracy," wrote a reporter who accompanied the troops to the Kennedy farm.

Lee either disagreed with that assessment or chose to downplay the documents; he barely mentioned them in his official report. But Governor Wise seized on the papers, portraying them as incendiary evidence of northern complicity in the attack. He read from the captured letters before a crowd at the Wager House in Harpers Ferry, where he stayed for two days, orating from the hotel porch to "Sons of Virginia!" Upon returning to Richmond, he delivered a long speech at the statehouse, declaring "I would have given my right arm to its shoulder" for Virginians to have defeated the insurgents on their own. "But, my fellow citizens, you must not imagine that this invasion was so insignificant, or that Commander Brown was mad because his force was so small."

Newspapers published selections from the captured documents, and Wise ordered them transcribed and entered into Virginia's official record just weeks after their discovery. In an accompanying ten-thousand-word address, he darkly conjured "a numerous host of enemies" for whom the twenty-two insurgents were "mere tools," sent ahead "to kindle the sparks of a general conflagration."

Wise, like Brown, wanted to shock and mobilize his countrymen and lead them to the ramparts—in his case, to *protect* southern white property and sovereignty. It therefore served his interests, just as it had Brown's, to inflate the size and menace of the Harpers Ferry attack. The two men also shared a taste for martial bluster. If he'd arrived in time to lead the counterattack, Wise claimed, he would have shown the insurgents "no quarter" in battle; he would have "tried the survivors, if any, by court martial," and "shot the condemned on the spot."

The governor's words were belied by his actual treatment of the prisoners. He protected Brown and his men from summary justice in Harpers Ferry and put them on trial in a civilian Virginia court. This required considerable legal legerdemain, since most of the violence had occurred at a federal armory, on land owned by the U.S. government. But Wise was intent on enabling Virginia to claim Brown's scalp, and in this he was aided by the passive executive in the White House.

Apart from dispatching federal troops to the scene, President Buchanan did little and said less about Harpers Ferry. Known as a "Northern man with Southern principles," he was content to let Virginians take the lead. As he later wrote the prosecutor who took charge of trying the insurgents, the question of jurisdiction in Harpers Ferry was "a matter quite indifferent to me."

And so, two days after the recapture of the engine house, the Virginia governor accompanied John Brown and the other prisoners, under heavy guard, past crowds crying "Lynch them!" and onto a train from Harpers Ferry to Charlestown, the Jefferson County seat, where Brown and his men would be jailed and tried. Wise also issued a thousand-dollar reward for the capture of John Cook, who was believed—incorrectly—to be Brown's chief lieutenant and still in command of an unknown force in the Maryland hills.

These fears were stoked by alleged evidence of Cook's contacts with local blacks. One of his supposed allies was an elderly woman who was arrested soon after the fighting ended on charges of having fed Cook during the fray and promised to spy on Harpers Ferry. "A supper basket was found in her hut ready to be carried into the mountains," read the newspaper report on her arrest. Another black woman was seized after telling someone she had visited Cook's house before the attack and heard him say "he would turn Harper's Ferry upside down."

To panicky whites, it began to seem plausible that the affable Yankee living in their midst for the past year had quietly aroused legions of slaves who might yet rise up. This prompted false alarms like the one at the farmhouse in Pleasant Valley, and gave urgency to the manhunt that followed the fighting at Harpers Ferry. Patrols fanned out across the hills and valleys between the Potomac and the Pennsylvania line, searching for "the notorious Captain Cook" and his guerrilla band.

THE MAN THEY HUNTED wasn't nearly so threatening as locals supposed. Cook had acted alone in sniping across the river during the Harpers Ferry fight, and he'd received little aid from Marylanders, apart from passersby he'd questioned in the road and an Irish family he visited for food and coffee. The intelligence he received from them was also flawed: they said not only that his comrades were trapped, but that John Brown was among the dead.

On Monday night, as darkness settled on the besieged engine house, Cook had delivered this sobering status report to the rest of Brown's men in Maryland. Together, after concluding that it would be "sheer madness" to attempt a rescue, they returned to the Kennedy farm for India-rubber blankets and other supplies, and then retreated into the mountain woods nearby.

The party consisted of Cook, Charles Tidd, and the three men who'd been left to guard the farm: Owen Brown, Barclay Coppoc, and Francis Meriam. With them was a slave from John Allstadt's estate who had been taken to Maryland to help transport arms. The other slaves who'd accompanied Brown's men into Maryland had fled back to Virginia upon learning the uprising was doomed. In the night, the last of Allstadt's freed slaves did the same, slipping away while the others slept for a few hours in the rain.

The next morning, fearing their location would be exposed, Cook and his four comrades trekked east to a parallel swell of the Blue Ridge. They then turned north and began traveling through the mountains toward Pennsylvania. The going was slow and the weather foul, first a cold rain and then an early snow. The men traveled only at night; by day, they hid in laurel thickets as mounted patrols galloped past in the valley below. They couldn't risk building a fire, and for food they had only a small supply of biscuits and sugar, supplemented by raw corn foraged from fields.

Within five days, the men were so hungry that they agreed to a desperate plan. One of them would approach a Maryland farmhouse and use the little money and barter they possessed to buy food. The obvious man for this mission was Cook, since "he could wield the glibbest tongue, and tell the best story," as Owen Brown later explained.

Owen and the others waited anxiously for several hours. When Cook finally returned, he said he'd "made himself very agreeable" to the farm family, dining with them and spinning tales about the hunting party he belonged to. He also brought back bread loaves, salt, boiled beef, and a pie, which made his fellow fugitives "exceedingly merry."

But this bounty quickly ran out, so Cook set off again. This time he descended into a valley near the Mason-Dixon Line. The others waited long into the night for his return, lingering until two A.M. and calling his name in the starlight. "Cook never came," Owen said.

Hoping he might have gone to a hideout near Chambersburg—the Pennsylvania town that Brown's band had used as a transit point for the Kennedy farm—the men decided to push on. They also hoped to get food from Mary Ritner, who ran the Chambersburg boardinghouse where John Kagi had stayed that summer. On reaching the house, shortly before dawn, Charles Tidd climbed a beanpole to rap on Mrs. Ritner's bedroom window. Upon seeing him, she motioned him away, whispering "Leave, leave!" The house was being watched by armed men.

Unbeknownst to Tidd and the others, Cook was already in custody just a few blocks away. His search for food the previous afternoon had led to a rural iron works, where he said he belonged to a hunting party and wanted to buy bacon. But one of the men he approached had seen wanted notices for Cook, and he communicated his suspicion to a colleague. Both were southern sympathizers and one of them was experienced at capturing fugitive slaves.

The two men offered to take Cook to a nearby store; en route, they overpowered him. On his person they found documents that erased any doubt about his identity. He carried a commission as a captain in Brown's army, sketches of roads near Harpers Ferry, and a piece of parchment attesting to the lineage of the antique pistol he had taken from Lewis Washington during the raid on the Virginian's plantation.

Bound and put in a wagon to Chambersburg, Cook tried to sweet-talk his captors, claiming he could pay them more than the official bounty. But the men took him before a judge, who committed Cook to the Chambersburg jail. A crowd of curious onlookers trailed the fugitive as he was escorted to prison, and among them were two abolitionist women who concocted a daring scheme. Carrying extra clothes, they planned to visit Cook in jail and dress him as a woman. Then one of the women would walk out of jail with Cook while the other remained in his cell.

But they were discouraged from this plan by the lawyer appointed to represent Cook. He told them that the prisoner wouldn't be handed over to Virginia authorities quickly or without a legal contest. He was wrong. A request for Cook's rendition arrived in the morning and at noon the manacled prisoner was put aboard a train for Charlestown, Virginia. His captors collected their $1,000 reward and Wise offered a new one of $500 for each of the men still at large.

Authorities also issued wanted notices describing the remaining fugitives on the basis of information Cook provided. The muscular and heavy-bearded Charles Tidd, the notice said, "looks like a fighting man, and his looks in this respect are in no way deceptive." Owen Brown was described as spare and freckled, with red whiskers. Barclay Coppoc had a light mustache and "a consumptive look." The even sicklier Francis Meriam "sometimes wears a glass eye" and had a face "blotched from the effects of Syphilis."

Cook may have provided this information knowing that the men would be long gone by the time the notice circulated. Meriam, so weak he couldn't walk much beyond Chambersburg, managed to slip aboard a train to Philadelphia and make his way home to Boston. After seeing him off, Charles Tidd, Owen Brown, and Barclay Coppoc continued their cross-country trek from Chambersburg, enduring rain and snow and subsisting on stolen chickens and apples. They finally found refuge with Quakers in northwest Pennsylvania. Only then did they learn the fate of those they'd left behind in Harpers Ferry, including the news that Owen's siblings Watson and Oliver were dead, and that Barclay's brother, Edwin, was alive but imprisoned.

They also learned that two other insurgents had taken flight. Albert Hazlett and Osborne Anderson, who had been posted at the arsenal across the street from the armory, had managed to slip away under cover of darkness or the heavy fighting around the engine house. After finding a boat, they made their way to Maryland and undertook their own hard journey through the mountains to Pennsylvania. The two men were even more conspicuous than the others, since Hazlett was white and Anderson black.

Hazlett, the rugged Kansas veteran who had apologized to Annie Brown for his tobacco spitting at the Kennedy farm, was overcome by exhaustion and blistered feet near Chambersburg and persuaded Anderson to go on alone. Hazlett then hitched a ride in a wagon and reached the Ritner boardinghouse, where he was quickly spotted and pursued. Described as being of "very rough and shabby appearance," he limped on for another thirty miles before being captured and relieved of a pair of

Osborne Anderson

revolvers and a bowie knife. Like Cook, he was sent to the jail in Charlestown.

Anderson, meanwhile, found shelter among free blacks and abolitionists in Pennsylvania and traveled north from there to his home in Canada. In his long flight from Harpers Ferry, the black fugitive had essentially followed the Underground Railroad from a slave state to a free country. He published a short account soon after his escape, "A Voice from Harper's Ferry." Despite the attack's failure, he wrote, John Brown "dug the mine and laid the train which will eventually dissolve the union between Freedom and Slavery."

IN LATE OCTOBER, WITH all of Brown's men dead, captured, or hiding in the North, the action shifted to the Jefferson County seat of Charlestown—a town extremely hostile to the insurgents now housed in its jail. Illustrative of the mood was the headline in the local *Independent Democrat* on the day of Brown's capture. THE INFERNAL DESPERADOES CAUGHT, AND THE VENGEANCE OF AN OUTRAGED COMMUNITY ABOUT TO BE APPEASED. The

Courthouse and street scene, Charlestown, 1859

newspaper's editor, like many other men in Charlestown, had taken part in the fighting.

On the day Brown was brought to jail, advertisements appeared in the local paper offering "Cash for Negroes" and seeking "MEN, WOMEN, BOYS, GIRLS, and FAMILIES, for the Southern markets." One of the slave dealers named in these ads was John Avis, who also served as the county jail keeper. This was the man now responsible for Brown and his fellow insurgents.

Avis, a Mexican War veteran, had also taken a prominent role in the fighting at Harpers Ferry. He was nonetheless considerate to his new inmates, treating them as he did all others. They were given fresh clothes, allowed to send and receive mail, and quartered close to Avis and his family, who occupied one part of the jailhouse, a two-story brick building with barred windows and a high-walled yard that otherwise resembled a private home. Brown and Aaron Stevens shared a ground-floor room that visitors described as large and well-lit; it was heated by a stove and furnished with chairs and a writing desk.

Diagonally across from the jail stood the county courthouse, a Greek Revival edifice fronted by Doric columns and topped by a bell tower. At the time of Brown's capture the circuit court for western Virginia was in autumn session; the session would end in another few weeks, not to resume until spring. If the insurgents weren't tried quickly, they would have to be kept under guard for months, a prospect few Virginians relished. "There is danger on the one hand of a rescue by their friends, and on the other of Lynch-law from the indignant populace," Governor Wise wrote on October 22.

While he fretted about security, his lead prosecutor, Andrew Hunter, worried that Aaron Stevens might "die of his wounds if we don't hang him promptly." The court should observe "all the judicial decencies," Hunter wrote Wise, "but at double quick time."

On October 25, exactly one week after their capture, Brown and his men were led between ranks of militiamen from the jail to the cannon-ringed courthouse. The town was swollen with soldiers and journalists. To accommodate the press, the telegraph line had been extended from Harpers Ferry to Charlestown. Fresh developments were quickly transmitted by wire to a national audience; as well, leading artists for publications such as *Leslie's* and *Harper's Weekly* provided a pictorial record, at a time when photographs weren't yet reproduced in newspapers and magazines.

This publicity worked to Brown's advantage. Even anti-abolitionist papers noted the swiftness of the proceedings and the defendants' questionable fitness for trial. "There is an evident intention manifested here to hurry the trial through, and to execute the prisoners as soon as possible," the *Baltimore American* noted upon the men's first appearance in court. Brown, manacled to Edwin Coppoc, looked "weak and haggard, with his eyes swollen from the effects of the wounds on his head," while Stevens was so feeble that he fainted during the initial testimony and had to lie on a mattress.

The first day's session concerned itself with a formality: whether there was enough evidence to call a grand jury. Brown nonetheless seized the moment to speak beyond the courtroom, answering a straightforward legal question with a short speech. "Virginians, I did not ask for any quarter at the time I was taken. I did not ask to have myself spared," he said. But, having been promised a fair trial by Governor Wise, he wanted no part in a legal charade that rushed him to judgment without time to prepare or recover from his wounds. "If you seek my blood, you can have it at any moment, without this mockery of a trial," he said. "I am ready for my fate."

His words had no practical effect. The court kept up the pace, assigning lawyers, selecting jurors, and summoning witnesses within twenty-four hours of the proceedings' commencement. But Brown's defiant, unflinching demeanor, in spite of his wounds and manacles, reinforced the impression he'd made while lying bloodied at the armory. He was "game," to use Governor Wise's cockfighting term, a courageous foe who commanded respect. "I have now little to ask," Brown stated that first day in court, "other than that I be not publicly insulted as cowardly barbarians insult those who fall into their hands." Brown may have misjudged many aspects of southern society, but he intuitively grasped—and identified with—its chivalric code of honor.

Virginians believed they were holding to their own high standards by conducting a trial in a civilian court, before the eyes of the nation, rather than administering "drum-head justice" in a closed military tribunal. All the legal "decencies" would be duly observed in the Charlestown court. But given the realities of antebellum society in Jefferson County and its surrounds, an impartial hearing for Brown and his men was impossible.

Richard Parker, the presiding judge, was a respected, by-the-book jurist. He was also a slave owner and a former paymaster at the Harpers Ferry armory, who stated in his opening instructions to the jury: "I will not permit myself to give expression to those feelings which at once spring up in every breast when reflecting on the enormity of the guilt" of the defendants, who had invaded "our common country" and shot down Virginians "without mercy." Then, having given expression to precisely those feelings, he reminded the jurors, most of whom were slaveholding farmers, that the defendants should be given "a fair and impartial trial."

Like Parker, the two lawyers appointed to defend Brown were competent and highly regarded—and, like him, they were slaveholders. They had also taken part in the military action at Harpers Ferry. The lead prosecutor, Andrew Hunter (another slaveholder), was related by marriage to Fontaine Beckham, the slain mayor of Harpers Ferry. And Hunter's son, Henry, was one of the gunmen who had burst into the

Wager House to avenge Beckham's shooting by dragging William Thompson to his death on the Potomac bridge.

As well, Andrew Hunter was a close associate of the governor and shared Wise's desire to implicate—and, if possible, indict—prominent Northerners. "What we aim at," Hunter stated, "is not only the destruction of these men whom we have in confinement," but "higher and wickeder game."

Virginians' ferocious hostility to abolitionism was reflected in the far-reaching indictment that Hunter drafted. It charged Brown and his men with first-degree murder, with conspiracy to induce slaves "to make insurrection against their masters," and with having "traitorously" levied war and rebellion against Virginia. Treason was generally understood as a crime against the nation, and none of the defendants were citizens of the state they'd allegedly betrayed. But Hunter cited Brown's Provisional Constitution as evidence that he and his men sought to usurp Virginia's laws and establish a new government. They did so, he added, "not having the fear of God before their eyes, but being moved and seduced by the false and malignant counsel of other evil and traitorous persons and the instigations of the devil."

The defendants were required to stand during the reading of the seven-page indictment, which took a full twenty minutes. Brown stood with difficulty and Stevens had to be held up by two bailiffs before returning to his mattress. "He has the appearance almost of a dying man; breathing with difficulty and panting for breath," one reporter wrote. The defendants pleaded not guilty and asked to be tried separately. Hunter elected to prosecute Brown first.

Brown sought a short delay, saying that his wounds had left him enfeebled and hard of hearing. But Judge Parker, eager to move the process along, denied this request (as he would almost every other defense request). Returned to jail during the lunch recess, Brown took to his bed and claimed he was too weak to get up for the afternoon session. So he was carried back to the courtroom on a cot, where he lay with his eyes closed and a blanket drawn to his chin, "determined to resist the pushing of his trial by all the means in his power," the *Baltimore American* reported.

Brown's theatrics heightened what was already a colorful courtroom scene. Hundreds of spectators packed the vast chamber, cracking

Charlestown courtroom with Brown on cot at left center

chestnuts and peanuts as they watched the legal drama. "The floor of the court, excepting within a few feet of the Judge, was inches deep, in places, with nut shells, and the noise of people moving about was like that which would be made by trampling on glass," wrote a reporter for the *New York Herald*. One of the prosecutors chewed tobacco, a wad sometimes slipping from his mouth; he showed up in court with his face bruised from a brawl the night before. Even the judge appeared casual, "comfortably reclining in his chair, his legs resting upon the table before him, amid the chaos of law-books, papers, and inkstands."

The legal proceedings were also irregular. Brown frequently lurched up from his cot to challenge a witness or make a pronouncement, before slumping back down and closing his eyes. His defense team kept changing: six different lawyers acted on his behalf in a trial that lasted less than five days. And the proceedings had barely gotten under way when a telegram arrived from a prominent citizen of Akron, Ohio, stating that a number of Brown's relatives had been committed to "a Lunatic Asylum" or died insane.

"These facts can be conclusively proven by witnesses residing here, who will doubtless attend the trial if desired."

THE INSANITY DEFENSE WAS a new but widely accepted doctrine in American courtrooms. In a sensational murder trial just months before Brown's, a New York congressman, Daniel Sickles, had successfully pleaded temporary insanity after shooting his wife's lover dead in a park in Washington, D.C. Brown, with his wild hair and even wilder scheme for slaves' liberation, fit many people's notion of a lunatic. "As mad as a March hare," opined the *Chicago Press and Tribune*, offering a typical view of Brown a few days after his capture.

The telegram from Akron also contained a certain amount of truth. Nineteen Ohioans later supported it by submitting affidavits about Brown's mental state. While these statements were collected in an obvious effort to win clemency for Brown, they attested to his family's long history of mental illness. A number of relatives on his mother's side had been committed to asylums. And two of Brown's children, Frederick and John junior, were clearly disturbed, though their instability may have been inherited from their mother, Dianthe, who was described as mentally afflicted.

More telling, perhaps, were the words used to describe Brown in the affidavits and other accounts of people who knew him well. They frequently called him "excitable" or a "monomaniac"—a term that Herman Melville applied to Captain Ahab. In early 1858, almost two years before the question of Brown's mental health arose in court, a free-state official in Kansas had written a striking letter to Franklin Sanborn, reporting that Brown was acting so oddly that some free-staters "openly express[ed] the opinion that one of his old fits of insanity has returned upon him."

Brown's own writing also spoke to his violent mood swings; he oscillated between periods of giddy, frantic activity and sloughs of despond that left him almost paralyzed. To modern eyes, this might suggest manic depression. So would Brown's recurrent grandiosity—his unassailable faith in his own plans and abilities, and his belief that he was "God's instrument," singled out for the liberation of slaves.

But diagnosing mental illness at a distance of a century and a half is a dubious exercise. Even if Brown gave signs of bipolar tendencies, there's no evidence he had hallucinations or other symptoms so severe that he could have been considered legally insane—in the parlance of Virginia's antebellum code, "an idiot, lunatic, *non compos*, or deranged."

In any event, Brown wanted no part of an insanity defense. As soon as his lawyer read the telegram from Ohio in court, he raised himself from his cot and objected. "I look upon it as a miserable artifice and pretext of those who ought to take a different course in regard to me," he said. "I am perfectly unconscious of insanity, and I reject, so far as I am capable, any attempt to interfere on my behalf on that score."

This pleased Virginians but left his lawyers little to argue in his defense. There was no real dispute over the facts of the case. Under Brown's leadership, the insurgents had seized the armory, taken hostages, armed slaves, and killed five men and wounded many others. At Brown's insistence, his lawyers elicited testimony that showed he had treated his hostages well and ordered his men not to shoot unarmed civilians. Brown felt this demonstrated that he never intended violence; he and his men had shed blood only in self-defense.

But to Virginians, this argument held no weight. At least one of those slain, Heyward Shepherd, was a noncombatant. And Brown could hardly have expected to seize the town, take hostages, and free and arm a legion of slaves without sparking a fight. The prosecution regarded Brown's defense as "too absurd to require argument" and didn't even bother to cross-examine the witnesses called on his behalf.

Though the trial testimony did little but confirm Brown's guilt, it provided moments that aroused the hundreds of white spectators. One witness testified to Brown's words about his provisional government, including mention of "an intelligent colored man elected as one of the members of the House." This notion caused a "sensation" in the courtroom, one reporter wrote. Another witness, John Allstadt, who had been taken hostage with his slaves and clearly loathed Brown, testified that the blacks in the engine house "were doing nothing, and had dropped their spears: some of them were asleep nearly all the time." The southern audience laughed, delighted by this stereotypical portrayal of blacks as lazy and docile.

A few witnesses expressed nobler sentiments. The Maryland officer, Captain John Sinn, was called by the defense and ended his testimony by stating: "As a Southern man, he came to state the facts about the case, so that Northern men would have no opportunity of saying that Southern men were unwilling to appear as witnesses in behalf of one whose principles they abhorred."

The last day of testimony brought one final surprise—the arrival of two eminent lawyers who had been recruited by Brown's supporters in the North. The trial had been so hasty that the attorneys arrived without having had a chance to so much as study the indictment. They'd also missed hearing the prosecution witnesses. But the judge was intent on forging ahead and allowed the prosecution to begin its closing arguments that same afternoon. When the defense's turn came, it could do little but argue technical points about jurisdiction and appeal to the jury to show "moral courage" and maintain Virginia's reputation for "chivalry unstained."

The closing arguments ended at one thirty on the afternoon of Monday, October 31, two weeks to the day after Brown's men had been trapped at the engine house. The jurors withdrew, but returned after just forty-five minutes, having put ballots in a hat and found their opinion was unanimous. The courtroom was now so packed that the crowd spilled into the hallway and outside the building's front door.

"Gentlemen of the Jury," the court clerk asked, "what say you, is the prisoner at the bar, John Brown, guilty or not guilty?"

"Guilty," the foreman replied.

"Guilty of treason, and conspiring and advising with slaves and others to rebel and murder in the first degree?"

"Yes."

There was no sound in the courtroom, "not the slightest expression of elation or triumph," reported the *New York Herald*. Brown, who had listened to the day's proceedings from his cot, often with his eyes shut, sat up to hear the verdict. Once it was read he "said not even a word, but, as on any previous day, turned to adjust his pallet, and then composedly stretched himself upon it."

Though the judge did not sentence Brown until a few days later, the verdict left little doubt about his fate. Convicted of three capital crimes, he appeared certain to hang. It also seemed likely that he would go to the gallows quickly, in company with his co-conspirators. The court began trying them immediately after Brown's verdict was handed down on Monday afternoon, and it would hastily convict three more of the insurgents before the week was out.

As the judge and prosecutor had hoped, Virginia was dispensing justice in "double quick time." Even the temporary telegraph office in Charlestown closed a few days after Brown's conviction, in expectation of a swift and uneventful conclusion to the affair.

BROWN, HAVING FAILED TO sway the Virginia jury, had thus far fared poorly in the North as well. Conservative, pro-southern organs like the *New York Herald* blasted Brown and his allies as "Nigger-Worshipping Insurrectionists." The middle-of-the-road *New York Times* called Brown "a fanatic; *sui generis*," and later termed him "a wild and absurd freak."

Papers strongly aligned with the antislavery cause were critical, too, and they sought distance from Brown's violent abolitionism. Horace Greeley's *New York Tribune* called Harpers Ferry a "deplorable affair" and "the work of a madman," adding that "the way to Universal Emancipation lies not through insurrection, civil war and bloodshed, but through peace, discussion, and the quiet diffusion of sentiments of humanity and justice." William Lloyd Garrison, editor of the radical but nonviolent *Liberator*, was sternly disapproving, calling the Harpers Ferry attack "misguided, wild, and apparently insane."

Worse still, Brown's innermost core of supporters had all but deserted him. Just after Brown's capture, Franklin Sanborn broke the news in a letter to another member of the Secret Six, Theodore Parker, who was in Italy sick with tuberculosis. "Our old friend struck his blow in such a way,—either by his own folly or the direction of Providence—that it has recoiled and ruined him, and perhaps those who were his friends," Sanborn wrote on October 22. By then, the teacher had fled Concord for Quebec, writing en route to Thomas Wentworth Higginson: "According to the advice of good friends and my own deliberate judgment I am to try change of air for my old complaint." Sanborn ended his note: "Burn this."

Two other members of the Secret Six soon followed Sanborn to Canada, even though a lawyer advised them that they were safe from arrest in Massachusetts. Frederick Douglass also fled north, and then left Canada for England on a previously planned trip. Though not a member of the Secret Six, Douglass was linked to Brown in papers found at the Kennedy farm, and Virginia authorities sought to apprehend him. "I have always been more distinguished for running than fighting," Douglass wrote in a letter from Canada to a New York newspaper, "and tried by the Harper's Ferry insurrection test, I am most miserably deficient in courage."

Douglass, at least, was forthright about his flight, and he called Brown "noble and heroic." Very different was the response of Gerrit Smith, the philanthropist who had bankrolled Brown from the start. He immediately destroyed all correspondence linking him to Brown and then, amid press speculation that he might be indicted, became so agitated that he was committed to the New York State Lunatic Asylum. Diagnosed as suffering from acute mania, Smith was treated with cannabis and morphine and quickly recovered his wits—though not, apparently, his memory. He denied any knowledge of, or complicity in, Brown's Virginia campaign, later stating that he had "but a hazy view of nearly the whole of 1859."

Samuel Howe, like Smith, was frequently named in letters published after Brown's capture. Yet he, too, loudly disclaimed any association with Harpers Ferry. "That event was unforeseen and unexpected by me," he wrote from Canada in a statement published by the *New York Tribune*. "It is still, to me, a mystery, and a marvel."

This disavowal enraged the combative preacher Thomas Wentworth Higginson, the only member of the Secret Six who didn't leave the country or take refuge in an asylum. It was "the extreme of baseness," he wrote, for the Six to deny knowledge of Brown's enterprise, and he judged Howe's disingenuous letter and Smith's alleged insanity as "two sad results of the whole affair."

He also complained to Sanborn, who returned from Canada but kept urging Higginson to stay quiet about their role in the insurrection. "Sanborn is there no such thing as *honor* among confederates?" Higginson fired back, disgusted that Brown and his men had suffered while "silent safe partners make haste to secure our good reputation by a *lie!*" He refused

Henry David Thoreau

to destroy Sanborn's letters, and signed one of his own: "There is no need of burning this."

WHILE HIGGINSON STEWED IN private, another New Englander went boldly public in defense of Brown. A few days after the Harpers Ferry attack, Henry David Thoreau told townspeople in Concord that he planned to give a speech supporting the jailed abolitionist. Though many citizens of the freethinking town had backed Brown strongly just months before, they now dreaded any association with Harpers Ferry. Local abolitionists discouraged Thoreau from speaking and town selectmen refused to ring a bell announcing his lecture. Undaunted, Thoreau rang the bell himself—on October 30, the eve of the abolitionist's conviction—before delivering a stirring oration that was published under the title "A Plea for Captain John Brown."

Harking back to his famous essay "Civil Disobedience," Thoreau cast Brown as an exemplar of principled resistance to authority. "Is it possible that an individual may be right and a government wrong?" he asked.

"Are laws to be enforced simply because they are made?" Brown, he said, had resisted unjust laws and stood up for human dignity, "knowing himself for a man, and the equal of any and all governments. In that sense he was the most American of us all."

Thoreau contrasted this individual heroism with the "cackling of political conventions" and the cravenness of the northern public, particularly "the herd" of commentators who condemned Brown or pronounced him "insane." Thoreau also mocked his Yankee neighbors who saw everything in terms of gain, and therefore felt that Brown had thrown his life away. "No doubt you can get more in your market for a quart of milk than for a quart of blood, but that is not the market that heroes carry their blood to," Thoreau said.

He reserved his greatest praise for the words spoken by Brown to the Virginians who had questioned him at the armory soon after his capture. All of the many antislavery speeches by northern congressmen, combined and boiled down, Thoreau said, "do not match for manly directness and force, and for simple truth, the few casual remarks of crazy John Brown" as he lay bleeding on the floor of the paymaster's office. As Thoreau memorably put it: "He could afford to lose his Sharpe's rifles, while he retained his faculty of speech, —a Sharpe's rifle of infinitely surer and longer range."

THREE DAYS LATER, ON November 2, Brown would show himself fully worthy of Thoreau's praise. Brown was now well enough to walk, though with difficulty, and during the court session that day he sat instead of lying on a cot. "It was late, and the gaslights gave an almost deathly pallor to his face," one reporter wrote. "He was like a block of stone." Brown remained impassive as the judge denied a defense motion seeking to overturn his verdict. Then the court clerk told Brown to rise and asked him if he had anything to "say why sentence should not be pronounced upon him."

This caught Brown off guard. He'd expected to be sentenced with the other prisoners, once they'd all been convicted. "He seemed to be wholly unprepared to speak at this time," one reporter wrote. If so, Brown recovered very quickly. Leaning slightly forward and resting his hands on a table, he spoke in a clear, distinct voice.

"I have, may it please the Court, a few words to say," he began. "In the first place I deny everything but what I have all along admitted, of a design on my part to free slaves. I intended certainly to have made a clean thing of that matter, as I did last winter when I went into Missouri and there took slaves without the snapping of a gun on either side, moving them through the country and finally leaving them in Canada. I designed to have done the same thing again on a larger scale. That was all I intended. I never did intend murder or treason, or the destruction of property, or to excite or incite slaves to rebellion, or to make insurrection."

This summary wasn't altogether true. In Missouri, one of Brown's men had shot a slaveholder dead. And the attack on Harpers Ferry was clearly intended as more than a large-scale reprise of his slave rescue. Brown later admitted as much in a letter, telling the prosecutor Andrew Hunter that he misspoke in court "in the hurry of the moment." His intent at Harpers Ferry had been to arm slaves to defend themselves within the South, rather than to "run them out of the slave States."

But the point was legally moot. As he continued speaking in court, Brown no longer sought to question the specifics of the prosecution's case. He even declared himself "entirely satisfied" with his treatment and praised the "truthfulness and candor" of the witnesses. What he challenged instead was the very basis of his indictment. Why was it a crime to try to free slaves?

"Had I interfered in the manner which I admit, and which I admit has been fairly proved," Brown said in his courtroom speech, "had I so interfered in behalf of the rich, the powerful, the intelligent, the so-called great, or in behalf of any of their friends, either father, mother, brother, sister, wife or children, or any of that class, and suffered and sacrificed what I have in this interference, it would have been all right; every man in this court would have deemed it an act worthy of reward rather than punishment."

Brown accepted his conviction under Virginia law. But he invoked another, higher code. "This Court acknowledges, too, as I suppose, the validity of the law of God. I see a book kissed here, which I suppose to be the Bible, or at least the New Testament. That teaches me that all things 'whatsoever I would men should do to me I should do ever so to them.' It teaches me, further, to 'remember them that are in bonds as bound with them.' I endeavored to act up to these instructions."

He had abided by the Golden Rule and the scriptural injunction to care for the afflicted. This was all he had done. To do otherwise would have been a much greater crime. "I believe that to have interfered as I have done, as I have always freely admitted I have done, in behalf of His despised poor, was no wrong but right."

This brought Brown to the climax of his speech—in effect, to the climax of his long struggle against slavery. "Now, if it is deemed necessary that I should forfeit my life for the furtherance of the ends of justice, and mingle my blood further with the blood of my children and with the blood of millions in this slave country, whose rights are disregarded by wicked, cruel and unjust enactments, I submit. So let it be done!"

BROWN SPOKE, IN ALL, for about three or four minutes. If his words had any effect on the judge, there was no sign of it. Parker moved immediately to sentencing. "You have been found by an impartial jury of your countrymen to be guilty of the offenses charged against you," he said. "In mercy to our own people—to protect them against similar invasions upon their rights—in mercy and by way of warning to the infatuated men of other States who, like you, may attempt to free our negroes by forcing weapons into their hands, the judgment of the law must be enforced against you."

Judge Parker then declared: "The sentence of the law is that you, John Brown, be hanged by the neck until you are dead." Furthermore, "for the sake of the example," the execution should occur in public rather than in the jail yard. He set December 2, a month hence, as the date for the hanging. "And may God have mercy on your soul."

Earlier in the court session, the many spectators crowded in the room had uttered execrations, calling Brown a "damned black-hearted villain" and other slurs. But they listened to his speech and sentencing with solemnity and silence. Then, after the judge had spoken, one man broke the quiet by clapping his hands. "This indecorum was promptly suppressed and much regret was expressed by citizens at its occurrence," a reporter wrote. The crowd also remained silent as the defendant returned to prison.

The first press reports on Brown's sentencing were likewise muted. Correspondents in the court faithfully recorded his words but made little comment on them. One wrote that Brown's "composure, and his quiet and truthful manner" commanded respect and even some sympathy. Another thought he "spoke timidly—hesitatingly, indeed—and in a voice singularly gentle and mild." A Virginian in the court described Brown's tone as "indifferent" and quoted only the speech's opening line.

The courtroom clerk didn't even bother to reproduce that much. His official record consisted of ten words. Brown, upon being asked if he had reason why judgment should not be passed against him, "said he had nothing but what he had before said."

In a sense, the clerk was right: Brown *had* said all of this before, in letters and in reply to his interrogators at the armory. Many elements of his speech, particularly his invocation of the Golden Rule, were decades-old touchstones for him. Brown may not have been fully prepared when the court called on him to speak in his own defense, but he'd been rehearsing for this moment his entire life.

And he had, at last, found the perfect stage, before a mostly hostile audience and a collection of correspondents who quickly transmitted the scene across the land. Brown's public speaking style often lacked punch, but in print, his words and manner carried tremendous force. In a speech of just six hundred words, without notes or apparent preparation, he had cut through decades of cant and equivocation over slavery. Moreover, he had done so, not from the safety of a northern pulpit or editorial page, but while standing in a slave state courtroom, on trial for his life.

"Has anything like it been said in this land or age," marveled a Philadelphia minister, writing the next day "with joy unutterable" to an abolitionist friend. "Slavery & Freedom brought face to face standing opposite; the one all black wrong, the other white as an angel."

In essence, Brown's speech had turned the case against him on its head. He had put his accusers on trial and pronounced *them* guilty, of crimes before God. He had also denied Virginians the righteous satisfaction of hanging a convicted felon. Feeling "no consciousness of guilt," he told the court, he would gladly go to the gallows for "the ends of justice," in solidarity with the slaves he had sought to free. Instead of pleading for his life, he made his death sentence a triumph. So let it be done!

Ralph Waldo Emerson, the most eminent intellectual of his day, hailed Brown's speech as one of the finest in history, and he would later call it

and the Gettysburg Address "the two best specimens of eloquence we
have had in this country." This praise reflected the strong shift in northern opinion that occurred following Brown's conviction and sentencing.
Emerson, like many others, had initially viewed Harpers Ferry with horror, writing that Brown "lost his head" and committed a "fatal blunder"
in attacking Virginia. Now, moved by Brown's words—and those of his
neighbor Thoreau—Emerson reconsidered his earlier stance and became
one of the abolitionist's greatest champions.

Like Thoreau, Emerson trafficked in ideal types. Years before, in an
essay titled "Heroism," he had conjured an "unschooled man" who feels
rather than thinks and "finds a quality in him that is negligent of expense,
of health, of life, of danger, of hatred, of reproach." Unafraid of suffering
and censure, and heedless of learned authority, Emerson's hero also had
to be persistent: "When you have chosen your part, abide by it, and do
not weakly try to reconcile yourself to the world." Above all, heroism
demanded certitude and self-reliance, right to the end. "Its ultimate
objects are the last defiance of falsehood and wrong, and the power to
bear all that can be inflicted by evil agents."

Brown seemed to exemplify these attributes, and once Emerson
embraced him, he did so without reserve. Brown's words conveyed "his
simple, artless goodness joined with his sublime courage," while his character fused the "perfect Puritan faith" and the revolutionary fervor of his
forebears. "He believes in two articles—two instruments, shall I say?—the
Golden Rule and the Declaration of Independence."

Emerson's loftiest praise came in his lecture "Courage," which he
delivered at the Music Hall in Boston five days after Brown's sentencing.
"None purer or more brave was ever led by love of men into conflict and
death," Emerson said. Brown represented nothing less than "the new
saint awaiting his martyrdom, and who, if he shall suffer, will make the
gallows glorious like the cross."

AS EMERSON AND OTHERS canonized Brown, the man himself, imprisoned in his cell, was more than playing his part. For most of his life, he
had shown little inclination to turn the other cheek; his own heroes
were mostly Old Testament warriors. But now he donned the mantle of

Brown in his prison cell

Christian martyr and inhabited the role with the steeliness he had brought to every other pursuit. Nothing would deter him from his glorious sacrifice—not family, not plots for his rescue, not weakness of spirit or resolve. In dying well, he would redeem all the tribulations of his difficult career, most particularly the failure at Harpers Ferry that had cost him so much, including his two young sons.

"I have been <u>whiped</u> as the saying <u>is</u>," Brown wrote his wife soon after his sentencing, "but am sure I can recover all the lost capital occasioned by that disaster; by only hanging a few moments by the neck; & I feel quite determined to make the utmost possible out of defeat. I am dayly & hourly striving to gather up what little I may from the wreck."

In this last great work of his life, Brown also found a new and potent weapon. At Harpers Ferry he had used guns and pikes; in court, he'd deployed the spoken word. Now, confined to a cell, he wielded his pen, aiming round after round of correspondence at friends, family, and supporters, clearly intending to hit a broader audience.

"You know that Christ once armed Peter," he wrote an admirer in one of many letters that quickly made its way into print. "So also in my case I think he put a sword into my hand, and there continued it so long as he saw best, and then kindly took it from me."

God had "often covered my head in the day of battle," he wrote a cousin, and must have spared him certain death in the engine house for a purpose. If it was not his destiny to be a triumphant warrior, like Gideon or David, or to die gloriously in battle, than the end of his being must be this: as a captive among the nonbelievers.

Brown felt no shame in dying a criminal at the hands of an unjust government. "Jesus of Nazareth suffered a most excruciating death on the cross as a fellon," he wrote his family, in what was meant as a consoling observation. "Think also of the prophets, & Apostles, & Christians of former days; who went through greater tribulations than you & I." His sacrifice, Brown added, "will do vastly more toward advancing the cause I have earnestly endeavored to promote, than all I have done in my life before." Or, as he put it plainly to his brother: "I am worth inconceivably more to hang than for any other purpose."

Brown's quest for martyrdom was greatly if unintentionally enhanced by those who had condemned him to death. Judge Parker, who had rushed the trial and turned down repeated requests for delays, could have sent Brown to the scaffold with equal dispatch. Instead, to allow ample time for the appeals process, and perhaps mindful of criticism that he'd tried Brown with unseemly haste, Parker granted the prisoner a full month of life and ordered him hanged outside the jail yard—steps that would make his end a protracted and public vigil. "No theatrical manager could have arranged things so wisely to give effect to his behavior and words," Thoreau observed.

Although he still felt weak from his wounds, Brown was determined to use every minute left him and wrote letters for hours each day. As he told one supporter, he wished he could offer "something more than words;

but it has come to that, I now have but little else to deal in." He also received a stream of visitors, many of them proslavery, and took time to patiently answer their questions and explain his views. When a reporter for the antiabolitionist *New York Herald* saw Brown a week after his conviction, he marveled at the prisoner's metamorphosis from "irascible" defendant to composed and reflective inmate, awaiting his fate "with that calm firmness which is the sure characteristic of a brave man."

Maintaining this courageous front was far more wrenching than Brown made it appear. At moments the mask fell away, revealing his doubts and fears. Mary Brown, upon learning of her husband's conviction, had quickly set off for Virginia; she was escorted part of the way by Thomas Wentworth Higginson, who hoped she might urge her husband to cooperate in a rescue attempt. But when Brown heard she was en route, he immediately tried to stop her.

"Mr. Brown says for gods sake dont let Mrs Brown come," one of his lawyers telegraphed Higginson from Virginia. Another lawyer wrote to her: "Mr. Brown fears your presence will undo the firm composure of his mind & so agitate him as to unman and unfit him for the last great sacrifice. He thinks it best to avoid the awful leave-taking which must precede the last act of his earthly existence & which might disturb the great serenity and firmness which he wills to have accompany him to the gallows."

In his own writing, Brown also expressed worry that Mary would deplete the family's "scanty means" in coming to Charlestown, and he didn't want her to become "gazing stock" for a hostile public. But his main concern was the effect she would have on him. "Her presence here will deepen my affliction a thousand fold," he wrote Higginson, in a letter he asked to be conveyed to his traveling wife. "I beg of her to be calm and submissive; & not go wild on my account. I lack for nothing & am feeling quite cheerful before I learned she talked of coming on." He urged her to abide by his wish, "out of pity to me."

Mary had reached Baltimore and was about to board a train for Virginia when she was persuaded to turn back. Brown wrote a letter thanking her for "heeding what may be my last, but earnest request" and asked her to stay calm as they faced this final trial. "In the world we must have tribulation: but the cords that have bound you as well as I; to Earth: have been many of them severed already." These losses included "the fall of our dear sons" at Harpers Ferry. Hoping to recover "all the lost capital" in death, Brown couldn't risk breaking down or wanting to live beyond the brief period allotted him.

But he would permit Mary to come later. "If after Virginia has applied the finishing stroke to the picture already made of me," he wrote, "you can afford to meet the expence & trouble of coming on here to gather up the bones of our beloved sons, & of your husband; and the people here will suffer you to do so; I should be entirely willing."

CHAPTER 11

——ᔕᔕᔕ——

A Full Fountain of Bedlam

O n November 10, 1859, as Brown wrote Mary about collecting his body, four other inmates were learning their fate in the courthouse across from the Charleston jail. Since their capture, not all of them had displayed Brown's passion for martyrdom. Edwin Coppoc said he had been misled about his leader's intentions and thought the attack was meant only to "run off slaves into a Free State." John Copeland made the same claim.

Copeland's lawyer also argued that he and the other black defendant, Shields Green, couldn't be charged with treason because the Supreme Court, in its notorious *Dred Scott* decision of 1857, had ruled that blacks were "beings of an inferior order" who possessed "no rights which the white man was bound to respect." Blacks, slave or free, were effectively noncitizens, and as such had no government to betray.

The prosecution acknowledged the logic of this argument and dropped the treason charge against the black men. But this victory by the defense proved hollow. Copeland and Green were found guilty of murder and inciting slaves; Coppoc was convicted of all charges.

John Cook's case appeared to offer more hope. For one thing, he had written a twenty-five-page confession that detailed his association with Brown, soft-pedaled his own role, and implicated prominent abolitionists. Further, Cook was well connected: his sister was married to Indiana's governor, a southern sympathizer who wrote obsequious letters to

Shields Green and John Copeland in prison cell with Albert Hazlett

Wise and came to Charlestown accompanied by a talented attorney to aid the defense.

The Indiana lawyer, Daniel Voorhees, gave a court address in which he declared slavery "more fully justified than ever before" by Brown's failure at Harpers Ferry. He also cast Cook as a "wayward, misled child" who had been exploited by a fanatical old man. "John Brown was the despotic leader and John E. Cook was an ill-fated follower of an enterprise whose horror he now realizes and deplores," Voorhees stated. "Cook simply obeyed—no more."

Voorhees's defense of the handsome, fair-haired youth with "a face for a mother to love, and a sister to idolize" moved some in the courtroom to tears. But it failed to sway the jurymen, who found Cook guilty of murder and inciting slaves. He, Coppoc, Green, and Copeland were then sentenced to hang on December 16, two weeks after their leader.

Judge Parker handed down these sentences on the final day of the circuit-court session. And he marked the occasion by expressing the relief and vindication that Virginians felt at the failure of the Harpers Ferry attack. "Happily for the peace of our whole land, you obtained no support from that quarter whence you so confidently expected it," he told the four men he sentenced on November 10. Each of the slaves forced to join the uprising had "hurried to place himself once more beneath the care and protection of his owner."

Parker's paternalistic message had, by then, become the refrain of leading Virginians. As they saw it, the attack illustrated not only the perfidy of abolitionists but also the fallacy of their belief that slaves were mistreated and desperate for freedom. "Those who were taken by force from their happy homes deserted their liberators," Governor Wise declared. "Not a slave around was found faithless."

Such testimonials, however, did not accord with all of the evidence that emerged after Brown's capture. They were further undercut by the behavior of white Virginians themselves. "The inhabitants are not by any means easy in their minds as to the temper of the slaves and free negroes among them," the *New York Herald* reported two weeks after the attack. "Colonel Washington who was one of Brown's hostages does not spend his nights at home, and we are assured that many other wealthy slave owners, whose residences lie at a distance from those of their neighbors, also regard it as prudent to lodge elsewhere for the present."

The *Herald* also noted whites' suspicion that local slaves "had at least cognizance of the plans of the marauders," and mentioned that one slave "had joined the rebels with a good will." This was a reference to Lewis Washington's coachman, Jim, who had been hired from a doctor in nearby Winchester. Jim was away from Washington's estate when Brown's men raided it, but he later joined the insurgents en route to Harpers Ferry, helped guard Hall's Rifle Works, and drowned while fleeing the Virginians who attacked the factory. Many locals, including a minister present at the scene, took Jim's behavior as evidence of his complicity with Brown's men.

One of John Allstadt's slaves, twenty-year-old Ben, also carried a pike at the rifle works. Though he quickly surrendered and told his captors he had been forced into guard duty, Ben was nonetheless taken to prison on suspicion of aiding the insurgents. He died in jail a week later, from what the county death register termed "Pneumonia and fright." A doctor who saw him in jail said Ben "manifested many of the symptoms which usually attend attacks of 'delirium tremens' such as nervous startings &

tremors, together with various hallucinations, among the most prominent of which was a constant dread of being killed by armed men."

This dread required no hallucinations to bring it on: Ben had almost been lynched upon his capture, and armed white men ringed the prison where he was held. Whatever disease killed him, it appears also to have struck his mother, Ary, who came to nurse him in jail and died a few weeks later, at the age of forty-five.

Their owner, John Allstadt, sought compensation from the state for property "destroyed by Civil War and Commotion." Jim's owner did likewise. These petitions included accounts of the slaves' "tractable and faithful" service to their masters, and of their value. John Avis, the jail keeper and slave dealer in Charlestown, priced Ben at $1,450. His mother was judged to be worth $600 "in the common market"; at auction "she would have sold for a much larger price."

There is no record of either owner receiving compensation for "being deprived of his property," as Allstadt put it. But the petitions show how little had been gained by the slaves caught up in Brown's effort to liberate them. Three were dead, while the surviving slaves taken from Washington and Allstadt were returned to bondage and showed signs of continuing to fear arrest.

Charles Tidd, who had accompanied a number of the liberated slaves into Maryland to transport arms, later described them as "ready & glad to be armed against their masters," and said two of them had planned to escape the next summer. During the fray, one of these men rode to the Kennedy farm to urge Brown's men posted at the hideout to "go over to the Ferry and help in the fight." Another carried Lewis Washington's shotgun. "But when they heard firing & then the rumor that all [were] killed, they slipped back & joined their masters," Tidd said.

Most white Virginians nonetheless maintained that slaves had fled Brown's men, or failed to join them, out of childlike devotion and terror. Only years later did some slaveholders acknowledge the unease they'd felt at the time. One farmer, Charles Conklyn, said the anxiety in Jefferson County after Harpers Ferry was greater even than during the Civil War. "It was not about John Brown, but about the fear—the uncertainty—as to how far disaffection might be spread among the negroes," he recalled. "In the towns it was comparatively a small matter—the danger—but the situation of country estates—and of women and children on country farms, was horrible, if insurrection was afoot. And the whole excitement arose from the uncertainty as to how far the negroes had been tampered with."

Though apprehension was greatest in the countryside, the towns were tense as well. Mary Mauzy, who witnessed the attack on the rifle works, wrote often to her daughter that fall with updates on the mood in Harpers Ferry. On November 10, she reported that guns were still turning up around town and all the children "have a warlike feeling." This included her son, who was too young to read and write but allowed by his father to carry a double-barreled pistol. "He says tell sister I've a pistol and I am going to shoot Niggers with it," Mary wrote.

Anxious whites that autumn also kept mulling the role played by "the great scamp Cook," as Mary's husband called the silver-tongued Yankee who had ingratiated himself with the Mauzy family and many others. In his written confession before trial, Cook said he had heeded Brown's order to tell no one of their plans, apart from one oblique conversation he had with four slaves near Harpers Ferry. "I asked them if they had ever thought about their freedom," Cook stated. "They replied, 'they thought they ought to be free,' but expressed doubts that they ever would be. I told them that time might come before many years, but for the present to keep dark and look for the good time coming."

Few whites believed this was Cook's only attempt to alert or incite blacks. Nor did white fears subside with Cook's sentencing. The very next day, mysterious fires started breaking out in Jefferson County, engulfing haystacks and outbuildings. As the blazes continued, they struck members of the jury that had convicted Brown, including the foreman, whose barn, corn crib, carriage, and hay burned on the night of November 17.

At first, locals attributed the fires to "Abolitionist incendiaries," acting in sympathy with the jailed insurgents. But when fires also broke out on slaveholders' properties in neighboring counties, whites blamed the "monstrous scoundrel," John Cook. "It is to his action we ascribe these fires—for he was the emissary to urge the negroes up," one of the fires' victims wrote Governor Wise, warning him that "Lynch will rule" if the convicted insurgent was shown any clemency.

THE HARPERS FERRY ATTACK had failed in military terms, but it had clearly evoked the deepest terror of white Virginians—that slaves would rise up in the night and slaughter them, just as Nat Turner's band had done in 1831. This fear spread well beyond Jefferson County. "There is considerable excitement here in reference to this insurrection," a resident of distant Augusta County, Virginia, wrote on November 14. "Many persons are selling, and sending their negros to the South."

Whites also became consumed, as they had after Turner's insurrection, by the image of northern infiltrators conspiring with blacks behind every barn and haystack. "They are panic stricken & fear their own shadows," James Hooff, the Jefferson County farmer, wrote of his neighbors. Even the veteran officer and West Pointer in command of the troops around Charlestown, Colonel J. Lucius Davis, succumbed to the panic. "There is a guerrilla war here; the property of five of the best citizens has been burnt," he telegraphed Governor Wise, asking for immediate reinforcements.

The fires also coincided with fresh warnings about plots to rescue the jailed insurgents. These had been pouring in since the moment of Brown's capture, along with scores of threatening letters directed at the Virginia executive. "Dishonorable Gov Wise," began a letter from a group calling itself Black Band of New York, "death to you if John Brown not pardoned." For added effect, the letter bore a skull and crossbones. Other letters threatened the South in general. "So sure as you hurt One hair of his head," an anonymous New Yorker wrote of Brown, "mark my word the following day you will see every City—Town and Village South of Mason & Dixon's line in Flames."

Most of these letters were hoaxes, often blatant ones. One, from Illinois, warned that a party of young women was on the way to Charlestown wearing "petticoats filled with powder, having slow matches attached." Others, sent to the Charlestown jail, included bribes for the sheriff, or coded rescue plans (one of them blotted with blood). These missives were handed over to the prosecutor, Andrew Hunter, who collated all the suspicious correspondence relating to Brown and his men. He also made notations on the letters such as "Evidently insane," "Contemptible Nonsense," "Anonymous Rescue, rather bold, consider," or "Deciphered. Significant."

As spurious as most of this correspondence was, it made a strong impression on Governor Wise, a man inclined from the start to see a vast northern conspiracy at work in Harpers Ferry. When a Virginia reverend and former classmate of Wise's urged him to spare Brown the gallows on grounds of insanity, the governor replied that the entire North seemed unhinged. "It is alarming not to my fears of peace, but to my patriotism, to read the bushels of letters from *like* maniacs that keep pouring in to me, as if from a full fountain of Bedlam," he wrote. "You people have no idea of the extent of this plot."

Wise also sent detectives to track down the escaped insurgents and gather intelligence on plots to free Brown. These and other sources generated ever graver alarms. One rumor told of up to a thousand armed men approaching from Ohio, led—improbably—by John Brown, Jr. By the time Colonel Davis pleaded for aid to combat the guerrillas he believed were lighting fires near Charlestown, Wise was only too ready to oblige. He quickly boarded a train himself, arriving in Charlestown on November 20 with four hundred soldiers. Another hundred and fifty men with cannon came the next day.

These reinforcements brought the force in and around Charlestown to about a thousand, straining the capacity of citizens to board and supply them. Soldiers made barracks of the courthouse, schools, churches, even graveyards. "Everything in the shape of business is suspended, and the inhabitants seem to do nothing but make efforts to provide for the military," the *Baltimore American* reported.

The patrols that fanned out across the countryside failed to turn up any guerrillas. Though a few slaves were arrested on suspicion of arson, none appear to have been charged. The true culprit was probably the strong winds and "too dry" weather that the farmer James Hooff noted in his daily diary that fall. Also, despite constant alarms—including reports "that there are rockets firing from all the mountains"—the rumored legions of Brown rescuers never appeared.

This left most soldiers in Charlestown with little to do, apart from frequent dress parades. Press reports described the troops passing the time by playing a game of chase called Fox and Hounds, posing for portraits at a "daguerreotype wagon," holding cotillions in their barracks, and rehearsing "tragedy from ancient and modern dramatists."

The Richmond Grays in Charlestown, 1859

One of these antic militiamen was a noted young actor named John Wilkes Booth. He had been in Richmond preparing for a play called *The Filibuster* when he noticed troops readying to board a train for Charlestown. Borrowing portions of two men's uniforms, Booth decided to play soldier and tag along. "He was a remarkably handsome man, with a winning personality and would regale us around the camp fire with recitations from Shakespeare," wrote a member of Booth's adopted unit, the Richmond Grays.

In later years, Booth would theatrically inflate the extent of his service in Jefferson County. He would also invoke John Brown as he devised his own daring plan to take violent action against a government he despised.

ALTHOUGH GOVERNOR WISE HAD clearly called out many more troops than needed, it turned out that his informants weren't entirely delusional in warning of a rescue attempt. Higginson and a few other diehards had dreamed of freeing Brown almost from the moment of his capture. One of the northern lawyers who arrived during the trial, George Hoyt, had actually gone to Virginia as a spy in an effort to gather information for a possible jailbreak. He made a detailed sketch of the prison, but a few days after his arrival he reported to a co-conspirator that Brown "positively refused his consent to any such plan," which in any event was hopeless due to the tight security. "*There is no chance* of his ultimate rescue," Hoyt wrote on October 30.

This failed to deter some would-be rescuers. One alleged plot involved a Kansas woman who would visit Brown's cell with a rescue plan hidden inside a wax ball in her mouth, which she would then transfer to the prisoner's mouth while kissing him. Another scheme called for an execution-day assault by revolutionary German émigrés, wielding "Orsini bombs"—spiked projectiles named for an Italian who had hurled them at Napoleon III in a failed assassination attempt the year before. There was also a plan to kidnap Governor Wise, bundle him aboard a boat in Richmond, and hold him hostage in exchange for Brown. These latter two plots actually reached the recruitment stage, but both were as expensive as they were outlandish. They were abandoned when sufficient money and men failed to materialize.

Legal attempts to save Brown from the gallows also foundered. Defense lawyers petitioned Virginia's Supreme Court to reconsider the verdict due to defects in the indictment; they also sought clemency on the basis of Brown's alleged insanity, supported by the affidavits from Ohioans who knew him and his family. This had a momentary effect on Governor Wise, who wrote a letter asking the head of Virginia's lunatic asylum to evaluate Brown. "If the prisoner is insane," Wise wrote, "he ought to be cured." But Wise immediately countermanded his own request; the letter was never sent.

Wise could still seek approval from the state legislature to commute Brown's death sentence. He was strongly urged to do so, and not only by the prisoner's supporters. "To hang a fanatic is to make a martyr of him and fledge another brood of the same sort," opined the pro-southern *Journal of Commerce,* in New York. Former president John Tyler, of Virginia, agreed. "Brown deserves to die a thousand deaths upon the Rack to end in fire and termination in Hell," he wrote Wise, but from "a point of political policy as cold as marble," hanging him would only aid the abolitionist cause. If Wise commuted the death sentence to life in prison, "the magnanimity of Virginia will be commended, and the wisdom of her Governor extolled, the enemy disarmed and the triumph of the Democracy secured."

Wise wrote long and considered replies to these appeals, including one by Lydia Maria Child, a prominent women's rights activist and self-described "uncompromising abolitionist." Their initially civil letters turned into a barbed exchange that was published in the *New York Tribune.* This in turn drew the ire of the wife of Virginia senator James Mason, who rebuked Child for supporting "the hoary-headed murderer of Harper's Ferry," whose success would "condemn women of your race" to "see their husbands and fathers murdered, their children butchered, the ground strewed with the brains of their babies." Child's correspondence with the Virginians was published as a tract by the American Antislavery Society and quickly sold 300,000 copies.

This and other exchanges only hardened Wise's conviction that Brown's northern sympathizers were culpable in the attack—if not literally, then in spirit. "I will not reprieve or pardon one man now after the letters I have rec'd from the North," Wise wrote to Andrew Hunter on November 6. He expressed a similar view to a Pennsylvanian who shared a train ride with him and was struck by the Virginian's fixation on northern opinion. "Gov. Wise told me there was one condition on which he would surrender Gen. Brown—which was that I should deliver up to him General Sympathy for execution in his stead. The Governor and the citizens are evidently more afraid of the latter than of the former."

Wise dwelled on northern sympathies again in an address to the Virginia Assembly. "Shall John Brown be pardoned, lest he might be canonized by execution of felony for confessed murder, robbery and treason in inciting servile insurrection in Virginia? Why a martyr? Because thousands applaud his acts and opinions, and glorify his crimes?" To Wise, the course was clear. "Sympathy was in insurrection, and had to be subdued more sternly than was John Brown."

The only possible brake on Wise's determination to hang Brown was the Supreme Court of Virginia, but on November 19 it unanimously rejected the appeal by Brown's lawyers. Wise and his troops reached Charlestown the next day, and on the twenty-first he visited Brown and the other prisoners. "Governor Wise left them," the *Baltimore American* reported, "with an injunction that they prepare for their doom, as under no circumstances whatever would the arm of the Executive be interposed in their behalf."

The *American* also reported that "Brown was still as determined as ever, justifying his course" at Harpers Ferry to the governor and "perfectly resigned to his fate." He had, after all, never asked for clemency, had rejected an insanity defense, and had discouraged rescue attempts. Even so, the Supreme Court decision, and Wise's visit, cleared away any remaining doubt that Brown's sentence would be carried out eleven days hence, on December 2.

AS HIS APPOINTMENT DATE with the gallows neared, the prisoner picked up the pace of his letter writing and moved to final matters.

"I have now been confined over a month, with a good opportunity to look the whole thing as 'fair in the face' as I am capable of doing; and I now feel it most grateful that I am counted in the least possible degree worthy to suffer for the truth," Brown wrote his children in North Elba the day after Wise's visit. "I want you all to 'be of good cheer.' This life is intended as a season of training, chastisement, temptation, affliction, and trial."

Despite his impending execution, Brown's health and mood improved. He found himself "able to sit up to read; & write pretty much all day: as well as part of the Night," he wrote his wife on November 26. He also hosted a plethora of new visitors, many of them soldiers posted to Charlestown who were curious to see the archvillain they'd come to guard. These callers included men who had fought against him at Harpers Ferry and even a few foes from Kansas. Brown spoke to them frankly about the evils of slavery, and relished playing the role of Christian teacher. As he wrote an admirer on the twenty-fourth: "I have many very interesting visits from pro-slavery persons almost daily, & I endeavor to improve them <u>faithfully, plainly, and kindly</u>. I do not think I ever enjoyed life better than since my confinement here."

The only company Brown could not abide was that of southern clergymen. One who tried to speak with him wrote in a letter: "He said that he would not receive the services of any minister of religion, for he believed that they, as apologists of slavery, had violated the laws of nature and of God, and that they ought first to sanctify themselves by becoming abolitionists, and then they might be worthy to minister unto him." Brown likewise told visiting Methodist ministers that "they had better pray for themselves."

He was more receptive to journalists, answering their questions on a range of topics. Asked by the *Baltimore American* for his views on "amalgamation," or interracial marriage, "he responded, that although he was opposed to it, yet he would much prefer a son or a daughter of his to marry an industrious and honest negro than an indolent and dishonest white man." Brown also gave written answers to questions posed by the *Independent Democrat,* one of the hostile local papers. Asked about his opinion of the justice meted out to him, Brown replied: "I feel no shame on account of my doom." Yet as a Calvinist, he could never be sure that he was among God's Elect.

Question: To what political party do you belong?
Answer: To God's party. (I think)

Brown also spoke of his spiritual doubts in a letter to Mary a week before his scheduled execution. "Life is made up of a series of changes: & let us try to meet them in the best maner possible," he wrote. "The near aproach of my great change is not the occasion of any particular dread. I trust that God who has sustained me so long; will not forsake me when I most feel my need of <u>Fatherly aid: & support</u>. Should he hide his face; my spirit will droop, & die: <u>but not otherwise</u>: be assured. My only anxiety is to be properly assured of my fitness for the company of those who are 'washed from <u>all filthiness</u>.'"

But his mind was not only on God. He ended the letter by telling Mary:

> If you <u>now feel</u> that you are <u>equal</u> to the undertaking do <u>exactly as</u> you
> FEEL <u>disposed to do</u> about coming to see me before I suffer. I <u>am</u>
> <u>entirely willing</u>.

> Your affectionate Husband

> John Brown.

CHAPTER 12

So Let It Be Done!

During his weeks in confinement, Brown was often asked about the failure of his attack on Harpers Ferry. What had gone wrong? In reply, Brown took full responsibility and faulted his own judgment. He had held tightly to the engine house instead of the Potomac bridge, and he had mistakenly believed his hostages would shield him from attack. But he repeatedly blamed his compassionate nature as well; as one reporter wrote after interviewing Brown, "It was a feeling of humanity that betrayed him." He had let the train full of frightened passengers go, and had been delayed in Harpers Ferry out of concern for the welfare of his prisoners.

However, Brown had come to terms with the failure of his intended mission. "I have been a good deal disappointed as it regards myself in not keeping up to my own plans; but I feel reconciled to that even; for Gods plan, was Infinitely better; no doubt; or I should have kept to my own," he wrote the Reverend H. L. Vaill, who had tutored him as a teenager. "Had Samson kept to his determination of not telling Delilah wherein his great strength lay; he would probably have never overturned the house."

The Samson reference was telling, as was another observation he made in his letter to Vaill. "I cannot believe that any thing I have done suffered or may yet suffer will be lost; to the cause of God or of humanity: & before I began my work at Harpers Ferry; I felt assured that in the worst event; it would certainly PAY."

This was a rare acknowledgment by Brown that he had ever harbored doubt about the prospects for his attack. It also gave substance to the suspicion of some observers that Brown had launched his strike knowing it was doomed. As William Lloyd Garrison wrote a friend on the day after Brown's conviction: "His raid into Virginia looks utterly lacking in common sense—a desperate self-sacrifice for the purpose of giving an earthquake shock to the slave system, and thus hastening the day for a universal catastrophe."

A first cousin of Brown's also questioned why his kinsman had gone "wading in blood" to inevitable defeat. "What you intended was an impossibility," the Reverend Heman Humphrey wrote him in prison. No one in his "right mind" would "have plunged headlong, as you did, into the lion's den, where you were certain to be devoured."

In reply, Brown assured Humphrey that he wasn't insane, and again made reference to Samson, referring to him as the "poor erring servant" of whom it was said, "He shall begin to deliver Israel out of the hands of the Philistines." As told in the Book of Judges, Samson, shorn of his strength by Delilah, was taken captive by the idolatrous Philistines, who gouged out his eyes and brought the shackled Israelite forth to entertain thousands of men and women at their temple in Gaza. Samson then asked God to "strengthen me just once more" before grasping the pillars of the temple and pulling it down on himself and all those gathered round. "Thus he killed many more as he died than while he lived."

Brown echoed this line in writing about Samson to Reverend Humphrey. "For many years I have felt a strong impression that God had given me powers and faculties, unworthy as I was, that he intended to use for a similar purpose. This most unmerited honor He has seen fit to bestow; and whether, like the same poor frail man to whom I allude, my death may be of vastly more value than my life is, I think quite beyond human foresight."

Northern admirers might cast Brown as a Christ figure, and he was willing to play that part. But the role he wrote for himself at the end was that of God's avenger, wounded and in bonds, triumphantly crying at the last, "Let me die with the Philistines!"

No single passage of Scripture defined Brown; in the course of his life, he took inspiration from a multitude of biblical figures. Nor is it possible to pinpoint when he first saw shades of Samson's story in his own. But he referred to Samson's "victory" in his writing well before Harpers Ferry, and his prison letters suggested he had mulled the parallels between the biblical hero and himself for many years.

Brown's identification with Samson also illuminated many aspects of his Virginia mission that otherwise defied explanation. The first mystery concerned his attack plan. What exactly was it? Brown's own version kept shifting. In court, he said he planned to run slaves north to freedom, as he'd done in Missouri. He later retracted this, saying he had hoped to arm slaves "without any bloodshed" so they could defend themselves in the South. At other times, he spoke of a mountain-based guerrilla campaign that would oppose U.S. troops if necessary and carve out a provisional state, ultimately toppling the government.

His men provided a more consistent picture of what *they* thought Brown intended, at least in the campaign's first stage. In their view, Brown planned to seize the armory, carry off its weapons, and quickly move back into the mountains with liberated slaves and any others who joined them. Some of Brown's men were also under the impression that similar strikes were to be made elsewhere in the South, by allied parties.

The detailed maps and other documents found at the Kennedy farm further suggested that Brown had well-laid plans for an extended campaign across the South. And his confidants described military preparations he had made over many years, including close study of historical precedents and sketches of mountain forts he intended to build.

But when Brown finally launched his strike, he gave little sign of pursuing any of his purported plans. Where was the mountain base he spoke of establishing, or the log redoubts he'd diagrammed for Frederick Douglass, Franklin Sanborn, and his own children? The Maryland schoolhouse and the Kennedy farm were meager strongholds, particularly if Brown envisioned large numbers of men following him back into the hills. With winter approaching, how would he feed and shelter those who flocked to his mountain refuge? For that matter, why did Brown fail to take even a modest supply of food for the small force he led across the Potomac?

Brown's behavior in Harpers Ferry didn't accord with his alleged plans, either. He said he had chosen to target the town because of its vast supply of arms. If so, why did he leave the town's hundred thousand guns untouched during the time he controlled the armory, arsenal, and rifle works? How did he plan to transport these weapons? And why was he bringing his own guns forward to the schoolhouse, when Harpers Ferry held an abundant store?

Brown's handling of civilians was also puzzling. He took white men hostage not only as a shield, but also to trade for able-bodied blacks. That, at least, is what he told his prisoners and, later, reporters. He ultimately collected about forty hostages, more than he could easily handle, and they gave him an ample pool from which to barter for black men. Yet Brown took no steps to trade any of his prisoners—not a single one.

Nor did he alert blacks to his intentions, either before or during the attack. He specifically cautioned Cook against doing so, and once the mission was under way, very few blacks apart from the slaves taken with Lewis Washington and John Allstadt had any way of knowing who the insurgents were or why they'd come. The great majority of slaves in Jefferson County lived on farms at some distance from Harpers Ferry. How were they to learn of Brown's crusade so they could join it?

Even more mysterious, and ultimately disastrous, was Brown's failure to budge from his position at Harpers Ferry. His supposed plan centered on mobility and surprise: a lightning strike on the armory, the swift liberation of plantation slaves, a move into the hills, and rolling attacks along the chain of mountains reaching into the South. But as soon as Brown took Harpers Ferry, he became completely immobile, barely moving for thirty hours after he breached the armory gate. He failed to properly secure the Potomac bridge, which was crucial to his maneuverability, and he concentrated most of his tiny force in a fortified but exposed position at the armory. The five men he posted at the rifle works were likewise stationary. Having established these vulnerable beachheads, as well as a smaller one at the arsenal, Brown proceeded to linger, for no discernible reason, until he was surrounded and massively outgunned.

Brown never gave satisfactory explanations for any of this behavior.

The claim that he had deviated from his plans because compassion compelled him to care for rail passengers and prisoners made little sense. He knew that trains stopped in town at night, and he had always intended to take hostages. Did he have no advance plan for dealing with these challenges? And if the welfare of civilians was his greatest concern, why did he refuse to surrender, or at least to release his prisoners, once it became apparent that his situation was utterly hopeless? Instead, despite ample warning and obvious preparations for an attack by troops outside, Brown chose to make a last stand in the engine house, endangering the hostages and his remaining accomplices, including his badly wounded son and two or three others who told him they wanted to lay down their arms.

Brown's surviving men couldn't explain his actions, either. Some of them said that their commander anticipated thousands of reinforcements. But no trace of this mysterious legion was ever found. "Captain Brown was all activity, though I could not help thinking at times he appeared somewhat puzzled," wrote Osborne Anderson, who got away.

Charles Tidd, another escapee, was less charitable. He felt Brown had attacked with too few men, failed to deliver on his promise to burn bridges, and then resisted the pleas of his men to withdraw. At one point during the battle, while moving arms into position in Maryland, Tidd went down to the Potomac bridge. "Some of the boys begged of me to go and try to persuade him that it was best to leave there, but I could not make him think so," he said. Kagi was likewise rebuffed. Of the sixteen men posted with Brown on the Virginia side of the Potomac that day, all but Osborne Anderson would be killed, or captured and sentenced to hang.

Four months later, having made his way to New England, Tidd told Annie Brown: "I sometimes feel as if the 'old man' murdered the boys, after all that was said against going to Harper's Ferry, and the opposition of the whole company, to think that he should have stayed there so long, until they were all taken or slaughtered." He also told Higginson that Annie's slain brothers, Watson and Oliver, had opposed their father's plan "most of all."

LONG AFTER THE INSURRECTION, another sibling, Salmon Brown, claimed to have warned his brothers about the risk of following their father into Harpers Ferry. "I said to the boys before they left: 'You know father. You know he will *dally* till he is trapped.'" Salmon blamed this vacillation on his father's chronic "horror of departing from the *order* that he fixed in his own mind. I felt that at Harper's Ferry this very thing would be likely to trap him. He would insist on getting everything arranged just to suit him before he would consent to make a move."

Salmon had fought with his father in Kansas and was regarded by one of his sisters as the most levelheaded of the Brown clan. His version of the Harpers Ferry debacle sounded plausible, particularly given his father's demonstrated inflexibility earlier in his career. But Salmon offered his analysis fifty years after Harpers Ferry, while explaining to a researcher why he'd stayed home when his father and brothers went ahead to Virginia.

More telling, perhaps, was another comment Salmon made in the same interview: "Father's idea in his Harper's Ferry movement, was to agitate the slavery question. Not to create an insurrection. The intention of the pikes was to strike terror—to make agitation." This disturbance, Salmon said, would spark the great conflict Brown believed was necessary to end slavery. "He wanted to bring on the war. I have heard him talk of it many times."

Though Salmon made this statement with considerable hindsight, it accorded with the testimony of many others who were close to Brown and knew of his plan. Richard Hinton, a Kansas ally who learned of the Virginia plot in the summer of 1858, wrote that the attack was intended to "strike terror into the heart of the slave States by the amount of the organization it would exhibit, and the strength it gathered." The Provisional Constitution, Hinton said, was not just a governing document. It was a scare tactic, "to alarm the Oligarchy by discipline and the show of organization."

That same summer, in 1858, Brown stayed at the home of a Kansas aid official, William Arny, who was later called to testify before the U.S. Senate. He said Brown derided eastern abolitionists as do-nothings and considered Republicans "of no account, for they were opposed to carrying the war into Africa; they were opposed to meddling with slavery in the States where it existed." About the same time, Brown told William Phillips, the Kansas correspondent of the *New York Tribune*, that Southerners and their allies in Washington would never "relinquish the machinery of this government into the hands of opponents of slavery." Brown believed the Slave Power was already preparing for armed separation. "We have reached a point where nothing but war can settle the question," Phillips quoted him as saying.

Brown may have genuinely believed that with twenty-one men and God as his defender, he could seize Harpers Ferry, carry off its arms, attract and sustain a large guerrilla army, and ultimately bring down the institution of slavery. But the manifest implausibility of this scheme, and Brown's failure to take the steps necessary to fulfill it, strongly suggest that he had a second plan.

"I expect to effect a mighty conquest, even though it be like the last victory of Samson," Brown had written Franklin Sanborn in 1858, eighteen months before Harpers Ferry. Even "in the worst event," he wrote from prison, he knew the attack "would certainly PAY." Whether or not his military plan succeeded, Brown believed his strike would shock the nation and shake down the pillars of slavery. And he was fully prepared to perish amid the rubble of a sinful society he had so long sought to destroy.

Brown's readiness to die at Harpers Ferry was also evident in the way he staged the mission. He quickly took possession of George Washington's sword and freed slaves belonging to the Founding Father's great-grandnephew. Lest anyone miss this symbolism, Brown left an ersatz suicide note, in the form of his "Declaration of Liberty by the Representatives of the Slave Population of the United States of America." The document not only quoted liberally from the 1776 model and cited the ways in which the promise of liberty had been betrayed, it promised a fight to the death and ended on an apocalyptic note: "Nature is mourning for its murdered, and Afflicted Children. Hung be the Heavens in Scarlet."

The declaration, rolled into a scroll, was part of the vast cache that troops found at the Kennedy farm. In the four years preceding his attack, Brown had obsessively covered his tracks, using aliases and coded language, hiding his whereabouts, and constantly lecturing his accomplices on the need for absolute loyalty and secrecy. Yet he set off for Harpers Ferry on the night of October 16 leaving behind trunks and carpetbags filled with incriminating documents. He even carried some on his person.

In the event of his death at Harpers Ferry, Brown wanted to ensure that the world knew his full design. When he was miraculously spared, Brown implicated himself as he lay bleeding on the floor of the paymaster's office. He spoke freely to his interrogators, even asking that the incendiary constitution he carried with him be read aloud. "It struck me at the time as very singular that he should so freely enter into his plans immediately," wrote Andrew Hunter, who was present for the questioning. "He seemed very fond of talking."

Though Brown refused to betray others, the paper trail he left at the Kennedy farm quickly did so, revealing a support network that included Gerrit Smith, his oldest benefactor. This careless exposure of his closest allies would seem out of character for Brown. But he gave a strong clue to his reasons for doing so in the advice he had offered years before to the League of Gileadites, the self-defense group he formed in 1851 to combat the Fugitive Slave Act.

"If you are assailed," Brown advised the Springfield blacks, "go into the houses of your most prominent and influential white friends with your wives, and that will effectually fasten upon them the suspicion of being connected with you, and will compel them to make a common cause with you, whether they would otherwise live up to their profession or not. This would leave them no choice in the matter."

By exposing his co-conspirators, Brown evidently hoped to pressure them to carry on the campaign should he die at Harpers Ferry. "Some would doubtless prove themselves true to their own choice; others would flinch," he had told the Gileadites. In the case of Gerrit Smith and others of the Secret Six, the initial response *was* to flinch. But in a broader sense, Brown was proved right. His actions forced a choice on antislavery Northerners: were they true to their convictions, or not? Though reluctant at first, much of the northern public ultimately came around to Brown and his cause.

One reason they did so was also alluded to in the abolitionist's advice to the Gileadites. "Nothing so charms the American people as personal bravery," he wrote in the 1851 document. "The trial for life of one bold and to some extent successful man, for defending his rights in good earnest, would arouse more sympathy throughout the nation than the accumulated wrongs and suffering of more than three millions of our submissive colored population."

EIGHT YEARS LATER, BROWN had followed his own advice almost to the letter. He demonstrated great bravery, earnestly defended his rights in court, and aroused tremendous sympathy. But he still faced the final sacrifice. "My present great anxiety is to get as near in readiness for a different field of action as I well <u>can</u>," he wrote a friend on November 28, four days before his execution.

The next day, he expressed his determination to die without clerical comfort. "I have asked to be spared from having any <u>mock</u>; <u>or hypocritical prayers made over me</u>, when I am publicly <u>murdered</u>," he wrote, "& that my only <u>religious attendants</u> be poor <u>little, dirty, ragged, bare headed, & barefooted Slave boys; & Girls</u>; led by some old <u>grey headed Slave Mother</u>."

Brown also readied himself for a final parting from his family. On November 30, he sat down to compose "what is probably the last letter I shall ever write to any of you." Most of the long letter consisted of religious and moral exhortation. "John Brown writes to his children to abhor with <u>undiing hatred</u>, also: that 'sum of all vilanies;' Slavery." He urged his "dear <u>shattered</u>: <u>& broken</u> family" to "cling to one another: "love <u>the whole remnant</u> of our once great family."

Brown, of course, was largely responsible for his clan's shattered state. He would soon add Mary to the lengthening list of widows in North Elba, and of the seven sons who had fought with him in Kansas and Virginia, three were now dead and two (Owen and John junior) were being hunted by authorities. Brown's guilt over having led, or misled, Oliver and Watson to their deaths at Harpers Ferry may have contributed to his trepidation over seeing Mary.

Understandably, she had expressed annoyance over being turned back in early November, a short way from Charlestown. "You have nursed and taken care of me a great deal; but I cannot even come and look at you," she wrote on November 13. Meanwhile, two other women had gone to "minister to your wants, which I am deprived of doing."

One of these women was the wife of a Boston judge who had gone with her husband to Charlestown during the trial and then briefly visited Brown in jail, where she mended his coat. The other was a New Jersey abolitionist, Rebecca Spring, who had impulsively headed to Charlestown with her son, bringing autumn leaves to brighten Brown's cell. "I do not want to do or say anything to disturb your peace of mind," Mary wrote her husband, "but O, I would serve you gladly if I could."

Rather than return all the way to North Elba, Mary had remained within close reach, mostly staying with abolitionist supporters in Philadelphia. A reporter who interviewed her that November described her as "tall, large, and muscular, giving the impression at first sight of a frame capable of great strength and long endurance." Though "quiet and retiring," she made an acute observation when asked about her husband's sanity. "He is always cool, deliberate, and never over hasty; but he has always considered that his first perceptions of duty, and his first impulses to action, were the best and safest to be followed. He has almost always acted upon his first suggestions."

While in Philadelphia, Mary enlisted the aid of an abolitionist minister to compose a letter to Governor Wise. "I do not ask for his life, dear as it is to us, and right worthy and honorable as I know him to be," she wrote the Virginia executive. "I ask for myself & my children that, when all shall be over, the mortal remains of my husband & his sons may be delivered to me for decent & tender interment among their kindred."

There was no assurance that this modest request would be granted. Like seven other insurgents killed at Harpers Ferry, Oliver had been dumped in an unmarked grave, at an undisclosed location; Watson's body had been carried off by medical students. Wise was strongly urged to dispose of their father in similar fashion. Medical students at the University of Virginia requested Brown's body for dissection, as did a Mississippi physician, who planned to display the skeleton: "I will rattle it through the New England States until I frighten every Scoundrel Abolitionist out of the country."

Even more ghoulish was the request of an anatomy professor at the Medical School of Virginia, in Richmond, who wrote the day after Brown's conviction: "We desire if Brown and his coadjutors are executed to add their heads to the collection in our museum. If the transference of the bodies will not exceed a cost of five dollars each we should also be glad to have them." Wise took note of this request, writing to Andrew Hunter the next day: "The Court may order the bodies to be given over to surgeons."

But Wise was evidently moved by Mary Brown's appeal, for he discarded any further consideration of handing her husband's body over for dissection or display. "Madam," he wrote her with characteristic chivalry, "Sympathizing as I do with your affliction, you shall have the exertion of my authority and personal influence to assist you in gathering up the bones of your sons and your husband."

Wise added that he took "not the slightest pleasure in the execution of any whom the laws condemn." He signed himself, "With tenderness and truth," and enclosed a copy of the order he'd written the same day to the commanding officer in Charlestown, instructing him to protect Brown's body "from all mutilation," place it "in a plain, decent coffin," and send it to Harpers Ferry for collection by Mary Brown.

GOVERNOR WISE WROTE THIS letter in Richmond on November 26, the same day Brown wrote Mary from Charlestown, saying that he was "entirely willing" to have her visit before his hanging. Upon receiving these encouraging dispatches, Mary immediately set off by train, with three Philadelphians, arriving in Harpers Ferry late on November 30, less than forty-eight hours before her husband's execution.

She was lucky to have gotten that far. In a final spasm of hypervigilance, Wise had cordoned off Jefferson County to guard against a last-minute rescue attempt. The authorities also feared the execution would become a public circus, undignified and hard to control. "I want you to take measures at once, to break up the exhibition and sale to passengers on our trains, at Harper's Ferry, of the pikes, or other weapons," W. P. Smith of the B & O wired a railroad agent. "I think this pike trade only adds to the excitement."

The railroad had to contend not only with souvenir sellers but also with "excursionists" who wanted to come "see Brown hung." One Boston tour operator requested reduced rates for a large party of Northerners and promised they would behave "with propriety." But he and others were turned away. "Under cover of such a crowd of pretended spectators, hundreds of armed assassins, coming with a view of attempting a rescue, could introduce themselves," Andrew Hunter warned the railroad, asking that no group tickets be sold.

On November 28, Virginia authorities went much further. Wise announced that the state would take control of the railroad line through Charlestown, "for the use and occupation of Virginia troops alone." He posted detectives at depots and on trains at other points, to guard against invasion. At Wise's instruction, military and civil authorities also issued a proclamation stating: "STRANGERS found within the County of Jefferson, and Counties adjacent, having no known and proper business here, and who cannot give a satisfactory account of themselves, will be at once arrested."

Wise, in effect, had declared martial law across a large swath of Virginia. Yet even this wasn't enough. Citing "information from various quarters" of plans to invade Virginia and rescue Brown, he wrote President Buchanan asking him to "take steps to preserve peace between the states." He sent copies of this dispatch to the governors of Maryland, Pennsylvania, and Ohio, adding: "Necessity may compel us to pursue invaders of our jurisdiction into yours."

Even the pliant Buchanan bucked at Wise's extraordinary request. The governor's alarm was "almost incredible," the president wrote in reply, and he was "at a loss to discover any provision in the constitution or laws of the United States" authorizing him to guard one state from another. As a token gesture, Buchanan agreed to send federal artillery to protect the U.S. arsenal at Harpers Ferry, but otherwise declared the security in place "sufficient for any emergency."

Undeterred, Wise secured the state borders on his own, ordering men posted "on the line of frontier" along the Potomac and Ohio Rivers. He also called out still more militia, bringing the total in Charlestown to about sixteen hundred men, equal to the civilian population. "The town looks to-day as if the times were revolutionary," a *New York Herald* correspondent reported on November 29. "Drums beating, music playing, flags waving, sentinels pacing." Even the new commander in charge of the area thought the force excessive. "There is no absolute need for half we have," he wired the governor.

The newly arrived troops included cadets from the Virginia Military Institute, accompanied by a professor, Major Thomas J. Jackson, who would soon earn the nickname Stonewall. His future Confederate com-

SO LET IT BE DONE!   245

mander, Robert E. Lee, also returned to the scene, in charge of the artillery sent by Buchanan. As before, Lee regarded fears of *the enemy* to be
greatly overblown, and he showed little enthusiasm at the prospect of
serving again in Harpers Ferry.

On the morning of December 1, Lee was introduced to Mary Brown,
who was seeking clearance to visit her husband in jail. Lee referred her to
the general in overall command of Virginia's troops. "It is a matter over
which I have no control & wish to take none," Lee explained in a letter to
his wife later that day.

The commander, General William Taliaferro, authorized Mary to
proceed to Charlestown, but only under the terms laid out by Governor
Wise. She must go alone, must be subject to the usual jail security, must
see Brown and no other prisoner, and must return promptly that evening
to Harpers Ferry, to await delivery of her husband's body.

RIDING IN A CARRIAGE and escorted by a number of cavalrymen,
Mary set off for Charlestown early on the afternoon of December 1. She
was greeted at the jail by a throng of curious onlookers and hundreds
of soldiers, with bayonets bristling and cannon at the ready. "There
seemed to be an evident intention to appall the poor woman with the
military majesty of the Commonwealth of Virginia," wrote the *Baltimore
American*.

Once inside the prison, Mary endured fifteen minutes of "stiff platitudes" from officials, including General Taliaferro, who "assured her that
if she should ever be disposed to visit Virginia again, he would cordially
invite her to Charlestown, where she would receive true Southern hospi-
tality." Finally, at four o'clock, after being searched by the jailer's wife,
Mary was taken to see her husband. As required, the jailer, John Avis,
was present.

"For some minutes they stood speechless—Mrs. Brown resting her head
upon her husband's breast, and clasping his neck with her arms," wrote a
correspondent who spoke to Avis. According to another report, "they were
so much affected that they were absolutely unable to utter a syllable." The
couple had last seen each other six months before, and they'd spent very

little time together in the four years since Brown's departure for Kansas in 1855.

"Wife, I am glad to see you," Brown said, breaking the silence. He had seemed emotional at first, but "was soon calm and collected." The couple spoke of their children, dead and alive, and moved quickly to practical matters. Brown suggested she gather up his body with that of their sons and also their neighbors, the Thompsons, burn off the flesh, and box the bones for transport to North Elba. Mary wasn't happy with this grim proposal and doubted she could get permission. "For my sake, think no more of such an idea," she said. Brown consented. He had only suggested the measure because he thought it would save money and guard against the odor of his decomposing corpse.

Brown told Mary he hoped she would remain in North Elba and spoke of the stone at the farm he wanted inscribed in his memory. He also discussed the disposition of his meager assets, which he had laid out in a will written earlier that day. He left a compass and other surveying tools to John junior, a silver watch to Jason, an opera glass and rifle to Owen (along with fifty dollars, "in consideration of his terible sufferings in Kansas: & his cripled condition from his childhood"), and his old family Bible to his eldest daughter, Ruth. His sons and other daughters were to receive "as good a coppy of the Bible as can be purchased at some Book store in New York or Boston at a cost of Five Dollars each." Brown also designated small sums from his father's estate to pay off debts still outstanding in Connecticut and Ohio.

Avis invited the Browns to supper with him and his family, and not long after dining on "simple jail fare," the couple was told that it was time for Mary to go. Brown, it was later reported, lost his composure for a moment and "showed a good deal of temper," as he wanted her to remain. But they had already been together four hours, longer than initially permitted, and the orders were for Mary to return to Harpers Ferry that night.

Avis gave them privacy at the end, or chose not to disclose much about their parting, beyond saying that Brown told his wife "God bless you," and that Mary replied, "Good bye, may Heaven have mercy on you." She then rode back to Harpers Ferry to wait at the Wager House, the hotel that had figured so prominently in the fight that ravaged her family.

AFTER HIS WIFE'S DEPARTURE, Brown wrote a final note to "MY DEAR WIFE," saying he wished to "bid you another Farewell: 'be of good cheer' and God Allmighty bless, save, comfort, guide, & keep; you, to 'the end.' Your Affectionate Husband." He enclosed the plain inscription he wanted etched on the old family monument at North Elba: "John Brown born May 9 1800 was executed at Charlestown, Va., December 2d 1859."

He also wrote his brother Jeremiah, noting that he could "only say a few words to you for want of time." He had sent Jeremiah $15.50, he said, "to refund to you what you had advanced to my boys on my account." Brown's many debts were trailing him to the grave and beyond. Even his horse and cart from the Kennedy farm had been seized in lieu of payment for the breakfasts he had ordered from the Wager House during his attack. He closed his note to Jeremiah: "Am quite cheerful & composed. Yours Ever J.B."

That same evening, Brown received a letter from Lora Case, a childhood neighbor and long-ago Bible-class student of his in Hudson, Ohio. Case asked for "something from your hand to look upon," offered to educate one of Brown's girls, and closed, "May God Almighty strengthen you as you are about to be offered up." Brown replied to Case in his final letter, dated Dec. 2, the day of his execution.

"Your most kind & cheering letter," he wrote, "compels me to steal a moment from those allowe[d] me; in which to prepare for my last great change to send you a few words." Brown took time to discuss faith—"Pure & undefiled religion before God & the Father is as I understand it: an active (not a dormant) principle"—and said he had no more role in educating his children. "I leave that now entirely to their excellent Mother." Brown signed himself, "Your Friend."

Brown's hanging was scheduled for eleven A.M. That morning, he dictated a codicil to his will, leaving his family any property of his that might be recovered from Virginia authorities, apart from items he had given his keepers. These included his prison Bible, left to John Blessing, a local baker who had shown him great kindness and provided the prisoners with cakes and oysters. In the Bible, Brown had marked a number of passages that were particularly significant to him, most of them related to persecution. Typical was this, from Ecclesiastes: "So I returned, and considered all the oppressions that are done under the sun: and behold the tears of such as were oppressed, and they had no comforter; and on the side of their oppressors there was power; but they had no comforter."

Brown also dispensed a small gift and a few parting words to his fellow prisoners, whom he was allowed to visit in their cells. "As soon as Brown entered," wrote a local editor with access to the jail, "he was again General Brown, and the prisoners his humble and devoted followers." Stopping first at the cell occupied by Shields Green and John Copeland, Brown scolded them for "false statements" he felt they'd made following their capture, about having been deceived as to the nature of his attack. Brown told them plainly that they had joined in it "of their own accord." At the next cell, he gave a similar reprimand to Edwin Coppoc, and heatedly contradicted Coppoc's cellmate, John Cook, who had stated in his confession that Brown sent him ahead to Harpers Ferry to gather intelligence.

"You know I opposed it when first proposed," Brown said, denying that he had sanctioned this mission.

"Your memory is very different from mine," Cook replied.

"I am right sir," Brown insisted.

Having rebuked his soldiers, Brown shook their hands, exhorted them to "die like men," and gave each man a quarter dollar, "telling them it would be of no use to him as his time was drawing very short."

Brown's last goodbye was to Aaron Stevens, his cellmate and loyal lieutenant. As they warmly clasped hands, Stevens said, "I feel it in my soul Captain that you are going to a better world." Brown agreed, and then added: "Stand up like a man—no flinching now. Farewell." Along with a quarter dollar, he left the brave but tempestuous Stevens a note quoting Proverbs: "He that is slow to anger; is better than the mighty; and that ruleth his Spirit, than he, that taketh a city."

A LITTLE BEFORE ELEVEN o'clock, Brown's jailers wrapped a cord around him, pinioning his arms just above the elbows, and escorted him from the building. Waiting outside was the wagon of an undertaker and furniture maker who occupied a building just beside the prison. In the bed of the open wagon lay a black walnut coffin enclosed in a poplar box. This was to be Brown's seat for his tumbrel ride.

Though it was early December, the weather was much finer than it had been six weeks before, when Brown drove a different wagon from the Kennedy farm to Harpers Ferry, inaugurating the attack that now led him to the gallows. On that October night, it had been wet and raw; now it was a sunny, springlike day with "a warm and dreamy haze," one reporter wrote. Locals flung open their windows; "just like a May morning, in Virginia, honey-bees were flying about and birds singing everywhere," recalled the undertaker's assistant, who rode at the front of Brown's wagon. Drawn by two horses, it traveled slowly east along George Street, flanked by lines of riflemen.

Brown riding on his coffin to the gallows

Brown, seated in back on his casket, appeared as calm and determined during the brief wagon ride as he had been in prison. According
to one account, the undertaker commented that he seemed "a game man,"
to which Brown replied that he'd never known fear. As the wagon neared
the gallows, the prisoner took in the sweeping view of undulating farmland and gentle mountains. "This is a beautiful country," he said. "I never
had the pleasure of seeing it before."

The site chosen for Brown's execution was a forty-acre field of rye and
corn stubble at the edge of Charlestown. It was not only convenient to
the jail but also almost bare of trees or other landmarks, "so as to prevent
any one being able to recognize it thereafter," wrote Andrew Hunter, who
had helped select it. The authorities wanted to ensure that the site of
Brown's hanging wouldn't become hallowed ground. To that end, the
scaffold was erected on the morning of the execution and taken down
immediately after.

Enclosed by a rail, the field now resembled a military parade ground.
White signal flags marked the position of each unit, and the troops
formed two large squares around the scaffold, which was also guarded
by cannon. Soldiers had marched onto the field and taken their places at
nine A.M., while cavalry patrolled the perimeter and other men occupied
posts in and around Charlestown. The overall force numbered about fifteen hundred.

This extraordinary security was ostensibly intended to prevent a
rescue attempt. But it also created a military buffer between Brown and
any civilians who wanted to witness his execution and possibly hear a
reprise of his courtroom speech. Initially, even reporters were to be kept
at a considerable distance from the scaffold; only at the last minute did
they prevail on authorities to let them come closer. Apart from visiting
dignitaries and well-connected citizens permitted onto the field, the
public could only glimpse the proceedings from distant buildings or
other spots hundreds of yards away. "Why this jealous caution?" wondered a reporter for the *New York Tribune*, who speculated that "it is
feared this old man's sturdy truths and simple eloquence will stir a fever
in the blood of all who listen."

As the wagon drew up to the gallows, observers who had waited two
hours in the field saw a rather unprepossing figure. Wearing a broad-

brimmed black slouch hat, Brown was dressed in the same disheveled dark suit he had worn in court. This funereal attire contrasted with his odd footwear: white socks and the blood-red "carpet slippers" he'd worn in prison.

Despite Brown's worn clothes, there was nothing spent about the man himself. On recognizing the town's mayor and the prosecutor standing near the gallows, he briskly addressed them: "Gentlemen, good bye." Then he swiftly ascended the scaffold with "the same imperturbable, wooden composure which had distinguished him at every step of his progress," the *Evening Star* of Washington reported.

Once on the platform, Brown obligingly positioned himself beneath the hanging rope. Facing south and a little east, toward the Shenandoah River, he had a commanding view of the crowded field, the rolling farmland beyond, and the gentle arc of the Blue Ridge Mountains. Born in the hard, stony hills of northwestern Connecticut, he would cast his last gaze at the fertile valley of Virginia. And his final company on the gallows would be, not the black children and slave mother he'd hoped for, but the portly, top-hatted sheriff, William Campbell, and the jailer and slave dealer, John Avis. Brown raised his pinioned arms to shake their hands, and then the two men tied his ankles, pulled a white hood over his head, and adjusted the noose around his neck. Avis asked Brown to step forward, onto the trap door.

"You must lead me, I cannot see," he said, in what one reporter called "the same even tone as if asking for a chair." Brown was equally composed when asked if he wanted a handkerchief to drop, to signal that he was ready to die. "No," he replied, "but do not detain me any longer than is absolutely necessary." Having fully prepared for this last great change, Brown was, as always, impatient for action. His last words were spoken "quietly & civilly" and without "the slightest apparent emotion."

But Brown's extraordinary resolve was now tested a final time. As he stood awaiting the sudden drop to his death, there was a long delay as the troops that had escorted him from prison found their place on the field. For an excruciating ten or fifteen minutes, Brown—hooded, noosed, and perched precariously atop the trapdoor—stood "upright as a soldier in position, and motionless," wrote a colonel posted by the scaffold. "I was

Brown on the gallows with the sheriff and jailer

close to him, and watched him narrowly, to see if I could detect any signs of shrinking or trembling in his person, but there was none."

Then, finally, the military maneuvers ended and the commander on the field said to the sheriff, "All ready, Mr. Campbell." The sheriff didn't hear him; the order had to be repeated. At last the sheriff raised a hatchet and cut the rope holding the trapdoor in place. Brown plunged through the floor of the scaffold but fell only a few feet. The rope was short—too short, apparently, to break his neck.

"With the fall his arms below the elbow flew up, hands clenched, & his arms gradually fell by spasmodic motions," wrote Major Thomas Jack-

Sketch of the execution by eyewitness Alfred Berghaus

son. A reporter for the *New York Tribune* observed: "There was but one spasmodic effort of the hands to clutch at the neck, but for nearly five minutes the limbs jerked and quivered." Then Brown's body went slack, swaying in a circle, the skirt of his coat fluttering in the breeze. "This motion," the *Evening Star* reported, gave Brown "the appearance of a corn-field scarecrow," so gaunt that his "limbs bore apparently not an ounce of surplus flesh, and thus did not fill out his clothes."

Doctors approached the swaying body, holding it still while pressing their ears to Brown's chest to make sure he was dead. Several teams of physicians took turns at this. Brown dangled for thirty-five minutes before he was cut down and his limp body finally placed in the coffin.

THE LARGE AUDIENCE IN the field had remained solemn and quiet throughout. "Of Sympathy there was none—of triumph no word nor sign," wrote David Strother, the *Harper's Weekly* artist and correspondent.

"The fifteen hundred soldiers stood mute and motionless at their posts." The spectators were nonetheless struck by the courage Brown had shown in death. "He behaved with unflinching firmness," wrote Major Jackson, who would soon become known for standing like a stone wall in battle. "Awful was the thought that he might in a few minutes receive the sentence 'Depart ye wicked into everlasting fire.'"

Nearby stood John Wilkes Booth, the actor who had joined a Richmond troop headed to Charlestown. "I was proud of my little part in the transaction," he later wrote, and glad to see the "trator" hanged. But he also regarded the abolitionist as "a brave old man" whose bold act had changed history. "John Brown was a man inspired, the grandest character of this century!" Booth told his sister in 1864, while ranting about Abraham Lincoln.

Another rabid defender of the South also viewed Brown with a mix of

Edmund Ruffin

awe and contempt. Edmund Ruffin was Virginia's foremost fire-eater, in some ways a mirror image of Brown. Sixty-five years old, with penetrating eyes and long white hair, Ruffin was an agriculturalist who had become a radical agitator for southern rights.

Ruffin described Brown as a "robber & murderer & villain of unmitigated turpitude," but welcomed his attack on Harpers Ferry, which he hoped would "stir the sluggish blood of the South" to take up arms and form an independent country. Traveling to "the seat of war," as he called Charlestown, Ruffin preached secession on the streets and borrowed the overcoat and arms of a Virginia cadet so he could get close to the gallows.

Later that day, Ruffin wrote in his diary that Brown had ascended the scaffold "with readiness & seeming alacrity. His movements & manner gave no evidence of his being either terrified or concerned." Ruffin was particularly impressed that Brown maintained his statuelike calm despite the "cruel & most trying infliction" of the long delay while he stood with the halter around his neck. "The villain whose life has thus been forfeited, possessed but one virtue," Ruffin concluded. "This is physical or animal courage, or the most complete fearlessness of & insensibility to danger & death. In this quality he seems to me to have had few equals."

This was remarkable testimony, coming from a Virginian who would now devote his energies to whipping the South into a secessionist fever—while brandishing one of Brown's pikes with a label that read: "*Sample of the favors designed for us by our Northern Brethren.*" Sixteen months after Brown's hanging, Ruffin would don a uniform again, this time to join in the attack on Fort Sumter that inaugurated four years of bloody civil war.

BROWN FORETOLD THIS CARNAGE himself just before going to the gallows. Authorities had informed him a few days earlier that he wouldn't be allowed to give a speech from the scaffold or write a public message intended for publication. "The object of this prohibition," the *New York Herald* explained, "is to avoid any further parade being made of his so called martyrdom." The order was redundant in any event. The military cordon around the gallows ensured that no one would hear any final

> *Charlestown, Va, 2ᵈ December, 1859.*
> *I John Brown am now quite <u>certain</u> that the crimes of this <u>guilty,</u> <u>land: will</u> never be purged <u>away;</u> but with Blood: I had <u>as I now</u> <u>think:</u> <u>vainly</u> flattered myself that without <u>very</u> much bloodshed: it might be done*

Brown's last prophecy

remarks he attempted, apart from soldiers and a few privileged observers close to the scaffold.

But Brown found other means to make his last thoughts known. A jail guard, Hiram O'Bannon, had asked the famous prisoner for his autograph. Instead, as Brown exited the jail on the morning of his execution, he handed O'Bannon a scrap of paper bearing a few lines of his distinctive, oddly punctuated script. Also characteristic was the terse, emphatic message it conveyed.

"I John Brown am now quite <u>certain</u> that the crimes of this <u>guilty,</u> <u>land: will</u> never be purged <u>away</u>; but with Blood."

Brown had a rhetorical habit of going on a beat too long, diluting the power of his words and muddying their meaning. He did this in his final message, adding a second line that was much gentler and almost apologetic in tone. "I had <u>as I now think: vainly</u> flattered myself that without <u>very much</u> bloodshed; it might be done."

But this was an unconvincing coda to the apocalyptic prophecy that preceded it. Brown had often stated his belief in blood sacrifice. In 1855, not long before moving to Kansas and launching his crusade against slavery, he had written to his family: "Should God send famin, pestilence, & war; upon this guilty hypocritical nation to destroy it; we need not be surprised."

In the years after Brown's death, Franklin Sanborn would become the abolitionist's most ardent champion, for decades defending Brown against every accusation and sanitizing some of his words and deeds. But when Sanborn reproduced his hero's violent final message he did so without varnish. Instead, Sanborn noted the scripture it echoed—"Without the shedding of blood there is no remission of sins"—and declared this the essence of "Brown's old-fashioned theology."

During one of their earliest conversations, Brown had told the Concord teacher that he believed the Golden Rule and the Declaration of Liberty meant the same: we must love our neighbor as our equal. He then proclaimed to his acolyte that it "would be better for a whole generation to die a violent death" than for this sacred doctrine to go unfulfilled. "Such was the faith," Sanborn concluded, "in which he died."

CHAPTER 13

Dissevering the Ties
That Bind Us

As John Brown rode atop his coffin to the gallows on December 2, northern admirers composed verse in his praise. "O Patriot true! O Christian meek and brave!" Bronson Alcott wrote in a sonnet to mark the occasion. His daughter, Louisa May, also felt moved to poetry: "Living, he made life beautiful, / —Dying, made death divine."

Unaware of Brown's blood-soaked prophecy, the Alcotts and others continued to celebrate what they saw as his Christ-like sacrifice. Herman Melville was a notable exception. Unable to support his family after the commercial failure of *Moby-Dick* and other works, the embittered novelist wrote fourteen lines that spoke to the dark future Brown had foretold.

In Melville's haunted imagining, Brown swayed from the beam, casting a gaunt shadow on the Shenandoah, his face hidden by the hangman's shroud.

> *But the streaming beard is shown*
> *(Weird John Brown),*
> *The meteor of the war.*

Melville's eerie poem, titled "The Portent (1859)," wasn't published until after Appomattox. But it captured a premonition that many Americans felt on the day of Brown's hanging. "Even now as I write, they are leading old John Brown to execution in Virginia for attempting to rescue slaves!" Henry Wadsworth Longfellow wrote in his diary on December 2. "This is sowing the wind to reap the whirlwind, which will come soon."

His words were echoed that night by a black preacher in Pittsburgh, at one of many "Martyr's Day" services held by African Americans. "From the firmament of Providence today, a meteor has fallen. It has fallen upon the volcano of American sympathies," J. S. Martin said, "and it shall burst forth in one general conflagration of revolution that shall bring about universal freedom."

Longfellow and Martin were ardent abolitionists, unlike George Templeton Strong, a New York lawyer who thought Brown was "cracked" and "justly" hanged. Even so, Strong acknowledged in his diary on December 2 that Brown's "name may be a word of power for the next half-century. It was unwise to give fanaticism a martyr. Why could not Virginia have condescended to lock him up for life in a madhouse?"

In communities across the North, citizens solemnly observed Brown's hanging with tolling bells, hundred-gun salutes, prayer meetings, and grandiloquent oratory. In Ohio, Akron businesses shut and Clevelanders hung the streets of their city in crepe. In Hartford, a statue of Liberty atop the statehouse dome was draped in black. One young Connecticut woman made a pilgrimage to Torrington, to spend the hour of Brown's execution at his birthplace. She found the weathered saltbox inhabited by an Irish family who knew nothing of Brown, but they allowed her to wander the house and take the door latch to the room in which her hero was born.

In Boston, four thousand people packed the Tremont Temple to honor Brown. Among the eulogies they heard was one by William Lloyd Garrison that showed how much the ground had shifted, even beneath those who had long opposed violence. "I am a non-resistant," Garrison reminded his audience, "yet, as a peace man—an 'ultra' peace man—I am prepared to say, 'Success to every slave insurrection at the South, and in every slave country.'" He went on: "Give me, as a non-resistant, Bunker Hill, and Lexington, and Concord, rather than the cowardice and servility of a Southern slave plantation."

This outpouring of northern anger and veneration went on for days, swelled by reports of Brown's demeanor on the day of his execution, including a false item in the *New York Tribune*, which claimed that he had kissed a black baby held up to him by its mother as he left the jail-house. Even George Templeton Strong wrote admiringly of Brown's "simplicity and consistency, the absence of fuss, parade and bravado, the strength and clearness" he showed to the end. "Slavery has received no such blow in my time as his strangulation."

The slow transit of Brown's body home from Virginia afforded a further opportunity for northern adoration. The day after the execution, Mary Brown boarded a train in Harpers Ferry and escorted her husband's coffin to Philadelphia, where the crowd awaiting the funeral train was so large that the mayor feared a riot. He arranged to send an empty hearse through the city to decoy the throng of Brown's admirers, while a separate wagon quietly carried the coffin directly aboard a boat for New Jersey.

Upon reaching New York City late that night, Brown's body was taken to an undertaker at a coffin factory in the Bowery. This conveyance was meant to be secret, but word quickly spread and "our entire block was filled with anxious men to see the body of *John Brown*," wrote the wife of the undertaker's assistant. She added: "When he come he was black in the face for they *slung* him in the coffin with all his clothes on with his head under his shoulder and the rope he was hung with in the coffin."

Pieces of the rope, along with screws from the coffin, quickly became prized relics. One man made off with a lock of Brown's hair. The under-taker washed the body and laid it on ice, then put a cravat collar around Brown's injured neck and placed him in a new walnut coffin for the onward journey. Mary escorted it by train to Vermont, with tolling bells and processions marking each stop. After taking a boat across Lake Champlain, she traveled by carriage through slushy snow to North Elba, where she arrived late on December 7.

The next day, family and neighbors gathered for Brown's funeral at his frame house beneath the Adirondack peak known as Cloud-Splitter. The mourners included four women widowed by the attack on Harpers Ferry: Mary and the young wives of Oliver Brown, Watson Brown, and William Thompson. The family of Lyman Epps, a black neighbor and friend of Brown's, opened the service by singing the abolitionist's favor-ite hymn, "Blow Ye the Trumpet, Blow."

Let all the nations know,
To earth's remotest bound,
The Year of Jubilee has come.

After a prayer and eulogies, mourners carried the coffin to Brown's grave site beside a rough granite boulder and lowered the box into the winter-hard ground. The funeral was entirely without pomp, as befitted the man. But one eulogist, the abolitionist orator Wendell Phillips, spoke eloquently to the hanged man's legacy. "History will date Virginia Emancipation from Harper's Ferry. True, the slave is still there. So, when the tempest uproots a pine on your hills, it looks green for months—a year or two. Still, it is timber, not a tree. John Brown has loosened the roots of the slave system; it only breathes, —it does not live, —hereafter."

ON THE DAY OF the funeral, Jefferson Davis of Mississippi gave his own prescient speech on the floor of the U.S. Senate. A new Congress had convened just three days after Brown's hanging and immediately fallen into heated debate over Harpers Ferry. Davis mocked Brown for claiming, in the Mississippian's words, "if we would allow him to take our niggers off without making any fuss about it, he would not kill anybody." But the issue was no longer Brown, per se; it was his beatification in the North, which Southerners had watched in horror.

So had many Northerners, particularly businessmen who had commercial ties to the South and feared the country's breakup. They organized enormous "Union meetings," to denounce Brown and declare allegiance to the Fugitive Slave Law and other southern totems. "FANATICISM REBUKED," read a flyer for a Union meeting in Philadelphia on December 7, which attracted six thousand people. There were similar rallies in Boston and New York, where speakers, including New York's mayor, hailed "the bond of commerce" between North and South.

But the demonstrations did little to allay southern fears, or to deter southern scaremongers who sought to exploit the region's alarm. A long-held southern suspicion was now hardening into conviction. The North, at heart, was abolitionist, and its leaders could not be trusted to uphold the constitutional protections afforded slavery.

"John Brown, and a thousand John Browns, can invade us, and the Government will not protect us," Jefferson Davis proclaimed in his December 8 speech to the Senate. If "we are not to be protected in our property and sovereignty, we are therefore released from our allegiance, and will protect ourselves out of the Union." Davis also issued a chilling threat: "To secure our rights and protect our honor we will dissever the ties that bind us together, even if it rushes us into a sea of blood."

Not all southern leaders shared this view, and some vehemently opposed it, including Governor Sam Houston of Texas, who had served with Davis in the Senate and thought him "as ambitious as Lucifer and cold as a lizard." But moderates were drowned out by the calls for separation that echoed across the South all through December 1859. In Virginia, Edmund Ruffin revived a dormant secessionist group, which declared Harpers Ferry the "last and crowning aggression of Northern usurpation and hatred." South Carolina reaffirmed its "right to secede" and sent a commissioner to lobby for a convention of slaveholding states. "The Harper's Ferry invasion, with the developments following it," the commissioner told Virginians, "prove that the north and the south are standing in hostile array."

With tensions rising in the winter of 1859–60, southern states massively increased their military budgets; they also cracked down on perceived infiltrators by barring postmasters from delivering "incendiary" materials and strictly policing book vendors and other "dangerous emissaries from the Northern states." Citizens conducted a witch hunt of their own. In Georgia alone that December, two "suspicious" book agents were lashed, a shoe peddler was tarred and feathered after "enticing negroes into his cellar at night and reading them all sorts of abolitionist documents," and a traveling map seller was lynched for allegedly preaching abolitionism to blacks.

"I do not exaggerate in designating the state of affairs in the Southern country as a reign of terror," the British consul in Charleston, South Carolina, wrote on December 9. "The Northern merchants and Travellers are leaving in great numbers."

A movement also arose in the South to "use, eat, drink, wear or buy nothing under the sun from north of the Mason and Dixon line," in the words of a legislative committee in Virginia. This boycott extended even to education. That December, southern medical students in Philadelphia voted "to secede in a body" from the city's medical schools "and go to Southern Colleges." About 250 students departed, arriving in Richmond to the cheers of five thousand Virginians and a welcome speech by Governor Wise, whose term was about to end.

In his final address to the Virginia Assembly, Wise declared "abolition a cancer eating into our very vitals." Even President Buchanan, whom Wise had supported, could no longer be counted on to defend southern rights. *"We must rely on ourselves,"* Wise concluded. *"I say then—To your tents! Organize and arm!"*

AS THE SOUTH MOBILIZED in the weeks following Brown's death, six of his accomplices still lingered in the Charlestown jail. Four of them were scheduled to hang on December 16. "The prisoners seem to have given up all hope, and look with great composure on their approaching fate," the *Baltimore American* reported. For at least two of the men, this wasn't in fact the case.

John Cook shared a room with Edwin Coppoc, their ankles shackled to a bolt on the floor. Cook passed time in prison reading Byron, writing poetry, and composing florid letters. "A dungeon bare confines me, a prisoner's cell is mine," he wrote his wife, who had taken refuge with his family in the North. "Yet there are *no bars* to confine the immortal mind, and *no cell* that can shut up the gushing fountain of undying love."

Coppoc's letters were more restrained. In his youth, he had been expelled from Quaker meeting for dancing and other "wayward tendencies"; now he wrote his mother to express regret for having taken up arms. "I have seen my folly too late, and must now suffer the consequences." On December 10 he told a friend about pies he and Cook had received. "So you may know that we live fat, but it is only fattening us up for the gallows rather poor consolation."

In their final days, a local paper reported, the two prisoners "professed a desire to be left alone, and not be interrupted by visitors, as they wish time for preparation to die." On December 15, the eve of execution, they and the other condemned men received clergymen. "Each expressed a hope of salvation in the world to come," the *American* wrote. "Cook and Coppoc were loudest in their professions of a change of heart, and in the hope of Divine forgiveness."

The two men were actually "playing possum." For about a week, they had been chiseling a hole in the wall of their cell, using a bedstead screw and a knife they'd borrowed from a jail guard to cut a lemon. The hole was concealed by one of their beds, and the bricks they dislodged were hidden in the room's potbellied stove. The men also succeeded in sawing off their shackles. On the night before their hanging, they crawled through the hole and onto a drain spout outside, quietly dropping to the prison yard, some twenty feet below.

Security had been eased somewhat in the days since Brown's execution, and the weather had turned foul; just a week prior to Cook and Coppoc's breakout, the night guard in the prison yard was withdrawn inside the jail due to the cold. But the escapees still had to scale the yard's fifteen-foot wall before they could reach the street beyond. To do so, they climbed atop a pile of timber—it was Brown's scaffold, which had been disassembled and stored in the yard until its intended reassembly, a few hours hence, for the hanging of his accomplices.

At just after eight P.M., a militiaman patrolling the street outside the prison glimpsed a figure rising above the wall. The head of a second man also appeared. The sentinel called out, received no answer, and fired. Coppoc immediately ducked down. Cook, daring to the end, appeared ready to jump into the street. But when the guard threatened to impale him with his bayonet, Cook followed Coppoc back into the prison yard, where both men were quickly seized.

"We do not wish that any one should be unjustly censured on our account," Cook and Coppoc stated in a signed confession intended to absolve their jailers, who were suspected of being too lenient or possibly having accepted bribes. "We received no aid from any person, or persons whatever."

The two men did, however, admit to having been given a second knife blade by a fellow prisoner, Shields Green. As a fugitive slave, Green was subject to special scorn from Virginians. He was also illiterate, and no one bothered to record more than a few of his thoughts and words in prison. Green's cellmate, John Copeland, received more favorable, if still racist, attention. David Strother thought the handsome, well-spoken Copeland "would make a very genteel dining-room servant." The prosecutor Andrew Hunter later wrote that the "copper-colored" Copeland "behaved himself with as much firmness as any of them and with far more dignity."

Hunter nonetheless confiscated some of the letters Copeland wrote from prison, evidently regarding them as incendiary. "I am so soon to stand and suffer death for doing what George Washington the so-called father of this great but slave-cursed country, was made a hero for doing," Copeland wrote his brother. "Washington entered the field to fight for the freedom of the American people—not for the white man alone."

On the day of his execution, he wrote his family: "Last night for the last time, I beheld the soft bright moon as it rose, casting its mellow light into my felons cell." The twenty-five-year-old nonetheless felt at peace. "We shall meet in Heaven, where we shall not be parted by the demands of the cruel and unjust monster Slavery."

At eleven A.M. on the raw, overcast morning of December 16, Copeland and Green followed Brown's path to the gallows, riding aboard their coffins to the same hanging field at the edge of Charlestown. Troops guarded the gallows, as before, but this time a minister accompanied the condemned onto the scaffold and recited a long prayer. When the drop came, Green died quickly, his neck apparently broken. But "Copeland seemed to suffer very much, and his body writhed in violent contortions for some time," the *New York Tribune* reported.

Before the hanging, Copeland's father in Oberlin had sent repeated pleas to Governor Wise, asking permission to retrieve his son's body. Wise's eventual reply, just four days before the execution, was curt: "Yes. To your orders to some white citizen. You can't come to this State yourself."

This gave Copeland's father little time to make the necessary arrangements; meanwhile, Wise notified a Virginia doctor that if "the Negro convicts are not demanded by the proper relatives," they could be handed over to a medical college. Immediately after their hanging, Copeland and Green were buried in a field near the gallows. They lay there for only a few minutes before students disinterred the bodies and carried them off for dissection at the medical school in Winchester, where two of the insurgents killed at Harpers Ferry had earlier been taken.

When the Copelands' agent, an Oberlin professor named James Monroe, arrived a few days later, he went to the medical school to try to recover the body. Faculty members agreed to turn Copeland over, but the students who had disinterred the body refused. As their representative told Monroe, "This nigger that you are trying to get don't belong to the faculty."

Even so, Monroe was given a tour of the college, including the dissecting room, where he was startled to see the body of Copeland's compatriot Shields Green. "A fine athletic figure, he was lying on his back," Monroe wrote, "the unclosed, wistful eyes staring wildly upward, as if seeking, in a better world, for some solution to the dark problems of horror and oppression so hard to be explained in this."

COPELAND AND GREEN'S WHITE jail mates received much more respectful treatment. An hour after the black men were hanged, Cook and Coppoc were taken from the jail, looking "remarkably cheerful," according to one reporter. Cook called out to those he recognized in the crowd outside, telling one, "Remember me to all my friends at the Ferry." As they neared the gallows, Coppoc's face assumed "a settled expression of despair" and tears streamed down Cook's cheeks. But both men strode firmly up the scaffold steps and listened to a final prayer without a tremor.

After the nooses and hoods had been placed over them, Cook said, "Stop a minute; where is Edwin's hand?" The jailer guided their hands together for a final shake. Cook "then waved his hand to the crowd around the gallows, and said, 'Good-bye, all!'"

To avoid a repeat of Copeland's slow strangling, the sheriff asked a doctor to carefully adjust the nooses "to expedite death." Both men died without a struggle. The undertaker who had driven Cook and Coppoc to the gallows retrieved their bodies and transported their coffins to Harpers Ferry. Coppoc's was collected by his uncle for burial at a Quaker graveyard in Ohio. Cook's was shipped to the family members in New York who had earlier taken in his teenaged wife, Virginia, whom he'd married in Harpers Ferry just eight months before.

Contrary to John Brown's stern instruction, Cook had told his wife before the Harpers Ferry attack about their plot to free slaves. Though she came from a proslavery family, Virginia later said she was "always at heart an Abolitionist" and she had kept her husband's plans secret. After his death, she went to work for Brown's abolitionist allies in Boston and later married a Union soldier. When a researcher tracked Virginia down fifty years after the attack, she said little about her brief marriage to Cook, except that he had "a great fondness for romance" and "would sit up for hours" telling her stories from the chivalric novels of Sir Walter Scott.

AFTER THE HANGINGS ON December 16, just two prisoners remained. Albert Hazlett, upon his capture in Pennsylvania, had claimed his name was Harrison and said he had no connection to Harpers Ferry. This fiction delayed his trial but isolated the semiliterate Hazlett from contact with friends and family outside prison. The trial of Aaron Stevens, Brown's stoic lieutenant and former cellmate, was delayed on technical grounds; during the waiting period, he wrote many letters, some of which were published in the North, as Brown's had been before.

"I had a very hard time of it," he wrote Annie Brown, describing the six bullet wounds from which he had miraculously recovered, "but I am as well now as ever except my face is paralyzed on one side, which prevents me from laughing on that side, and my jaw bone was thrown out of place and my teeth do not meet as they did before."

Reporters and other visitors to the jail also continued to describe Stevens as a darkly handsome Spartacus, a chained gladiator so majestic that even a lawyer gushed, "Such black and penetrating eyes! Such an expansive brow! Such a grand chest and limbs!" With the other jailed insurgents dead, apart from the obscure Hazlett, Stevens became a cause célèbre to Brown's faithful in the North, particularly women.

"We feel an increased and *intense* interest in you," wrote an Ohio woman, who signed herself, "*Forever* yours in sympathy & affection." "I have looked at your likeness," another Ohio stranger wrote, "and I admire you I *love* you." Others yearned to mother him, most especially Rebecca Spring, the forty-eight-year-old New Jersey woman who had boldly gone to visit Brown in prison and had been smitten by his cellmate. She called Stevens a "regular young lion" and sent him apples, figs, and an evergreen bouquet, along with letters addressing him as "My dear little boy."

Stevens appreciated the attention and answered Spring in kind, as "Your son in the bonds of love, truth, friendship and righteousness." But his true passion was reserved for the one woman who seemed immune to his charms: Jennie Dunbar, the music teacher he had met in Ohio before embarking for the South.

"My love is very warm and there is no deceite about me, and I want a woman to *love* me, with all her soul," he'd written her in one of several amorous letters from the Kennedy farm. Stevens carried a picture of her into battle in Harpers Ferry and kept writing her from prison, "hoping that I am not *forgotten*."

He wasn't alone in extolling Jennie Dunbar. Others described her as intelligent, extremely independent, and physically stunning. "A rare and delicate type," one writer called her, "with great eyes full of pathos, with exquisite contours, with a glory of dark hair." When Stevens showed her picture to his comrades at the Kennedy farm, they had hurried to send their regards.

Dunbar was sympathetic to the insurrectionists' cause, and she was part of the close-knit abolitionist community in northeastern Ohio that had served as Brown's main weapons depot and muster station in the lead-up to Harpers Ferry. She taught music to John Brown, Jr.'s, wife, translated John junior's secret correspondence into numbered code, and often visited the farm family with whom Stevens boarded in the spring and summer of 1859.

Though Dunbar had enjoyed singing and playing music with Stevens, she was taken aback by his sudden professions of love from Maryland and Virginia. As a friend of Dunbar's put it in a letter: "He did not seem to think anymore of her than any one else before he went away." Dunbar didn't respond to Stevens's letters for months, and when she finally wrote him in prison in December, her words were mostly spiritual. "Be of good cheer as possible, believing that 'all things work together for good, to those who serve the Lord.'" She also wished she could come "to cheer you with *spoken* words of affection and appreciation," and closed: "With tenderest sympathy, I bid you Good-Bye. Jennie."

Undeterred, Stevens wrote her back immediately, saying that her words were "pure spring water, to a *thirsty soul*." But she didn't reciprocate and left it to a mutual friend to explain her feelings. "She loves you as a brother for your noble principles," wrote Julia Lindsley, the Ohio woman at whose home Stevens had stayed.

In February 1860, after four months in prison, Stevens and Hazlett went on trial; both were quickly convicted. Asked whether he had anything to say before sentencing, Stevens spoke of slavery: "When I think of my brothers slaughtered and my sisters outraged, my conscience does not reprove me for my actions. I shall meet my fate manfully." He and Hazlett were sentenced to hang a month later, on March 16, 1860.

Stevens also followed Brown in refusing ministerial comfort. He was devoted to Spiritualism, a creed that questioned the authenticity of the Bible and the divinity of Christ. His personal "god and Savior," he wrote, was "*good actions*" and "I expect to receive a free pass to the Spirit-World," where he would be able to communicate with those he had known and loved.

To his uncle, Stevens wrote that he was soon "to *dance* on *nothing*. It is rather a queer way to leave this world, but if a person must die, because he *loves man & justice*, why I think it becomes one of the best of deaths." He added: "I think now, from what I have seen, that the way we were trying to do away with Slavery is not the best way, but I had to get this experience before I knew it." He expressed some regret to his brother as well: "I have a desire to live yet awhile for I am young yet and have just learnt how to live."

Some of his supporters still hoped to save him. Thomas Wentworth Higginson assembled a band of armed men in southern Pennsylvania, but then abandoned the rescue mission when heavy snow and tight security made it too risky. The Ohio farm wife Julia Lindsley began a petition drive, urging Virginia's governor to commute the death sentence. Many others had sent similar pleas, but the Ohioans decided to deliver theirs in person, and they prevailed on Jennie Dunbar to act as emissary.

Traveling alone, she reached Richmond just two days before the execution. Governor John Letcher, who had replaced Wise, received her cordially, "supposing her to be the affianced bride of Mr. Stevens," a newspaper reported. But he told her Stevens was "the worst of John Brown's men" and he would not commute the sentence.

"I left him, with what feelings, I cannot tell," Dunbar later wrote. "Hope had not quite died till then."

The next day she went to Charlestown, arriving on the afternoon before the execution—Stevens's twenty-ninth birthday. His sister Lydia had arrived a few days before, prompting him to write their brother, "She is all nerve which is more than I can say of myself." But when Lydia brought Jennie Dunbar to his cell, Stevens seemed transformed. In his last letter to her before the attack on Harpers Ferry, he had dreamed of living "to see thy lovly face wonce more." Now, in a prison cell on the eve of his hanging, he had gotten his wish.

"Mr. Stevens rose from the side of the bed where he had been sitting, and came forward as well as he could for the chain around his ankles," Dunbar wrote. "He did not speak and I could not have done so had I tried."

Stevens's composed sister broke the silence and "we all recovered ourselves pretty soon," Dunbar went on. They shared the apples, maple sugar, and cheese she'd brought him from Ohio, and the mood turned incongruously cheerful. "The near approach of death seemed not to be thought of," she wrote. Stevens sang with them, read aloud about Spiritualism, and performed a phrenological exam of his sister's head. The two women ate supper at the jail and stayed until ten P.M. "He is in the best of spirits, talks, laughs and sings just as he used to do when life was bright before him," Dunbar wrote Julia Lindsley late that night.

She and Lydia returned to the jail the next morning for a breakfast consisting mostly of oysters, which Stevens had requested for his final meal. "He was talking to us as if he were to meet us again soon," Dunbar wrote. "He sent for a brush and polished his shoes, saying he 'wished to look well when he ascended the scaffold.'"

This was too much for his sister, who ran from the room and "wept convulsively." Lydia's anguish, Dunbar wrote, "more even than grief for him, moved me, and the tears forced themselves to my eyes."

But Stevens remained stoic, urging them not to grieve, and soon after their departure he and Hazlett climbed atop their coffins for the wagon ride to the gallows. "Both exhibited great firmness," the *New York Times* reported, and "persisted in refusing all the kindly offices of the ministry in their last moments."

Still, the man who had survived six bullet wounds was not easy to kill. When the drop came, "Hazlett seemed to die very easily," a Baltimore paper reported, but Stevens "struggled for a considerable time, and appeared to suffer very much."

Like Brown, Stevens had left a message before going to the gallows, though his was not in writing. In accordance with Stevens's and Hazlett's wishes to be buried in "a free land," their coffins were shipped to the New Jersey home of Rebecca Spring, who had taken such an interest in the prisoners. Before the burial in a nearby cemetery, Stevens's coffin was opened to cut a lock of his hair. "Attached to the button-hole of Stevens' coat by red and blue ribbons was a plain black India rubber ring," the *New York Herald* reported, "but for whom it was intended his friends were not informed." A woman at the funeral wrote Higginson, "It apparently was a last thought, conceived too late for explanation."

Jennie Dunbar was present at Stevens's funeral and was described in news reports as his fiancée. Annie Brown believed this to be true. She had grown close to Stevens at the Kennedy farm, had corresponded with him in prison, and met Dunbar a few months after his hanging, at a ceremony for Brown and his men in North Elba. While there, Dunbar told Annie that she had broken her engagement to Stevens in prison, just hours before his execution. According to Annie, Dunbar knew that "as soon as he entered the spirit world," he would know she didn't love him, and "her conscience would not let her deceive him."

But Stevens was a persistent suitor, and he evidently died in hope, carrying a ring with him to the gallows. Two months later, his friends in Ohio held a "circle" to communicate with his spirit. At one point, the medium "seemed to suffer about the throat," wrote a woman present at the séance, and "beckoned to Jennie to take a seat by her side." The medium held Dunbar's hand as Stevens reported that "he died very hard but it did not injure the soul." He then "addressed Jennie very kindly."

As Stevens had told her in his letters, he would await her in the Spirit-Land, bearing "the love of Soul, who's depth is to the end of time."

Immortal Raiders

They all called him crazy then;
who calls him crazy now?

—Henry David Thoreau,
"The Last Days of John Brown," 1860

The hanging of Stevens and Hazlett on March 16, 1860, was greeted with relief by the Virginians whom Brown and his men had attacked exactly five months before. "The curtain has at last fallen upon the closing scene of the Harper's Ferry tragedy," a Charlestown paper observed, "and we will indulge the hope, that with it terminates forever all organized interference with the constitutional rights of the South."

But the execution of the last jailed insurgents terminated little except their lives and the duties of their guards. Nationally, Harpers Ferry and its aftermath had exposed a gaping crevasse; nothing now seemed capable of bridging it. The "knell of the Union" that Jefferson had first heard forty years earlier, during the debate over Missouri, could no longer be hushed.

Abraham Lincoln, who was emerging that March as a contender for the presidency, labored to hold the Union together. But in his failure to do so, and in his eventual conversion to Brown's cause, he personified the nation's transformation between 1859 and 1865. At the time of the Harpers Ferry attack, Lincoln was a second-tier candidate for the Republican nomination, so lightly regarded that newspapers often rendered his first name as "Abram." Like many in the North, he admired Brown's courage and antislavery conviction but condemned his resort to violence. He also grasped the nation's fear of disunion and war, and used Harpers Ferry to position himself as a safely moderate choice in the Republican field.

"John Brown's effort was peculiar," he told leading Republicans at New York's Cooper Institute in February, 1860. "It was an attempt by white men to get up a revolt among slaves, in which the slaves refused to participate. In fact, it was so absurd that the slaves, with all their ignorance, saw plainly enough it could not succeed."

Reiterating the Republican position on slavery—to oppose the institution's spread but "to let it alone where it is"—he addressed southern fears directly. "You charge that we stir insurrections among your slaves. We deny it; and what is your proof? Harper's Ferry! John Brown!! John Brown was no Republican; and you have failed to implicate a single Republican in his Harper's Ferry enterprise."

Brown was indeed no Republican, and Lincoln no abolitionist. Though the two men shared certain traits, including a Calvinist upbringing on the frontier, Lincoln had very different views on race and emancipation. Born in the slave state of Kentucky, he believed the institution would die of its own accord, and he favored resettling freed blacks in Africa, just as Jefferson and others had proposed decades earlier.

"I am not, nor ever have been in favor of bringing about in any way the social and political equality of the white and black races," he stated during his 1858 debates with Stephen Douglas. Citing a "physical difference between the races" that made such equality impossible, he added: "I as much as any other man am in favor of having the superior position assigned to the white race."

Such attitudes were broadly in line with the white northern mainstream and served Lincoln well in the anxious aftermath of Harpers Ferry. So did the militancy of the Republican frontrunner, Senator William Seward, of New York, who was famous for having spoken of "an *irrepressible conflict*" that would make the nation all slaveholding or entirely free. Southerners and their northern allies repeatedly cited this remark after Harpers Ferry. In their telling, Seward had called for an abolitionist crusade, of which Brown and his men were the inevitable vanguard.

Lincoln had many political assets, including his "Rail-Splitter" image of backwoods self-reliance. But his deft handling of the slavery issue, amid the fallout from Harpers Ferry, did much to secure his surprise, third-ballot victory over Seward at the Republican convention in May 1860. The party also wrote into its platform Lincoln's rebuke of Brown, adopting a resolution to "denounce the lawless invasion by armed force of the soil of any State or Territory, no matter under what pretext, as among the gravest of crimes."

IN THE SOUTH, HOWEVER, Republicans' pledge of noninterference with slavery fell on deaf ears. Fire-eaters, emboldened by the secessionist fever that broke out after Brown's hanging, led a walkout at the Democratic convention when delegates refused to endorse extreme guarantees for slaveholders. In the end, the two factions nominated separate candidates, while disaffected moderates formed a third party and nominated a Tennessean who drained support from both Democratic candidates.

The Republicans, needing only to hold their northern base, ran a cautious campaign; Lincoln gave no speeches and barely left Springfield, Illinois. This made electoral sense, but it served to further isolate North from South. There was little national discussion of the brewing crisis, and almost no Republican presence below the Mason-Dixon Line, where Southerners dismissed or wildly misrepresented Lincoln's views on slavery. All that mattered was his denunciation of the institution as a great evil, and his leadership of a "Black Republican" party that Southerners had long since caricatured as an abolitionist cabal, intent on waging a "war of extermination" against slavery everywhere.

The depth of the sectional divide became apparent that fall, when Lincoln won all but one northern state, in most cases easily. This gave him enough electoral votes to win the presidency in the crowded field, even though he received less than 40 percent of the popular vote and had almost no support in the South (in eleven states, Republican ballots weren't even available).

Mary Chesnut, the South Carolina diarist, was on a train the day after the election when news of Lincoln's victory swept her car. The response was electric, she wrote, with everyone agreeing a Rubicon had been crossed. The election result would reprise, on a national level, the terror in Virginia the previous fall.

"Now that the black radical Republicans have the power I suppose they will Brown us all," one passenger cried. Chesnut added in her diary: "No doubt of it."

SOUTH CAROLINIANS DIDN'T WAIT to have their fears confirmed. Six weeks after the election, delegates meeting in Charleston voted unanimously to repeal the state's ratification of the U.S. Constitution in 1788: "The union now subsisting between South Carolina and the other States, under the name of 'The United States of America,' is hereby dissolved."

Six other Deep South states quickly followed South Carolina out of the Union. In formal declarations explaining their secession, the states often cited Harpers Ferry and made clear their core grievance. "Our position is thoroughly identified with the institution of slavery," Mississippians stated. "There was no choice left us but submission to the mandates of abolition, or a dissolution of the Union."

In February 1861, the secessionists formed the Confederate States of America and elected Jefferson Davis as president. They also adopted a "Provisional Constitution," outlining the laws of their breakaway government. Sixteen months earlier, Southerners had pointed to Brown's Provisional Constitution as evidence of treason. Now they were in rebellion themselves.

Virginians, however, balked at joining the Confederacy, at least initially. This hesitation irked Henry Wise, who was eager as always to be at the forefront. As delegates in Richmond debated secession that April, the former governor secretly convened a band of conspirators, appointing himself as commander. Their mission: to seize the federal armory at Harpers Ferry before the U.S. government fortified it.

The next day, having dispatched his men, Wise returned to the secession meeting and brandished a pistol, telling delegates: "Blood will be flowing at Harper's Ferry before night." On April 18, six days after South Carolinians shelled Fort Sumter and exactly eighteen months after Brown's capture, Wise's allies took over the government works at Harpers Ferry, amid cries of treason from townspeople who wanted Virginia to stay in the Union. Delegates in Richmond voted to secede that same day and belatedly sent troops to assist in Wise's raid. The newly Confederate

Burning of the arsenal at Harpers Ferry

state acquired thousands of federal guns and hauled the factory's machines and tools to an armory in Richmond.

Before surrendering the government works, federal guards torched the arsenal, and in June, Confederates completed the job, burning the stripped armory and rifle factory. Born with John Brown at the turn of the nineteenth century, the Harpers Ferry armory had outlived him by less than two years. One of its few surviving structures was the little brick engine house that had served as his headquarters.

The men who had led U.S. marines in the attack on the engine house, Robert E. Lee and J.E.B. Stuart, were now Confederate officers, opposing federal troops. So was Thomas "Stonewall" Jackson, who had watched Brown hang. In 1862, Jackson returned to Harpers Ferry and won a battle that resulted in the largest surrender of U.S. troops in American history until World War II.

But the town itself was no longer much of a prize. Earlier that year, Union troops had retaliated against Confederate sniper fire from the town by burning the Wager House, the Gault House saloon, and other buildings from which Virginians had battled Brown and his men. The major who carried out the burning was Hector Tyndale, an abolitionist who had escorted Mary Brown when she traveled to Virginia in 1859 to bring home her husband's remains.

THE MEMORY OF BROWN'S body also lived on, in song. Early in the war, Massachusetts troops marched to the tune of a popular hymn, improvising their own lyrics, which ran, in part:

> *John Brown's body lies a-mouldering in the grave ...*
> *He's gone to be a soldier in the army of the Lord,*
> *His soul is marching on!*

The poet Julia Ward Howe first heard the marching song in the fall of 1861. Married to Samuel Howe of the Secret Six, she regarded Brown as a "holy and glorious" martyr and was moved to compose new lyrics. Though her version of the song made no mention of Brown, it was infused with his crusading spirit.

> *Mine eyes have seen the glory of the coming of the Lord:*
> *He is trampling out the vintage where the grapes of wrath are*
> *   stored;*
> *He hath loosed the fateful lightning of His terrible swift sword:*
> *His truth is marching on.*

Howe's "Battle Hymn of the Republic" was to become the anthem of the Union, a righteous call to answer God's trumpet and crush the serpent's head. But in one respect, her lyrics—like the man she honored—were ahead of their time. In late 1861, when Howe composed the "Battle Hymn," the Union hadn't yet embraced the stirring line "As he died to make men holy, let us die to make men free."

Through six months of war, Abraham Lincoln had held to his long-standing pledge of noninterference with slavery in the South. He was fighting to preserve the Union, not to free slaves. For Lincoln, this wasn't simply a matter of principle or constitutional duty. The northern public wasn't ready to fight for emancipation, and he needed the support of slaveholding border states such as Maryland and Kentucky, which hadn't seceded and were crucial to the war effort.

But slaves themselves quickly upset Lincoln's policy. They fled their owners and streamed to Union-held positions in the South. Many expressed eagerness to join the northern fight. Abolitionists urged Lincoln to free and enlist these refugees, and some officers in the field effectively did so, refusing to return them to their owners and employing the fugitives at forts and camps.

Still, Lincoln wouldn't budge from his policy. Fugitive slaves were "contraband of war"—property seized from the enemy—and nothing more. He would not wage a war for liberation.

"Emancipation," the president declared in December 1861, "would be equivalent to a John Brown raid, on a gigantic scale."

BUT LINCOLN WAS A self-questioning man; unlike Brown, he was willing to reconsider his views when they butted against circumstance. In 1862, as the South secured one battlefield victory after another, he reversed course, intent on doing whatever was necessary to win the war. Assailing slavery would bring the North both manpower and European support, while at the same time weakening the southern war effort. Once he decided to change his policy, Lincoln awaited an elusive northern victory to announce it, lest his shift seem an act of desperation.

Fittingly, the crucial battle occurred just seven miles from the Kennedy farm, where Brown and his men had launched their assault on slavery three years before. On September 17, 1862, after driving north across the Potomac, Robert E. Lee's Confederate army met a massive Union force by Antietam Creek, outside the Maryland town of Sharpsburg. The clash left 23,000 dead and wounded men strewed across cornfields and sunken farm roads—the bloodiest single day of combat in American history. The roar of battle was so great that it could be heard ten miles away in Harpers Ferry.

Neither army was driven from the field. But a day after the battle, Lee led his battered army back into Virginia, ending the southern offensive. Lincoln then signed the Emancipation Proclamation, which was formally issued on January 1, 1863. As of that date, slaves in states "in rebellion against the United States, shall be then, thenceforward, and forever free."

The edict's impact was more symbolic than real. The slaves declared free were under Confederate control, beyond the reach of the federal government. But the proclamation nonetheless marked a sea change in the war and its ultimate aims. "God bless Abraham Lincoln and give God the glory for the day of Jubilee has come," Mary Brown wrote from North Elba six days after the proclamation.

Lincoln's decree also stated that "the people so declared to be free" would be "received into the armed service of the United States." Circulars were issued, one of them urging "able-bodied COLORED MEN" to "fight for the STARS AND STRIPES." At the top, the announcement said "ALL SLAVES were made FREEMEN" by Lincoln; at the bottom appeared the original version of the "John Brown Song."

At one point, Lincoln even looked to Brown's attack as a tactical model. Told by Frederick Douglass that Southerners had doubtless kept news of the proclamation from their slaves, Lincoln proposed organizing "a band" of black scouts, "whose business should be somewhat after the original plan of John Brown." They would go behind enemy lines, carrying news of emancipation and urging slaves "to come within our boundaries."

But the advance of Union armies made this measure unnecessary. Hundreds of thousands of slaves flocked to freedom, and black enlistment boosted the Union Army and Navy by 200,000 men. Brown's dream of arming blacks to fight for their freedom was realized not at Harpers Ferry, but in the trenches of Petersburg, Virginia, and the lowlands of South Carolina, where the first regiment of freed slaves was led by Thomas Wentworth Higginson, the minister-warrior and most stalwart of the Secret Six.

"I had been an abolitionist too long, and had known and loved John Brown too well," Higginson wrote, "not to feel a thrill of joy at last on finding myself in the position where he only wished to be."

BY WAR'S END, BROWN'S prophecy before the gallows would also be fulfilled. And it was Lincoln, yet again, who recapitulated Brown's vision, that the "crimes of this guilty land" could only be purged with blood. The president echoed this most eloquently in March 1865, after four years of battle and the deaths of over 600,000 men. "This mighty scourge of war," he said, was the "woe due" the nation for slavery. If God willed that the carnage continue "until every drop of blood drawn with the lash, shall be paid by another drawn with the sword," then this was the true and righteous judgment of the Lord.

Six weeks later, the fighting was finally over and Lincoln lay dead, shot in Ford's Theatre by John Wilkes Booth, who had watched Brown hang. Harpers Ferry and Lincoln's assassination became bookends to the great national bloodletting over slavery. And in death, the reluctant Emancipator was joined to the abolitionist he had distanced himself from six years before. "Lincoln and John Brown are two martyrs, whose memories will live united in our bosoms," wrote a black newspaper editor in New Orleans.

Later that year, the nation ratified the first change to the U.S. Constitution since 1804. The Thirteenth Amendment abolished slavery; the Fourteenth and Fifteenth Amendments, ratified a few years later, extended full citizenship rights to blacks. In 1859, Americans had howled at the absurdity of Brown's constitution, particularly its provision for blacks holding political office. A decade later, one of the signatories to Brown's document, Isaac Shadd, joined the first wave of black officeholders in the Reconstruction South, rising to the speakership of the Mississippi House of Representatives.

ANOTHER SIGNATORY TO BROWN'S constitution was Osborne Anderson, the black printer who had survived the fighting in Harpers Ferry. He recruited black soldiers in the Civil War and died soon after it, from tuberculosis. Shortly before his death, Anderson revisited Harpers Ferry with friends, "for the purpose of pointing out to them the field of their maneuvres under Capt. Brown."

Three other men who escaped capture in 1859 also served in the war. Barclay Coppoc, whose brother Edwin hanged, enlisted at the war's start and died soon after, when Confederates derailed his troop train. Charles Tidd, the Kansas veteran who had opposed Brown's attack plan, enlisted in the summer of 1861 and died at the front six months later, from disease. Francis Meriam, the sickly Bostonian who had arrived at the Kennedy farm with much-needed money, became a captain of black troops in South Carolina. Wounded in the leg, he survived the war, only to die a few months after its end.

The last of the escapees, Brown's partly crippled son Owen, spent the war years in the North, far from the battlefield. But Annie Brown, who had joined her father and brothers as a fifteen-year-old, wanted desperately to serve. "What a pity it is that I belong to the *weaker sex*, for if I were *only* a *man* then I could go to war," she wrote in a letter in 1862. "I want to go and would if they would accept me."

The next year she found a way, returning south as a teacher of freed slaves in Union-held territory in Virginia. While there, she attended a black Sunday school that had been established on the seized plantation of Henry Wise, the former governor who had been so intent on hanging her father. His now freed slaves were among those being educated at missionary schools on his property.

As for Wise himself, he had finally gotten his wish to lead Virginians in battle. Appointed a brigadier general, he rashly predicted that "Yankees would break and run" at the first sight of advancing rebels. Instead, under his incompetent and cantankerous command, Wise's men were routed in Virginia and North Carolina—rare Confederate defeats in the East during 1861 and 1862.

At war's end, Wise was indicted for treason along with Robert E. Lee and other Virginia rebels. Lee sought amnesty, but Wise followed Brown's example, denying any guilt and refusing to plead with his accusers. "I could stand prouder on the gallows even," he wrote, "than I could *on any condition of servile submission.*"

The treason charge was eventually dropped, and Wise ultimately renounced the institution he had fought so hard to defend. "God knew that we could be torn away from our black idol of slavery only by fire and blood and the drawn sword of the destroying angel of war," he stated in 1866, sounding very much like the man he'd hanged in 1859.

IN THE INTERVENING YEARS, Brown's body had lain a-mouldering in North Elba, but his family was no longer with him. Mary left the struggling property behind in 1863, writing that she hoped to give her daughters "a chance to do something for themselves in a new country that they cannot have here." She headed west, writing soon after her departure: "I very much regret that I ever spent a cent on that farm."

The little money Mary possessed was a legacy of her husband's hanging. Abolitionists created a John Brown Fund to support the family, with donations coming from as far afield as Haiti. Mary received several thousand dollars, and when she and four children reached northern California in 1864, neighbors raised additional money to help her buy land and build a cottage.

She lived in California until her death twenty years later, in relative comfort and peace. But there was one gruesome postscript to her loss at Harpers Ferry. In 1882, when Mary was visiting Chicago, an Indiana doctor offered to return the remains of her son Watson, who had been killed near the engine house and carried off for dissection and display at the medical school in Winchester. The doctor had served in Virginia during the war and recovered Watson's remains before Union troops burned the medical school to the ground in 1862.

"Four of his finger joints on one hand and all the toes of one foot had already been cut off and carried away by relic seekers," a reporter wrote of Watson's partly preserved body, consisting of the skeleton, nerves, and blood vessels. The body had a bullet hole corresponding to Watson's fatal belly wound. The family collected the remains for belated burial in North Elba, beside Brown and another son, Frederick, killed in Kansas.

Owen Brown, the last of the twenty-one men who had joined his father at the Kennedy farm, died in 1889, having spent his final years as a hermit on a mountainside in California. But Annie Brown lived on, well into the twentieth century, outlasting her many siblings and everyone else directly connected to the 1859 plot.

"She was born to suffer and yet endure," John Brown, Jr., had written six months after Harpers Ferry, when Annie was still afflicted with "bone-crushing sorrow," not only for her father and brothers but for an unnamed sweetheart who, her siblings believed, was among those killed in the attack.

In 1864, Annie moved with her mother to California, where she continued to teach black children and married an older man. For a short time she seemed "wonderfully happy," a friend wrote. But her husband became alcoholic, abusive, and unable to work, leaving Annie struggling

Brown's four surviving sons in old age, Owen at lower right

to support their eight children. "He just sits and smokes and growls and snarls nearly all the time," Annie wrote Franklin Sanborn, whose school in Concord she had briefly attended. "I married the man for what I thought he was or might be, not for what he has proved to be."

Though desperately poor, in debt, and often ill herself, Annie did not want to become "an object of charity" to admirers of the Brown family. She sold the few relics and letters of value she possessed, "to buy bread and clothing for my children," and she told her offspring little about her father or Harpers Ferry. Annie "wished to live their lives with them—not the old, sad one that was gone," she said, and so she "shut the past away."

But as her children grew up and her siblings died, Annie began to talk and write freely about the ten weeks she had spent as housekeeper and "watchdog" for Brown's band. That long-ago summer, her sixteenth, was the most stirring passage of Annie's difficult life, and she recalled every detail, right down to her insect bites and the exact layout of the log house. Mostly, though, she spoke of the men she had concealed, vividly describing their appearance, idiosyncrasies, favorite songs, and fears of what lay ahead.

"People who never did a heroic deed themselves are very particular as to how heroes behave," she wrote. Having "waited upon them, watched and cared for them," she knew Brown's men as "neither saints nor the worst of sinners." They were high-spirited, vulnerable young idealists, as she had been herself.

Part of Annie had died with them in 1859, despite the fame and assistance accorded her family. Though abolitionists paid for her to attend fine schools and board with families like the Alcotts, "I used to lock myself in my room and lay and roll on the floor, in the agony of a tearless grief for hours at a time," she wrote. "The honor and glory that some saw in the work, did not fill the aching void that was left in my heart, losing so many loved ones."

Annie carried that grief into widowhood and old age. She was "easily upset," a niece wrote of her aged aunt's visits. "She always called herself 'The Last Survivor.'" In 1926 there appeared a small dispatch from the Associated Press: "Death Comes to Last Brown of Harper's Ferry." At the age of eighty-two, Annie had died after a serious fall. Newspapers reported, incorrectly, that she had witnessed her father's execution. But the coroner's certificate revealed a curious detail. Sixty-seven years after Brown's hanging, his loyal daughter had died of a broken neck.

THE TOWN ANNIE'S FATHER had attacked in 1859 never fully recovered from the trauma, either. As Brown had discovered, Harpers Ferry was easy to seize and hard to hold. It changed hands a dozen times in the Civil War, with passing armies repeatedly burning the river bridges and bombarding the town from surrounding hills. "The larger portion of the houses all lie in ruins and the entire place is not actually worth $10," a Massachusetts soldier wrote his mother in 1863.

The Harpers Ferry that emerged from the ruins of war was an ironic counterpoint to the antebellum community that had fought Brown in 1859. Jefferson County wasn't even part of Virginia anymore. It belonged to *West* Virginia, a new state carved out of the old during the Civil War, in support of the Union and its cause. Former slaves poured into the ravaged town, and by war's end, it was a refugee camp, with tents filling the grounds of the burned armory.

A few years earlier, it had been a crime to teach slaves how to read and write. Now, a black school arose, founded by northern Baptists, and in 1867 it became Storer College, an institution mainly devoted to training black teachers. Its first dormitory was called Lincoln Hall.

The armory engine house in the late nineteenth century

For many years, another building stood on the Storer campus: the brick engine house where Brown made his last stand. In the decades after his attack, it was chipped at by souvenir hunters, painted with the words "John Brown's Fort," and disassembled for exhibit at the World's Fair in Chicago before finally returning to Harpers Ferry.

White townspeople who trickled back after the Civil War, including families whose members had fought against Brown, valued the fort as a tourist attraction for their beleaguered community. One early visitor was Thomas Wentworth Higginson, who honeymooned in Harpers Ferry following his second marriage in 1879 and found the town "shabby and ruined." Two years later, another prominent backer of Brown's arrived: Frederick Douglass, invited to speak at the fourteenth anniversary of Storer College.

The former slave and militant abolitionist found himself "upon the very soil" Brown "had stained with blood," he wrote, "and among the very people he had startled and outraged and who a few years ago would have hanged me in open daylight to the first tree." Sitting just behind Douglass on the speaker's platform was Andrew Hunter, whose prosecution of Brown and his men had sent them to the gallows in nearby Charlestown.

Douglass nonetheless proceeded to give the most rousing celebration of Brown ever delivered. "His zeal in the cause of my race was far greater than mine—it was as the burning sun to my taper light," Douglass said. "I could live for the slave, but he could die for him."

Douglass's speech was given added force by his acknowledgment of the doubts he had harbored about Brown. Describing their first meeting in Springfield, he confessed to having felt "a little disappointed at the appearance of this man's house," a barely furnished abode on the back street of a working-class district, where Douglass joined Brown's family for a repast of potatoes, cabbage, and soup. But he had come to recognize the significance of this humble household. "In its plainness it was a truthful reflection of its inmates: no disguises, no illusions, no make-believes here, but stern truth and solid purpose."

At first, Douglass had also been taken aback by Brown's consuming hatred of slavery, unusual in a white man. "He saw the evil through no

mist or haze," Douglass said. "Against truth and right, legislative enactments were to his mind mere cobwebs—the pompous emptiness of
human pride—the pitiful outbreathings of human nothingness." For
Brown, slavery was a state of war and must be met in kind.

This, too, Douglass had resisted. He told of their last meeting in the
Chambersburg quarry, when Douglass "could see Harper's Ferry only as
a trap of steel" and refused to join Brown. He also conceded to his audience that Brown's nighttime invasion of their town could fairly be
regarded as "cold-blooded and atrocious."

But for all that, Douglass had come "to pay a just debt long due," to
"vindicate" the man he had doubted and ultimately abandoned. The attack
on Harpers Ferry was an awful price that had to be paid—"the answering back of the avenging angel to the midnight invasions of Christian
slave-traders on the sleeping hamlets of Africa." Nothing less, Douglass
said, could force the nation to face its great wrong. "Slavery had so
benumbed the moral sense of the nation that it never suspected the pos-
sibility of an explosion."

Once Brown lit the fuse, less with his actions than with the moral
clarity of his words, Southerners were unable to extinguish it. "They
could kill him," Douglass told his audience, "but they could not answer
him." In the war that followed, the Union's armies had "found it necessary to do on a large scale what John Brown attempted to do on a small
one." Douglass therefore regarded Harpers Ferry, not Fort Sumter, as
the true start of the nation's great conflict. "If John Brown did not end
the war that ended slavery, he did at least begin the war that ended
slavery."

All this was apparent in retrospect, when war and emancipation had
come to seem inevitable. But Douglass closed his speech by returning to
the autumn of 1859, to remind his audience how the events of that fall
had changed history.

"Until this blow was struck, the prospect for freedom was dim, shadowy and uncertain. The irrepressible conflict was one of words, votes, and
compromises. When John Brown stretched forth his arm the sky was
cleared. The time for compromises was gone—the armed hosts of freedom
stood face to face over the chasm of a broken Union—and the clash of

arms was at hand." The South, no longer able to steer the nation, "drew the sword of rebellion and thus made her own, and not Brown's, the lost cause of the century."

These words didn't sit well with some whites in his audience. Andrew Hunter had been close to Governor Wise and others whom Douglass criticized in his oration. Hunter's home had also been a casualty of the "lost cause," burnt by northern troops on the orders of his own cousin, a Union commander. At points during the speech, Douglass later wrote, Hunter "condemned my sentiments as they were uttered."

But the prosecutor surprised Douglass once the speech was over. Hunter shook his hand, "commended me for my address, and gave me a pressing invitation to visit Charlestown," offering to share details about "the sayings and conduct of Captain Brown while in prison and on trial." Hunter said he still disapproved of the attack, but admired Brown's "manliness and courage."

This overture was all the more astonishing for its timing. By 1881, the year of Douglass's address, postwar Reconstruction had given way to resurgent white supremacy. Former Confederates were regaining power across the South, and many whites in Jefferson County wanted to join in this restoration of the old regime. In Harpers Ferry, Ku Klux Klansmen had harassed black students at Storer College.

But for the moment, at least, Douglass allowed himself to feel hopeful about the revolution Brown had unleashed. "The abolition of slavery has not merely emancipated the negro, but liberated the whites," he wrote of his warm reception at Harpers Ferry.

DOUGLASS'S OPTIMISM WOULD PROVE misplaced. As Jim Crow laws took firm hold in the 1880s and 1890s, Harpers Ferry itself became a symbol and shrine in the struggle for civil rights. In 1906, black activists walked barefoot at dawn to the engine house, carrying candles. "Here on the scene of John Brown's martyrdom," they resolved, "we reconsecrate ourselves, our honor, our property to the final emancipation of the race which John Brown died to make free."

Those who had died with Brown also received belated recognition.

On the fortieth anniversary of Harpers Ferry, the eight insurgents whose bodies had been dumped in unmarked pits by the Shenandoah were disinterred. Their remains, along with those of Aaron Stevens and Albert Hazlett, removed from their graves in New Jersey, were then reburied in North Elba, beside those of John and Watson Brown.

These reunited raiders included two black men whose families had carried on their struggle for freedom and dignity. One of them was Dangerfield Newby, who had hoped to rescue his wife and children from slavery in Virginia. Newby's brother joined the Union Army and died in the long battle for Petersburg, which preceded Lee's surrender at Appomattox. Newby's widow, Harriett, who had been sold south to Louisiana with some of their children, found her way at war's end to a Freedmen's Bureau camp. She married a fellow refugee from Virginia and they returned to their home state, as free people. Harriett raised a large family—including most of the children she'd had by Dangerfield—while her husband farmed and acquired land, becoming a substantial property holder.

The second black man interred at North Elba was Lewis Leary, the harness maker from Ohio who had been shot in the Shenandoah. His young widow, Mary, received a few hundred dollars from a local John Brown Fund and married an ardent Brown supporter, Charles Langston. They moved to Kansas, and in old age Mary raised a grandson, wrapping him in a bullet-riddled shawl she said her first husband had worn during the fight at Harpers Ferry.

"My grandmother," the grandson later recalled, "held me on her lap and told me long, beautiful stories about people who wanted to make the Negroes free." She also took the youngster to Osawatomie, site of Brown's battle during the days of Bleeding Kansas.

That boy was Langston Hughes, who grew up to become a leading figure in the Harlem Renaissance and one of the most celebrated poets of the twentieth century. Hughes kept his grandmother's shawl and never forgot her stories of Lewis Leary, "who went off to die with John Brown." In 1931, he wrote a poem addressed to black Americans; "October the Sixteenth" took its title from the date in 1859 when the raiders embarked on their night march from the Kennedy farm.

Perhaps
You will remember
John Brown.

John Brown
Who took his gun,
Took twenty-one companions,
White and black,
Went to shoot your way to freedom
Where two rivers meet
And the hills of the
North
And the hills of the
South
Look slow at one another—
And died
For your sake.

Now that you are
Many years free,
And the echo of the Civil War
Has passed away,
And Brown himself
Has long been tried at law,
Hanged by the neck,
And buried in the ground—
Since Harpers Ferry
Is alive with ghosts today,
Immortal raiders
Come again to town—
Perhaps,

You will recall
John Brown.

—mm—

The Toll from the Raid
on Harpers Ferry

Raiders killed in action:
Dangerfield Newby, shot in the street, Oct. 17, 1859
William Leeman, shot in Potomac River, Oct. 17, 1859
Watson Brown, shot in the street, Oct. 17, 1859
John Kagi, shot in Shenandoah River, Oct. 17, 1859
Lewis Leary, shot in Shenandoah River, Oct. 17, 1859
William Thompson, shot on Potomac bridge, Oct. 17, 1859
Steward Taylor, shot in engine house, Oct. 17, 1859
Oliver Brown, shot in engine house, Oct. 17, 1859
Jeremiah Anderson, bayoneted in engine house, Oct. 18, 1859
Dauphin Thompson, bayoneted in engine house, Oct. 18, 1859

Raiders captured:
John Brown, wounded in engine house, hanged Dec. 2, 1859
Shields Green, captured in engine house, hanged Dec. 16, 1859
Edwin Coppoc, captured in engine house, hanged Dec. 16, 1859
John Copeland, captured in Shenandoah River, hanged Dec. 16, 1859
John Cook, captured in Pennsylvania, hanged Dec. 16, 1859
Aaron Stevens, wounded in street, hanged March 16, 1860
Albert Hazlett, captured in Pennsylvania, hanged March 16, 1860

Raiders escaped:
Barclay Coppoc, died in Civil War, 1861
Charles Tidd, died in Civil War, 1862
Francis Meriam, wounded in Civil War, died 1865
Osborne Anderson, recruiter in Civil War, died 1872
Owen Brown, died 1889

Others:

Jim, slave who joined raiders, drowned near rifle works, Oct. 17, 1859

Ben, slave freed by raiders, captured at rifle works, died in prison from "Pneumonia & fright," Oct. 25, 1859

Ary, Ben's mother, died after caring for him in prison, Nov. 17, 1859

Killed by raiders:

Heyward Shepherd, porter, shot on Potomac bridge, Oct. 17, 1859

Thomas Boerly, grocer, shot in street, Oct. 17, 1859

George Turner, farmer, shot in street, Oct. 17, 1859

Fontaine Beckham, mayor, shot near engine house, Oct. 17, 1859

Luke Quinn, marine, shot at engine house, Oct. 18, 1859

Wounded by raiders:

Edward McCabe, Harpers Ferry laborer, shot Oct. 17, 1859

Samuel Young, Charlestown militia, shot Oct. 17, 1859

George Murphy, Martinsburg militia, shot Oct. 17, 1859

George Richardson, Martinsburg militia, shot Oct. 17, 1859

G. N. Hammond, Martinsburg militia, shot Oct. 17, 1859

Evan Dorsey, Martinsburg militia, shot Oct. 17, 1859

Nelson Hooper, Martinsburg militia, shot Oct. 17, 1859

George Woollett, Martinsburg militia, shot Oct. 17, 1859

Matthew Rupert, marine, shot at engine house, Oct. 18, 1859

Author's Note

Spelling and punctuation weren't yet standardized during much of the period covered by this book, and John Brown's usage was irregular even for his time. As a result, many scholars and printers have cleaned up his writing, particularly by correcting grammatical errors and substituting italics for his ceaseless underlining. When quoting from original documents in Brown's hand, I've rendered his words exactly as they appeared. When quoting from transcriptions of his letters—in some cases, all that survives—I've chosen to better convey his actual writing style by replacing italics with underscores.

Harper's Ferry, as the town was known in the eighteenth and nineteenth centuries, lost the apostrophe in its name due to a change in post office policy. When quoting from historical documents, I have used the old form; in all other cases it is Harpers Ferry. Charlestown's name has also changed slightly, to present-day Charles Town; I have used the former throughout. And both towns now lie in West Virginia, which was formed during the Civil War. When referring to events before this change, I have referred to the towns as being part of Virginia.

Notes

Material related to Brown and Harpers Ferry is widely scattered in libraries, archives, museums, and other sites from New York to California. Over the years, many documents have been reproduced, sometimes in slightly different form. Whenever possible, I have quoted from the original handwritten sources. But in some instances, the citations below refer to transcriptions or copies, particularly those available in the wonderfully rich and accessible Clarence Gee Collection at the Hudson Library and Historical Society in Ohio.

Three other collections deserve special mention. The Oswald Garrison Villard papers at Columbia University are an almost bottomless trove. Particularly valuable are the interviews done by Villard's intrepid researcher, Katherine Mayo, in the early 1900s. The Kansas State Historical Society is equally indispensable, and the best place to research the many players apart from Brown who figure in this story. The historical society also has one of the best online archives I came across in my research: http://www.kansasmemory.org/.

In West Virginia, Boyd Stutler, like Clarence Gee, was an indefatigable compiler of Brown material. The West Virginia State Archives has digitized most of Stutler's collection, as well as his correspondence and articles over many decades. For the monomaniacal, there is no better place to lose oneself in every detail of Brown's story, as Stutler did, than by browsing his

collection at http://www.wvculture.org/HiStory/wvmemory/imlsintro
.html.

Manuscript Collections

Boston Public Library, Boston, Mass.
　　Thomas Wentworth Higginson Papers
Chicago Historical Society, Chicago, Ill.
　　John Brown Family Papers
Columbia Rare Book Library, Columbia University, New York, N.Y.
　　Oswald Garrison Villard John Brown Papers
The Gilder Lehrman Institute of American History, New York, N.Y.
　　Gilder Lehrman Collection
Harpers Ferry National Historical Park, Harpers Ferry, W.Va.
Historical Society of Pennsylvania, Philadelphia, Pa.
　　Ferdinand J. Dreer Collection
　　Miscellaneous John Brown Papers
Houghton Library, Harvard University, Cambridge, Mass.
　　Franklin Sanborn Papers
Hudson Library and Historical Society, Hudson, Ohio
　　Clarence Gee Collection
Jefferson County Museum, Charles Town, W.Va.
　　John Brown Collection
Kansas State Historical Society, Topeka, Kans.
　　John Brown Collection
　　Adair Family Collection
　　Richard Hinton Papers
Ohio Historical Society, Columbus, Ohio
　　John Brown, Jr., Papers
　　Oliver Brown Papers
Robert W. Woodruff Library, Atlanta University, Atlanta, Ga.
　　John Brown Collection
Special Collections Research Center, Syracuse University, Syracuse, N.Y.
　　Gerrit Smith Papers
State Library of Virginia, Richmond, Va.
　　John Brown's Raid: Records and Resources
West Virginia State Archives, Charles Town, W.Va.
　　Boyd Stutler Collection

Abbreviations Used in the Notes

BPL: Boston Public Library
BSC: Boyd Stutler Collection, West Virginia State Archives
HFNHP: Harpers Ferry National Historical Park
HLHS: Hudson Library and Historical Society
HSP: Historical Society of Pennsylvania

KSHS: Kansas State Historical Society
OGV: Oswald Garrison Villard John Brown Papers
RWL: Robert W. Woodruff Library

Prologue: October 16, 1859

1 "Men, get on": Osborne P. Anderson, "A Voice from Harper's Ferry" (Boston: printed for the author, 1861), 31. See also Annie Brown Adams in Franklin Sanborn, *Recollections of Seventy Years* (Boston: The Gorham Press, 1909), 177–78. Some observations of landscape are taken from my own retracing of the route on the night of October 16, 2009, with Dennis Frye, the chief historian at the Harpers Ferry National Historical Park.

1 "When in the course": "A Declaration of Liberty," H. W. Flournoy, ed., *Calendar of Virginia State Papers,* vol. 9, *The John Brown Insurrection* (Richmond, Va., 1893), 275–79. Also see Richard Hinton, *John Brown and His Men* (New York: Funk & Wagnalls, 1894; Michigan Historical Reprint Series, 2005), 637–43.

2 "Open the gate!": testimony of Daniel Whelan, Jan. 6, 1860, Report of the Select Committee of the Senate Appointed to Inquire into the Late Invasion and Seizure of the Public Property at Harper's Ferry ("Mason Report"), 36th Cong., 1st Sess., 1860; BSC.

2 "I came here": ibid.

4 "infidels": Aaron Stevens to James Redpath, Dec. 17, 1859, KSHS, among other examples. Stevens told Redpath "all were infidels but three or four." Brown's son Oliver also wrote approvingly of "infidels," which sometimes referred to those who had left their church over slavery (June 18, 1859, to wife Martha; HLHS).

4 "HOW WOULD": *Baltimore American,* Nov. 14, 1859, citing the list first published in the *New York Express.* The first reference I can find to the "John Brown Raid" was in the *New York Herald,* Dec. 9, 1859, and this phrase appeared sporadically in 1860. But "John Brown's Raid" didn't become the norm until after the Civil War.

4 "I do not suppose": *The Collected Works of Abraham Lincoln,* vol. 3 (New Brunswick: Rutgers University Press, 1953), 181. Lincoln said this on Sept. 18, 1858, during his famous debates with Stephen Douglas.

5 "even if it rushes": Jefferson Davis, Remarks to U.S. Senate, Dec. 8, 1859, *Congressional Globe,* 36th Cong., vol. 1 (Washington, D.C.: John C. Rives, 1860), 69.

5 "In firing his gun": Archibald Grimké, *William Lloyd Garrison: The Abolitionist* (New York: Funk & Wagnalls, 1891), 367. For a discussion of Garrison and Brown, see Henry Mayer's outstanding *All on Fire: William Lloyd Garrison and the Abolition of Slavery* (New York: St. Martin's Press, 1998), particularly 494–505.

Chapter 1: School of Adversity

9 "for want of": This and other statements by Owen Brown are quoted from Clarence S. Gee, "Owen Brown's Autobiography," HLHS. John Brown's birthplace no longer stands, but a plaque marks the site on a small road near Torrington, Connecticut. For more on Owen Brown, tanning and shoemaking, and the Torrington

area at the time of Brown's birth, see David Ross Bennett, *The John Brown Birthplace* (Westport, Conn.: Torrington Historical Society, 2002).

11 "I cannot tell you": John Brown to Henry L. Stearns, July 15, 1857, in Oswald Garrison Villard, *John Brown, 1800–1859: A Biography Fifty Years After* (Boston: Houghton Mifflin, 1910), 1. For Henry Stearns's account, see "Why John Brown Wrote the Letter to Me," Oct. 26, 1902, BSC.

11 "I came with": "Owen Brown's Autobiography," HLHS.

11 Brown on his early life: John Brown to Henry L. Stearns, July 15, 1857, in Villard, *John Brown*, 2–5.

12 "worldly": This and other Sabbath rules adopted in 1819 are in "Minutes of the First Congregational Church, Hudson, Ohio, 1802–1837," 6–7, HLHS.

12 "did open his house": "Records of the Congregational Church in Hudson," 71, HLHS.

13 "the conversation": James Foreman to James Redpath, Dec. 28, 1859, KSHS.

13 Stubbornness, temper, and vanity: John Brown to Henry L. Stearns, July 15, 1857, in Villard, *John Brown*, 2–5.

14 "Species of": Charles Pinckney, quoted in Walter A. McDougall, *Freedom Just Around the Corner: A New History, 1585–1928* (New York: Harper-Collins, 2004), 317.

14 "moral and political": Thomas Jefferson to Thomas Cooper, Sept. 10, 1814, quoted in David McCullough, *John Adams* (New York: Simon & Schuster, 2001), 633. More of the letter is at the Monticello website: http://www.monticello.org/site/jefferson/quotations-slavery-and-emancipation.

15 "This momentous question": Thomas Jefferson to John Holmes, April 22, 1820, Library of Congress.

16 "Eternal war": John Brown to Henry L. Stearns, July 15, 1857, in Villard, *John Brown*, 4.

16 "Some Persons": "Owen Brown's Autobiography," HLHS.

16 "used to hang about": John Brown to Henry L. Stearns, July 15, 1857, in Villard, *John Brown*, 2.

17 "An inspired paternal ruler": George B. Delamater, undated manuscript, OGV. For more on Brown in Pennsylvania, see "John Brown Pennsylvania Citizen," by Ernest Miller (Warren, Pa.: Penn State Press, 1952).

17 Brown and corporal punishment: Salmon Brown on Jason Brown, BSC; interview with Jason Brown, in OGV; Salmon Brown, "My Father, John Brown," in *The Outlook*, Jan. 25, 1913; Lou V. Chapin, "The Last Days of Old John Brown," *Overland Monthly*, April 1899; and James Foreman to James Redpath, Dec. 28, 1859, KSHS.

17 "little folks": John Brown to Mary Ann Brown, Nov. 26, 1838, BSC.

17 "strangeness": Louis DeCaro, Jr., *"Fire from the Midst of You"* (New York: New York University Press, 2002), 69, 300. See also Robert McGlone, *John Brown's War Against Slavery* (New York: Cambridge University Press, 2009), 162–63.

17 "a difficulty about her heart": John Brown to Seth Thompson, Aug. 13, 1832, RWL.

18 "with instruments": John Brown to Owen Brown, Aug. 11, 1832, HLHS.

18   "great bodily pain": John Brown to Seth Thompson, Aug. 13, 1832, RWL.

18   "Farewell Earth": interview with Jason Brown, OGV. Also see "Monument Inscriptions," HLHS.

18   "I have been growing numb" and "Getting more & more unfit": John Brown to Seth Thompson, Aug. 13, 1832, RWL.

18   For more on Brown's proposal to Mary Day, see interview with Sarah Brown, OGV.

18   "Remedy for": *Ohio Cultivator*, April 15, 1846, BSC.

18   "In summer": John Brown Memorandum Books, BPL.

18   "I am running": John Brown to Seth Thompson, January 6, 1828, RWL.

18   "I was unable": John Brown to Seth Thompson, Nov. 3, 1832, RWL.

18   "I have been": John Brown to Seth Thompson, March 1, 1834, RWL.

19   "I have aroused": John Brown to Owen Brown, June 12, 1830, HLHS. See also Boyd Stutler, "John Brown and the Masonic Order," BSC.

Chapter 2: I Consecrate My Life

20   Nat Turner quotes: Kenneth Greenberg, ed., *The Confessions of Nat Turner and Related Documents* (Boston: Bedford Books, 1996), 38–57. See also my own "Untrue Confessions," *The New Yorker*, Dec. 13, 1999.

22   "Tell a man": Henry Mayer, *All on Fire*, 112. Also, the free black activist David Walker published his fiery "Appeal" in 1829, calling on blacks to violently overthrow their masters.

23   "with the express": Governor John Floyd, quoted in Greenberg, *Confessions of Nat Turner*, 107.

23   "I take higher ground": John C. Calhoun, "Speech on Slavery," U.S. Senate, *Congressional Globe*, 24th Cong., 2nd Sess. (Feb. 6, 1837), 157–59. On George Fitzhugh, see C. Vann Woodward's introductory essay in 1959 to *Cannibals All! or, Slaves Without Masters*, online at http://www.ditext.com/woodward/fitzhugh.html. See also Paul Finkelman, ed., *Defending Slavery: Proslavery Thought in the Old South* (New York: Bedford/St. Martins, 2003).

23   "The first step": Mayer, *All on Fire*, 218.

24   "I have been trying": John Brown to Frederick Brown, Nov. 21, 1834, BSC.

24   "non-resistant": Archibald Grimké, *William Lloyd Garrison*, 367.

24   "I deny the right": Mayer, *All on Fire*, 121.

24   "all on fire": ibid., 119–20. In full: "I have need to be *all on fire*, for I have mountains of ice about me to melt."

24   "Total with": ibid., 50.

25   "resist not evil": Matthew 5:38–39.

25   "Here before God": Edward Brown, in Louis Ruchames, ed., *A John Brown Reader* (London: Abelard-Schuman, 1959), 189. For another account of the meeting, see Lora Case, *Hudson of Long Ago* (Hudson, Ohio: The Hudson Library and Historical Society, 1963), 53–54.

25   "He asked": Franklin Sanborn, ed., *The Life and Letters of John Brown* (Boston: Roberts Bros., 1891), 39, 138.

26 "dead to the world": Salmon Brown, "My Father, John Brown," in *The Outlook*, Jan. 25, 1913.

26 "held firmly": ibid.

26 "There was": John Brown, Jr., quoted in Oswald Villard, *John Brown*, 45–46.

26 "The sword": Judges 6–8.

27 "I do think": John Brown to Seth Thompson, Dec. 30, 1836, RWL.

27 "The prospect": John Brown to Seth Thompson, July 10, 1839, RWL.

27 "flat down": John Brown to Seth Thompson, July 21, 1840, RWL.

27 Ohio bankruptcy details: "Bankruptcy Inventory," BSC. Brown was named in more than twenty lawsuits in the Portage County, Ohio, Court of Common Pleas between 1820 and 1845, mostly for unpaid debts (Villard, *John Brown*, 36–37).

27 "abandon anything": James Foreman to James Redpath, Dec. 28, 1859, KSHS.

27 "Unworthily": John Brown to George Kellog, Aug. 27, 1839, HLHS.

28 "many faults": John Brown to family, Dec. 5, 1838, BSC.

28 "the sharer of my poverty": John Brown to Mary Brown, March 7, 1844, BSC.

28 John Brown on children's deaths: John Brown to John Brown, Jr., Sept. 25, 1843, HLHS. In his diary, Brown sketched the floor plan of one of his family's many dwellings; he included a chamber labeled "sick room." Memorandum Books, BPL.

28 "a calamity": Salmon Brown, "My Father, John Brown."

28 "I felt": John Brown to Franklin Sanborn, Feb. 24, 1858, in Sanborn, *The Life and Letters*, 444.

Chapter 3: A Warlike Spirit

29 "You have a": "Phrenological Description of John Brown as Given by O. S. Fowler," February 27, 1847, KSHS.

29 "fixedness": Franklin Sanborn, "Comment by a Radical Abolitionist," *Century Magazine*, July 1883, 414. See also Salmon Brown, "My Father, John Brown": "Father was strongly fixed in most of his habits. . . . It was always difficult for him to fit himself to circumstances; he wanted conditions to change for him."

30 "I sometimes": John Brown to Owen Brown, Dec. 10, 1846, in Franklin Sanborn, *The Life and Letters of John Brown*, 22. Also see John Brown to John Brown, Jr., May 23, 1845: "I hope that entire leanness of soul may not attend any little success in business," HLHS.

30 Douglass descriptions: Frederick Douglass, *Autobiographies* (New York: Library of America, 1994), 715–16.

31 "for the emancipation": Douglass, *Autobiographies*, 717–18.

32 "Though a white gentleman": Stephen Oates, *To Purge This Land with Blood: A Biography of John Brown* (Amherst: University of Massachusetts, 1984), 63.

32 "purity": See *Graham's Lectures on Chastity* (Glasgow: Royalty Buildings, 1900). Graham's beliefs were the origin of the now familiar Graham cracker.

32 "There are yet two places": Henry H. Garnet to Frederick Douglass, *North Star*, (Rochester, N.Y.), Dec. 8, 1848.

32 On Brown's surveying work in western Virginia, see Boyd Stutler, "John Brown and the Oberlin Lands," *West Virginia History*, vol. 12, April 1951.

33 "I can think": John Brown to Owen Brown, Jan. 10, 1849, KSHS.

34 Dana recollections: Richard Henry Dana, Jr., "How We Met John Brown," *The Atlantic Monthly*, July 1871, 1–9.

34 "if lost": John Brown to John Brown, Jr., Nov. 4, 1850, in Sanborn, *The Life and Letters*, 75.

34 "follies": John Brown to Mary Brown, March 7, 1844, BSC.

34 "verry considerable . . . sometimes chide": ibid.

34 "rather an invalid": Dana, "How We Met John Brown," 5.

34 "she must do something": John Brown, Jr., to John Brown, Sept. 18, 1849, Houghton Library.

34 "a Scrofulous humor": ibid.

35 "never believed": Mary Brown to John Brown, Jr., Sept. 25, 1849, Ohio Historical Society.

35 "plunge, douche": Ruggles advertisement, 1847, in *North Star*, HLHS. See also DeCaro, *"Fire from the Midst of You,"* 182–85.

35 "If you can send me" and "I went to hear": Mary Brown to John Brown, Jr., Nov. 8, 1849, BSC.

36 "It is an existing": Henry Mayer, *All on Fire*, 403.

36 "*The workingmen*": Emory Holloway, ed., *The Uncollected Poetry and Prose of Walt Whitman*, vol. 1 (New York: Doubleday, 1921), 172.

37 "It now seems": John Brown to Mary Brown, Nov. 28, 1850, in Sanborn, *The Life and Letters*, 106–7.

37 the United States League of Gileadites: "Words of Advice," in Hinton, *John Brown and His Men*, 585–88.

37 "Let the first blow": ibid.

38 "Cuba must be . . . a basin of water": Jefferson Davis, May 5, 1848, *Congressional Globe*, 30th Cong., 1st Sess., 599.

38 "I want these countries": Jeffrey Rogers Hummel, *Emancipating Slaves, Enslaving Free Men* (Peru, Ill.: Open Court Publishing, 1996), 96.

38 "doughfaces": This phrase is believed to have arisen at the time of the Missouri Compromise and came to refer to Northerners who held southern principles.

38 "Slavery": Horace Greeley in the *New York Tribune*, Jan. 11, 1854.

39 "forever prohibited": Missouri Compromise (1820). Full text at http://www.our documents.gov/doc.

39 "I could travel": William McFeely, *Frederick Douglass* (New York: Norton, 1995), 188.

40 "My thoughts are murder": Henry David Thoreau, *The Journal of Henry D. Thoreau* (New York: Dover, 1962), entry for June 16, 1854.

40 "a covenant": William Lloyd Garrison, *The Liberator*, July 7, 1854. Also see Mayer, *All on Fire*, 445.

40 "atrocious plot": *National Era* (Washington, D.C.), Jan. 24, 1854.

40 "grasping, skin-flint": Virgil Dean, ed., *Kansas Territorial Reader* (Topeka: Kansas State Historical Society, 2005), 224.

40 "Pukes": Michael Fellman, *Inside War: The Guerrilla Conflict in Missouri During the American Civil War* (New York: Oxford, 1990), 13, 271. Fellman suggests the name might be related to the malarial bottomlands of Missouri. For a classic characterization of Pukes, see William Phillips, *The Conquest of Kansas* (Boston: Phillips, Sampson and Co., 1856), 28–29.

40 "disposed to go": John Brown to John Brown, Jr., Aug. 21, 1854, OGV.

41 "If I were not": ibid.

41 "more likely to benefit": John Brown to his children, Sept. 30, 1843, HLHS.

41 "Every Slaveholding State": John Brown, Jr., to John Brown, May 20, 24, 1855, HSP.

41 "exhibit": ibid.

42 "We need them more": ibid.

42 "Every day strengthens": John Brown, Jr., to John Brown, May 5, 1855, Houghton Library.

42 "He has something": Owen Brown to S. L. Adair and family, Aug. 8, 1855, KSHS.

Chapter 4: First Blood

43 "I *certainly*" and other descriptions of Kansas beauty: Wealthy Brown to Ruth Brown, June 12, 1855, Beinecke Library, Yale University.

43 "The prairies": John Brown, Jr., to John Brown, June 22, 1855, KSHS.

43 "shivering": Oswald Villard, *John Brown*, 88.

43 "we were all": John Brown to Mary Brown, Oct. 13, 1855, KSHS.

44 "thinking it would afford": John Brown, "brief history of John Brown otherwise (old B) & his family: as connected with Kansas," HSP.

44 "I think, could I hope": John Brown to his family, Sept. 4, 1855, KSHS.

44 "You are all": John Brown to Mary Brown and his children, Oct. 13, 1855, KSHS.

45 "We will continue": General Stringfellow, "Squatter Sovereign," August 28, 1855, in Villard, *John Brown*, 93.

45 "Guns, Revolvers": John Brown to family, Aug. 15, 1855, HLHS.

45 "Hearing that trouble": John Brown to Owen Brown, Oct. 19, 1855, HLHS.

45 "shanties": John Brown to Mary Brown, Nov. 30, 1855, BSC.

45 "silently suffered us to pass": John Brown letter in *Akron Beacon-Journal*, Dec. 20, 1855, in Louis Ruchames, *A John Brown Reader*, 97–101.

46 "Our men have so much": Wealthy Brown to Mary Brown, January 6, 1856, in Villard, *John Brown*, 127.

46 "to live rather slim": Oliver Brown to family, Jan. 6, 1856, Ohio Historical Society.

46 "we got on": Mary Brown to John Brown, May 20, 1856, Ohio Historical Society.

46 "Father seems": Wealthy Brown to Owen Brown, March 19, 1856, HLHS.

46 "Should that take": John Brown to family, Feb. 1, 1856, KSHS.

46 Pierce quotations: Nicole Etcheson, *Bleeding Kansas: Contested Liberty in the Civil War Era* (Lawrence: University of Kansas, 2004), 91, and Pierce, "State of the Union," December 31, 1855, at http://millercenter.org/scripps/archive/speeches/detail/3730.

47 "Hellish enactments": John Brown to Joshua Giddings, Feb. 20, 1856, in Villard, *John Brown*, 131.

47 "I have no desire": John Brown to family, April 7, 1856, KSHS.

47 "Matters": John Brown to Samuel Adair, April 22, 1856, HLHS.

48 Buford quotes: "The Buford Expedition to Kansas," Walter Fleming, *The American Historical Review*, October 1900, 38–48.

48 "We are constantly": Florella Adair to family, May 16, 1856, OGV.

48 "law-abiding": I. B. Donaldson, "Proclamation," in Villard, *John Brown*, 143.

48 "Draw your revolvers": David Atchison, "Speech to Pro-Slavery 'Soldiers,' " May 21, 1856, KSHS.

49 "Now something": interview with Jason Brown, OGV.

49 "commit": Oates, *To Purge This Land with Blood*, 129.

49 "There was a signal": interview with Owen Brown, Feb. 27, 1880, Houghton Library.

49 Charles Sumner quotations: *Appendix to the Congressional Globe*, 34th Cong., 1st Sess., May 19, 1856.

49 "a libel on": "Isaac Bassett: A Senate Memoir," U.S. Senate website: http://www.senate.gov/artandhistory/art/special/Bassett/tdetail.cfm?id=17.

50 "lashed into submission": *Richmond Enquirer*, quoted in Mary Norton et al., eds., *A People and a Nation*, vol. 1 (Boston: Houghton Mifflin, 2005), 370.

50 "The men went": interview with Salmon Brown, OGV.

50 "Northern army": "Report of the Special Committee Appointed to Investigate the Troubles in Kansas," House Report No. 200, 34th Cong. (Washington, D.C.: Cornelius Wendell, 1856), 1193–99. The report includes affidavits by the families attacked that night.

50 "My husband": ibid., 1793.

50 "An old man": ibid., 1195.

51 "I want you to tell me the way": ibid., 1198.

51 "You are our prisoner": ibid.

51 "You have neighbors?" ibid.

52 "His fingers": ibid., 1195.

52 "Sherman's skull": ibid., 1197.

53 "tenderfoot": interview with Salmon Brown, OGV.

53 Jason Brown confronting John: Jason Brown statement to F. G. Adams, April 2, 1884, OGV; also see Jason Brown, letter to *Lawrence* (Kansas) *Journal*, Feb. 8, 1880, OGV.

53 "Father never": interview with Salmon Brown, OGV.

53 "old man Doyle": Ruchames, *A John Brown Reader*, 202.

54 "For what purpose": Salmon Brown to William Connelley, Nov. 6, 1913, BSC. He spoke of this also in a letter to Franklin Sanborn, Nov. 17, 1911, BSC. See also interview with Salmon Brown, OGV.

54 "death for death," and "restraining fear": John Brown, Jr., to *Cleveland Leader*, Nov. 29, 1883. Also see "John Brown of Osawatomie; A History, Not an Apology," HLHS.

54 "I left for fear": Report of the Special Committee, 1198.

54 "taken from their beds": Samuel Adair to brother and sister, May 23, 1856, OGV.

55 "I never lie down": William Stanley Hoole, ed., "A Southerner's Viewpoint of the

Kansas Situation, 1856–1857: The Letters of Lieutenant Col. A. J. Hoole, C.S.A.,"
Kansas Historical Quarterly, Feb. 1934, 43–56.

55 "LET SLIP THE DOGS": *Border Times* (Westport, Missouri), May 27, 1856, in
Villard, *John Brown*, 189.

55 "He wanted": interview with Salmon Brown, OGV.

55 "thought it": interview with Owen Brown, June 27, 1880, Houghton Library.

55 "felt terribly": Salmon Brown to William Connelley, May 28, 1913, BSC.

55 "When I came": Villard, *John Brown*, 165.

56 "spells": Annie Brown to Thomas Wentworth Higginson, Nov. 29, 1859, BPL.

56 "subjected himself to the most dreadful": John Brown, "brief history of John
Brown," HSP.

56 "the most terrible shock": Jason Brown in Sanborn, *The Life and Letters*, 273, and
1880 statement in OGV.

56 "he became quite insane": John Brown to family, June 1856, Ruchames, *A John
Brown Reader*, 103.

56 "You cannot easily imagine": Rev. Adair to "Dear Bro. & Sis. Hand," May 23,
1856, OGV. Feeling badly exposed, the Adairs also came to resent John's handling of money sent from Ohio. "One letter from father stated 'I wish to have
Adairs folks have a share,'" Florella Adair wrote, "but he seemed to need it all &
took it" (Florella Adair to "Dear Brother & Sister," Nov. 9, 1856, HLHS).

56 Redpath quotations: James Redpath, *The Public Life of Captain John Brown*
(Boston: Thayer and Eldridge, 1860), 106–7.

57 "I went to take": Clay Pate, "John Brown as Viewed by Clay Pate," BSC.

57 "He is not": William Phillips, *The Conquest of Kansas*, 332.

58 For the details of the Browns' diet, see Bondi File, OGV. Also, see Salmon
Brown, "After the Battle of Black Jack," BSC, and Salmon Brown to William
Connelley, May 28, 1913, BSC.

58 "We have": John Brown to family, June 1856, in Ruchames, *A John Brown Reader*,
104.

58 For details on the chaos of Kansas, see Nicole Etcheson's *Bleeding Kansas*.
Etcheson's book is the best study of the conflict. She quotes a territorial governor
saying of his job, "You might as well attempt to govern the devil in hell" (131).

58 "This has proven": John Brown, Jr., to father and brother, Sept. 8, 1856, KSHS.

59 "God sees it": interview with Jason Brown, OGV. The code phrase "into Africa"
may have derived from the South's large black population. But in "A Footnote to
John Brown's Raid" (*Virginia Magazine of History and Biography*, vol. 67, Oct.
1959, pp. 396–98), Phil Milhous points out another possible source. Brown's
reading included a popular work of ancient history by Charles Rollin, which tells
of the Sicilian warrior Agathocles, who devised a daring plan to "make Africa the
seat of war" by besieging Carthage. He set off with only fifty men and two of his
sons, telling them "the only way to free their country, was to carry the war into the
territories of their enemies," and, further, that the oppressed natives "would run in
crowds to join them on the first news of their arrival; that the boldness of their
attempt would alone disconcert the Carthaginians, who had no expectation of
seeing an enemy at their gates." This sounds very much like what Brown intended.

Chapter 5: Secret Service

60 "Captain Brown of Osawatomie": This is how Sanborn introduced him in Massachusetts. Stephen Oates, *To Purge This Land with Blood*, 195. See also Franklin Sanborn, *The Life and Letters of John Brown*, 374.

60 "You need not": John Brown to wife and children, Oct. 11, 1856, BSC.

61 "death was": Owen Brown to John Brown, March 27, 1856, KSHS.

61 "Your unfaithful Parent": ibid.

61 "to witness": John Brown to Owen Brown, March 26, 1856, HLHS.

61 "errand": John Brown Speaking Notes, March 1857, KSHS.

61 "There is a divining": Franklin Sanborn, *Recollections of Seventy Years*, vol. 1 (Boston: Richard G. Badger, 1909), 83. Sanborn later proposed to Emerson's daughter and was refused. For more on Sanborn and his role as gatekeeper of Brown's memory, see R. Blakeslee Gilpin, *John Brown Still Lives!* (Chapel Hill: University of North Carolina Press, 2011).

62 "He did not": Sanborn, *Recollections*, 112.

62 "pent-up fire": ibid.

62 "suppressed yet metallic" and other Alcott comments: Odell Shepard, ed., *The Journals of Bronson Alcott* (Boston: Little Brown & Co., 1938), 316.

63 "I should hate": Walter Muir Whitehill, "John Brown of Osawatomie in Boston, 1857," *Proceedings of the Massachusetts Historical Society*, vol. 69, 263–64.

63 "moral magnetism": Mary Stearns to Franklin Sanborn, April 1885, in Sanborn, *The Life and Letters*, 510.

63 "it suddenly seemed": ibid.

64 "John Brown": Sanborn, *The Life and Letters*, 381.

64 "Minute Men": John Brown to Heman Humphrey, April 18, 1857, HLHS.

64 For John Brown's fund-raising pitch, see John Brown Speaking Notes, March 1857, KSHS.

64 "I have no other income": John Brown to Amos Lawrence, March 19, 1857, in Oswald Villard, *John Brown*, 280.

64 "I fully sympathize" and other apologetic quotes: John Brown to Mary Brown, Nov. 2, 1855, Nov. 23, 1855, KSHS.

65 "to learn, & practice": John Brown, quoting from Mary's letter in his reply to her, March 31, 1857, BSC.

65 "in remembrance of": John Brown to Ellen Brown, May 13, 1857, BSC.

65 "I prize it": John Brown to Mary Brown, March 12, 1857, KSHS.

65 "If I should never": John Brown to Mary Brown, May 27, 1857, BSC.

65 "OX" and "Oxentricity": note at bottom of letter of Owen Brown to his sisters, Nov. 27, 1859, Houghton Library. In his diary, reprinted in the *Richmond Daily Whig*, Oct. 29, 1859, Owen wrote: "I dispute and contradict my father in any and everything." A copy is in OGV.

66 "for the settlers": testimony of Charles Blair, Mason Report, A121.

66 "Kansas butter knifes": Oliver Brown to family, May 16, 1857, KSHS.

66 "I furnished that money": John Brown to Hugh Forbes, June 22, 1857, HSP. In an earlier letter, Brown called Forbes "a distinguished Scotch officer" (John Brown to John Brown, Jr., April 15, 1857, BSC).

67 "It is not easy": Franklin Sanborn to John Brown, Aug. 28, 1857, RWL.

67 "How to act": John Brown to "Dear Brother & Sister Adair," Oct 5, 1857, HLHS.

67 "In immediate": John Brown to George Luther Stearns, Aug. 8, 1857, in Villard, *John Brown*, 297.

67 "small school": John Brown to Franklin Sanborn, Aug. 27, 1857, BSC.

67 "Do you mean": Franklin Sanborn to John Brown, Sept. 14, 1857, RWL.

68 "If you want": John E. Cook's confession. This was widely published in newspapers after the Harpers Ferry attack. It also appears in Richard Hinton, *John Brown and His Men*, 700–714.

68 "*Here we found*": ibid.

68 "Guerrilla warfare": John Brown Memorandum Books, BPL.

69 the Hole: James P. Noffsinger, *Harpers Ferry, West Virginia: Contributions Towards a Physical History* (U.S. Department of the Interior, 1958), 206. The first white resident of what became Harpers Ferry was a squatter known as "Peter in the Hole." He was bought out by Robert Harper, a Pennsylvania millwright, in 1747. In 1763, the town was incorporated as "Shenandoah Falls at Mr. Harper's Ferry."

69 "one of the most": Thomas Jefferson, *Notes on the State of Virginia* (New York: Library of America, 1984), 143.

69 "This spot affords": George Washington to Timothy Pickering, Sept. 16, 1795, in Jared Sparks, *The Writings of George Washington*, vol. 11 (Boston: Charles Tappan, 1846), 69.

69 "There is not a spot": George Washington to James McHenry, May 6, 1798, in W. W. Abbot, ed., *The Papers of George Washington, Retirement Series*, vol. 2 (Charlottesville: University of Virginia, 1998), 253. For more on George Washington's visions for the Potomac, see Joel Achenbach, *The Grand Idea* (New York: Simon & Schuster, 2002).

71 "make a dash" and other quotes about discussions with Brown: Forbes to Samuel Gridley Howe, May 14, 1858, in *New York Times*, Oct. 28, 1859.

72 "He was very pious": *New York Herald*, Nov. 1, 1859.

72 "protégé": testimony of Richard Realf, Mason Report, A090.

72 "drunken riot": Irving Richman, *John Brown Among the Quakers, and Other Sketches* (Chicago: R. R. Donnelley, 1894), 24: "He, together with three comrades, was sentenced to death for participation in what is called in his sentence 'a drunken riot and mutiny against a major of the regiment.'" For more details, see Court Martial Case Files, War Department Office of the Judge Advocate General, May 21, 1855, National Archives. Kit Carson was one of the witnesses against Stevens.

72 "The persons": John Brown to Mary Brown, Dec. 30, 1857, BSC.

72 "Some warm words": John Cook's confession.

72 "after a good deal": Hinton, *John Brown and His Men*, 702.

72 "11 desperadoes": Owen Brown's diary, Dec. 3, 1857, in *New York Times*, Oct. 24, 1859. Other portions printed in *Richmond Daily Whig*, Oct. 29, 1859; copy in OGV.

72 "Lyceums": L. F. Parsons to "Dear Friends Redpath & Hinton," Dec. 1859, KSHS.

72 "Cold, wet, and snowy": Owen Brown's diary, Dec. 8, 1857, in *New York Times*, Oct. 24, 1859.

73 "War College": "Scrap in handwriting of Owen Brown," BSC. See also L. F. Parsons to "Dear Friends Redpath & Hinton," Dec. 1859, KSHS, which tells of training with "Col. Whipple as Drillmaster."

73 "legislatures": ibid.

73 "censure . . . for hugging girls": Owen Brown's diary, *Richmond Whig*, Oct. 29, 1859, OGV.

73 "the worse": Moses and Charlotte Varney to "My dear friends Whipple & Tidd," May 10, 1858, *Calendar of Virginia State Papers: The John Brown Insurrection*, State Library of Virginia. George Gill, another of Brown's men, later wrote that Tidd "became quite notorious for his amours" in Iowa (Gill to Richard Hinton, undated manuscript, KSHS, 20). For more on the band's stay in Iowa, see Jeannette Mather Lord, "John Brown: They Had a Concern," *West Virginia Archives and History*, April 1959, 163–83, BSC, and Richman, *John Brown Among the Quakers*.

74 "secret service": John Brown to Thomas Wentworth Higginson, Feb. 2, 1858, BPL.

74 "His whole time": Douglass, *Autobiographies*, 756.

74 "Courage, courage . . . the great work of my life": John Brown to wife and children, Jan. 30, 1858, in Ruchames, *A John Brown Reader*, 118.

74 "Kansas is": John Brown, Jr., to E. B. Whitman, Feb. 1858, KSHS.

74 "When you look": John Brown to John Brown, Jr., Feb. 4, 1858, BSC.

74 "I want to get": ibid.

75 "I now want": John Brown to Thomas Wentworth Higginson, Feb. 2, 1858, BPL.

75 "I am always": Thomas Wentworth Higginson to John Brown, Feb. 8, 1858, BPL.

75 "Rail Road": John Brown to Thomas Wentworth Higginson, Feb. 12, 1858, BPL.

75 "I have been told": John Brown to Thomas Wentworth Higginson, Feb. 2, 1858, BPL.

76 "I have written": John Brown to Theodore Parker, Feb. 2, 1858, in Sanborn, *The Life and Letters*, 435.

76 "bends towards": Frances Cobbe, ed., *The Collected Works of Theodore Parker*, vol. 2 (London: N. Trubner & Co., 1867), 48.

76 "I long to see": Thomas Wentworth Higginson to John Brown, May 1, 1859, BPL. For more on Higginson, and also his relationship with Emily Dickinson, see Brenda Wineapple's riveting *White Heat* (New York: Knopf, 2008).

77 "Hope died": Edward J. Renehan, Jr., *The Secret Six: The True Tale of the Men Who Conspired with John Brown* (New York: Crown, 1995), 31.

77 "no boaster": Ralph Waldo Emerson, *The Complete Works of Ralph Waldo Emerson*, vol. 10 (Boston: Houghton Mifflin, 1911), 504.

78 "Our friend": Franklin Sanborn to Thomas Wentworth Higginson, Feb. 23, 1858, BSC.

78 "secret committee": Sanborn, *The Life and Letters*, 514. The group had no formal name and was sometimes called the "Secret Committee of Six." See Jeffery Rossbach, *Ambivalent Conspirators* (Philadelphia: University of Pennsylvania Press, 1982), 142–44.

78 "wealth, luxury": "Old Brown's Farewell," BSC.

78 "manifest hopelessness": Sanborn, *The Life and Letters*, 439.

78 "If God be for us": ibid.

78 "dangerous": ibid, 445.

78 "milk-and-water": testimony of William Arny, Mason Report, 88.

79 "He is of the stuff": Samuel Gridley Howe to John Forbes, Feb. 5, 1859, in *Letters and Recollections of John Murray Forbes*, vol. 1 (Boston: Houghton, Mifflin & Co., 1900), 178.

79 "The slave": Gerrit Smith to Joshua Giddings, March 25, 1858, in Renehan, *Secret Six*, 147.

Chapter 6: This Spark of Fire

80 "wool business" and the "mill": For example, see Franklin Sanborn to Thomas Wentworth Higginson, Feb. 23, 1858, which also mentions "woolen machinery" (BSC).

80 "a very quiet convention" and "true friends": confession of John Cook, in Richard Hinton, *John Brown and His Men*, 703.

80 "flock": Franklin Sanborn, *The Life and Letters of John Brown*, 457.

80 "to state the object": "Journal of the Provisional Constitutional Convention," *Calendar of Virginia State Papers*, 271.

81 "a plan for organization": ibid.

81 "Whereas, Slavery": John Brown, "Provisional Constitution and Ordinances for the People of the United States," ibid., 278–88.

81 "no rights": *Dred Scott v. Sandford*, 60 U.S. 393 (1857), online at http://caselaw.lp .findlaw.com/scripts/getcase.pl?court=US&vol=60&invol=393.

82 "Every man was anxious": Charles Moffett, quoted in "Extracts on John Brown in Canada," BSC.

82 "elected by acclamation": "Journal of the Provisional Constitution Convention," *Calendar of Virginia State Papers*, 273.

82 "Had a good": John Brown to Mary Brown, May 12, 1858, BSC.

82 "There is the most abundant": John Brown to John Brown, Jr., April 8, 1858, BSC.

82 "Hariet Tubman": ibid.

83 "had the blues" and other quotes: Salmon Brown to "Dear Folks," Dec. 28, 1856, BSC.

83 "quit running around": ibid.

83 "I should be": John Brown to family, May 1, 1858, HLHS.

83 "O my daughter": John Brown to family, Jan. 30, 1858, in Ruchames, *A John Brown Reader*, 117–18.

83 "Dear father": Ruth Brown Thompson to John Brown, Feb. 20, 1858, HLHS.

83 "My whole heart": Henry Thompson to John Brown, April 21, 1858, KSHS.

83 "I hope you": Ruth Brown Thompson to John Brown, April 21, 1858, KSHS.

84 "New England humanitarians": Hugh Forbes to *New York Herald*, Nov. 1, 1859.

84 "they were not": Thomas Wentworth Higginson, "Memorandum," BPL. Brown added, "They held the purse and he was powerless without them."

84 "blind": ibid.

84 "I do not wish": Gerrit Smith to Franklin Sanborn, July 26, 1858, in Sanborn, *The Life and Letters*, 466. For more on Forbes's disclosures, see testimony of Henry Wilson and Samuel Gridley Howe, Mason Report.

85 "He would have": Salmon Brown to William Connelley, Dec. 2, 1913, BSC.

85 "suavity itself": George Gill to Richard Hinton, undated manuscript, 21, KSHS.

85 "rage for talking": For Cook's lack of discretion, see Richard Realf to Brown, May 31, 1858, KSHS.

85 "to see how things": John Cook's confession, Hinton, *John Brown and His Men*, 703.

86 "Rifles": Meriwether Lewis to Thomas Jefferson, April 20, 1803, Library of Congress. Other Lewis and Clark details: Stephen Ambrose, *Undaunted Courage* (New York: Simon & Schuster, 1996), 248–29. The "Experiment" didn't work and was abandoned by the Missouri River.

86 "lock, stock" and "common hands": Merritt Roe Smith, *Harpers Ferry Armory and the New Technology* (Ithaca: Cornell University Press, 1980), 67–68, 239.

86 "coal smoke": Thomas Yoseloff, ed., *Voyage to America: The Journals of Thomas Cather* (New York: A. S. Barnes, 1961), 28.

86 "offensive matter": "Board of Health for Harpers Ferry," *The Constitutionalist*, June 12, 1839, HFNHP.

86 "hallooing or rioting" and "throwing stones": By-Laws & Ordinances of the Corporation of Harper's Ferry, HFNHP. The ordinances also prohibited swine, dogs, "and sluts running at large in the street," and forbade "dirt, filth, manure or rubbish, to be and remain in the streets."

87 "mere machines": Merrit Roe Smith, *Harpers Ferry Armory*, 272.

87 "with a ghastly": Joseph Barry, *The Strange Story of Harper's Ferry: With Legends of the Surrounding Country* (Martinsburg, W.Va.: Thompson Brothers, 1903), 26.

88 "I was really pleased": Mary Mauzy to daughter, Dec. 18, 1859, HFNHP.

88 "his patriarchal disguise": James Redpath, *The Public Life of Captain John Brown*, 199.

88 "I have done": John Brown to Ruth and Henry Thompson, May 10, 1853, HLHS.

88 "was never": John Brown to John Brown, Jr., Sept. 9, 1858, in Villard, *John Brown*, 358.

89 Quotations from the *New York Tribune*: "Old Brown's Parallels," *New York Tribune*, Jan. 28, 1859.

89 "The closer we got": George Gill to Richard Hinton, "1860 or '61—early," KSHS.

89 "BROWN'S RESCUED": *New York Tribune*, March 18, 1859.

90 "most ready": Villard, *John Brown*, 386.

90 "He has begun": Franklin Sanborn to Thomas Wentworth Higginson, Jan. 19, 1859, in Sanborn, *The Life and Letters*, 492.

90 "to pursue": Stephen Oates, *To Purge This Land with Blood*, 262.

90 "set his mill": Sanborn, *The Life and Letters*, 493.

90 "The entire success": John Brown to Samuel Gridley Howe, March 1, 1858, Houghton Library.

90 "liberated": Villard, *John Brown*, 391.

90 "would give two dollars": Redpath, *Public Life of Captain John Brown*, 239.

90 "The Captain leaves us": Odell Shepard, *The Journals of Bronson Alcott*, 316.

91 "glittering gray-blue eyes": Sarah Forbes Hughes, ed., *John Murray Forbes: Letters and Recollections* (Boston: Houghton Mifflin, 1899), 179–82.

91 "monomania": William Lawrence, *Life of A. A. Lawrence* (Freeport, N.Y.: Greenwood, 1971; originally published 1888), 130.

92 George Gill is quoted from his letters to Richard Hinton, KSHS, in particular July 7, 1893. Also see interview with George Gill, OGV.

92 Charles Blair is quoted from his testimony, Mason Report, A124–25.

93 "Wishing you": Charles Blair to John Brown, June 10, 1859, *Calendar of Virginia State Papers*, 324.

93 "We leave here": John Brown to "J. Henrie, Esq.," June 30, 1859, ibid.

Chapter 7: My Invisibles

97 "Good morning, gentlemen": This and other Unseld quotes are from his testimony, Mason Report, A001–A012.

98 "Nothing going on": Jeremiah Anderson to "Dear Brother," July 5, 1859, KSHS.

99 "John Henrie Esquire": John Brown to John Kagi, July 27, Aug. 10, and Sept. 10, 1859, HSP.

100 "had far more": Franklin Keagy to Richard Hinton, March 27, 1893, KSHS. See also Franklin Keagy to Franklin Sanborn, March 24, 1891, BSC.

101 "Tomorrow": Cook to "Iowa Family," July 3, 1859, KSHS.

101 "as a good time": Franklin Sanborn, *The Life and Letters*, 468.

101 "have the freight": *Calendar of Virginia State Papers*, 330.

101 "almost disqualified": John Brown, Jr., to John Brown, May 1, 1858, in Villard, *John Brown*, 406.

101 "Please say to Mr.": "John Smith" to "J. Henrie Esq.," July 23, 1859, HSP.

102 "hands": John Brown to "John Henrie Esquire," undated, HSP, and to "Dear friends all," Aug. 6, 1859, HSP.

102 "Hardware": John Brown, Jr., to John Kagi, July 23, 1859, HSP.

102 "mining" and "I had supposed": John Brown, Jr., to "Friend Henrie," Sept. 8, 1859, HSP.

102 "I expected": Luke Parsons to John Kagi, May 16, 1859, *Calendar of Virginia State Papers*, 301.

102 "Don't you do it": interview with Luke Parsons, OGV.

102 "I find it": John Brown to Mary Brown, July 5, 1859, in Oswald Villard, *John Brown*, 404–5.

103 "Mother *would not go*": Statement of Annie Brown Adams, written for Franklin Sanborn, Nov. 1886, Chicago Historical Society.

104 "in the enjoyment": ibid.

104 "Sometimes in the night": "Kennedy Farm Notes," OGV.

104 "I always blush": statement of Annie Brown Adams, Chicago Historical Society.

104 "the outlaw girl": ibid.

104 "had a good excuse": ibid.

105 "plague and torment": ibid.

105 "earnest, kind-looking": Annie Brown Adams to Garibaldi Ross, Dec. 15, 1887, Gilder Lehrman Collection.

106 "After bidding": Thomas Featherstonhaugh, *John Brown's Men* (Harpers Ferry, W.Va.: Harrisburg, 1899), 13.

106 "a sort": statement of Annie Brown Adams, Chicago Historical Society.

106 "much more": Annie Brown Adams to Richard Hinton, May 23, 1893, KSHS.

106 "i Received": Albert Hazlett to "Dear Sir," July 14, 1859, *Calendar of Virginia State Papers*, 308.

106 "that he had nearly": statement of Annie Brown Adams, Chicago Historical Society.

106 "chronic roamer": interview with Charles Whipple, OGV.

107 "no place for a young man": Stevens to "Dear Sister," June 30, 1853. He writes of baked beans and apple pie in a letter to his sister, Jan. 25, 1855. Both are in Gilder Lehrman Collection.

107 "drunken riot": Court Martial Case Files, May 21, 1855, War Department Office of the Judge Advocate General, National Archives, Washington, D.C.

107 "The grate battle is begun": Stevens to "Dear Brother," Oct. 3, 1857, Gilder Lehrman Collection.

107 "the finest specimen": S. K. Donovan, "A Pennsylvania Man's Recollections of Stevens," OGV. Donovan was a reporter for the *Baltimore Exchange* and one of the first correspondents on the scene after the raid on Harpers Ferry.

107 "Jenny": Aaron Stevens to Jennie Dunbar, Sept. 1, 1859, KSHS.

107 "We are rather": ibid.

107 "furniture" and "very particular": Villard, *John Brown*, 419.

108 "skulk into the kitchen": ibid., 418.

108 "my invisibles": Annie Brown Adams to Alexander Ross, undated, Gilder Lehrman Collection. At other times she capitalized "Invisibles"; see, e.g., Franklin Sanborn, *Recollections of Seventy Years*, 172.

108 "Press nobly on": captured letter published in the *Charleston Mercury*, Oct. 26, 1859.

108 "all no where": unsigned letter to "friend Ed," Aug. 6, 1859, *Calendar of Virginia State Papers*, 300.

108 "I suppose": William Leeman to family, Aug. 14, 1859, KSHS.

108 "a Secret Asosiation": William Leeman to "Dear Mother," Oct. 2, 1859, KSHS.

109 "I do hope": John Brown to John Kagi, Aug. 11, 1859, HSP.

109 "I have discovered": testimony of John Floyd, Mason Report, A250–52.

109 "Besides": ibid. For an account from the perspective of the Quakers who warned Floyd, see B. F. Gue, "John Brown and His Iowa Friends," *The Midland Monthly* (Des Moines, Iowa), Feb. 1897, copy in BSC.

110 "I begin": John Brown to John Brown, Jr., Aug. 1859, in Sanborn, *The Life and Letters*, 535–36.

110 "They were all": John Brown, Jr., to "Friend Henrie," Aug. 17, 1859, *Calendar of Virginia State Papers*, 325.

110 "too fat": John Brown, Jr., to "Friend J.H.," Aug. 7, 1859, HSP.

110 "associations": John Brown, Jr., to "Friend Henrie," Aug. 27, 1859, *Calendar of Virginia State Papers*, 315.

110 "I spent": ibid., 317.

111 "If friend": ibid.

111 "Northern tour": John Brown, Jr., to "Friend J.H.," Aug. 7, 1859, HSP.

111 "It is my chief": Steward Taylor to "Dear Friend," July 3, 1859, *Calendar of Virginia State Papers*, 301.

111 "seem a slave stampede": Hinton, *John Brown and His Men*, 673.

111 "It seemed to be": Annie Brown Adams to Richard Hinton, June 7, 1894, KSHS.

111 "all of our men": Sanborn, *Recollections*, 182–83.

112 "It nearly broke": "Conversation with ———," Feb. 10, 1860, BPL. Higginson later disclosed that this conversation was with Charles Tidd.

112 *"Dear Sir"*: Note of Owen Brown, HSP.

113 "Give a slave": Hinton Notes, Houghton Library.

113 "There was no": Anderson, "A Voice from Harper's Ferry," 23.

113 "they were only": George Gill to Richard Hinton, undated manuscript, 44, KSHS. African Mysteries was also known as the Order of the Men of Oppression.

114 "He thought": statement of Annie Brown Adams, Chicago Historical Society.

115 "His face wore": For Douglass's account of the meeting at the quarry, see his *Autobiographies*, 758–60.

116 "wen": Annie Brown Adams, quoted in Sanborn, *Recollections*, 174.

117 "buy her off": statement of Annie Brown Adams, Chicago Historical Society.

117 "they were some friends": ibid.

117 "used her power": ibid.

117 "taking the dishes": ibid.

117 "When there was": Villard, *John Brown*, 420.

117 "He was impatient": Annie Brown Adams, quoted in Sanborn, *Recollections*, 179. For more on Newby, see the remarkable study by Philip Schwarz, *Migrants Against Slavery: Virginians and the Nation* (University Press of Virginia, 2001), 149–68. Schwarz has tracked down every available document to reconstruct Newby's story.

118 "Oh, Dear": Harriett Newby to Dangerfield Newby, April 11, 1859, *Calendar of Virginia State Papers*, 310.

118 "commenced to *Crall*": Harriett Newby to Dangerfield Newby, April 22, 1859, ibid, 311.

118 "Dear Dangerfield": ibid, 310–11.

119 "I want you": Harriett Newby to Dangerfield Newby, Aug. 16, 1859, ibid., 311.

119 "Post of Duty": Aaron Stevens to "Jenny," Oct. 7, 1859, KSHS.

119 "Parts unknown": Dauphin Thompson to brothers and sisters, Sept. 4, 1859, Gilder Lehrman Collection.

119 "I think of you all day": Watson Brown to wife, Sept. 8, 1859, in Sanborn, *The Life and Letters*, 542–43.

120 "They nearly all": Sanborn, *Recollections*, 177.

120 "He knew": statement of Annie Brown Adams, Chicago Historical Society.

120 "very intimate": Annie Brown Adams, quoted in Sanborn, *Recollections*, 177.

120 "tall," "fine-looking," and so forth: Sanborn, *Recollections*, 177; Annie Brown Adams to Richard Hinton, May 23, 1893, KSHS; statement of Annie Brown Adams, Chicago Historical Society; interview with Annie Brown Adams, OGV.

120 "first lover": Lou Chapin, "The Last Days of Old John Brown," *Overland Monthly*, April 1899.

120 "a perfect": statement of Annie Brown Adams, Chicago Historical Society.

120 "took a fancy": undated note and letter from Los Gatos, Dauphin Thompson file, OGV.

120 "I know your sister": statement of Annie Brown Adams, Chicago Historical Society.

120 "Mother and Father": Annie Brown Adams to Richard Hinton, May 23, 1893, KSHS.

120 "mothers, sisters": statement of Annie Brown Adams, Chicago Historical Society.

121 "We were": Anderson, "A Voice from Harper's Ferry," 25.

121 "Of course": statement of Annie Brown Adams, Chicago Historical Society.

121 "Home Again": Sanborn, *Recollections*, 180.

121 "I want you": John Brown to family, Oct. 1, 1859, BPL.

122 "Sharp's rifle": Hugh Forbes, *Extracts from the Manual for the Patriotic Volunteer* (New York: W. H. Tinson, 1857). The story of the Ritner girl peering through the keyhole is told in Virginia Ott Stake, *John Brown in Chambersburg* (Chambersburg: Franklin Co. Heritage, 1977), 31–32.

122 "General Orders": October 10, 1859, *Calendar of Virginia State Papers*, 274–75.

122 "A Declaration of Liberty": ibid., 275–79.

123 "just the right time": This and other quotations of Kagi's about the timing of the attack are from John Kagi to John Brown, Jr., Oct. 10, 1859, in Villard, *John Brown*, 422.

123 "He goes to": Franklin Sanborn to Thomas Wentworth Higginson, Oct. 6, 1859, BPL.

123 "half-crazy": Thomas Wentworth Higginson to Richard Hinton, March 15, 1895, KSHS.

124 "white men alone": John Copeland to his brother, Dec. 10, 1859, quoted in Franny Nudelman, *John Brown's Body* (Chapel Hill: University of North Carolina Press), 68.

124 "business operation": Franklin Sanborn to Thomas Wentworth Higginson, Oct. 13, 1859, BPL. Also see John Cook confession: "The attack was made sooner than it was intended, owing to some friends in Boston writing a letter finding fault with the management of Capt. B, and what to them seemed his unnecessary delay and expense."

125 "this is perhaps": Charles Tidd letter, quoted in *Bangor* (Maine) *Daily Whig & Courier*, Nov. 17, 1859.

125 "I am now": William Leeman to his mother, Oct. 2, 1859, KSHS.

125 "to worrie": ibid.

125 "Home," "peculiar condition," and other quotes in this passage: Oliver Brown to
     Martha Brown, Oct. 9, 1859, Houghton Library.

125 "I sometimes think": Watson Brown to Belle Brown, undated, in Sanborn, *The
     Life and Letters*, 549.

125 "a few more lines" and other Stevens quotes: Aaron Stevens to "Jenny," Oct. 7,
     1859, KSHS.

Chapter 8: Into the Breach

For press accounts of the events of October through December 1859, I have in almost
all cases cited original newspaper reports. But many of the reports were reprinted in
abridged form in two publications compiled soon after the raid. See *The Life, Trial and
Execution of Captain John Brown: Known as "Old Brown of Ossawatomie," with a Full
Account of the Attempted Insurrection at Harper's Ferry* (New York: Robert M. De
Witt, 1859), and Thomas Drew, *The John Brown Invasion: An Authentic History of the
Harper's Ferry Tragedy*, a series of pamphlets that are available online at BSC.

127 "HEAD-QUARTERS": *Calendar of Virginia State Papers*, 324.

127 "In pursuance": ibid.

127 "applicable": Osborne Anderson, "A Voice from Harper's Ferry," 28.

128 "Throughout": ibid.

128 "You all know": ibid., 29.

129 "Men, get": ibid., 31.

129 "Come, boys!": ibid., 32.

129 "They all felt": Franklin Sanborn, *Recollections of Seventy Years*, 177–78. See also
     "Kennedy Farm Notes," OGV, in which Annie reports that Osborne Anderson
     told her: "It seemed like a funeral march the night we left the house and went
     down to Harper's Ferry. We all shook hands with, and bade the boys who stayed
     behind at the house, goodbye. The Coppoc brothers embraced, kissed one another
     and parted like they felt they would never meet again."

129 "Which way?" and "Not far": "Statement of Patrick Higgins," *Baltimore Ameri-
     can*, Oct. 21, 1859. See also Oswald Garrison Villard, "How Patrick Higgins Met
     John Brown," OGV, and interview with Higgins by Thomas Featherstonhaugh,
     KSHS.

130 "Lock your doors": "Statement of W. W. Throckmorton," *New York Herald*, Oct. 24,
     1859.

130 "I was nearly": Daniel Whelan testimony, Mason Report, A021.

130 "I knew Cook well": ibid, A022.

131 "The head": ibid.

131 "I want to free": ibid.

133 "by the servants": Washington is quoted from his testimony, Mason Report,
     A029–39, and in the *Baltimore American*, Oct. 25, 1859. Lewis Washington's
     account books are at the Jefferson County (West Virginia) Museum, Charles
     Town.

136 "Murder!": D. E. Henderson to David Strother, Oct. 19, 1859, RWL. See also testimony of John Allstadt, Mason Report, A040–41.

136 "merely a robbing party": Washington is quoted from the Mason Report, A034.

138 "newly fitted up": *Virginia Free Press,* Oct. 13, 1859. On May 5, the paper had reported that the hotel was losing business because "the Bar had apparently become the main attraction."

138 "gypsy wagon" and "some rowdies": "Statement of W. W. Throckmorton."

138 "Stand and deliver!": *Baltimore American,* Oct. 28, 1859.

138 "I am shot": ibid. Little is known about Shepherd. According to the 1860 census, he left a widow and five children in Winchester, Virginia. See Mary Johnson, "An 'Ever Present Bone of Contention': The Heyward Shepherd Memorial," *West Virginia History,* 1997, 1–26.

139 "There he goes now!": *Baltimore American,* Oct. 28, 1859.

140 "Passengers": *New York Herald,* Oct. 24, 1859.

140 "It was filled": Simeon Franklin Seely, letter to his wife, Oct. 17, 1859, West Virginia and Regional History Collection, West Virginia University Libraries. See also the letter of Oct. 20, 1859, from a Maryland woman, telling of what train passengers saw, in "An Account of the John Brown Raid," *Maryland Historical Magazine,* June 1944, 162–63, Maryland Historical Society.

140 "Never mind": testimony of John Starry, Mason Report, A024.

141 "was to free": *Baltimore American,* Oct. 29, 1859.

141 "You will furnish": "Statement of W. W. Throckmorton." Additional information about the food is from the Harpers Ferry National Historical Park (interview with Thomas Allstadt in West Virginia Folklore File). See also Lewis Washington's testimony, Mason Report: he feared eating the food because it "may be drugged."

141 "have to be rather rough": "Statement of W. W. Throckmorton."

141 "You no doubt wonder": *Baltimore American,* Oct. 28, 1859.

142 "Express train": A. J. Phelps to W. P. Smith, Oct. 17, 1859, *Correspondence Relating to the Insurrection at Harper's Ferry* (Annapolis: B. H. Richardson, 1860), at Western Maryland Historical Library, www.whilbr.org.

142 "The leader of those men": ibid.

142 "The Captain" and "he expected": ibid.

142 "strapping negroes": *Baltimore American,* Oct. 18, 1859.

142 "escape with their booty": *Harper's Weekly,* Nov. 5, 1859.

142 Passengers flinging notes: *New York Herald,* Oct. 19, 1859.

143 Newspaper headlines from Oct. 18, 1859: *New York Herald, Baltimore American, New York Times.*

143 "something startling": Douglass, *Autobiographies,* 759.

144 "to get the citizens": testimony of John Starry, Mason Report, A025. For more on Boerly and shooting, see George Mauzy letter to "My dear Children," Dec. 3, 1859, HFNHP; Mauzy writes of Boerly and his neighbor: "When they made the first attack at Taylor's corner upon the guard at the Arsenal gate, & from whence the latter recd a dead shot by a negro with a Sharps rifle." See also Joseph Barry, *The Strange Story of Harper's Ferry,* 51–52.

144 Byrne exchange: testimony of Terence Byrne, Mason Report, A013–A020.

146 "should not be interrupted": For this and other exchanges with Cook, see the testimony of Lind Currie, Mason Report, A054–A059.

147 "I had an umbrella": For Byrne's exchanges with Leeman and Thompson, see the testimony of Terence Byrne, Mason Report, A016–17.

148 "Thompson came up": John Cook confession.

148 "I heard a good deal": ibid.

148 "bad management": *Baltimore American,* Oct. 28, 1859.

148 "It was not": ibid.

148 "From Brown": "Copeland's Confession," *New York Herald,* Nov. 5, 1859.

149 "sticks wrapped": "Notes of Personal Interviews with Graham made by Dr. Thomas Featherstonhaugh for Richard J. Hinton," KSHS. See also testimony of Archibald Kitzmiller, Mason Report, A049–50. He says there were a hundred "faggots" in the wagon.

149 "sharpshooter": David Potter, *The Impending Crisis, 1848–1861* (New York: Harper & Row, 1976), illustration 42.

149 "Father and the others": Jennie Chambers, "What a School Girl Saw of John Brown's Raid" (Harriman, Tenn.: Pioneer Historical Society, 1902), 5. See also Alexander Boteler, "Recollections of the John Brown Raid by a Virginian Who Witnessed the Fight," *Century Magazine,* July 1883, 405.

150 "rode out in haste": journals of James Lawrence Hooff, entry for Oct. 17, 1859, Virginia Historical Society.

150 "any negro": *Virginia* (Charlestown) *Free Press,* Aug. 11, 1859.

150 "for remaining in the Commonwealth": ibid., Aug. 20, 1857.

151 "armed bands": "Some personal recollections of 'John Brown's Raid' by an Eye-witness," HFNHP. This unsigned manuscript is by one of the men sent across the river to attack the bridge. See also D. E. Henderson to David Strother, Oct. 19, 1858, RWL.

151 "Every man": "Some personal recollections."

153 "if I thought": Harriett Newby to Dangerfield Newby, Aug. 16, 1859, *Calendar of Virginia State Papers,* 311. A lane close to where Newby fell was known at the time as Hog Alley. Mary Mauzy wrote her daughter on October 17, 1859, "Those wreches that were killed lay in the street until the hogs began to tear them up" (HFNHP). According to the *Richmond Daily Dispatch,* Oct. 20, 1859: "The ball went through his throat, tearing away all the great arteries, and killing him instantly. . . . His body was left in the street up to noon yesterday; exposed to every indignity that could be heaped upon it by the excited populace." See also Barry, *The Strange Story of Harper's Ferry,* 81–82.

154 "well guarded": Franklin Sanborn, "Personal Reminiscences of John Brown," Remarks at the Reunion of the Anti-Slavery Men and Women (Boston, April 7, 1897), Houghton Library.

154 "strange doctrine": ibid.

154 "Some valuable hints" and "deep and narrow": John Brown Memorandum Books, BPL.

155 "in each direction": "Conversation with Tidd," Feb. 10, 1860, BPL.

156 "I want you": testimony of Terence Byrne, Mason Report, A018.

156 "You are": testimony of Lewis Washington, Mason Report, A035.

156 "It's getting too hot": *Baltimore American*, Oct. 29, 1859.

157 "His answers": Christine Fouke, "Interesting Letter from Miss Fouke, of Harpers-Ferry," *Virginia Free Press*, Dec. 8, 1859.

157 "I am as good": Court Martial Case Files, May 21, 1855, War Department Office of the Judge Advocate General, National Archives.

157 "You would be the first": testimony of Lewis Washington, Mason Report, A036. For more on Stevens, see interview with E. B. Chambers, who said "Stevens was the gamest man in the lot" and "walked on without flinching till he was shot down. It takes nerve to do that" (OGV).

157 "was in possession": testimony of John Starry, Mason Report, A025.

158 "I can possibly": *New York Times*, Oct. 26, 1859.

158 "I have been": ibid.

158 "show temper": testimony of Brua at Brown's trial, *New York Tribune*, Oct. 29, 1859. On Watson after the shooting, see testimony of John Dangerfield, *New York Tribune*, Oct. 31, 1859.

158 "did not consider": *New York Herald*, Oct. 24, 1859.

159 "I seen big": Patrick Higgins to E. P. Stevens, Nov. 5, 1899, OGV. See also interview with John Thomas Allstadt, OGV. He said Chambers and another man stood "in an upper window of the Galt House, watching Stevens until he should come well within range. As the moment arrived, they broke the glass in order to fire true. Stevens fell." He pulled himself up on one knee and fired a second volley. "He lay for perhaps half an hour, there in the road. Then he was carried to the Wager House."

159 "A large, exceedingly": *Baltimore American*, Oct. 19, 1859.

159 "brawny shoulders": *New York Tribune*, Oct. 20, 1859.

159 "the Negroes": *Baltimore American*, Oct. 19, 1859.

159 "One life for many": "An Account of the John Brown Raid," *Maryland Historical Magazine*, June 1944, 163.

160 "Devil may care": George Gill to Richard Hinton, undated, KSHS.

160 "we will not want": Leeman to family, Aug. 14, 1859, KSHS. On the depth of the Potomac: "Very few places in the river at that period of the year contained over two feet of water" (L. T. Moore to Thomas Hughes, Nov. 2, 1880, BSC).

161 "Don't shoot!": *Baltimore Clipper*, Oct. 19, 1859.

161 "Oh my dear": *Richmond Dispatch*, Oct. 29, 1859.

161 "floating upon": *The Sun* (Baltimore), Oct. 19, 1859.

162 "Our men" and "dragged him": Mary Mauzy to daughter, Oct. 17, 1859, HFNHP. See also Joseph Crane to David Strother, Oct. 25, 1859, BSC.

162 "Be cheerful": John Kagi to "My Dear Father & Sister," Sept. 24, 1859, KSHS.

163 "wept like": interview with Mrs. C. M. Langston, May 27, 1908, OGV.

163 "thought that we": John Copeland to Addison Halbert, Dec. 10, 1859, "The John Brown Letters Found in the Virginia State Library in 1901," *Virginia Magazine of History and Biography*, Oct. 1902, 170.

163 "So enraged": Charles White, "John Brown's Raid at Harpers Ferry: An Eyewitness Account," *Virginia Magazine of History and Biography*, Oct. 1959.

163 "fighting on my own hook": *New York Daily Tribune*, Oct. 29, 1859. For the episode of the train official seized by drunken townspeople, see J. Rosengarten, "John Brown's Raid," BSC.

164 "The old man": "Statement of W. W. Throckmorton."

164 "greatly excited": ibid.

164 "If he keeps": interview with John Allstadt, OGV.

164 "That man is down": *New York Times*, Oct. 26, 1859.

165 "When Beckham": *New York Herald*, Oct. 24, 1859.

165 "Shoot him!": ibid.

165 "covered his face": *New York Tribune*, Oct. 29, 1859.

165 "nervous chill": Christine Fouke is quoted from her letter to the *St. Louis* (Missouri) *Republican*, reprinted in the *Baltimore American*, Dec. 6, 1859.

165 "You may kill me": *New York Tribune*, Oct. 29, 1859.

165 "Before he fell": ibid.

165 "fired and": ibid.

165 "probably dying": ibid.

166 "we could have ended": *Baltimore American*, Oct. 24, 1859.

167 "There": Currie testimony at Cook's trial, reported in *Baltimore American*, Nov. 11, 1859.

167 "very rapid and continuous": testimony of Lind Currie, Mason Report, A057.

167 "I thought": This and other quotes about Cook's sniping are from John Cook's confession.

167 "It's all up": *Baltimore American*, Oct. 31, 1859.

167 "We could not": Edwin Coppoc letter, Nov. 22, 1859, quoted in Richard Hinton, *John Brown and His Men*, 488.

168 "he suffered": ibid.

168 "spoke no word": Edwin Coppoc to Mary Brown, Nov. 1859, OGV.

168 "You can hardly": Oliver Brown to Martha Brown, Oct. 9, 1859, Houghton Library.

168 "She had been a wife": Annie Brown Adams to Alexander Ross, Dec. 18, 1887, Gilder Lehrman Collection.

168 "She was willing": Mary Brown to J. M. McKim, March 6, 1860, HLHS.

168 "Who commands": Boteler, "Recollections of the John Brown Raid by a Virginian Who Witnessed the Fight," *Century Magazine*, July 1883, 399–411.

168 Terms of surrender: Col. Baylor to Gov. Wise, Oct. 22, 1859, *Governor's Message and Reports of the Public Officers of the State* (Richmond: William Ritchie, 1859), State Library of Virginia.

169 "In consideration": ibid.

169 "take him": testimony of Captain Sinn, *New York Tribune*, Oct. 31, 1859.

169 "that he & his men": report of Col. Edward Shriver, from "In Readiness to Do Every Duty Assigned," Gregory Stiverson, ed., in *Archives of Maryland*, Annapolis, 2000.

169 "He thought he was": *Baltimore American*, Oct. 31, 1859.

169 "The terms": Col. Baylor to Gov. Wise, October 22, 1859, *Governor's Message and Reports*.

169 "Our troops": ibid.

170 "Every man": *Baltimore American,* Oct. 31, 1859.

170 "If the man": *New York Tribune,* Oct. 31, 1859.

171 "For the first": *Shepherdstown* (Virginia) *Register,* Jan. 14, 1860, OGV.

171 "badly scared": *Baltimore American,* Oct. 29, 1859.

171 "No, my son": testimony of Terence Byrne, Mason Report, A019.

171 "to endure a little longer": *Baltimore Clipper,* Oct. 20, 1859.

171 "treason": *New York Daily Tribune,* Oct. 31, 1859.

172 "saying he": *New York Daily Tribune,* Oct. 20, 1859.

172 "extraordinary nerve": *Baltimore American,* Oct. 19, 1859.

Chapter 9: I Am Nearly Disposed of Now

173 "armed abolitionists": A. J. Phelps to W. P. Smith, Oct. 17, 1859, *Correspondence Relating to the Insurrection at Harper's Ferry,* Western Maryland Historical Library.

173 "Your dispatch": ibid., W. P. Smith to A. J. Phelps, Oct. 17, 1859.

173 "My dispatch": ibid., A. J. Phelps to W. P. Smith, Oct. 17, 1859.

174 "Matter": ibid., W. P. Smith to J. B. Ford, Oct. 17, 1859.

174 *"His Excellency"*: ibid., J. W. Garrett to James Buchanan, Oct. 17, 1859. On Stuart's finding Lee buying castor oil, see "Extract from letter of Dr. Roy Bird Cook," Aug. 16, 1952, HLHS.

175 "He has left": Francis Raymond Adams, Jr., "An Annotated Edition of the Personal Letters of Robert E. Lee, April 1855–April, 1861" (Ph.D. thesis, University of Maryland, 1955), 542. For more on the Lee and Custis slaves, see Elizabeth Brown Pryor, *Reading the Man: A Portrait of Robert E. Lee Through His Private Letters* (New York: Viking, 2007), 260–61.

175 "a wise Merciful": Robert E. Lee to his wife, December 27, 1856. Available at http://fair-use.org/robert-e-lee/letter-to-his-wife-on-slavery.

175 "the scene": Emory M. Thomas, "'The Greatest Service I Rendered the State': J.E.B. Stuart's Account of the Capture of John Brown," *Virginia Magazine of History and Biography,* July 1986, 352. Stuart's Jan. 31, 1860, letter about his service at Harpers Ferry is at the Virginia Historical Society. For more on the marines, see Bernard Nalty, "'At All Times Ready . . .': The Marines at Harper's Ferry" (U.S. Marine Corps, 1959).

176 "Have given": W. P. Smith to L. M. Cole, Oct. 18, 1859, *Correspondence Relating to the Insurrection.*

176 "party of Banditti": Lee, quoted in Thomas, "The Greatest Service," 346.

176 "the persons": Colonel Lee's report, Mason Report, 43–44.

176 "cautioned": Thomas, "The Greatest Service," 353. Also see Colonel Lee's report, Mason Report, 41.

176 "The people are terribly excited": unsigned telegram to Washington, Oct. 18, 1859, *Correspondence Relating to the Insurrection.*

177 "All eyes": Edward White, "Eyewitness at Harpers Ferry," *American Heritage,* Feb. 1975.

177 "opened the door": Thomas, "The Greatest Service," 353.

177 "You are" and the rest of conversation between Stuart and Brown: Boteler, "Recollections of the John Brown Raid," *Century Magazine,* July 1883, 407.

177 "he could expect" and "would sell": *New York Herald*, Oct. 24, 1859.

177 "Is that your" and "Yes": Boteler, "Recollections of the John Brown Raid," 407.

178 "It was evident": *New York Herald*, Oct. 24, 1859.

178 "reechoed" and "oppressive silence": Boteler, "Recollections of the John Brown Raid," 409.

178 "There was": testimony of Terence Byrnes, Mason Report, A020.

178 "One man surrenders!": ibid.

179 "When I heard": *Shepherdstown* (Virginia) *Register*, Jan. 14, 1860, OGV.

179 "cried for quarter": *New York Tribune*, Oct. 31, 1859.

179 "they picked": ibid.

180 "There's Brown!": Boteler, "Recollections of the John Brown Raid," 410.

180 "Quicker than thought": Israel Green, "The Capture of John Brown," *North American Review*, Dec. 1885.

180 "Instinctively": ibid. See also Thomas, "The Greatest Service," which quotes Stuart: "Green complained to me afterwards that his sword was so dull (being a common dress sword) he could not hurt Brown with it." For more details on the storming, see Israel Green File, OGV. For evidence of shooting, despite Lee's orders, see testimony of Lewis Washington, Mason Report, A038, and report of Col. Robert Baylor, who wrote that "a heavy volley was fired in by the marines," in *Governor's Message and Reports*.

180 "The whole": Colonel Lee's report, Mason Report, 42.

180 "the breathless": Edward White, "Eyewitness at Harper's Ferry."

180 "I never saw": W. P. Smith to J. W. Garrett, Oct. 18, 1859, *Correspondence Relating to the Insurrection*.

181 "I embraced": *Shepherdstown* (Virginia) *Register*, Jan. 14, 1860, OGV.

181 "stepped daintily": Edward White, "Eyewitness at Harper's Ferry."

181 "Colonel Washington": A.R.H. Ranson, "The John Brown Raid," *The Sewanee Review*, Oct. 1913.

181 "The crowd": *Baltimore American*, Oct. 19, 1859.

181 "vomiting gore": Barry, *The Strange Story of Harper's Ferry*, 80. See also notes on J. Graham, OGV, describing Anderson pinned to wall and turning over.

181 "Gentlemen": Cecil Eby, ed., "The Last Hours of the John Brown Raid: The Narrative of David H. Strother," *Virginia Magazine of History and Biography*, April 1965, 173.

181 "Well it takes": Barry, *The Strange Story of Harper's Ferry*, 52.

182 "Duty, sir": C. W. Tayleure to John Brown, Jr., June 15, 1879, KSHS.

182 "feelingly": *Baltimore Clipper*, Oct. 20, 1859.

182 "Keep up": Watson Brown to Belle Brown, Oct. 14, 1859, quoted in Sanborn, *The Life and Letters*, 549.

182 "a mere boy": "The Last Hours of the John Brown Raid," 173.

182 "with his hands": "David Hunter Strother's Lecture on John Brown in Cleveland, 1868," West Virginia and Regional History Collection, West Virginia University Libraries.

182 "gaunt": ibid.

182 "The old man's": ibid.

182 "upon": Colonel Lee's report, Mason Report, 45.

183 "if the wounded": *New York Herald*, Oct. 21, 1859.

183 "the great work": John Brown to wife and children, Jan. 30, 1858, in Louis Ruchames, *A John Brown Reader*, 118.

184 "a corpse": Craig M. Simpson, *A Good Southerner: The Life of Henry A. Wise of Virginia* (Chapel Hill: UNC Press, 2001), 20.

185 "The Governor": "David Hunter Strother's Lecture on John Brown in Cleveland, 1868." There is some confusion about the sequence of interviews in the paymaster's office. It appears that Wise and Hunter conducted the first, a few hours after Brown's capture, and may also have been present for the second, longer interview by James Mason and others.

185 "Old Brown": *Baltimore American*, Oct. 21, 1859 (citing the *Richmond Enquirer*).

185 "You are in": ibid.

185 "He was singularly free": Andrew Hunter, "John Brown's Raid," *Publications of the Southern History Association*, July 1897, 167.

185 "He is the gamest": *Baltimore American*, Oct. 21, 1859.

185 "He is a bundle": *Baltimore American*, Oct. 26, 1859.

186 "No sign of weakness": *Baltimore American*, Oct. 21, 1859.

186 "SEN. MASON—How": For this and other quotations from the interview, I have drawn on reports in the *New York Herald* and the *Baltimore American* on Oct. 21, 1859. A reporter from the *Cincinnati Gazette* was also present.

186 "I think you": *Baltimore American*, Oct. 21, 1859.

186 "I want you to": ibid.

187 "You had better": ibid. Other details and the quotation about the plan of government and the carpetbag are from Andrew Hunter, "John Brown's Raid."

Chapter 10: His Despised Poor

191 "The boards": "The Last Hours of the John Brown Raid," *Virginia Magazine of History and Biography*, April 1965, 176. The anecdote about Christine Fouke collecting Fontaine Beckham in a wheelbarrow appeared in the *New York Herald*, Oct. 21, 1859.

191 "A dog": "The Last Hours of the John Brown Raid," 173. The dead insurgents were buried "together like a parcel of dead dogs," one local wrote (George Mauzy to Burtons, Dec. 3, 1859, HFNHP). A woman who witnessed the burial "said the men were buried much as an equal number of dead animals would have been" (*Milwaukee Sentinel*, Nov. 5, 1899). See also Thomas Featherstonhaugh, "The Final Burial of the Followers of John Brown," *New England Magazine*, April 1901.

192 "The work": W. P. Smith to J. W. Garrett, Oct. 18, 1859, *Correspondence Relating to the Insurrection at Harper's Ferry*, Western Maryland Historical Library.

192 "The result": Colonel Lee's report, Mason Report, 42.

192 "shaking": *New York Herald*, Oct. 21, 1859.

192 "To arms!": *Baltimore American*, Oct. 21, 1859.

193 "for the scene": Colonel Lee's report, Mason Report, 43.

193 "all the necessaries": ibid., 42. For an inventory of the seized arms and equipment,

see the list accompanying the testimony of Archibald Kitzmiller, Mason Report, A051–52.

193 "done up": *Baltimore Clipper*, Oct. 20, 1859.

193 "answering": *Baltimore Sun*, Oct. 26, 1859, OGV.

194 "the existence": *Baltimore Clipper*, Oct. 20, 1859.

194 "Sons of Virginia!": J. Rosengarten, "John Brown's Raid," BSC.

194 "I would have given": *Baltimore American*, Oct. 24, 1859.

194 "a numerous": Governor Wise, "Speech to Assembly," Dec. 5, 1859, in *Governor's Message and Reports of the Public Officers of the State*.

194 "no quarter": ibid.

195 "Northern man": David Potter, *The Impending Crisis, 1848–1861* (New York: Harper & Row, 1976), 141.

195 "a matter": Brian McGinty, *John Brown's Trial* (Cambridge, Mass.: Harvard University Press, 2009), 82.

195 "Lynch them!": James Redpath, *The Public Life of Captain John Brown*, 286.

195 "A supper basket": *New York Herald*, Oct. 21, 1859.

195 "he would turn": *New York Herald*, Oct. 25, 1859.

195 "the notorious": *Baltimore American*, Oct. 23, 1859.

196 "sheer madness": "John Cook's confession," in Richard Hinton, *John Brown and His Men*, 711.

196 "he could wield": "Owen Brown's Escape from Harper's Ferry," *Atlantic Monthly*, March 1874, 353. Most of the details of the escape are from Owen's vivid account.

196 "made himself": ibid.

196 "exceedingly merry": ibid.

197 "Cook never came": ibid., 354.

197 "Leave, leave!": ibid., 356. For more on Cook's capture, see the *Baltimore American*, Oct. 28–29, 1859. For women who wanted to rescue him from jail, see the article by Cook's lawyer, A. K. McClure, "An Episode of John Brown's Raid," *Lippincott's Magazine*, Sept. 1883, 279–87.

198 "looks like": "A Proclamation by the Governor," Nov. 3, 1859, *Calendar of Virginia State Papers*, 90.

198 "a consumptive": ibid.

198 "sometimes": ibid.

198 "very rough": *New York Herald*, Oct. 22, 1859.

199 "dug the mine": Osborne Anderson, "A Voice from Harper's Ferry," 62.

199 "INFERNAL DESPERADOES": *Independent Democrat* (Charlestown), Oct. 18, 1859.

200 "Cash for Negroes" and "MEN, WOMEN": *Virginia Free Press*, Oct. 13, 1859. The ad referring to Avis states that he is "authorized to buy for a gentleman's use on his own plantation 50 NEGROES" and that he can be reached at the Charlestown jail. The town was named for Charles Washington, who had laid it out in 1786, calling the main thoroughfares "George" and "Washington" in honor of his famous older brother. The Washingtons and other early settlers were transplants from the Virginia Tidewater, and Charlestown grew into a farming and horse-racing center

with four times as many slaves as Harpers Ferry. For more on local history, the Jefferson County Museum in Charles Town has an excellent collection.

201 "There is danger": Governor Wise to Col. Lucius Davis, Oct. 22, 1859, Governor Henry A. Wise Executive Papers, State Library of Virginia.

201 "die of his wounds": Andrew Hunter to Gov. Wise, Oct 22, 1859, Governor Wise Executive Papers, State Library of Virginia.

201 "There is an evident": *Baltimore American*, Oct. 26, 1859.

201 "weak and haggard": ibid.

201 "Virginians": ibid.

202 "If you seek my blood": ibid.

202 "I have now": ibid.

202 "drum-head justice": Andrew Hunter, quoted in *Baltimore American*, Nov. 1, 1859.

202 "I will not": *Virginia Free Press*, Oct. 20, 1859.

203 "What we aim": J. E. Norris, *History of the Lower Shenandoah Valley* (Chicago: A. Warner and Co., 1890), 443–44. Historians have speculated that Hunter may have had another purpose in bringing the treason charge. Virginia's governor could unilaterally pardon or lessen the punishment of men sentenced to death for murder or incitement of slaves. He didn't have this power in the case of treason.

203 For quotations from the indictment, see Records of Jefferson Co. Circuit Court Clerk's Office, BSC, available online at www.wvculture.org/history/johnbrown/jbjeffcc.html.

203 "He has": *Baltimore American*, Oct. 27, 1859.

203 "determined to resist": *Baltimore American*, Oct. 28, 1859.

204 "The floor": *New York Herald*, Nov. 10, 1859.

204 "comfortably": *New York Tribune*, Nov. 5, 1859.

204 "a Lunatic": For the telegram and an excellent discussion of the law as it related to insanity, see McGinty, *John Brown's Trial*, 132–35.

205 "As mad as": *Chicago Press and Tribune*, Oct. 21, 1859.

205 "excitable": For descriptions of Brown's "insanity," see Villard, *John Brown*, 508, and interviews with John Whedon, Robert Thompson, and Benjamin Waite, OGV. On monomania, see testimony of John Andrews, Mason Report, A192: "I noticed that the old gentleman in conversation scarcely regarded other people, was entirely self-poised, self-possessed, sufficient to himself, and appeared to have no emotion of any sort, but to be entirely absorbed in an idea, which preoccupied him and seemed to put him in a position of transcending an ordinary emotion and ordinary reason."

205 "openly": E. B. Whitman to Franklin Sanborn, Jan. 16, 1858, KSHS.

205 "God's instrument": Louis DeCaro, *Fire from the Midst of You*, 248. See also letter of H. C. Gill, June 1, 1892, quoted in Irving Richman, *John Brown Among the Quakers*, 29: "He told me repeatedly, while talking, that he believed he was an instrument in the hands of God." My speculation about manic depression draws on an interview with Dr. Earle Silber of Chevy Chase, Md., as well as on other sources.

206 "an idiot": Code of Virginia, 1849, cited in McGinty, *John Brown's Trial*, 133.

206 "I look upon": Robert De Witt, *The Life, Trial and Execution of Captain John Brown*, 8.

206 "too absurd": *New York Tribune*, Nov. 1, 1859.

206 "an intelligent": De Witt, *The Life, Trial and Execution of Captain John Brown*, 13.

206 "were doing": ibid., 16.

207 "As a Southern": *Baltimore American*, Oct. 31, 1859.

207 "moral courage": De Witt, *The Life, Trial and Execution of Captain John Brown*, 31.

207 "Gentlemen of the jury" and other quotes on the verdict: *New York Herald*, Nov. 1, 1859, and De Witt, 34–35.

208 "Nigger-Worshipping": William Rasmussen and Robert Tilton, *The Portent: John Brown's Raid in American Memory* (Richmond: Virginia Historical Society, 2009), 39.

208 "a fanatic" and "a wild and absurd": *New York Times*, Nov. 3 and 21, 1859: "In common with the whole North, we have been astonished at the immense outcry raised over that wild and absurd freak of a hard-headed, strong-willed fanatic."

208 a "deplorable": *New York Tribune*, Oct. 19, 1859.

208 "misguided, wild": *Liberator*, Oct. 21, 1859, quoted in Villard, *John Brown*, 473.

208 "Our old friend": Franklin Sanborn to Theodore Parker, Oct. 22, 1859, Houghton Library. Sanborn would later change his mind, writing Parker on Nov. 14, 1859, "The *failure* is a success; it has done more for Freedom than years of talk could" (BPL).

208 "According": Franklin Sanborn to Thomas Wentworth Higginson, Oct. 21, 1859, BPL.

209 "I have always": Frederick Douglass to the *Rochester* (New York) *Democrat and Republican*, Oct. 31, 1859; the same letter was published in the *New York Tribune*, Nov. 4, 1859.

209 "noble and heroic": ibid.

209 "but a hazy": letter of Gerrit Smith, March 21, 1860, in Ralph Harlow, "Gerrit Smith and the John Brown Raid," *American Historical Review*, Oct. 1932, 32–60. For an excellent discussion of Smith's illness and treatment, see John Stauffer, *The Black Hearts of Men* (Cambridge, Mass.: Harvard University Press, 2001), 238–45, 261–62. Also see "The 'Black Dream' of Gerrit Smith, New York Abolitionist," by John R. McKivigan and Madeleine Leveille, *Library Associates Courier* (Syracuse University), fall 1985, 51–76. Smith's correspondence—and litigation—over claims that he knew more than he let on can be found in the Houghton Library, and in the Smith Papers, Syracuse University.

209 "That event": Samuel Gridley Howe to *New York Tribune*, Nov. 16, 1859.

209 "extreme" and "two sad results": Thomas Wentworth Higginson, draft of letter to Samuel Gridley Howe, Nov. 15, 1859, BPL. This letter appears not to have been sent, but Higginson wrote the same to Sanborn, who quotes it in a letter back to Higginson, Nov. 17, 1859, BPL.

209 "Sanborn is there": Thomas Wentworth Higginson to Franklin Sanborn, November 1859, BPL.

210 "There is no need": Thomas Wentworth Higginson to Lysander Spooner, Nov. 28, 1859, quoted in Edward Renehan, *The Secret Six*, 219.

210 "Is it possible": Thoreau's "A Plea for Captain John Brown" was widely published and has been repeatedly anthologized, though often in abridged form. The version

from which I have quoted is at http://www.transcendentalists.com/thoreau_plea
_john_brown.htm.

211 "It was late" and "block of stone": *New York Tribune*, Nov. 5, 1859.

211 "say why sentence": *New York Herald*, Nov. 3, 1859.

211 "He seemed to be": *New York Tribune*, Nov. 5, 1859.

211 "I have" and other quotes from Brown's speech: *New York Herald*, Nov. 3, 1859,
     and *Baltimore American*, Nov. 3, 1859. The two accounts differ only slightly.

212 "in the hurry": John Brown to Andrew Hunter, Nov. 22, 1859, in Franklin Sanborn,
     The Life and Letters of John Brown, 584.

213 "You have been found" and other quotations of Parker's: Jefferson County Court
     Records, OGV.

213 "damned": *New York Tribune*, Nov. 5, 1859.

213 "This indecorum": *Baltimore American*, Nov. 3, 1859.

214 "composure": *New York Herald*, Nov. 3, 1859.

214 "spoke timidly": *New York Tribune*, Nov. 3, 1859.

214 "indifferent": Cleon Moore to David Hunter Strother, Nov. 4, 1859, BSC.

214 "said he": Jefferson County Court Records, BSC.

214 "Has anything": William Henry Furness to J. M. McKim, Nov. 3, 1859, quoted in
     Villard, *John Brown*, 646–47.

214 "no consciousness" and "ends of justice": Brown's speech to the court, Nov. 2,
     1859, in *New York Herald*, Nov. 3, 1859.

215 "the two best": Ralph Waldo Emerson, *The Complete Works of Ralph Waldo
     Emerson*, vol. 8 (Boston: Houghton Mifflin, 1911), 125. This appears in the essay
     "Eloquence."

215 "lost his head" and "fatal blunder": Ralph Waldo Emerson to William Emerson,
     Oct. 23, 1859, in Ralph Rusk, ed., *Letters of Ralph Waldo Emerson*, vol. 5 (New
     York: Columbia University Press, 1939), 178.

215 "unschooled" and other quotes from the essay "Heroism": Ralph Waldo Emer-
     son, *Essays: First Series* (1841). E-text at University of Virginia Library, http://
     etext.virginia.edu/toc/modeng/public/EmeEssF.html.

215 "his simple, artless" and Emerson's other observations concerning Brown: Emer-
     son, "Remarks at a Meeting for the Relief of the Family of John Brown, Novem-
     ber 18, 1859," in *The Complete Works*, vol. 10.

215 "He believes in two articles": quoted in John J. McDonald, "Emerson and John
     Brown," *New England Quarterly*, Sept. 1971, 383.

215 "None purer": James Elliot Cabot, *A Memoir of Ralph Waldo Emerson*, vol. 2
     (Boston: Houghton Mifflin, 1888), 597. Cabot notes that Emerson omitted these
     lines from a published version of the essay ten years later, "distance of time hav-
     ing brought the case into a juster perspective." For more on Emerson and Tho-
     reau and their impact, see David S. Reynolds, *John Brown, Abolitionist: The Man
     Who Killed Slavery, Sparked the Civil War, and Seeded Civil Rights* (New York:
     Knopf, 2005), 344–47, 363–36.

216 "I have been": John Brown to Mary Brown, Nov. 10, 1859, HSP.

217 "You know": John Brown to "My Dear Friend E.B.," Nov. 1, 1859, in Louis
     Ruchames, *A John Brown Reader*, 137.

217 "often covered my head": John Brown to Rev. Heman Humphrey, Nov. 25, 1859,
     in Ruchames, *A John Brown Reader*, 158.

217 "Jesus of Nazareth": John Brown to family, Nov. 8, 1859, HSP.

217 "will do vastly more": ibid.

217 "I am worth": John Brown to Jeremiah Brown, Nov. 12, 1859, in Ruchames, *A
     John Brown Reader*, 142.

217 "No theatrical": Thoreau, quoted in Franny Nudelman, *John Brown's Body*, 18.

217 "something more": John Brown to Rebecca Spring, Nov. 24, 1859, quoted in letter
     from Spring to Mary Brown, Dec. 1, 1859, BSC.

218 "irascible": *New York Herald*, Nov. 10, 1859.

218 "Mr. Brown": George Sennott telegram to Thomas Wentworth Higginson, Nov.
     5, 1859, BPL.

218 "Mr. Brown fears": George Hoyt to Mary Brown, Nov. 11, 1859, BSC.

218 "scanty means": John Brown to family, Nov. 8, 1859, HSP.

218 "gazing stock": ibid.

218 "Her presence here": John Brown to Thomas Wentworth Higginson, Nov. 4, 1859
     (contents forwarded by Samuel Gridley Howe in letter to Higginson, Nov. 9,
     1859), BPL.

218 "heeding": John Brown to Mary Brown, Nov. 10, 1859, HSP.

218 "In the world": ibid.

219 "If after": ibid.

Chapter 11: A Full Fountain of Bedlam

220 "run off slaves": Thomas Drew, "The John Brown Invasion," 36, BSC.

220 "beings of": *Dred Scott v. Sandford*, 60 U.S. 393 (1857).

221 "more fully": Voorhees is quoted in Charles S. Voorhees, ed., *Speeches of Daniel
     W. Voorhees* (Cincinnati: Robert Clark & Co., 1875), 1–26.

221 "a face": ibid., 12. See also *Virginia Free Press*, Nov. 17, 1859, which reported that
     some were carried away by the "magic eloquence of Mr. Voorhees," and "the
     sternest men had their hearts so opened that they wept like women."

221 "Happily": *Virginia Free Press Extra*, Nov. 11, 1859, BSC.

222 "Those who were": Oswald Villard, *John Brown*, 469.

222 "The inhabitants": *New York Herald*, Nov. 1, 1859.

222 "had at least": ibid. See also Charles White, "John Brown's Raid at Harper's
     Ferry": "One negro was drowned—a slave—the only one of whom we have
     doubts as to his complicity with them—& that because he ran with them."

222 "Pneumonia and fright": Office of the Circuit Court, Jefferson County, West
     Virginia, BSC. See also *Virginia Free Press*, Nov. 3, 1859.

222 "manifested many of": "Petition John H. Allstadt of Jefferson County Virginia
     for compensation to the extent of the value of two negro slaves, his property,
     deceased from fright at their capture at night, by John Brown's party," Jan. 9,
     1860, Dept. of Military Affairs, State Library of Virginia.

223 "destroyed by Civil War": ibid.

223 "tractable and faithful": "Memorial of W. McP. Fuller of Winchester Frederick

Co. praying indemnity for the loss of his slave Jim at the Harpers Ferry Invasion," Jan. 5, 1860, State Library of Virginia.

223 "in the common market": "Petition John H. Allstadt."

223 "being deprived of his property": ibid.

223 "ready & glad": "Conversation with Tidd," Feb. 10, 1860, BPL.

223 "go over": "Owen Brown's Escape from Harper's Ferry," *Atlantic Monthly*, March 1874, 345.

223 "But when they heard firing": "Conversation with Tidd," BPL.

223 "It was not": interview with Charles Conklyn, OGV.

224 "have a warlike": Mary Mauzy letter to her daughter, Nov. 10, 1859, HFNHP.

224 "the great scamp Cook": ibid.

224 "I asked them": "John Cook's confession," Hinton, *John Brown and His Men*, 712.

224 "Abolitionist incendiaries": *Baltimore American*, Nov. 12, 1859.

224 "monstrous scoundrel": *Virginia Free Press*, Nov. 10, 1859. The paper also called him a "consummate villain" who insinuated himself among trusting Virginians so he could "whisper the blessings of freedom into the ears of our slaves, and to prepare them to aid in the blow that was to be struck for their liberation."

224 "It is to his": J. W. Ware to Henry Wise, Nov. 13, 1859, BSC.

225 "There is considerable excitement": B. S. Brooke to John T. Blake, Nov 14, 1859, in online archives, *The Valley of the Shadow*, Valley Personal Papers, http://valley .lib.virginia.edu/. Panic also spread to other states, including Maryland, Tennessee, Kentucky, and Georgia, where it was feared "a squad of Brown's emissaries" were hiding near Pine Mountain (*New York Tribune*, Nov. 21, 1859).

225 "They are": Journal of James Hooff, Nov. 18, 1859, Virginia Historical Society.

225 "There is a": *New York Herald*, Nov. 20, 1859. The excitable Colonel Davis had previously alerted Wise of the jail defenses: "If attack be made, the prisoners will be shot by the inside guards" (Villard, *John Brown*, 520).

225 "Dishonorable Gov Wise" and other threats: Governor's Office, Letters Received, Henry A. Wise, State Library of Virginia, and "The John Brown Letters Found in Virginia State Library 1901," *Virginia Historical Magazine of History and Biography*, Jan. 1902, 273–82.

225 "Contemptible Nonsense" and other notations: ibid.

226 "It is alarming": Gov. Wise to Rev. James McKennan of Wheeling, undated, copied from original by Clarence Gee, HLHS.

226 "Everything": *Baltimore American*, Nov. 26, 1859.

226 "too dry": Journal of James Hooff, Nov. 3, 1859. He also comments on dryness and wind on Nov. 10, Nov. 14, and Nov. 17.

226 "that there are rockets": John Thompson to wife, Nov. 27, 1859, Virginia Historical Society. Thompson wrote that he was about to go on patrol, adding "If any thing happens good bye darling, take care of mother." Nothing happened that night. Thompson died five years later, in the Battle of the Wilderness.

226 "daguerreotype wagon" and "tragedy": *Baltimore American*, Nov. 23–24, 1859.

227 *The Filibuster*: Michael Kaufmann, *American Brutus: John Wilkes Booth and the*

Lincoln Conspiracies (New York: Random House, 2004), 105. A further discussion of Booth and Brown appears on 103–7.

227 "He was a remarkably": George Libby, "John Brown and John Wilkes Booth," in *The Confederate Veteran*, April 1930.

228 "positively refused": Villard, *John Brown*, 512.

228 "*There is no*": ibid.

228 "Orsini bombs": J. W. LeBarnes to Thomas Wentworth Higginson, Nov. 22, 1859, BPL. This letter also speaks of the scheme to kidnap Wise. On November 28, LeBarnes telegraphed "projects abandoned."

228 "If the prisoner": Gov. Wise to Francis Stribling, Nov. 10, 1859, quoted in McGinty, *John Brown's Trial*, 243.

229 "To hang": Villard, *John Brown*, 501.

229 "Brown deserves": John Tyler to Henry Wise, November 2 and 9, 1859, HSP.

229 "uncompromising abolitionist": Lydia Maria Child to Gov. Wise, Oct. 26, 1859, in "Correspondence between Lydia Maria Child and Gov. Wise and Mrs. Mason of Virginia," BSC.

229 "the hoary-headed": Eliza Mason to Lydia Child, Nov. 11, 1859, in *Letters of Lydia Maria Child* (Boston: Houghton Mifflin, 1883), 280.

229 "I will not": Gov. Wise to Andrew Hunter, Nov. 6, 1859, in *Magazine of History*, Aug. 1908, HLHS.

229 "Gov. Wise told me": *Baltimore American*, Nov. 30, 1859.

229 "Shall John Brown": The quotations from Wise in this passage are from his speech to the Assembly on Dec. 5, 1850, in *Governor's Message and Reports of the Public Officers of the State*.

230 "Governor Wise left": *New York Herald*, Nov. 23, 1859.

230 "I have now": John Brown to his children, Nov. 22, 1859, in Louis Ruchames, *A John Brown Reader*, 150.

230 "able to sit up": John Brown to Mary Brown, Nov. 26, 1859, in Ruchames, *A John Brown Reader*, 159.

231 "I have many": John Brown to Rebecca Spring, Nov. 24, 1859; an extract appears in a letter Spring wrote to Mary Brown, Dec. 1, 1859, BSC.

231 "He said": Father Michael Costello to Father Harrington, Feb. 11, 1860, HFNHP.

231 "they had better pray": Cleon Moore to David Strother, Nov. 4, 1859, BSC.

231 "amalgamation": *Baltimore American*, Nov. 23, 1859.

231 "I feel no": *Independent-Democrat* (Charlestown, Va.), Nov. 22, 1859, OGV.

231 "Question": ibid.

231 "Life is made up": John Brown to Mary Brown, Nov. 26, 1859, in Ruchames, *A John Brown Reader*, 159–60.

232 "If you <u>now feel</u>": ibid.

Chapter 12: So Let It Be Done!

233 "It was a": *Baltimore American*, Oct. 24, 1859, citing interview by *Spirit of Jefferson* (Charlestown).

233 "I have been": John Brown to Rev. H. L. Vaill, Nov. 15, 1859, in Louis Ruchames, *A John Brown Reader*, 143–44.

233 "I cannot believe": ibid.

234 "His raid": William Lloyd Garrison to Oliver Johnson, Nov. 1, 1859, in Walter Merrill, *The Letters of William Lloyd Garrison* (Cambridge, Mass.: Harvard University Press, 1971), 661.

234 "wading in blood": Rev. Heman Humphrey to John Brown, Nov. 20, 1859, in Sanborn, *The Life and Letters of John Brown*, 602.

234 "poor erring servant" and "He shall begin": John Brown to Rev. Heman Humphrey, Nov. 25, 1859, in Ruchames, *A John Brown Reader*, 157–58.

234 "strengthen me just once more": Judges 16:30.

234 "For many years": John Brown to Heman Humphrey, Nov. 25, 1859, in Ruchames, *A John Brown Reader*, 157.

235 "without any bloodshed": John Brown to Andrew Hunter, Nov. 22, 1859, in Sanborn, *The Life and Letters*, 584. On Brown's men and what they thought, see, for instance, the confession of John Copeland, who stated he thought there would be a similar attack "in Kentucky about the same time" (*New York Herald*, Nov. 5, 1859). Also, see the testimony of Richard Realf, who said Brown believed "slaves would immediately rise" and join him as he worked diagonally south through the mountains from Maryland to Alabama, expanding his provisional state. Mason Report, A096–98.

237 "Captain Brown was all": Osborne Anderson, "A Voice from Harper's Ferry," 36.

237 "Some of the boys begged": statement of Annie Brown Adams, Chicago Historical Society.

237 "I sometimes feel": ibid.

237 "most of all": "Conversation with Tidd," Feb. 10, 1860, BPL.

237 "I said to": interview with Salmon Brown, OGV.

238 "Father's idea": ibid.

238 "strike terror": Richard Hinton, "An Interview with John Brown and Kagi," in Hinton, *John Brown and His Men*, 673.

238 "to alarm the": ibid., 675.

238 "of no account": testimony of William Arny, Mason Report, A088.

239 "relinquish": William A. Phillips, "Three Interviews with Old John Brown," *Atlantic Monthly*, Dec. 1879, quoted in Hinton, *John Brown and His Men*, 681.

239 "I expect": John Brown to Franklin Sanborn, Feb. 24, 1858, in Sanborn, *The Life and Letters*, 444.

239 "in the worst": "John Brown to Rev. H. L. Vaill, Nov. 15, 1859, in Ruchames, *A John Brown Reader*, 143–44.

239 "Declaration of Liberty" and "Nature is mourning": Hinton, *John Brown and His Men*, 637, 643.

240 "It struck me at the time": testimony of Andrew Hunter, Mason Report, A060.

240 "If you are assailed" and other advice: Hinton, *John Brown and His Men*, 585–88.

241 "My present": John Brown to D. R. Tilden, Nov. 28, 1859, in Ruchames, *A John Brown Reader*, 162.

241 "I have asked": John Brown to Mary Stearns, Nov. 29, 1859, RWL.

241 "what is probably": John Brown to family, Nov. 30, 1859, in Ruchames, *A John Brown Reader*, 164–66.

241 "You have nursed": Mary Brown to John Brown, Nov. 13, 1859, OGV.

241 "minister to your": ibid.

242 "I do not": ibid.

242 "tall, large" and other descriptions of Mary: interview by Theodore Tilton in the *Independent* (New York), Nov. 17, 1859, extracted in *Virginia Free Press*, Dec. 1, 1859.

242 "He is always cool": ibid.

242 "I do not ask": Mary Brown to Governor Wise, Nov. 21, 1859, HSP.

242 "I will rattle": W. Hicks to Governor Wise, Nov. 19, 1859, Governor Henry Wise Executive Papers, State Library of Virginia. See also, Dr. Bickle to Gov. Wise, Nov. 1859, HSP.

242 "We desire": Dr. A. E. Peticolas to Andrew Hunter, Nov. 1, 1859, HLHS.

242 "The Court": Gov. Wise to Andrew Hunter, Nov. 2, 1859, HLHS.

243 "Madam": Gov. Wise to Mary Brown, Nov. 26, 1859, HSP.

243 "from all mutilation": Gov. Wise to Major-Gen. Taliaferro, Nov. 26, 1859, HSP.

243 "entirely willing": John Brown to Mary Brown, Nov. 26, 1859, in Ruchames, *A John Brown Reader,* 159–60.

243 "I want you": W. P. Smith to A. P. Shutt, Nov. 20, 1859, *Correspondence Relating to the Insurrection at Harper's Ferry.*

243 "excursionists": Josiah Perham to President/Superintendent of B&O, Nov. 7, 1859, *Correspondence Relating to the Insurrection at Harper's Ferry.*

243 "Under cover": Andrew Hunter to B&O President, Nov. 25, 1859, *Correspondence Relating to the Insurrection at Harper's Ferry.*

244 "for the use": *New York Herald,* Nov. 30, 1859.

244 "STRANGERS": *Baltimore American,* Nov. 30, 1859.

244 "information from various quarters": Gov. Wise to Pres. Buchanan, Nov. 25, 1859, *Governor's Message and Reports of the Public Officers of the State.*

244 "Necessity may": Gov. Wise to the Governors of Maryland, Pennsylvania, and Virginia, Nov. 25, 1859, *Governor's Message and Reports of the Public Officers of the State.*

244 "almost incredible": Pres. Buchanan to Gov. Wise, Nov. 28, 1859, *Governor's Message and Reports of the Public Officers of the State.*

244 "on the line": Governor Wise's order, Nov. 24, 1859, in Villard, *John Brown,* 523.

244 "The town": *New York Herald,* Nov. 29, 1859.

244 "There is no": Major-General William B. Taliaferro to Gov. Wise, Dec. 2, 1859, in Villard, *John Brown,* 527.

245 *"the enemy":* Robert E. Lee to his wife, Dec. 1, 1859, quoted in Francis Adams, *An Annotated Edition of the Personal Letters of Robert E. Lee,* 551–52.

245 "It is a matter": ibid.

245 "There seemed to be an evident": *Baltimore American,* Dec. 3, 1859.

245 "stiff platitudes": *New York Tribune,* Dec. 6, 1859.

245 "assured": ibid.

245 "For some minutes": ibid.

245 "they were": *Evening Star* (Washington, D.C.), Dec. 2, 1859.

246 "Wife, I am": *New York Tribune,* Dec. 6, 1859.

246 "was soon": *Baltimore American*, Dec. 3, 1859.

246 "For my sake": *New York Tribune*, Dec. 3, 1859. The December 4, 1859, *New York Herald* quotes an "official" who adds: "His sole object was to prevent inconvenience in their transportation, and avoid any disagreeable odor."

246 "in consideration": John Brown's will, Dec. 1, 1859, is in HSP.

246 "as good": ibid.

246 "simple jail fare": *New York Tribune*, Dec. 3, 1859.

246 "showed a": Andrew Hunter, "John Brown's Raid," 178.

246 Final exchange: *New York Herald*, Dec. 3, 1859, and *Evening Star* (Washington D.C.), Dec. 3, 1859.

247 "MY DEAR WIFE": John Brown to Mary Brown, Dec. 2, 1859, in Villard, *John Brown*, 553.

247 "John Brown": John Brown note, headed "To be inscribed on the old family monument at North Elba," HSP.

247 "only say": John Brown to Jeremiah Brown, Dec. 1, 1859, BSC.

247 "something from": Lora Case to John Brown, Nov. 28, 1859, in James Redpath, *Echoes of Harpers Ferry* (New York: Arno Press, 1969), 423–24.

247 "Your most": John Brown to Lora Case, Dec. 2, 1859, in Clarence Gee, "John Brown's Last Letter," *Ohio History*, Sept. 1930, courtesy of Louis DeCaro. See also Lora Case, "Hudson of Long Ago," HLHS.

248 "So I returned": Ecclesiastes 4:1. For a complete list, see "J.B.'s Marked Texts from the Blessing Bible," OGV.

248 "As soon": *Virginia Free Press*, Dec. 8, 1859.

248 "false statements" and "of their own accord": *Virginia Free Press*, Dec. 8, 1859.

248 "You know I opposed": ibid.

248 "die like men" and "telling them": ibid.

248 "I feel it in my soul": ibid.

248 "Stand up like a man": ibid.

248 "He that is slow": John Brown to Aaron Stevens, Dec. 2, 1859, Gilder Lehrman Collection.

249 "a warm": David Strother, unpublished account of execution, Virginia Historical Society.

249 "just like a May": Louis Starry, quoted in J. Hampton Baumgartner, "Fifty Years After John Brown" (Baltimore: Baltimore and Ohio Railroad Co., 1909), 8, HFNHP.

250 "a game man": *Virginia Free Press*, Dec. 8, 1859.

250 "This is a beautiful": *New York Herald*, Dec. 3, 1859.

250 "so as": "Recollections of Prosecuting Attorney Andrew Hunter," *The Times-Democrat* (New Orleans), Sept. 6, 1887.

250 "Why this jealous": *New York Tribune*, Dec. 3, 1859.

251 "carpet slippers": *Evening Star*, Dec. 3, 1859.

251 "Gentlemen": *Baltimore American*, Dec. 3, 1859.

251 "the same": *Evening Star*, Dec. 3, 1859.

251 "You must": *New York Herald*, Dec. 3, 1859.

251 "the same even": *Evening Star*, Dec. 3, 1859.

251 "No": *New York Herald*, Dec. 3, 1859.

251 "quietly": David Strother, unpublished account of execution, Virginia Historical Society.

251 "upright as a soldier": J.T.L. Preston, "The Execution of John Brown," *The Southern Bivouac*, Aug. 1886, BSC.

252 "All ready": *Evening Star*, Dec. 3, 1859.

252 "With the fall": James I. Robertson, Jr., *Stonewall Jackson: The Man, the Soldier, the Legend* (New York: Simon & Schuster, 1997), 198–99.

253 "There was": *New York Tribune*, Dec. 3, 1859.

253 "This motion": *Evening Star*, Dec. 3, 1859.

253 "Of Sympathy": David Strother, unpublished account of execution, Virginia Historical Society.

254 "He behaved": Robertson, *Stonewall Jackson*, 199.

254 "I was proud": John Rhodehamel and Louise Taper, *"Right or Wrong, God Judge Me": The Writings of John Wilkes Booth* (Springfield: University of Illinois Press, 1997), 125.

254 "trator": ibid., 60.

254 "a brave": Asia Booth Clarke, *John Wilkes Booth, A Sister's Memoir*, Terry Alford, ed. (Jackson: University Press of Mississippi, 1996), 81.

254 "John Brown was": ibid., 88.

255 "robber & murderer": William Kauffman Scarborough, ed., *The Diary of Edmund Ruffin*, vol. 1 (Baton Rouge: Louisiana State University Press, 1972), 366–67. As an agriculturalist, Ruffin was famous for an 1832 article, "Essay on Calcareous Manures."

255 "stir the sluggish blood": ibid., 348.

255 "the seat of war": ibid., 361.

255 "with readiness" and other execution quotes: ibid., 368–71.

255 *"Sample of the favors"*: ibid., 368.

255 "The object": *New York Herald*, Dec. 4, 1859.

256 "I John Brown": "Final Statement," Chicago Historical Society.

256 "Should God": John Brown to family, Jan. 23, 1855, Chicago Historical Society.

257 "Without": Hebrews 9:22.

257 "Brown's old-fashioned": Sanborn, *The Life and Letters*, 620.

257 "would be better": ibid. Brown's final note passed from Hiram O'Bannon to the jailer John Avis to a collector, Alexander Ross, who exhibited it at the World's Fair in Chicago in 1892–93. See Boyd Stutler to Dr. David Hearns, April 21, 1953, BSC. The note was barely reported at the time of Brown's hanging; the only mentions I can find are in *Charleston* (S.C.) *Courier, Tri-Weekly* on Dec. 15, 1859, and *Lowell* (Massachusetts) *Daily Citizen and News*, on Dec. 20, 1859. The first prominent mention was in Franklin Sanborn's article "The Virginia Campaign of John Brown," *Atlantic Monthly*, Dec. 1875, 721.

Chapter 13: Dissevering the Ties That Bind Us

258 "O Patriot True!": Paul Finkelman, ed., *His Soul Goes Marching On* (Charlottesville: University of Virginia Press, 1995), 315.

258 "Living, he made": Louisa May Alcott, "With a Rose, That Bloomed on the Day of John Brown's Martrydom," *The Liberator*, Jan. 20, 1860. Alcott made note of writing the verse in her diary on Dec. 2, 1859, but was less enthusiastic about hosting the Brown girls while they attended Sanborn's school in Concord. "John Brown's daughters came to board, and upset my plans of rest and writing. . . . I had my fit of woe up garret on the fat rat-bag" (Ednah Cheney, ed., *Louisa May Alcott: Her Life, Letters, and Journals* [Boston: Roberts Brothers, 1890], 105, 127).

258 "But the streaming": The poem and an excellent analysis of it can be found in Zoe Trodd and John Stauffer, *Meteor of War*, 246–48.

258 "Even now as I write": diary entry for Dec. 2, 1859, in Samuel Longfellow, *Life of Henry Wadsworth Longfellow, with Extracts from His Journals and Correspondence* (Boston, 1886), vol. 2, 347. In the same entry he wrote of Brown's hanging: "This will be a great day in our history; the date of a new Revolution,—quite as much needed as the old one."

259 "Martyr's Day" and "From the firmament": Trodd and Stauffer, *Meteor of War*, 213–17.

259 "cracked," "justly," and "name may be": Allan Nevins and Milton Thomas, eds., *The Diary of George Templeton Strong* (New York: Macmillan, 1952), 465, 473. Foreigners also sensed that the United States would be forever changed by Brown's hanging. The French novelist Victor Hugo wrote in a letter on December 2 that "the murder of Brown" would open an "irreparable fault" in the Union, "which would in the end tear it asunder" (Trodd and Stauffer, 169). The anecdote about the Connecticut woman's visit to Brown's birthplace is from Sarah Pritchard to "Mr. Kilborn," May, 6, 1900, BSC.

259 "I am a non-resistant": *The Liberator*, Dec. 16, 1859.

260 "simplicity and consistency": Nevins and Thomas, *Diary of George Templeton Strong*, 474. See also Samuel May to Lydia Maria Child, Jan. 13, 1860, BSC. "If John Brown erred in the plan which he devised his subsequent conduct has well nigh converted the nation."

260 "our entire block" and "When he come": Louisa Williamson to Jedidiah Williamson, Dec. 8, 1859, BSC. See also "Notes on John Brown's Body in New York," BSC. For the funeral train's arrival in Philadelphia, see *Baltimore American*, Dec. 6, 1859.

260 "Blow Ye the Trumpet" and other details of Brown's funeral: *New York Tribune*, Dec. 13, 1859.

261 "History will date": *New York Weekly Tribune*, Dec. 17, 1859.

261 "if we would allow him": Jefferson Davis, remarks to the U.S. Senate, Dec. 8, 1859, quoted in Trodd and Stauffer, *Meteor of War*, 261.

261 "Union meetings" and "FANATICISM REBUKED": William Rasmussen and Robert Tilton, *The Portent* (Richmond: Virginia Historical Society, 2009), 58.

261 "the bond of commerce": ibid, 60.

262 "John Brown, and a thousand" and "even if it rushes": Davis, remarks to the U.S. Senate, in Trodd and Stauffer, *Meteor of War*, 260.

262 "as ambitious as Lucifer": Henry Mayer, *All on Fire*, 515.

262 "last and crowning aggression": Trodd and Stauffer, *Meteor of War*, 256.

262 "right to secede": "Resolution of South Carolina," Dec. 27, 1859, State Library of
Virginia.

262 "The Harper's Ferry invasion": address of the Hon. C. G. Memminger to State of
Virginia, Jan. 19, 1860, OGV.

262 "incendiary" and "dangerous emissaries": *New York Herald*, Dec. 19, 1859.

262 "suspicious" and "enticing negroes": *Baltimore American*, Dec. 6, 16, 1859. The
lynching is described in the *Baltimore American*, Dec. 16, 1859.

262 "I do not exaggerate": Doris Kearns Goodwin, *Team of Rivals* (New York: Simon
& Schuster, 2005), 227.

262 "use, eat, drink": Finkelman, *His Soul Goes Marching On*, 157.

263 "to secede in a body": *Baltimore American*, Dec. 22, 1859.

263 "abolition a cancer" and "*We must rely*": Gov. Wise speech to Assembly, Dec. 5,
1859, *Governor's Message and Reports of the Public Officers of the State* (Richmond: William F. Ritchie, 1859), State Library of Virginia.

263 "The prisoners seem": *Baltimore American*, Dec. 15, 1859.

263 "A dungeon bare": *Baltimore American*, Dec. 13, 1859.

263 "wayward tendencies": Jeannette Mather Lord, "John Brown: They Had a Concern," *West Virginia History*, April 1959, BSC.

263 "I have seen my folly": *Baltimore American*, Dec. 13, 1859.

263 "So you may know": Irving Richman, *John Brown Among the Quakers*, 51.

263 "professed a desire": *Virginia Free Press*, Dec. 22, 1859.

263 "Each expressed a hope": *Baltimore American*, Dec. 17, 1859.

264 "playing possum": ibid. This and the paper of December 19 have details of the
breakout. A Kansas ally of Brown later said that a free-state fighter had sneaked
into Charlestown, claimed to hate abolitionists, and been hired as a jail guard.
He conspired with Cook and Coppoc to be posted outside the yard wall on the
night of December 14. But their escape was delayed a day and, as a result, the
Kansan wasn't on duty. See Villard, *John Brown*, 571, and Hinton, *John Brown
and His Men*, 396–97.

264 "We do not wish": *Virginia Free Press*, Dec. 22, 1859.

265 "would make a very genteel": *Harper's Weekly*, Nov. 12, 1859.

265 "copper-colored" and "behaved himself": Andrew Hunter, "John Brown's Raid,"
188. He added: "If it had been possible to recommend a pardon for any of them,
it would have been for this man."

265 "I am so soon to stand": John Copeland to his brother, Dec. 10, 1859, quoted in
Nudelman, *John Brown's Body*, 68, and *Ashtabula Sentinel*, Dec. 21, 1859.

265 "Last night": For full text of this and other Copeland letters, see http://www
.oberlin.edu/external/EOG/Copeland/copeland_letters.htm. Also, in slightly
different form, Intercepted Letters, Gov. Wise Executive Papers, State Library of
Virginia, and "The John Brown Letters Found in Virginia State Library 1901,"
Virginia Historical Magazine of History and Biography, April 1903, 383–84, and
October 1902, 170–71.

265 "Copeland seemed to suffer": *New York Weekly Tribune*, Dec. 17, 1859.

265 "Yes. To your orders": The telegrams from Copeland's father, and Henry Wise's reply on December 12, are in the John Copeland file, OGV.

265 "the Negro convicts are not": Gov. Wise, note on back of request for bodies from Dr. Edmund Mason, Dec. 14, 1859, Executive Papers, State Library of Virginia.

266 "This nigger that you are": James Monroe, *Thursday Lectures, Addresses and Essays* (Oberlin, Ohio: Edward J. Goodrich, 1897), 170.

266 "A fine athletic figure": ibid., 175. For an excellent discussion of the treatment of black bodies in the nineteenth century, see Nudelman, *John Brown's Body*.

266 "remarkably cheerful": from the report in the *Cincinnati Gazette*, Dec. 16, 1859, BSC.

266 "Remember me to all my friends": ibid.

266 "a settled expression of despair": ibid.

266 "Stop a minute": *New York Herald*, Dec. 17, 1859.

266 "then waved his hand": *Shepherdstown* (Virginia) *Register*, Dec. 24, 1859, BSC.

266 "to expedite death": *Virginia Free Press*, Dec. 22, 1859.

267 "always at heart": interview with Virginia Kennedy Cook Johnston, 1908, OGV.

267 "a great fondness": ibid.

267 "I had a very hard time": Aaron Stevens to Annie Brown, Jan. 5, 1860, Gilder Lehrman Collection.

267 "Such black and penetrating": George Hoyt to Thomas Wentworth Higginson, Oct. 31, 1859, extracted in letter from Higginson to Brown family, Nov. 4, 1859, BSC.

267 "We feel an increased": Mary Miller to Aaron Stevens, Feb. 3, 1860, KSHS.

267 "I have looked": E. F. Curtis to Aaron Stevens, Feb. 28, 1860, KSHS.

267 a "regular young lion": Rebecca Spring to Thomas Wentworth Higginson, Jan. 23, 1860, BPL.

267 "My dear little boy": For this and other correspondence, see Sarah Barkin, *Rebecca Buffum Spring and the Politics of Motherhood in Antebellum America* (Rochester, N.Y.: University of Rochester Libraries, 2006).

268 "Your son in the bonds": ibid.

268 "My love is very warm": Aaron Stevens to Jennie Dunbar, Sept. 1, 1859, KSHS.

268 "hoping that I am": Aaron Stevens to Jennie Dunbar, Dec. 3, 1859, KSHS.

268 "A rare and delicate type": Katherine Mayo, "A Lieutenant of John Brown," *New York Evening Post*, 1909, clipping in BSC.

268 "He did not seem": Ellis Lindsley to James Redpath, Feb. 29, 1860, KSHS.

268 "Be of good cheer": Jennie Dunbar's statements are from her letter to Aaron Stevens, Dec. 13, 1859, OGV. This letter incorporates an earlier one she wrote on November 12 and didn't send until December.

268 "pure spring water": Aaron Stevens to Jennie Dunbar, Dec. 20, 1859, KSHS.

268 "She loves you as a brother": Julia Lindsley to Aaron Stevens, Feb. 9, 1860, KSHS. See also Ellis Lindsley to James Redpath, Feb. 29, 1860, telling of Dunbar's refusal to accept money as the "soul bride" of Stevens.

269 "When I think": *Ashtabula Sentinel*, Feb. 22, 1860.

269 "god and Savior" and "good actions": Aaron Stevens to "My Dear Brother," Feb. 20, 1860, Gilder Lehrman Collection.

269 "I expect": Aaron Stevens to "My Dear Sister," Jan. 18, 1860, Gilder Lehrman Collection.

269 "to *dance* on *nothing*" and "I think now": Aaron Stevens to "Unkcle James," Dec. 11, 1859, quoted in "The John Brown Letters Found in the Virginia State Library."

269 "I have a desire to live": Aaron Stevens to "My Dear Brother," Feb. 23, 1860, Gilder Lehrman Collection.

269 "supposing her to be": *Ashtabula Sentinel*, March 28, 1860, OGV.

269 "the worst of": ibid.

269 "I left him": Jennie Dunbar to James Redpath, May 7, 1860, OGV.

270 "She is all nerve": Aaron Stevens to "Dear Brother," March 8, 1860, KSHS.

270 "to see thy lovly face": Aaron Stevens to Jennie Dunbar, Oct. 7, 1859, KSHS.

270 "Mr. Stevens rose": Jennie Dunbar to James Redpath, May 7, 1860, OGV.

270 "we all recovered ourselves": ibid.

270 "The near approach of death": ibid. For more on the prison visit, see interview with Lydia Stevens Pierce, 1908, OGV.

270 "He is in the best of spirits": Jennie Dunbar to Julia Lindsley, March 15, 1859, KSHS. See also "Notes from Jennie Dunbar's Letter—visit to A.D.S.," May 7, 1860, KSHS, and Jennie Dunbar manuscript, "An Echo," July 1908, in OGV.

270 "He was talking to us": Jennie Dunbar's account of the morning of the execution is in her letter to James Redpath, May 7, 1860, OGV.

270 "Both exhibited": *New York Times*, March 17, 1860.

270 "Hazlett seemed to die": Baltimore report quoted in *Carlisle* (Pa.) *American Volunteer*, March 22, 1860.

271 "a free land": from "Bury Me in a Free Land," a poem Aaron Stevens copied for Jennie Dunbar in prison, KSHS. See also Rebecca Spring to Annie Brown, March 26, 1860, Houghton Library.

271 "Attached to the button-hole" and "for whom it was": *New York Herald*, March 19, 1860.

271 "It apparently was": Carrie Andrews to Thomas Wentworth Higginson, March 29, 1860, BPL.

271 "as soon as he entered": Annie Brown Adams to Richard Hinton, June 7, 1894, KSHS. She also told of this in a letter to Alexander Ross, April 2, 1889, Gilder Lehrman Collection.

271 "seemed to suffer": The account of the séance appears in a letter from Julia Lindsley to Lydia Pierce, May 19, 1860, KSHS.

271 "the love of Soul": Aaron Stevens to Jennie Dunbar, Dec. 20, 1859, KSHS. In the same letter he writes of "knowing that we shall ere long meet in the Spirit-land."

In 1861, Dunbar moved to Minnesota, where she told no one of her ties to the Browns or to Stevens. She married and lived in anonymity until an article about Stevens appeared in a New York paper, fifty years after Harpers Ferry, describing the music teacher as his "lover." For more see the interview with Jennie Dunbar Garcelon, 1908, OGV.

Epilogue: Immortal Raiders

272 "The curtain has": *Virginia Free Press*, March 22, 1860.

272 "Abram": Adam Goodheart, *1861* (New York: Knopf, 2011), 40.

273 "John Brown's effort": The address at Cooper Institute, Feb. 27, 1860, appears in Roy Basler, ed., *The Collected Works of Abraham Lincoln* (New Brunswick: Rutgers University Press, 1953), vol. 3, 522–50. Lincoln later credited this speech, and a dignified Mathew Brady portrait taken the same day, with getting him elected. Campaigning in Kansas on the day of Brown's hanging, Lincoln stated that "We can not object" to the execution, "even though he agreed with us in thinking slavery wrong. That cannot excuse violence, bloodshed and treason."

273 "I am not, nor ever": For quotations from the Douglas debates, I've drawn on Eric Foner, *The Fiery Trial* (New York: Norton, 2010), 108.

273 "an *irrepressible conflict*": William Seward, quoted in Doris Kearns Goodwin, *Team of Rivals*, 191. See also page 227, for a typical attack on Seward after Harpers Ferry; as the Tennessee legislature declared, Brown and his men were "the natural fruits of this treasonable 'irrepressible conflict' doctrine, put forth by the great head of the Black Republican party." Seward was also tarnished by controversy in the winter of 1859–60 over the speakership of the House and Hinton Helper's inflammatory book about slavery, *The Impending Crisis of the South and How to Meet It*. See Elizabeth Varon, *Disunion!* (Chapel Hill: University of North Carolina Press, 2008), 311–12, 331–32.

274 "denounce the lawless": The Republican Party platform is available at http://cprr .org/Museum/Ephemera/Republican_Platform_1860.html.

274 "Black Republican" and "war of extermination": Potter, *The Impending Crisis*, 448. For more on the 1860 election, see Douglas Egerton's excellent *Year of Meteors* (New York: Bloomsbury, 2010).

274 "Now that the black radical": diary entry, Nov. 8, 1860, in Isabella Martin and Myrta Lockett Avary, eds., *A Diary from Dixie, as Written by Mary Boykin Chesnut* (New York: D. Appleton & Co., 1905), 1.

275 "The union now subsisting": South Carolina Ordinance of Secession, Dec. 20, 1860, quoted in Walter Edgar, *South Carolina: A History* (Columbia: University of South Carolina Press, 1998), 324.

275 "Our position is thoroughly": Mississippi's "Declaration of Immediate Causes," quoted in Charles Dew, *Apostles of Disunion* (Charlottesville: University of Virginia Press, 2001), 12.

275 The provisional constitution of the Confederacy is available at http://avalon.law .yale.edu/19th_century/csa_csapro.asp.

275 "Blood will be flowing": Wise, quoted in *Encyclopedia Virginia*, an online publication of the Virginia Foundation for the Humanities: www.encyclopediavirginia .org/Virginia_Constitutional_Convention_of_1861. For more on the burning of the arsenal, see George Mauzy to "Mr. Burton," April 19, 1861, HFNP. The destruction of the buildings at the Point by Hector Tyndale and his men was reported in the Feb. 10, 1862, *New York Tribune*, which wrote of the burning: "John Brown's ghost is marching on."

277 *"John Brown's body"*: Franny Nudelman, *John Brown's Body*, 14.

277 "holy and glorious": ibid., 167. See also Nudelman's discussion of Julia Ward Howe and the song, 164–68.

277 "As he died to make": This was the penultimate line in the version of Howe's song first published on the cover of the *Atlantic Monthly* in February 1862.

278 "Emancipation would be equivalent": *New York Herald*, Dec. 10, 1861. Lincoln added: "Our position is surrounded with a sufficient number of dangers already. Abolition would throw against us, irrevocably, the four states of Missouri, Kentucky, Virginia, and Maryland." He also overruled an edict by a western commander, John C. Frémont, freeing slaves in Missouri. See Goodwin, *Team of Rivals*, 391–94.

278 "in rebellion against": The Emancipation Proclamation is available on the National Archives site: http://www.archives.gov/exhibits/featured_documents/emancipation_proclamation/.

279 "God bless Abraham": Mary Brown to Mary Stearns, Jan. 7, 1863, BSC.

279 "able-bodied COLORED": undated circular, HSP.

279 "a band" and "whose business": Douglass, *Autobiographies*, 796–97.

279 "I had been": Brenda Wineapple, *White Heat: The Friendship of Emily Dickinson and Thomas Wentworth Higginson* (New York: Knopf, 2008), 125.

279 "This mighty scourge": Lincoln's Second Inaugural Address, Foner, *The Fiery Trial*, 325.

280 "Lincoln and John Brown": *New Orleans Tribune*, April 22, 1865, quoted in Carolyn Harrell, *When the Bells Tolled for Lincoln* (Macon: Mercer University Press, 1997), 75.

280 "for the purpose of": J. D. Enos, introduction to second edition of Osborne Anderson's "A Voice from Harper's Ferry," 1873, BSC. For more on Anderson in his later years, see Eugene Meyer, "Sole Survivor," *Washington Post*, Dec. 12, 2004.

281 "What a pity": Annie Brown Adams to Richard Hinton, Feb. 16, 23, 1862, in Bonnie Laughlin-Schultz, "'Could I Not Do Something for the Cause?' The Brown Women, Antislavery Reform, and the Memory of Militant Abolitionism" (Ph.D. diss., Indiana University, 2009). Annie wrote William Lloyd Garrison about her desire to teach "Contrabands" in a letter of June 9, 1863 (BSC). On her attending Sunday school on the plantation of Henry Wise, see her April 13, 1879, letter to Alexander Ross, Gilder Lehrman Collection.

281 "Yankees would break": James McPherson, *Battle Cry of Freedom* (New York: Oxford University Press, 1988), 317.

281 "I could stand prouder": Craig Simpson, *A Good Southerner* (Chapel Hill: University of North Carolina Press, 1985), 303.

281 "God knew": ibid., 301–2.

281 "a chance to do": Mary Brown to Mary Stearns, Aug. 4, 1863, BSC.

282 "I very much regret": Mary Brown to Owen Brown, Jan. 31, 1864, HLHS. For more on family's move west see Jean Libby, ed., *John Brown's Family in California* (Palo Alto: Allies for Freedom, 2006).

282 "Four of his finger joints": "A John Brown Reminiscence," by a reporter for the *Indianapolis Daily Journal*, undated, KSHS. See also Dr. Jarvis Johnson affidavit

in Thomas Featherstonhaugh, *John Brown's Men* (Harrisburg, Pa.: Harrisburg Publishing Co., 1899), 19–21, and John Brown, Jr., to Wealthy Brown, Sept. 10, 1882, Gilder Lehrman Collection. Mary had intended to retrieve Watson's and Oliver's bodies in 1859, but one had been carried off and the other buried in a mass grave, making it hard to identify.

282 "She was born": John Brown, Jr., to Mary Stearns, May 1, 1860, BSC.

282 "bone-crushing sorrow": Ruth Brown Thompson to Mary Stearns, April 22, 1860, BSC. In Lou Chapin, "The Last Days of John Brown," Ruth states of Annie: "Among those who died that bloody night was her first lover. She went about the house pale, silent and tearless."

282 "wonderfully happy": Sarah Wall to "Dear Friend," Dec. 7, 1884, KSHS.

283 "He just sits": Annie Brown Adams to Franklin Sanborn, Dec. 23, 1894, BSC.

283 "I married the man": ibid.

283 "an object of": ibid. In a letter of September 25, 1892, to Sanborn she refused to go to the Chicago World's Fair, stating: "I may be a relic of John Brown's raid on Harper's Ferry, but I do not want to be placed on exhibition with other relics and curios."

283 "to buy bread": Annie Brown Adams to Rev. Joshua Young, April 19, 1899, in "Extracts from letters written by the Brown family," BSC.

283 "wished to live" and "shut the past": Galley proof, "The Trip to Annie Brown Adams," unpublished article by Katherine Mayo, BSC. See also Mayo's interview with Annie Brown Adams, 1908, in OGV.

284 "watchdog": Richard Hinton, *John Brown and His Men*, 245.

284 "People who never did a heroic deed": Katherine Mayo notes on Mrs. Annie Brown Adams, 1908, OGV.

284 "waited upon them": Annie Brown Adams, quoted in Franklin Sanborn, *Recollections of Seventy Years*, 177.

284 "neither saints": ibid.

284 "I used to lock myself" and "The honor and glory": Annie Brown Adams to Alexander Ross, Dec. 28, 1887, Gilder Lehrman Collection.

284 "easily upset" and "The Last Survivor": Mary Fablinger to Boyd Stutler, June 14, 1949, BSC.

284 "Death Comes": Associated Press dispatch, datelined Eureka, Calif., Oct. 5, 1926, HLHS. The coroner's certificate, dated Oct. 3, 1926, is from the California Dept. of Public Health, copy in HLHS. It notes that she also suffered from carcinoma of the lip.

285 "The larger portion": quoted in Barbara Post, "Beyond John Brown: Jennie Chambers and Harpers Ferry" (master's thesis, Duke University, 2007), 55, HFNP. For more on Harpers Ferry during and just after the war, see James Noffsinger, *Contributions Towards a Physical History*, 45–52, HFNHP. On the engine house, see Clarence Gee, "John Brown's Fort," *West Virginia History*, Jan. 1958, BSC. On Storer, see Vivian Verdell Gordon, "A History of Storer College," *The Journal of Negro Education*, Autumn 1961, 445–49.

286 "upon the very soil" and "first tree": Douglass, *Autobiographies*, 885.

286 "His zeal": For Douglass's speech, I've drawn on "An Address by Frederick

Douglass, at the Fourteenth Anniversary of Storer College" (Dover, N.H.: Morning Start Job Printing House, 1881).

288 "condemned my sentiments": Douglass, *Autobiographies*, 886. For the burning of Hunter's home on July 17, 1864, see J. E. Taylor, *With Sheridan Up the Shenandoah Valley in 1864* (Dayton, Ohio: Morningside House, 1989), 53.

288 "commended me": Hunter is quoted in Douglass, *Autobiographies*, 885–86. Douglass regretted being unable to accept the invitation, writing, "I could not doubt the sincerity with which it was given."

288 "The abolition of": ibid., 885.

288 "Here on the scene": This occurred at a meeting of the Niagara Movement, described in David Levering Lewis, *W.E.B. Dubois: Biography of a Race* (New York: Henry Holt, 1993), 328–29. The resolution, written by Dubois, appears in W.E.B. Dubois, *The Autobiography of W.E.B. Dubois* (New York: International Publishers, 1968), 249. For more on Brown's memory and early civil rights movement, see chapter four of R. Blakeslee Gilpin, *John Brown Still Lives!*

288 On the disinterment and reburial of raiders in 1899, see Thomas Featherstonhaugh, "The Final Burial of the Followers of John Brown," *New England Magazine*, April 1901, 133–34.

289 Newby relations: see Schwarz, *Migrants from Slavery*, 149–68, and Scott Casper, *Sarah Johnson's Mount Vernon* (New York: Hill and Wang, 2008), 171–73. Harriett's second husband, William Robinson, later worked at Mount Vernon, which was owned before the war by a cousin of Lewis Washington's, whose plantation Brown's men raided. See also, "The Life and Death of Dangerfield Newby," Jefferson Co. Black History Preservation Society, 2005.

289 "My grandmother": Langston Hughes, *The Big Sea* (New York: Hill & Wang, 1967), 17. He recounts the story of the shawl on page 12 and says it was sent to his grandmother a few weeks after Leary's death, "full of bullet holes." He later notes that he inherited the shawl and kept it with his manuscripts in a safe-deposit vault in New York. For description of his grandmother wrapping him in the shawl, see Mark Scott, "Langston Hughes of Kansas," *The Journal of Negro History*, 1981, 4–5.

289 "who went off to die": Langston Hughes, *I Wonder As I Wander* (New York: Octagon Books, 1990), 309.

289 "October the Sixteenth": This title, and the version I have quoted, are from the poem's first publication, in *Opportunity*, Oct. 31, 1931. It was later retitled and published, in slightly different form, as "October 16: The Raid." The revised version is in Arnold Rampersad and David Roessel, eds., *The Collected Poems of Langston Hughes* (New York: Vintage Books, 1995), 141–42, and a discussion of the differences from the original is on page 639.

Selected Bibliography

This is a partial list of books I used in my research, an abbreviated guide for those who want to do more reading. Citations for other materials appear in the endnotes, where I have also commented on some of the works below.

Achenbach, Joel. *The Grand Idea: George Washington's Potomac and the Race to the West*. New York: Simon & Schuster, 2002.

Anderson, Osborne P. "A Voice from Harper's Ferry." Boston: printed for the author, 1861.

Avery, Elijah. *The Capture and Execution of John Brown*. Chicago: Hyde Park Bindery, 1906.

Banks, Russell. *Cloudsplitter*. New York: Harper Perennial, 1999.

Barry, Joseph. *The Strange Story of Harper's Ferry*. Martinsburg, W.Va.: Thompson Brothers, 1903.

Blight, David. *Race and Reunion: The Civil War in American Memory*. Cambridge, Mass.: Belknap Press, 2001.

Carton, Evan. *Patriotic Treason*. Lincoln: University of Nebraska Press, 2006.

Clinton, Catherine. *Harriet Tubman: The Road to Freedom*. New York: Little, Brown, 2004.

Dean, Virgil, ed. *Kansas Territorial Reader*. Topeka: Kansas State Historical Society, 2005.

DeCaro, Louis A. *"Fire from the Midst of You": A Religious Life of John Brown*. New York: New York University Press, 2002.

———. *John Brown: The Cost of Freedom*. New York: International Publishers, 2007.

Dew, Charles. *Apostles of Disunion*. Charlottesville: University Press of Virginia, 2001.

Douglass, Frederick. *Autobiographies*. New York: Library of America, 1994.

Dubois, W.E.B. *John Brown*. Philadelphia: George W. Jacobs & Co., 1909.

Earle, Jonathan. *John Brown's Raid on Harpers Ferry*. New York: Bedford/St. Martins, 2008.

Egerton, Douglas. *Year of Meteors*. New York: Bloomsbury, 2010.

Etcheson, Nicole. *Bleeding Kansas: Contested Liberty in the Civil War Era*. Lawrence: University of Kansas, 2004.

Faust, Drew Gilpin. *James Henry Hammond and the Old South*. Baton Rouge: Louisiana State Press, 1982.

Fellman, Michael. *Inside War: The Guerrilla Conflict in Missouri During the American Civil War*. New York: Oxford University Press, 1990.

Finkelman, Paul, ed. *His Soul Goes Marching On*. Charlottesville: University of Virginia Press, 1995.

Finkelman, Paul, and Peggy Russo, eds. *Terrible Swift Sword*. Athens: Ohio University Press, 2005.

Flournoy, H. W., ed. *Calendar of Virginia State Papers: The John Brown Insurrection*. Richmond, Va., 1893.

Foner, Eric. *The Fiery Trial*. New York: Norton, 2010.

Furnas, J. C. *The Road to Harpers Ferry*. New York: William Sloane, 1959.

Gilpin, R. Blakeslee. *John Brown Still Lives! America's Long Reckoning with Violence, Equality, and Change*. Chapel Hill: University of North Carolina Press, 2011.

Goodheart, Adam. *1861: The Civil War Awakening*. New York: Knopf, 2011.

Hinton, Richard. *John Brown and His Men*. New York: Funk & Wagnalls, 1894. Michigan Historical Reprint Series, 2005.

Howe, Daniel Walker. *What Hath God Wrought*. New York: Oxford University Press, 2007.

Libby, Jean, with Hannah Geffert and Evelyn Taylor. *John Brown Mysteries*. Missoula, Mont.: Pictorial Histories Publishing, 1999.

Malin, James. *John Brown and the Legend of Fifty-six*. Philadelphia: American Philosophical Society, 1942.

Mayer, Henry. *All on Fire: William Lloyd Garrison and the Abolition of Slavery*. New York: St. Martin's Press, 1998.

McCurry, Stephanie. *Confederate Reckoning*. Cambridge, Mass.: Harvard University Press, 2010.

McFarland, Gerald. *A Scattered People*. New York: Pantheon, 1985.

McFeely, William. *Frederick Douglass*. New York: Norton, 1991.

McGinty, Brian. *John Brown's Trial*. Cambridge, Mass.: Harvard University Press, 2009.

McGlone, Robert. *John Brown's War Against Slavery*. New York: Cambridge University Press, 2009.

McPherson, James. *Battle Cry of Freedom*. New York: Oxford University Press, 1988.

Nevins, Allan. *The Ordeal of the Union*. New York: Scribners, 1947–71.

Noffsinger, James. *Harpers Ferry, West Virginia: Contributions Towards a Physical History*. Philadelphia: U.S. Department of the Interior, 1958.

Nudelman, Franny. *John Brown's Body: Slavery, Violence, and The Culture of War.* Chapel Hill: University of North Carolina Press, 2004.

Oakes, James. *The Radical and the Republican.* New York: Norton, 2007.

Oates, Stephen. *To Purge This Land with Blood: A Biography of John Brown.* Amherst: University of Massachusetts, 1984.

Phillips, William. *The Conquest of Kansas.* Boston: Phillips, Sampson and Co., 1856.

Potter, David. *The Impending Crisis, 1848–1861.* New York: Harper & Row, 1976.

Pryor, Elizabeth Brown. *Reading the Man: A Portrait of Robert E. Lee Through His Private Letters.* New York: Viking, 2007.

Quarles, Benjamin. *Allies for Freedom.* New York: Oxford University Press, 1974.

———, ed. *Blacks on John Brown.* Urbana: University of Illinois Press, 1972.

Rasmussen, William, and Robert Tilton. *The Portent: John Brown's Raid in American Memory.* Richmond: Virginia Historical Society, 2009.

Redpath, James. *Echoes of Harper's Ferry.* New York: Arno Press, 1969.

———. *The Public Life of Captain John Brown.* Boston: Thayer and Eldridge, 1860.

Renehan, Edward, Jr. *The Secret Six: The True Tale of the Men Who Conspired with John Brown.* New York: Crown, 1995.

Report of the Select Committee of the Senate Appointed to Inquire into the Late Invasion and Seizure of the Public Property at Harper's Ferry. 36th Cong., 1st Sess. (1860). In BSC; referred to in notes as "Mason Report."

Reynolds, David. *John Brown, Abolitionist: The Man Who Killed Slavery, Sparked the Civil War, and Seeded Civil Rights.* New York: Knopf, 2005.

Rhodehamel, John, and Louise Taper. *"Right or Wrong, God Judge Me": The Writings of John Wilkes Booth.* Springfield: University of Illinois Press, 1997.

Robertson, James, Jr. *Stonewall Jackson: The Man, the Soldier, the Legend.* New York: Simon & Schuster, 1997.

Rossbach, Jeffery. *Ambivalent Conspirators.* Philadelphia: University of Pennsylvania Press, 1982.

Ruchames, Louis, ed. *A John Brown Reader.* London: Abelard-Schuman, 1959.

Sanborn, Franklin. *The Life and Letters of John Brown.* Boston: Roberts Bros., 1891.

———. *Recollections of Seventy Years.* Boston: Gorham Press, 1909.

Schwarz, Philip. *Migrants Against Slavery: Virginians and the Nation.* Charlottesville: University Press of Virginia, 2001.

Shepard, Odell, ed. *The Journals of Bronson Alcott.* Boston: Little, Brown, 1938.

Simpson, Craig. *A Good Southerner: The Life of Henry A. Wise of Virginia.* Chapel Hill: University of North Carolina Press, 2001.

Smith, Merritt Roe. *Harpers Ferry Armory and the New Technology.* Ithaca: Cornell University Press, 1980.

Stauffer, John. *The Black Hearts of Men.* Cambridge, Mass.: Harvard University Press, 2001.

Stavis, Barrie. *John Brown: The Sword and the Word.* London: A. S. Barnes, 1970.

Swanson, James. *Manhunt.* New York: Harper Perennial, 2007.

Trodd, Zoe, and John Stauffer, eds. *Meteor of War: The John Brown Story.* Maplecrest, N.Y.: Brandywine, 2004.

Varon, Elizabeth. *Disunion! The Coming of the American Civil War, 1789–1859*. Chapel Hill: University of North Carolina Press, 2008.

Villard, Oswald Garrison. *John Brown, 1800–1859: A Biography Fifty Years After*. Boston: Houghton Mifflin, 1910.

Wineapple, Brenda. *White Heat*. New York: Knopf, 2008.

Wood, Gordon. *Empire of Liberty*. New York: Oxford University Press, 2009.

Acknowledgments

Midnight Rising is a departure from my previous books, which weaved between past and present. This one stays firmly rooted in the nineteenth century. As a result, I owe a special debt to historians and librarians who eased my passage from ink-stained journalist to pencil-smudged archival rat.

Thanks first to David Blight, the director of the Gilder Lehrman Center for the Study of Slavery, Resistance, and Abolition. Three years ago he urged me to pursue this project, despite my lack of expertise, and introduced me to Blake Gilpin, a young historian who has inspired me throughout. Blake is about to publish his first book, *John Brown Still Lives!*, a pioneering study of the memory and myth-making of Brown from the 1850s to the present.

Through David and Blake, I entered the wider world of "Browniacs," a dedicated community of academics, independent scholars, and others who share a passion for the abolitionist's story. Louis DeCaro, the author of *"Fire from the Midst of You,"* has been very generous in sharing his sources and insights, as he also does at http://abolitionist-john-brown.blogspot.com/. Bonnie Laughlin-Schultz has been another invaluable resource, particularly on Annie Brown Adams, my favorite figure in the Harpers Ferry drama. Bonnie's upcoming book on the Brown women and abolitionism will greatly expand the male-centered universe of Brown scholarship.

The story of the black raiders at Harpers Ferry also remains to be fully told, and Philip Schwarz's work is a model in this regard. Through painstaking research over many years, he has pieced together the extraordinary life of Dangerfield Newby, who hoped to free his wife and children from slavery. Like Bonnie, Phil has been extraordinarily generous, calmly booting up his computer database to answer my every query.

Jonathan Earle and Karl Gridley were kind enough to guide me through the Kansas mud to Pottawatomie Creek, Black Jack, and Osawatomie. Jonathan also shared his vast knowledge of antebellum politics, the subject of his upcoming book, *The Election of Abraham Lincoln and the Revolution of 1860*. Among the other scholars I consulted, I'd like to thank Richard Blackett, Evan Carton, William Cooper, Caleb McDaniel, Franny Nudelman, John Stauffer, and Brenda Wineapple for their wisdom and companionship. Thanks also to Jean Libby, for a disc of hard-to-find *Baltimore Clipper* stories and for keeping me abreast of all things Brown at http://www.alliesforfreedom.org/.

In this era of budget cutting, librarians labor under severe constraints. So I'm especially grateful to those who shared their scarce time and resources to show me the ropes. Gwen Mayer at the Hudson Library and Historical Society in Ohio gave me unfettered access to the library's vault—as well as the key to its photocopy machine and a very warm welcome to the Western Reserve. Mary Beth McIntire and Craig Moore made things easy for me at the State Library of Virginia, as did William Obrochta and Frances Pollard at the Virginia Historical Society. I'd also like to thank Andrea Jackson and Kayin Shabazz at the Robert Woodruff Library in Atlanta; Kimberly Reynolds at the Boston Public Library; Virgil Dean and the reference librarians at the Kansas State Historical Society; Alyson Barrett-Ryan at the Gilder Lehrman Collection; and the accommodating staff of the Rare Book & Manuscripts Library at Columbia University.

Along with librarians, the unsung heroes of Brown research are the hardworking employees of the National Park Service. There is no better place to learn about Brown and engage with history than at the Harpers Ferry National Historical Park in West Virginia. Park ranger David Fox combines an encyclopedic knowledge of Harpers Ferry with contagious enthusiasm for its story. I've visited David many times, and he's responded to my countless questions and theories with unfailing thoughtfulness and good humor. The park's chief historian, Dennis Frye, led me on a night march from the Kennedy farm that was a highlight of my research, and his provocative insights on the Civil War will appear in his upcoming book, *Antietam Addressed*. Thanks also to Michelle Hammer for help in navigating the park's archives, and to Susan Collins at the nearby Jefferson County Museum in Charles Town, for access to the museum's underutilized trove of Brown-related documents.

As always, I owe a debt beyond measure to my editor at Macmillan, John Sterling, and to my literary agent, Kristine Dahl. I've collaborated with John and Kris for over a decade, and they're simply the best: upbeat, rigorous, and tremendous fun, even when I'm not. John, with his lean frame, piercing eyes, and monomaniacal devotion to his task, would make an excellent movie Brown, if Chris Cooper and Tommy Lee Jones are unavailable. Thanks also to Jolanta Benal, the world's finest copy editor, and to Emi Ikkanda for much-needed help tracking down illustrations.

Finally, once again, I'm grateful to friends and family for their counsel, jokes, and tolerance during the years it took me to write this book. Thanks to Dr. Earle Silber for his reflections on Brown's mental state: to Christina Bevilacqua for her unparalleled knowledge of Melville; to Ron Nemirow and Erin Shay for Scrabble and Scotch; to my parents, Elinor and Norman Horwitz, for reading this book when it was barely readable; to my sons, Nathaniel and Bizu, for memorizing Brown's courtroom speech and reminding me the world does not revolve around him; and most of all, to my wife, Geraldine, who led me to this subject in the first place, endured its execution, and remains the love of my life.

Illustration Credits

105 Courtesy of the Kansas State Historical Society. Originally published in *Frank Leslie's Illustrated Newspaper*, Nov. 26, 1859.

106 Courtesy of the West Virginia State Archives, Boyd B. Stutler Collection.

106 Courtesy of the West Virginia State Archives, Boyd B. Stutler Collection.

106 Courtesy of the West Virginia State Archives, Boyd B. Stutler Collection.

114 Courtesy of the Collection of the New-York Historical Society, Negative # 35765.

118 Courtesy of the West Virginia State Archives, Boyd B. Stutler Collection.

121 Courtesy of the Kansas State Historical Society.

121 Courtesy of the West Virginia State Archives, Boyd B. Stutler Collection.

124 Courtesy of the West Virginia State Archives, Boyd B. Stutler Collection.

124 Courtesy of the West Virginia State Archives, Boyd B. Stutler Collection.

128 Courtesy of Harpers Ferry National Historical Park, Harpers Ferry, W.Va.

133 Courtesy of the Library of Congress Prints and Photographs division.

133 Collection of the author.

137 Courtesy of Jim Glymph, Avon Bend, W.Va.

146 Courtesy of the West Virginia State Archives, Boyd B. Stutler Collection. Originally published in *Harper's Weekly*, Nov. 12, 1859.

155 Courtesy of the West Virginia State Archives, Boyd B. Stutler Collection.

160 Courtesy of the West Virginia State Archives, Boyd B. Stutler Collection.

175 Courtesy of the Library of Congress Prints and Photographs division.

175 Courtesy of the West Virginia State Archives, Boyd B. Stutler Collection.

179 Courtesy of Harpers Ferry National Historical Park, Harpers Ferry, W.Va. Originally published in *Frank Leslie's Illustrated Newspaper*, Oct. 29, 1859.

183 Courtesy of the West Virginia State Archives, Boyd B. Stutler Collection. Originally published in *Harper's Weekly*, Nov. 5, 1859.

184 Courtesy of the Library of Congress Prints and Photographs division.

199 Courtesy of the Kansas State Historical Society.

200 Courtesy of the West Virginia State Archives, Boyd B. Stutler Collection. Originally published in *Frank Leslie's Illustrated Newspaper*, Nov. 19, 1859.

204 Courtesy of Harpers Ferry National Historical Park, Harpers Ferry, W.Va. Originally published in *Harper's Weekly*, Nov. 12, 1859.

210 Courtesy of the Concord Free Library, Concord, Mass.

216 Courtesy of the West Virginia State Archives, Boyd B. Stutler Collection. Originally published in *New York Illustrated News*, Dec. 10, 1859.

221 Courtesy of the Kansas State Historical Society. Originally published in *Frank Leslie's Illustrated Newspaper*, Dec. 10, 1859.

227 First Virginia Regiment (Richmond Grays) in Charlestown, Va., 1859. Courtesy of the Cook Collection, Valentine Richmond History Center.

249 Courtesy of the West Virginia State Archives, Boyd B. Stutler Collection. Originally published in *Frank Leslie's Illustrated Newspaper*, Dec. 17, 1859.

252 Courtesy of the Virginia Military Institute Archives.
253 Courtesy of the Virginia Historical Society.
254 Courtesy of the Virginia Historical Society.
256 Courtesy of the West Virginia State Archives, Boyd B. Stutler Collection.
276 Courtesy of Harpers Ferry National Historical Park, Harpers Ferry, W.Va. Originally published in *Harper's Weekly*, May 11, 1861.
283 Courtesy of the West Virginia State Archives, Boyd B. Stutler Collection.
285 Courtesy of Harpers Ferry National Historical Park, Harpers Ferry, W.Va.

Index

Page numbers in *italics* refer to illustrations.